VIZ GRAPHIC NOVEL

SILENT MÖBIUS ™

VOL. 5

STORY AND ART BY **KIA ASAMIYA**

1999 A.D.

On a visit to Japan for work on a shadowy project, the hermetic magician Gigelf Liqueur becomes involved in a disaster. A gate is opened to another world—the world of Nemesis, home of evil entities known as Lucifer Hawks who visited our Earth in ancient times. Soon afterward, Gigelf Liqueur is never seen again.

2023 A.D.

Tokyo has become a mega-city, but sightings of the mysterious and murderous Lucifer Hawks are on the rise. In response, Rally Cheyenne forms a special police group known as the A.M.P.—Attacked Mystification Police Department. With the help of second-in-command Lebia Maverick, Shinto priestess Nami Yamigumo, and cyborg "megadyne" Kiddy Phenil, the A.M.P. monitors and combats the infestation. For Rally Cheyenne, the matter is personal; for she is the child of a Lucifer Hawk and a human mother, and her sister, Rosa, willingly vanished long ago into her father's dark world.

2026 A.D.

Two new members join the A.M.P.: Yuki Saiko, an inexperienced psychic, and Katsumi Liqueur, who is blessed or cursed with her father's magical powers. Finding herself a target because of her abilities, Katsumi gradually learns more about her father's legacy, but there is still much more to be revealed.

2028 A.D.

Mana Isozaki, a highly skilled friend of Rally Cheyenne's, becomes the A.M.P.'s new acting commander. They need the extra manpower, because their enemies' strength is increasing…

MEET THE A.M.P

NAMI YAMIGUMO
IDENTITY: Priest

Heir to the House of Yamigumo and inheritor of its divine Ki-Rin dagger, Nami was put in the care of Rally Cheyenne at the age of 15 to develop her powers. A Shinto priestess, she can call upon many kinds of shamanic magic.

KATSUMI LIQUEUR
IDENTITY: Sorcerer

Katsumi is the daughter of the great magician Gigelf Liqueur, who was responsible for bringing the Lucifer Hawks to Earth. She has inherited many of his powers, as well as the living weapon known as Grospoliner, king of swords.

LEBIA MAVERICK
IDENTITY: Visionaire

Lebia Maverick specializes in computer operations; cybernetic systems in her body allow her to mentally enter 'computer logic space.' Her data bank is stored in an orbital satellite, giving her a memory capacity 3000 times that of an ordinary visionaire and far beyond a normal human being's.

RALLY CHEYENNE
IDENTITY: Superintendent

The product of crossbreeding between a Lucifer Hawk and a human woman, Rally used her powers to turn the A.M.P. into the human race's strongest defense. She now acts as the A.M.P.'s liason to the government, leaving day-to-day operations to her hand-picked replacement, Mana Isozaki.

YUKI SAIKO
IDENTITY: Psychic

The youngest member of the A.M.P., Yuki was raised in a secret project to develop ESPer weapons. She has rejected the violent aspect of her training, and relies mostly on her intuition and precognitive abilities.

MANA ISOZAKI
IDENTITY: Commander

The most recent and mysterious addition to the A.M.P., she is second in rank only to Rally Cheyenne. A stern, highly capable officer, she uses a form of magic derived from Indian Buddhism.

KIDDY PHENIL
IDENTITY: Cyborg

In 2023, detective Kiddy Phenil was nearly killed in combat by a megadyne (cyborg). She was saved by a combat-graft which replaced 70% of her body with bionic parts, giving her super-strength, but making her into what she hated most.

This volume contains the monthly comics SILENT MÖBIUS: KARMA #1 through #7 in their entirety.

STORY AND ART BY KIA ASAMIYA

ENGLISH ADAPTATION BY FRED BURKE, TOSHIFUMI YOSHIDA & AKIKO YAGI

Touch-Up Art & Lettering/Wayne Truman (p.5-73) & Dan Nakrosis (p.74-243)
Cover Design/Hidemi Sahara
Graphics & Layout/Sean Lee
Editor/Jason Thompson

Managing Editor/Annette Roman
Editor-in-Chief/Hyoe Narita
Publisher/Seiji Horibuchi
Senior Sales Manager/Ann Ivan
Senior Marketing Manager/Dallas Middaugh

Printed in Canada

Published by Viz Communications, Inc.
P.O. Box 77010 ▪ San Francisco, CA 94107

10 9 8 7 6 5 4 3 2 1

First printing, October 2000

Vizit our web sites at **www.viz.com**, **www.pulp-mag.com**, **www.animerica-mag.com**, and our Internet magazine at **www.j-pop.com**!

CONTENTS

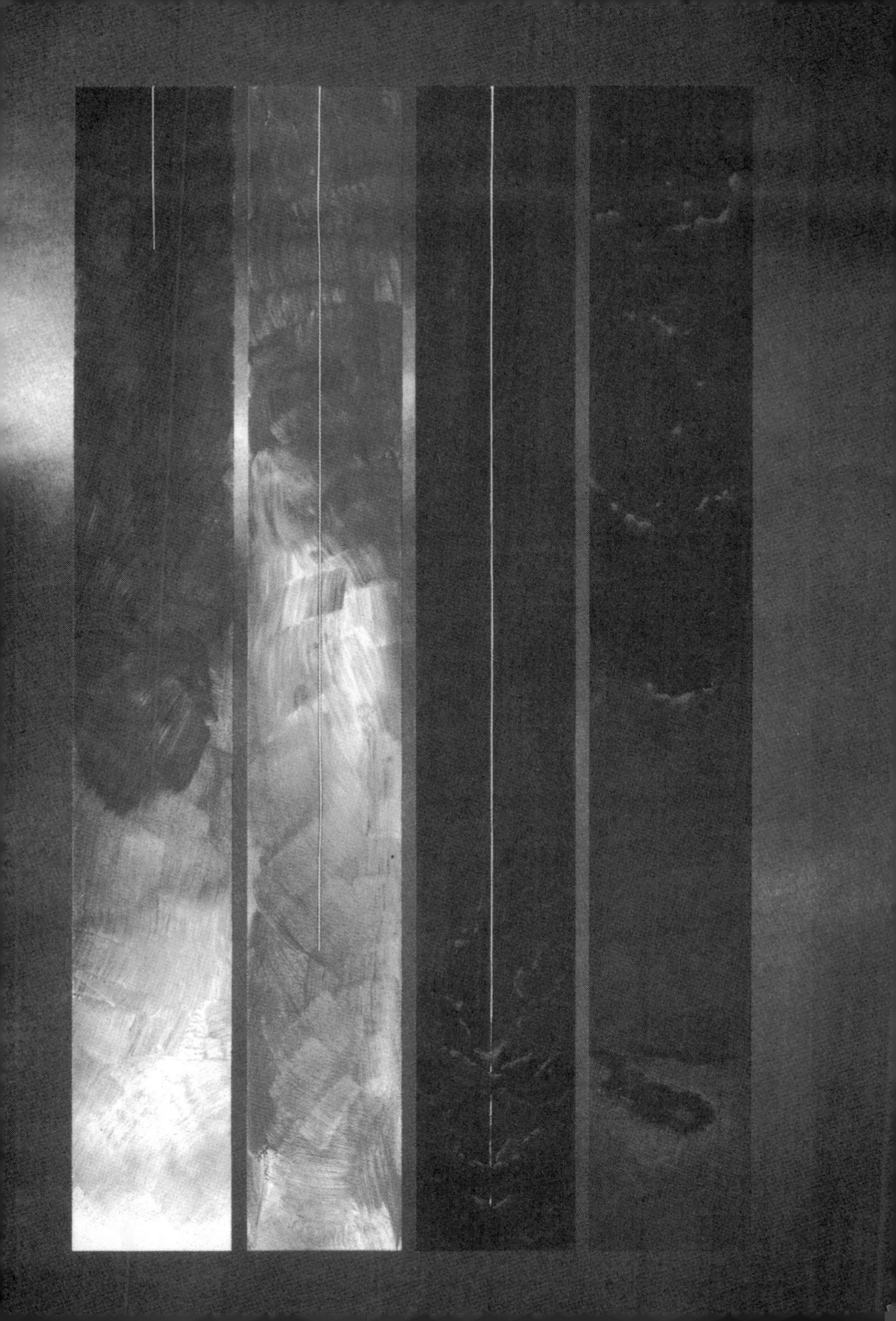

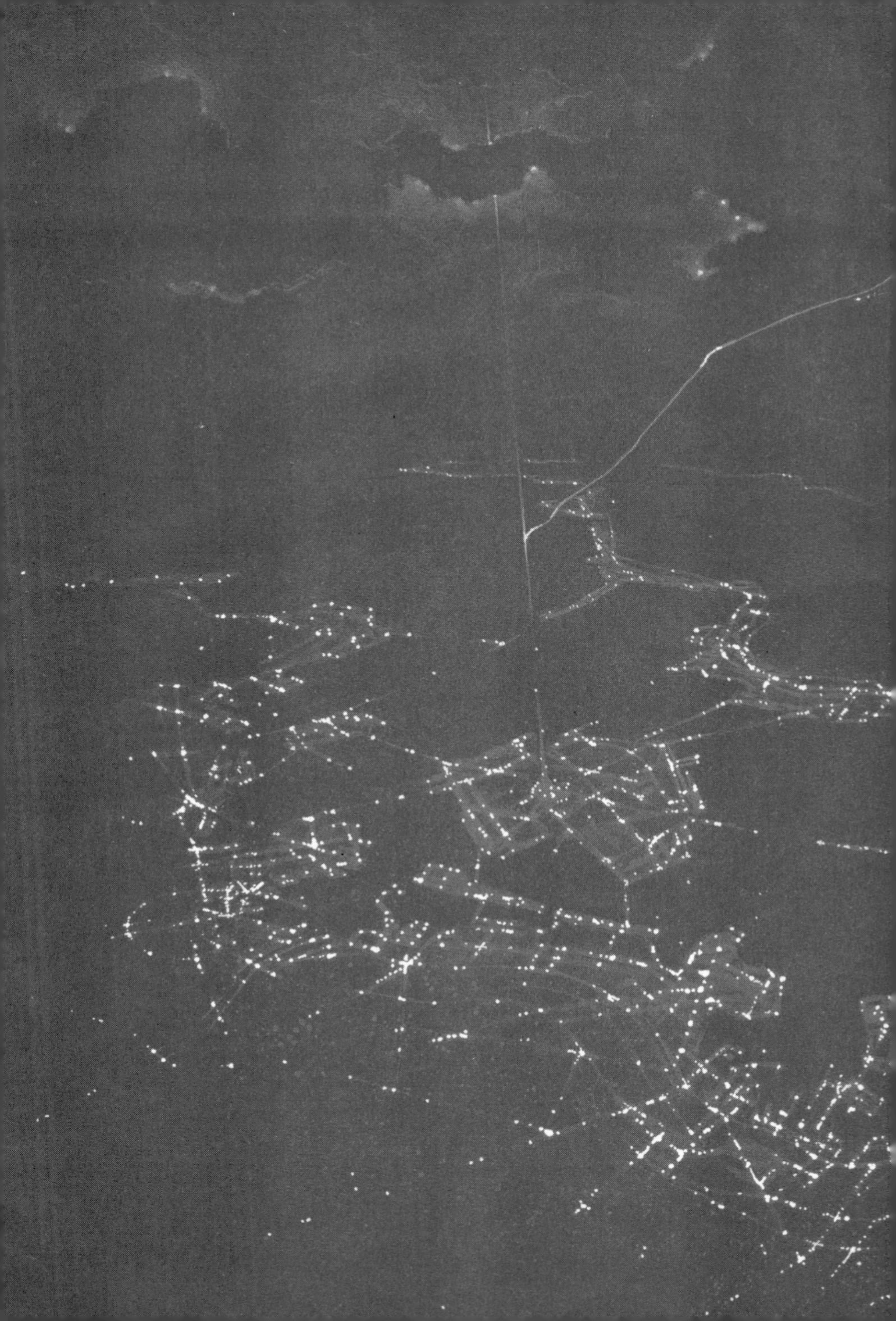

CHAPTER 13:
KARMA

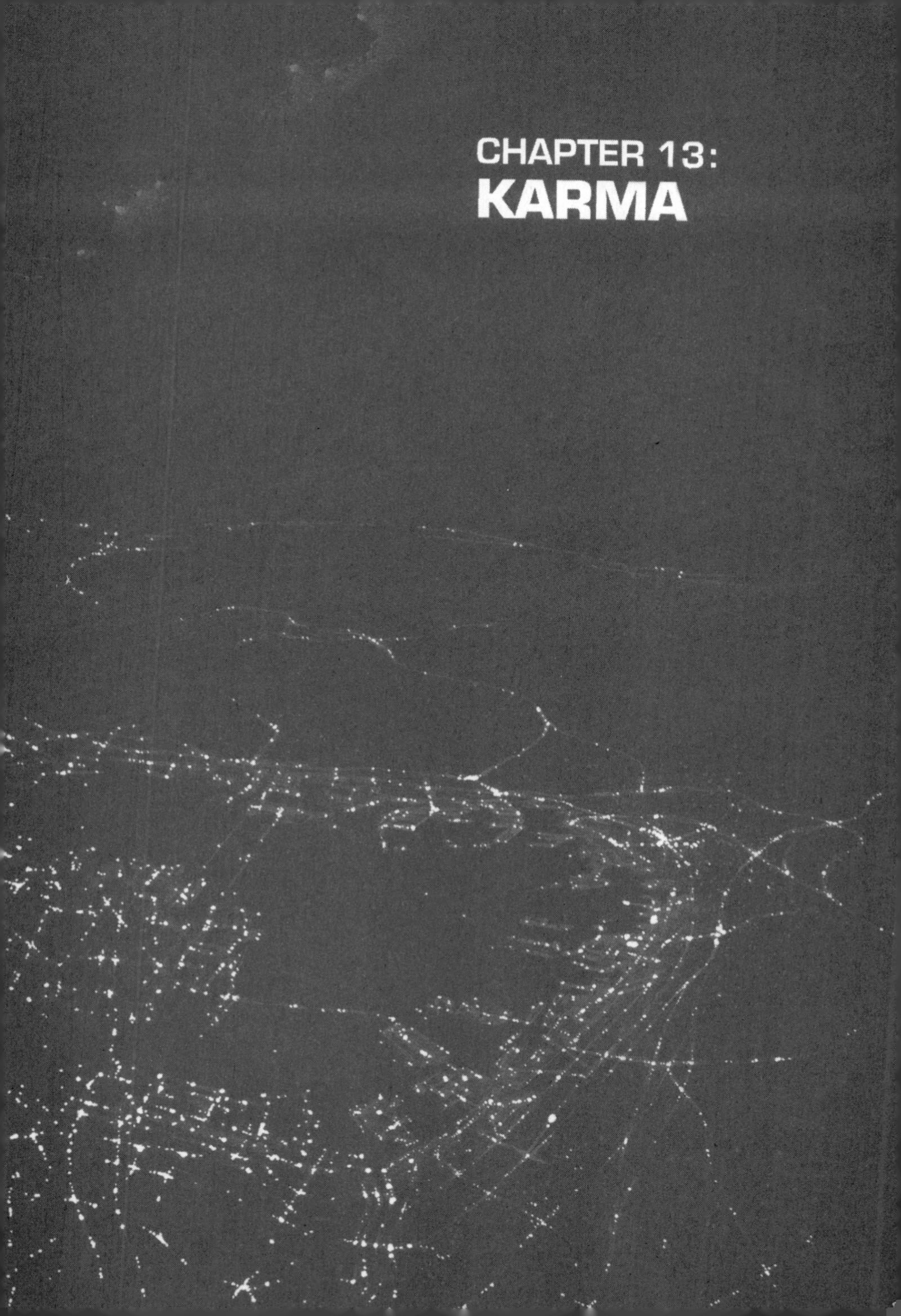

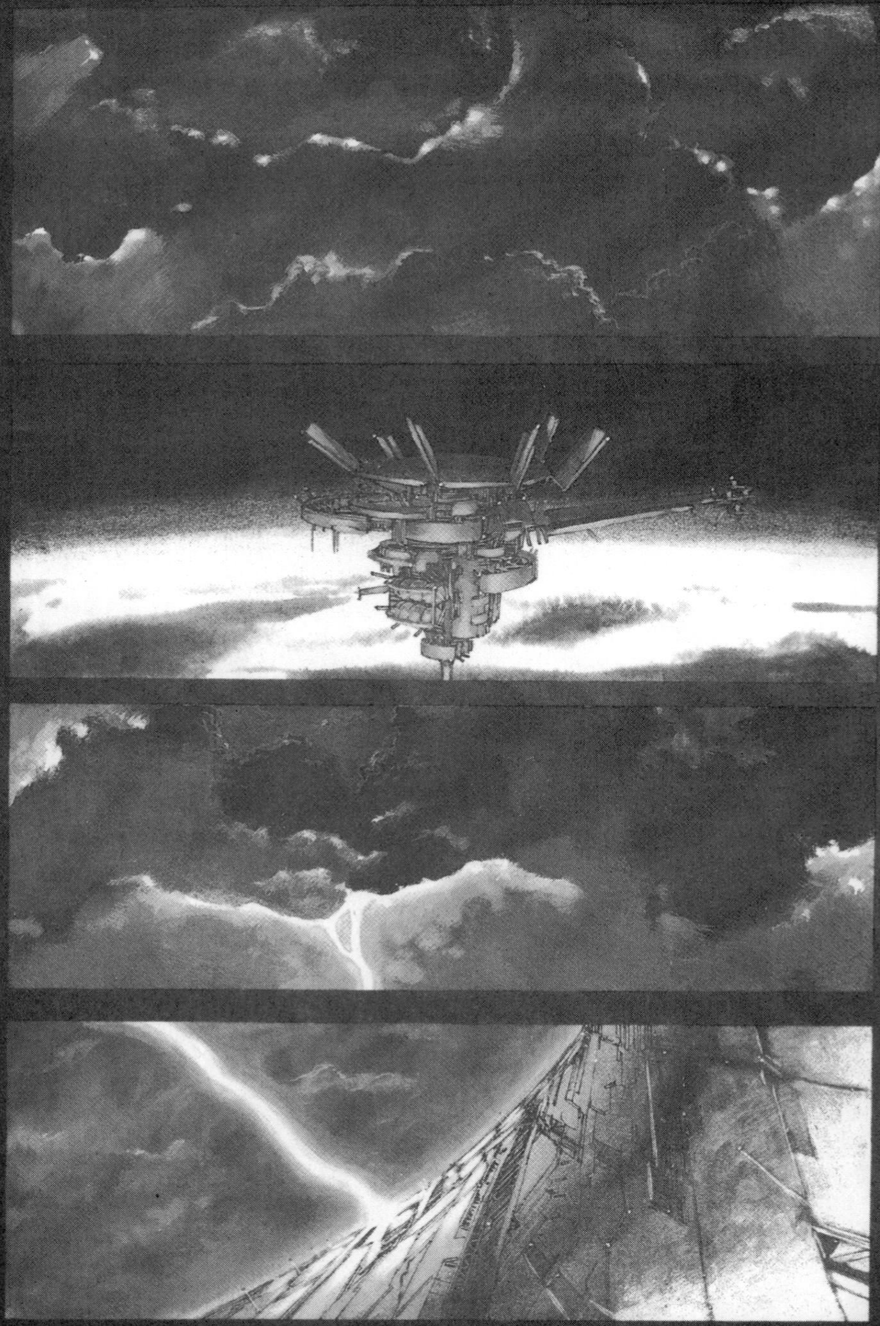

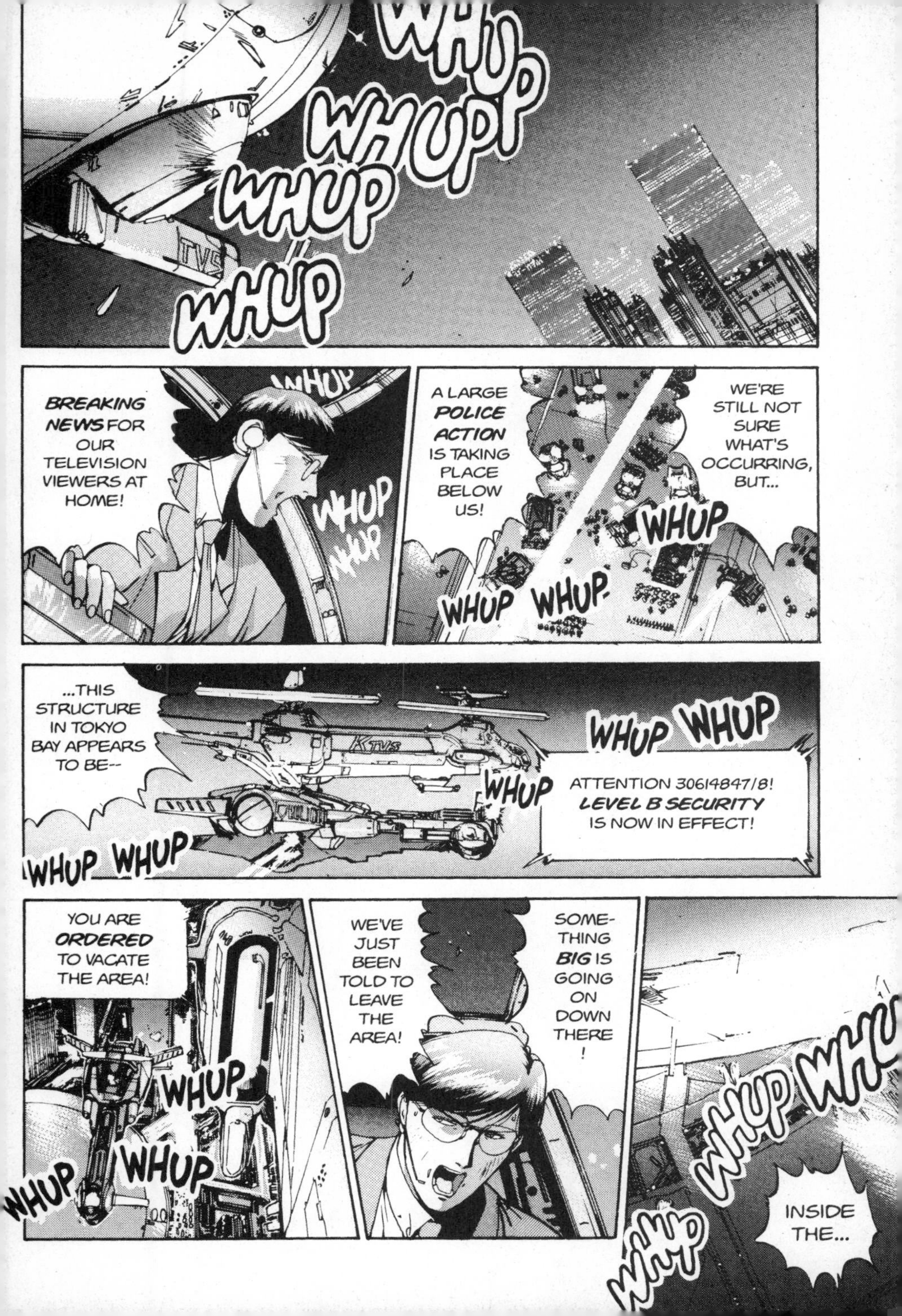
WHUP
WHUPP
WHUP
WHUP
WHUP
BREAKING NEWS FOR OUR TELEVISION VIEWERS AT HOME!
WHUP
WHUP
A LARGE POLICE ACTION IS TAKING PLACE BELOW US!
WE'RE STILL NOT SURE WHAT'S OCCURRING, BUT...
WHUP
WHUP
WHUP
...THIS STRUCTURE IN TOKYO BAY APPEARS TO BE--
WHUP WHUP
WHUP
ATTENTION 30614847/8! LEVEL B SECURITY IS NOW IN EFFECT!
WHUP WHUP
YOU ARE ORDERED TO VACATE THE AREA!
WHUP
WHUP
WHUP
WE'VE JUST BEEN TOLD TO LEAVE THE AREA!
SOME-THING BIG IS GOING ON DOWN THERE!
WHUP
INSIDE THE...

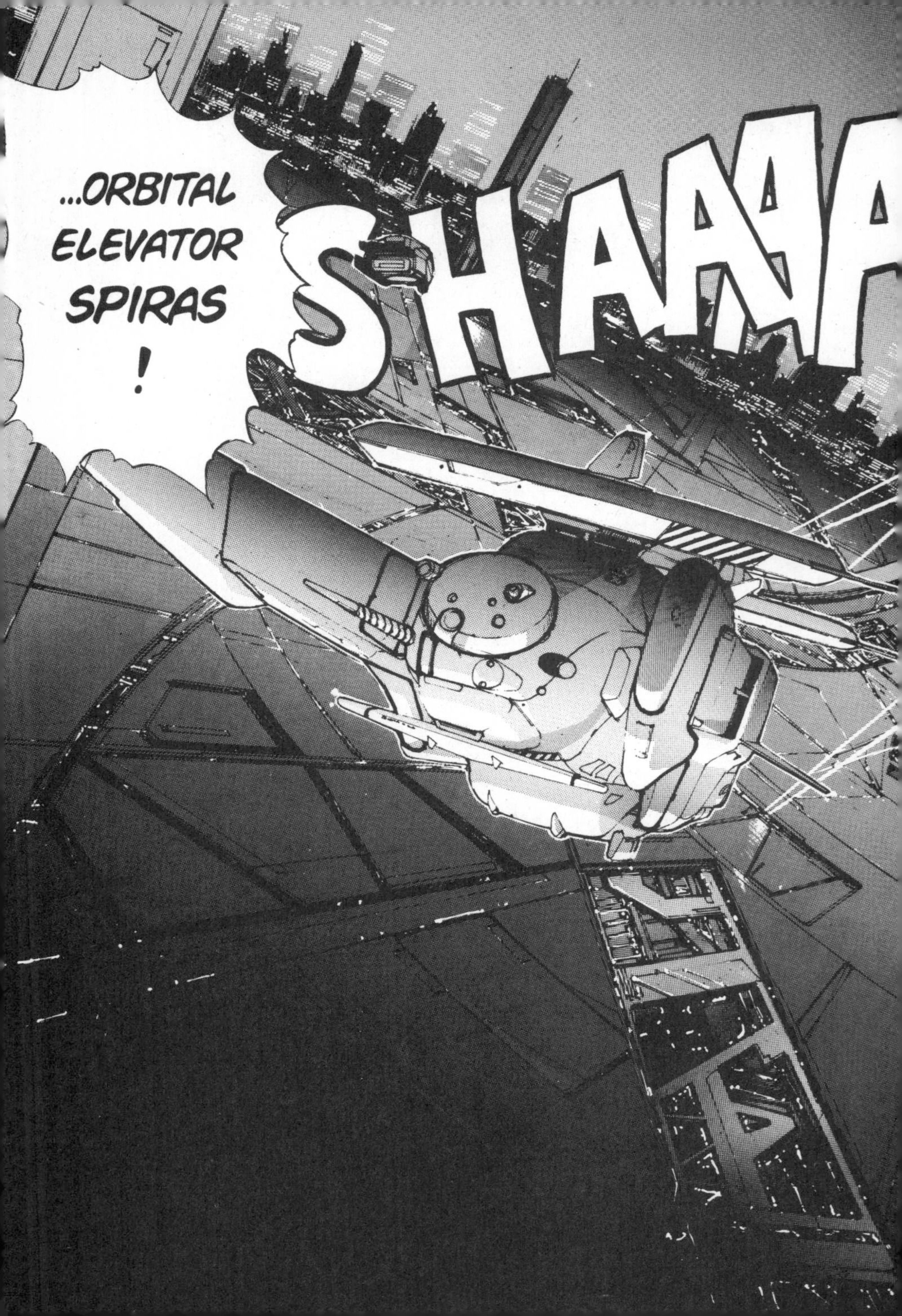
...ORBITAL ELEVATOR SPIRAS !
SHAAAA

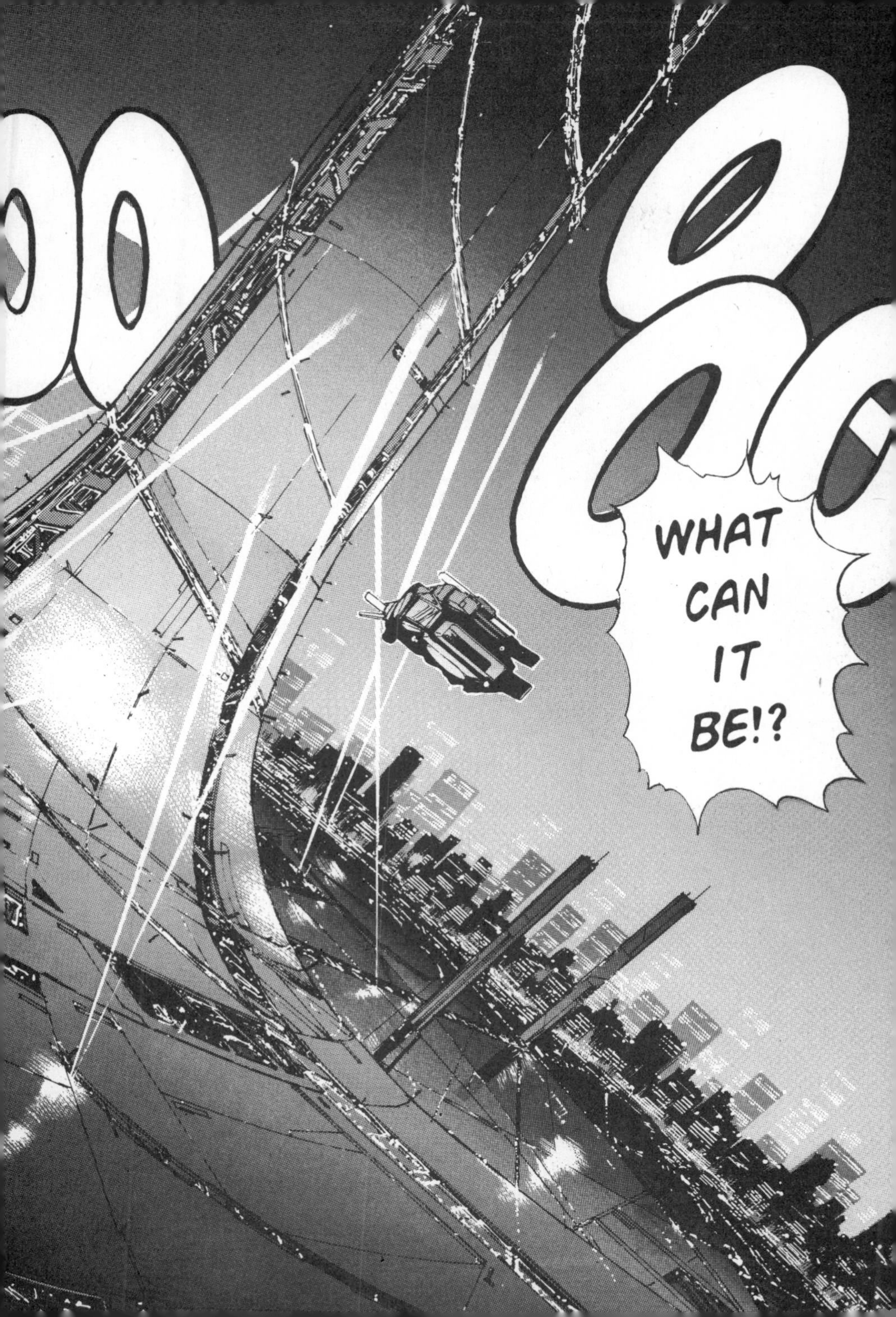
WHAT CAN IT BE!?

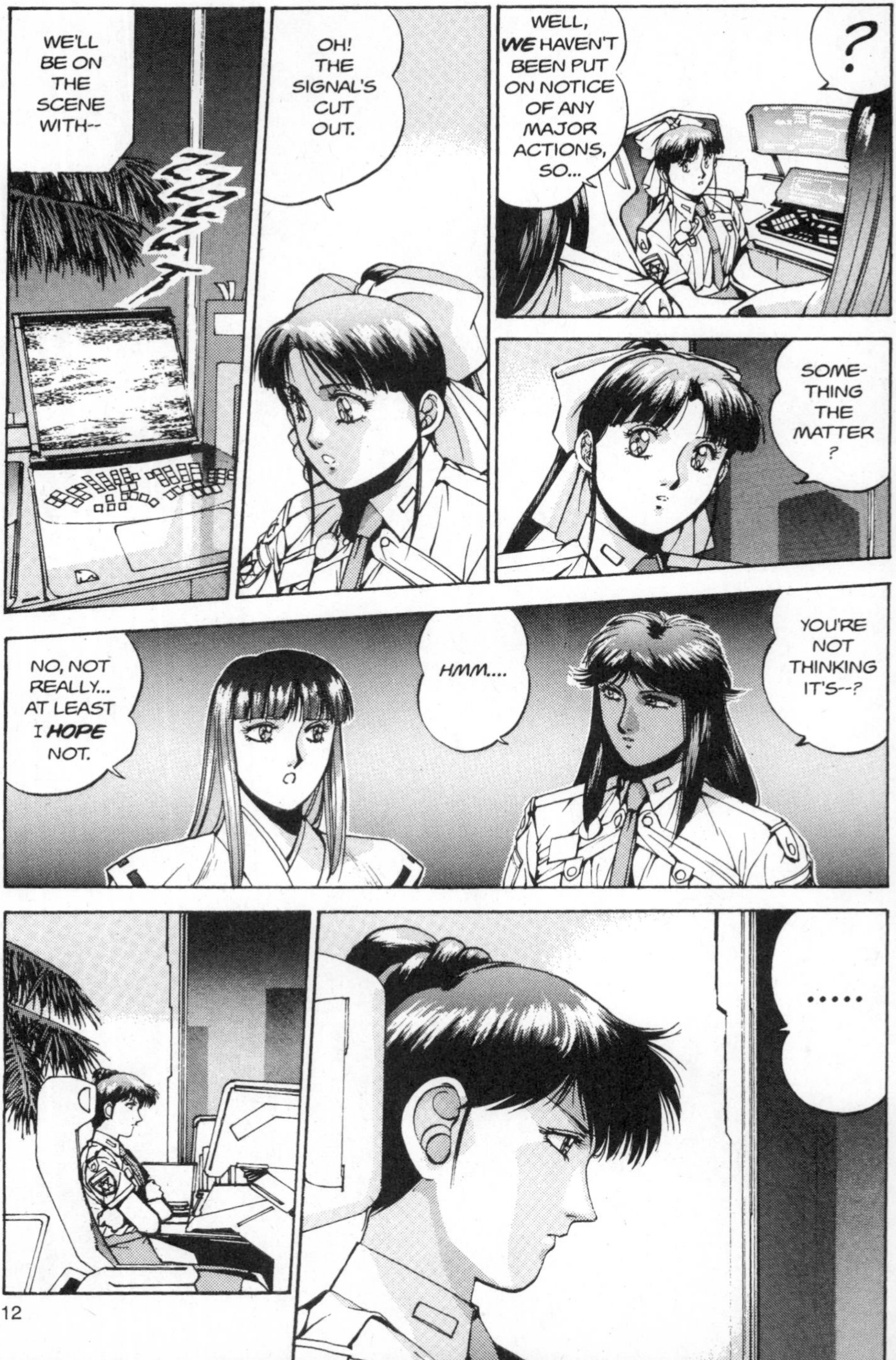

WE'LL BE ON THE SCENE WITH--
ZZZZZZT
OH! THE SIGNAL'S CUT OUT.
WELL, **WE** HAVEN'T BEEN PUT ON NOTICE OF ANY MAJOR ACTIONS, SO...
?
SOMETHING THE MATTER?
NO, NOT REALLY... AT LEAST I **HOPE** NOT.
HMM....
YOU'RE NOT THINKING IT'S--?
.....

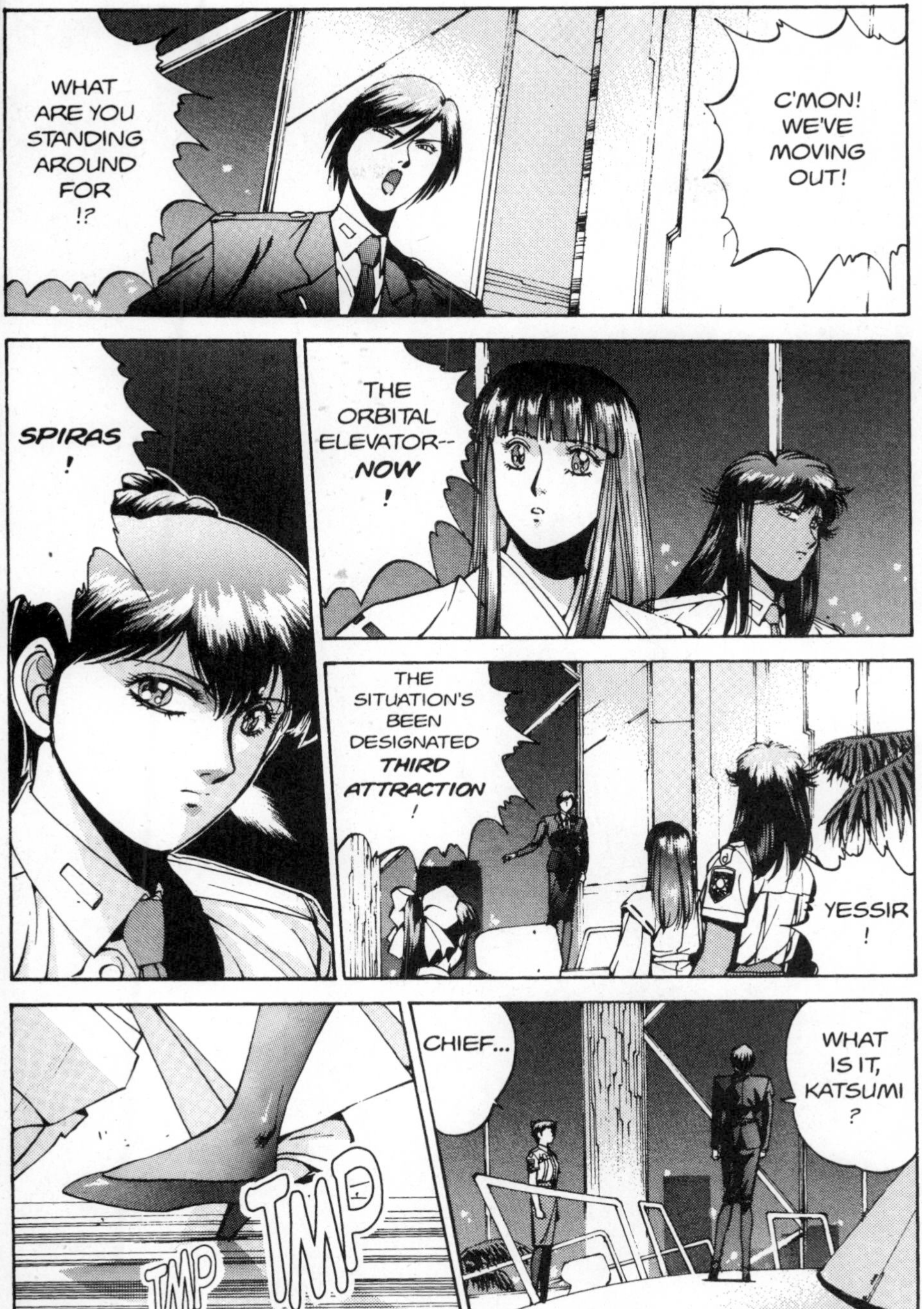
WHAT ARE YOU STANDING AROUND FOR !?
C'MON! WE'VE MOVING OUT!
SPIRAS !
THE ORBITAL ELEVATOR-- NOW !
THE SITUATION'S BEEN DESIGNATED THIRD ATTRACTION !
YESSIR !
TMP TMP
CHIEF...
WHAT IS IT, KATSUMI ?

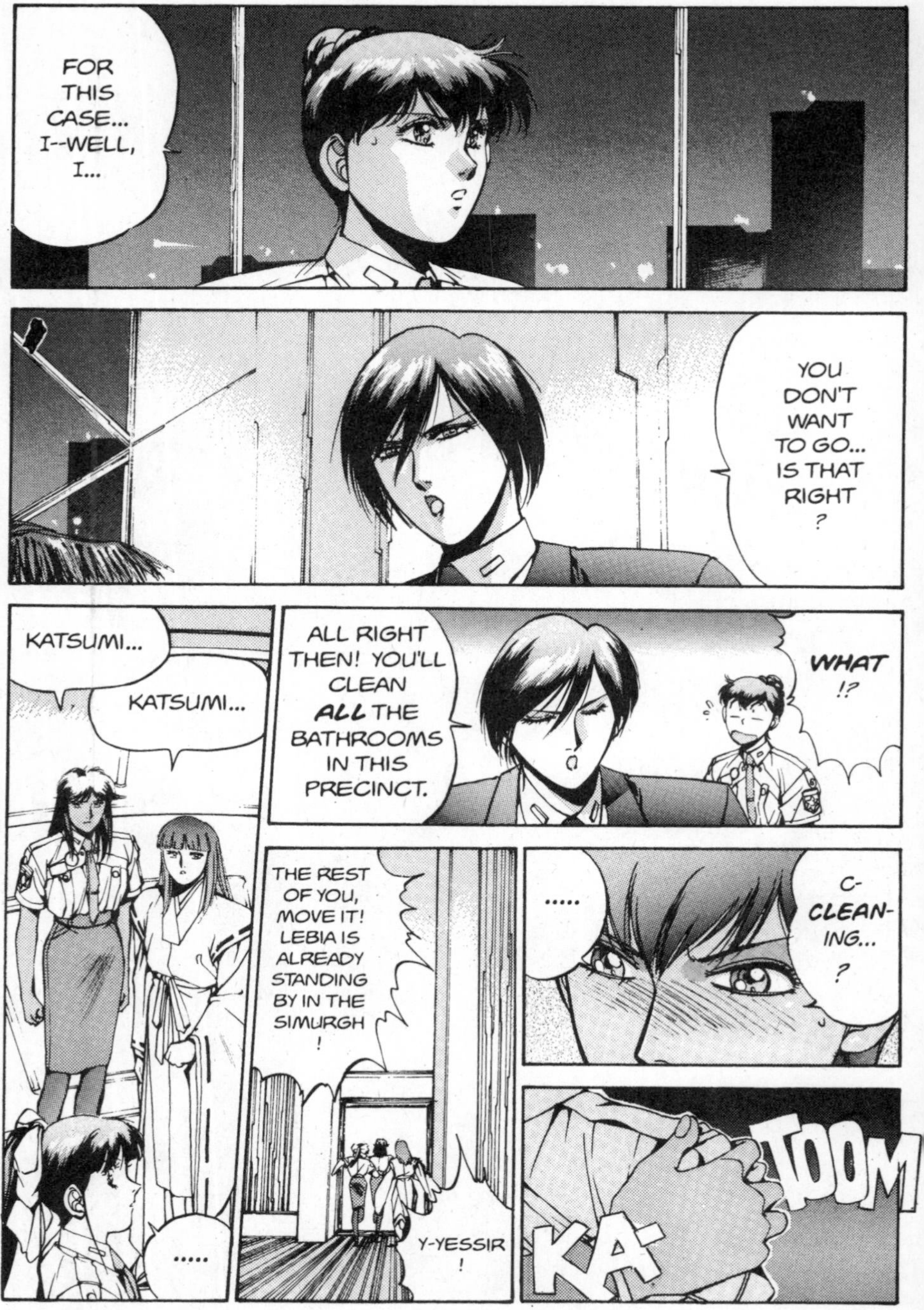
FOR THIS CASE... I--WELL, I...
YOU DON'T WANT TO GO... IS THAT RIGHT?
KATSUMI...
KATSUMI...
.....
ALL RIGHT THEN! YOU'LL CLEAN ALL THE BATHROOMS IN THIS PRECINCT.
WHAT!?
THE REST OF YOU, MOVE IT! LEBIA IS ALREADY STANDING BY IN THE SIMURGH!
Y-YESSIR!
.....
C-CLEANING...?
KA-
TOOM

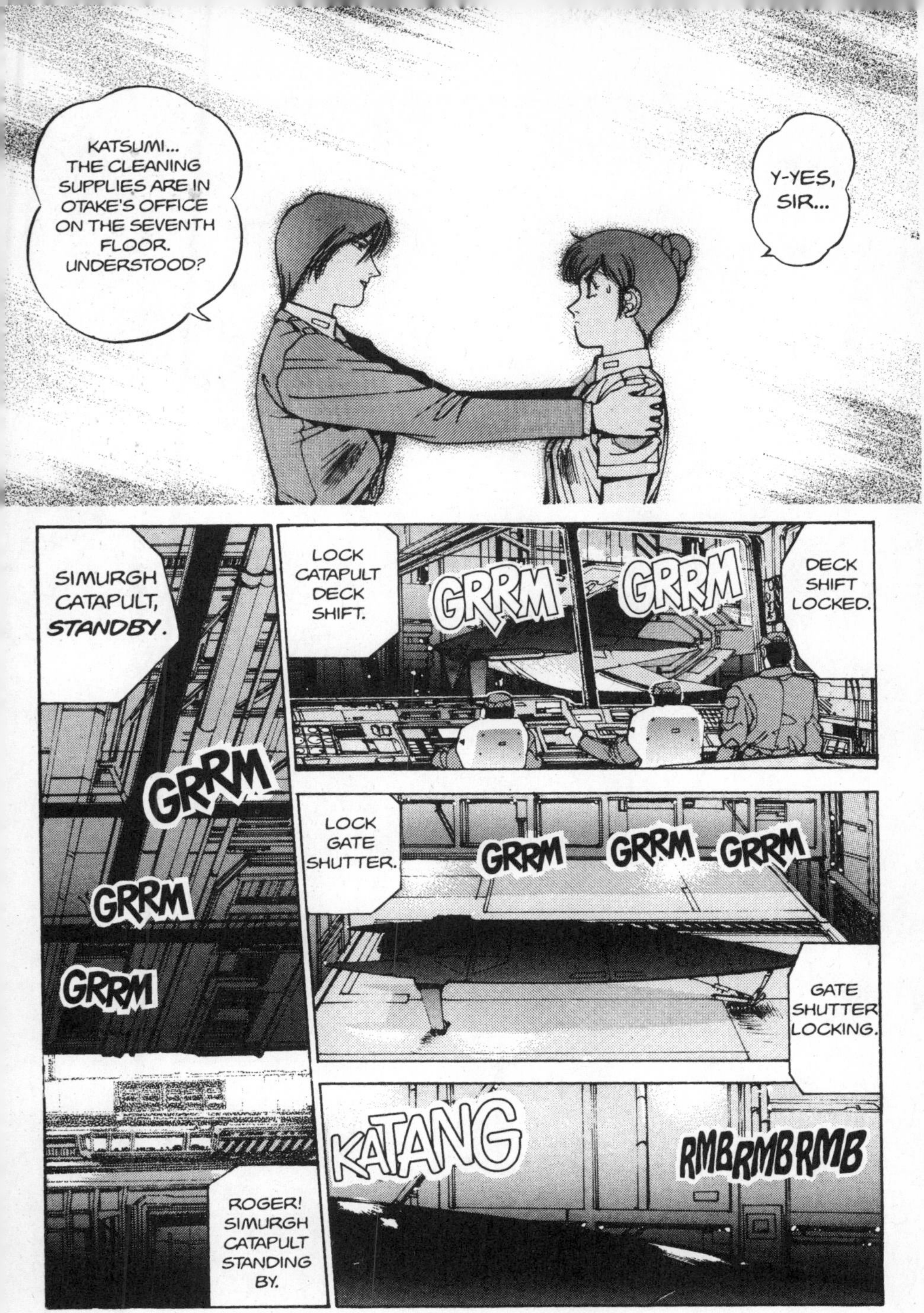
KATSUMI... THE CLEANING SUPPLIES ARE IN OTAKE'S OFFICE ON THE SEVENTH FLOOR. UNDERSTOOD?
Y-YES, SIR...
SIMURGH CATAPULT, **STANDBY**.
GRRM
GRRM
GRRM
LOCK CATAPULT DECK SHIFT.
GRRM GRRM
DECK SHIFT LOCKED.
LOCK GATE SHUTTER.
GRRM GRRM GRRM
GATE SHUTTER LOCKING.
ROGER! SIMURGH CATAPULT STANDING BY.
KATANG
RMBRMBRMB

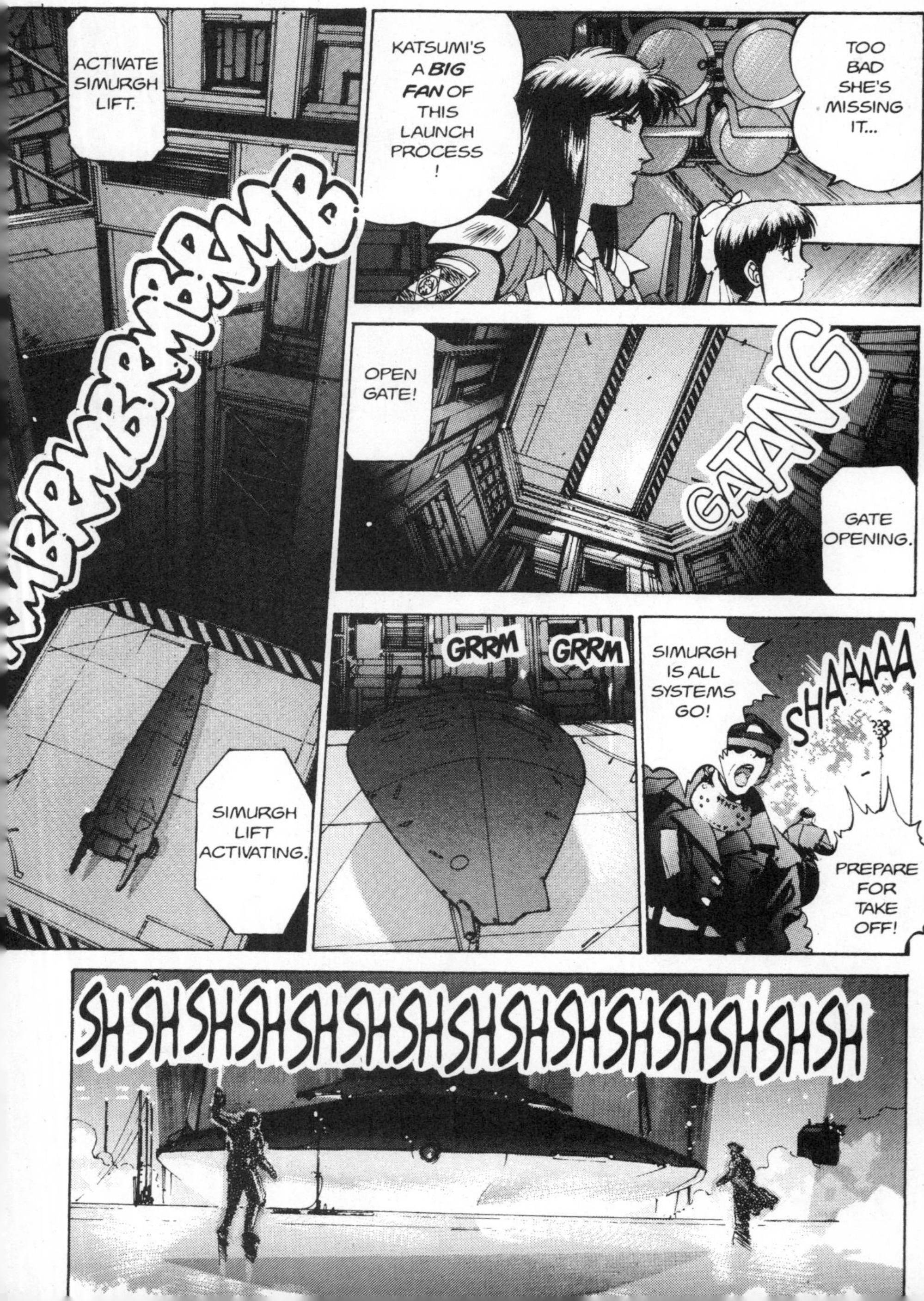
ACTIVATE SIMURGH LIFT.
BRMBRMBRMBRMB
KATSUMI'S A **BIG FAN** OF THIS LAUNCH PROCESS!
TOO BAD SHE'S MISSING IT...
OPEN GATE!
GATANG
GATE OPENING.
SIMURGH LIFT ACTIVATING.
GRRM GRRM
SIMURGH IS ALL SYSTEMS GO!
SHAAAAA
PREPARE FOR TAKE OFF!
SHSHSHSHSHSHSHSHSHSHSHSHSH

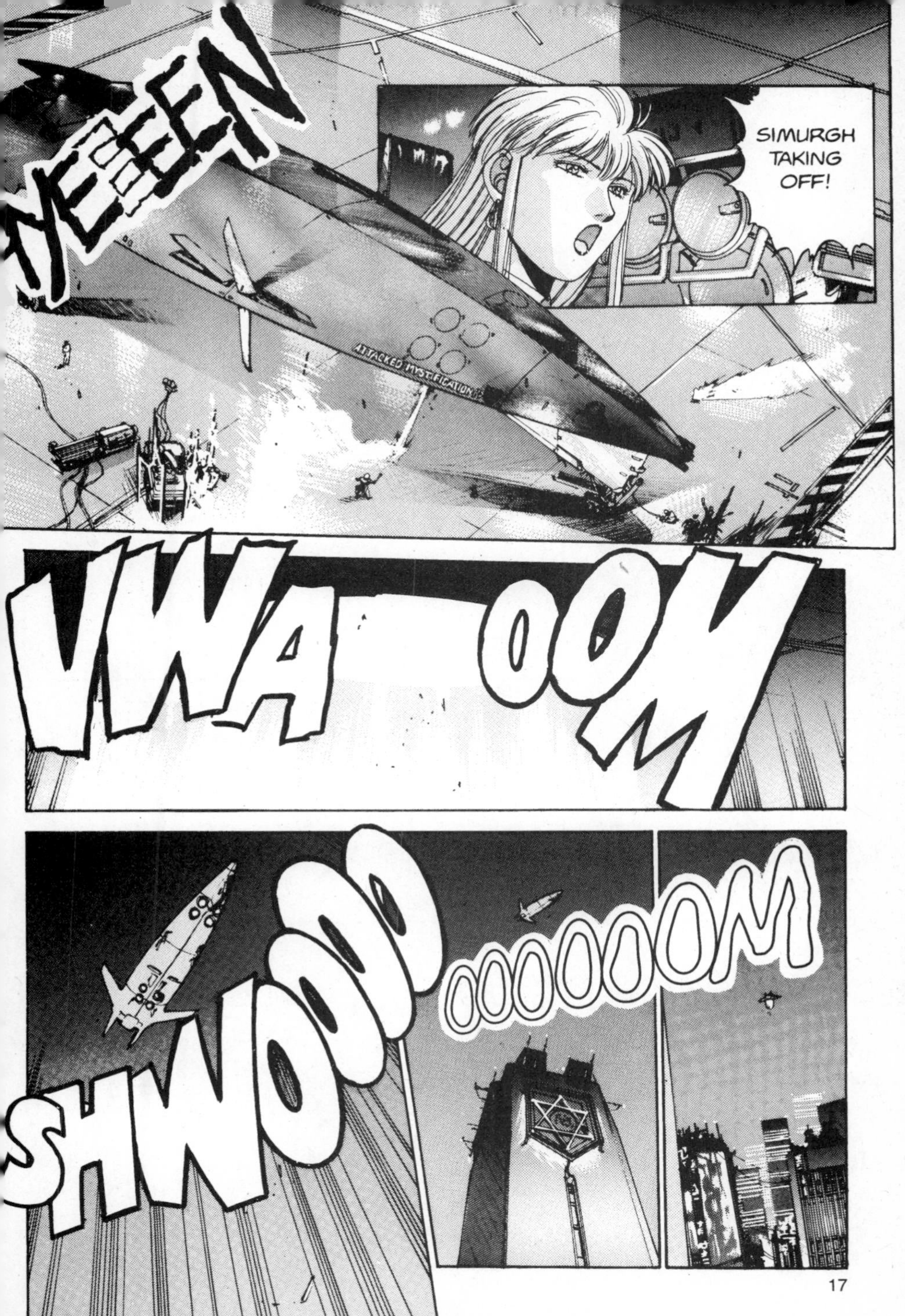
YEEEN
SIMURGH TAKING OFF!
ATTACKED MYSTIFICATION
VWA OOM
SHWOOOOO
OOOOOOOM

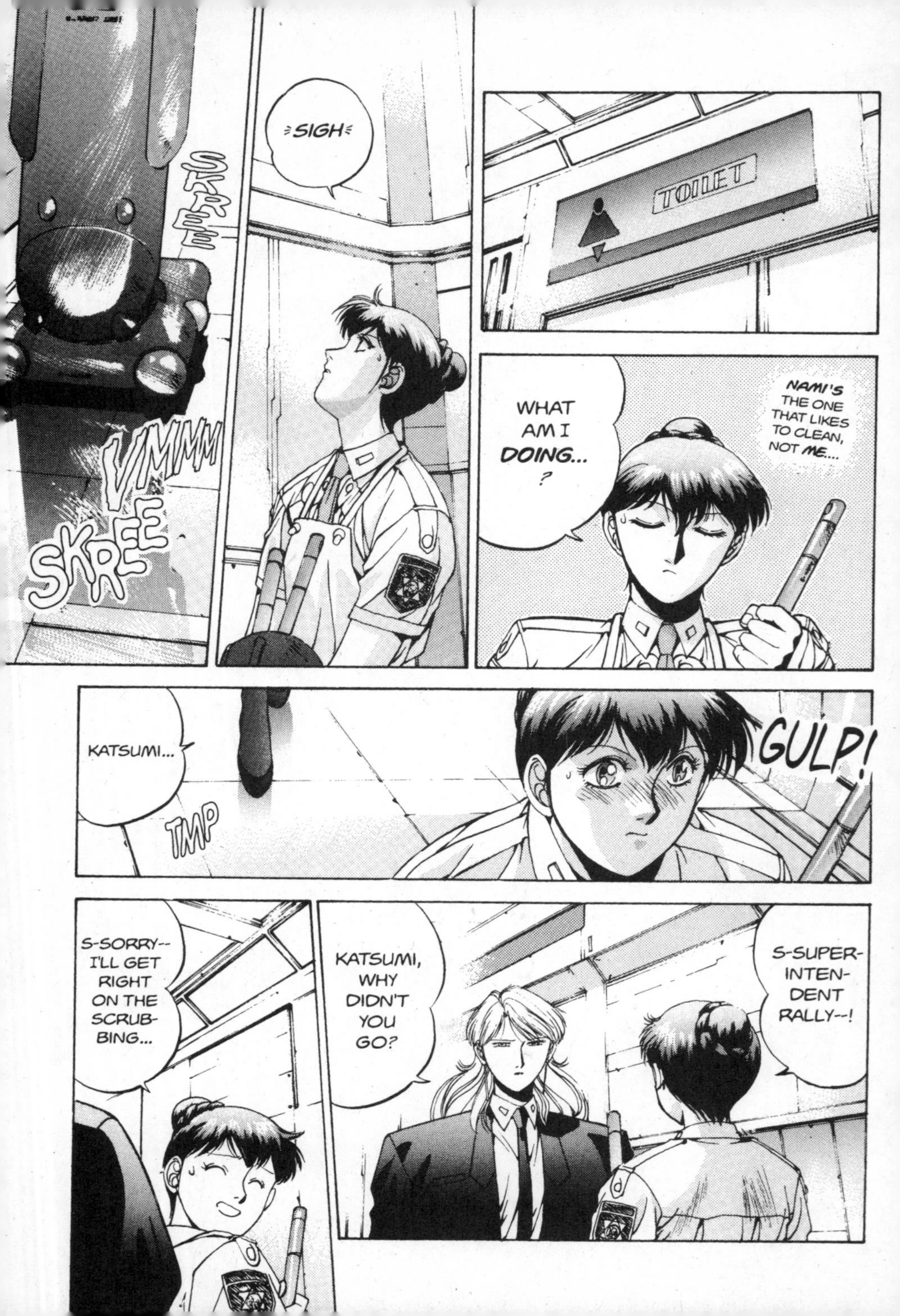
SKREE
VMMM
SKREE
SIGH
TOILET
WHAT AM I DOING...?
NAMI'S THE ONE THAT LIKES TO CLEAN, NOT ME...
KATSUMI...
TMP
GULP!
S-SORRY-- I'LL GET RIGHT ON THE SCRUB-BING...
KATSUMI, WHY DIDN'T YOU GO?
S-SUPER-INTEN-DENT RALLY--!

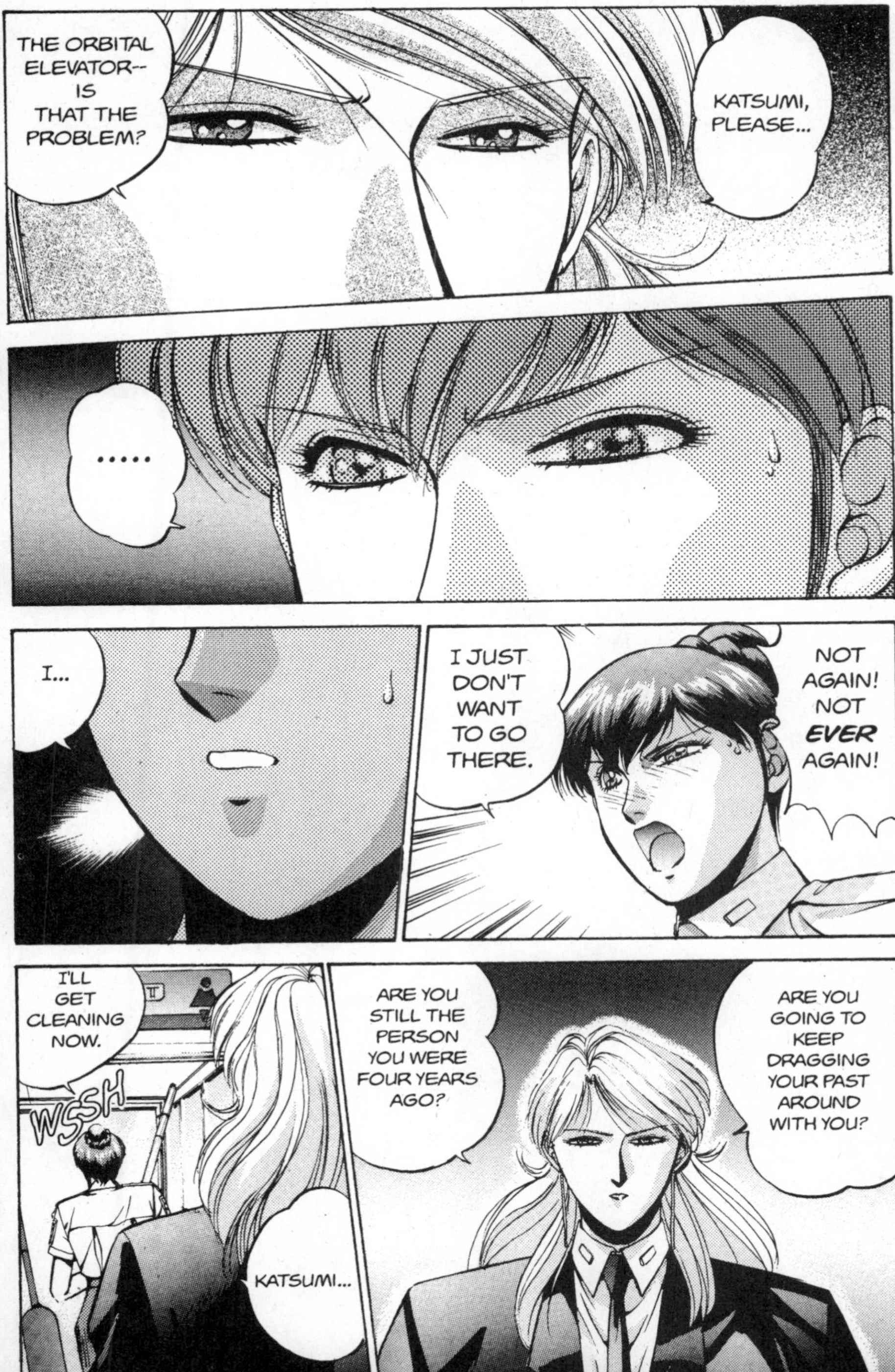
THE ORBITAL ELEVATOR-- IS THAT THE PROBLEM?
KATSUMI, PLEASE...
.....
I...
I JUST DON'T WANT TO GO THERE.
NOT AGAIN! NOT EVER AGAIN!
I'LL GET CLEANING NOW.
WSSH
ARE YOU STILL THE PERSON YOU WERE FOUR YEARS AGO?
ARE YOU GOING TO KEEP DRAGGING YOUR PAST AROUND WITH YOU?
KATSUMI...

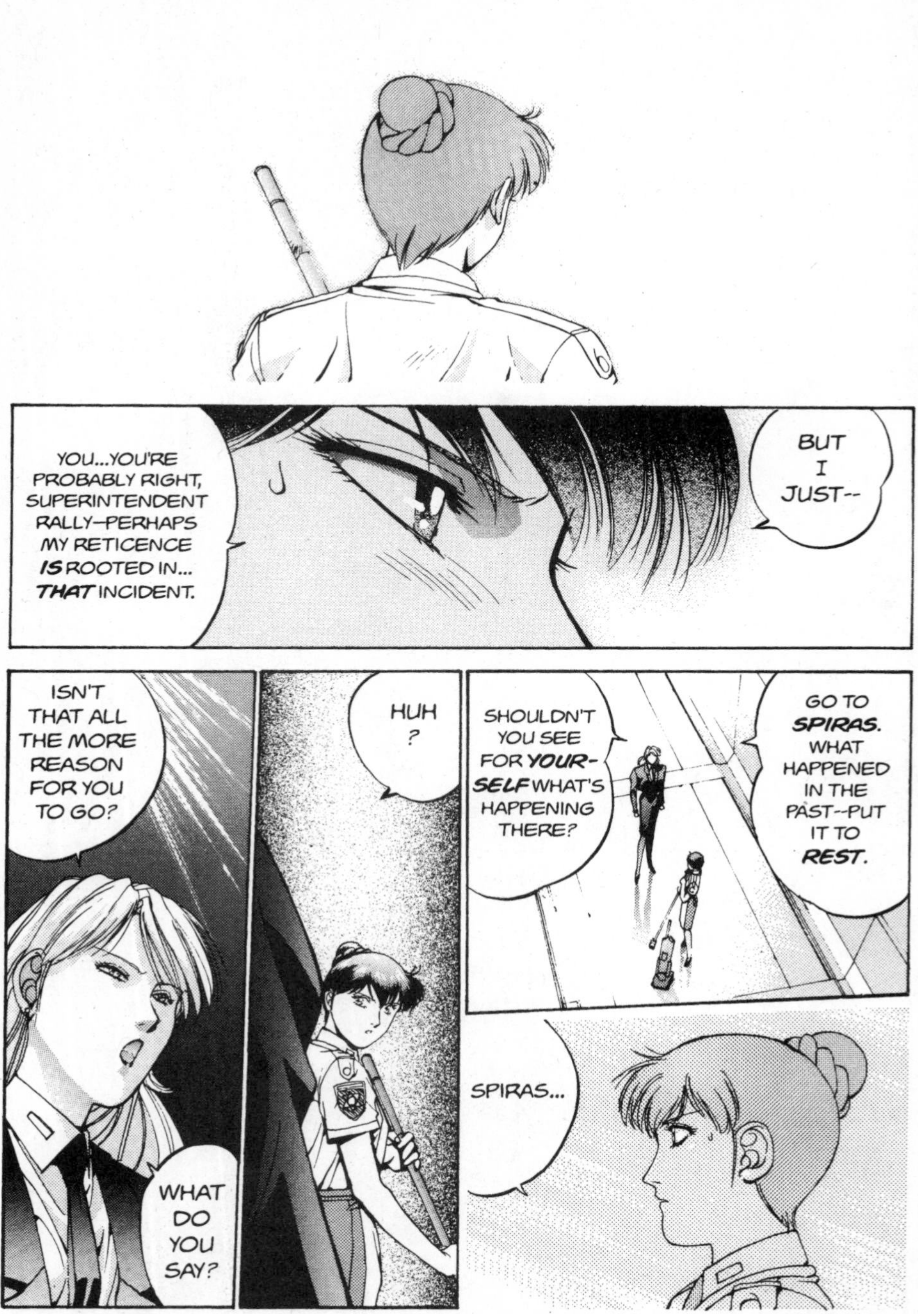
YOU...YOU'RE PROBABLY RIGHT, SUPERINTENDENT RALLY--PERHAPS MY RETICENCE **IS** ROOTED IN... **THAT** INCIDENT.
BUT I JUST--
ISN'T THAT ALL THE MORE REASON FOR YOU TO GO?
WHAT DO YOU SAY?
HUH ?
SHOULDN'T YOU SEE FOR **YOURSELF** WHAT'S HAPPENING THERE?
GO TO **SPIRAS**. WHAT HAPPENED IN THE PAST--PUT IT TO **REST**.
SPIRAS...

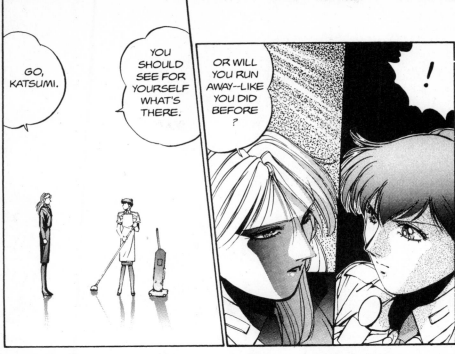

GO, KATSUMI.

YOU SHOULD SEE FOR YOURSELF WHAT'S THERE.

OR WILL YOU RUN AWAY--LIKE YOU DID BEFORE?

!

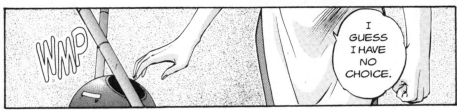

WMP

I GUESS I HAVE NO CHOICE.

I'LL GO!

BACK TO SPIRAS!

GOOD...

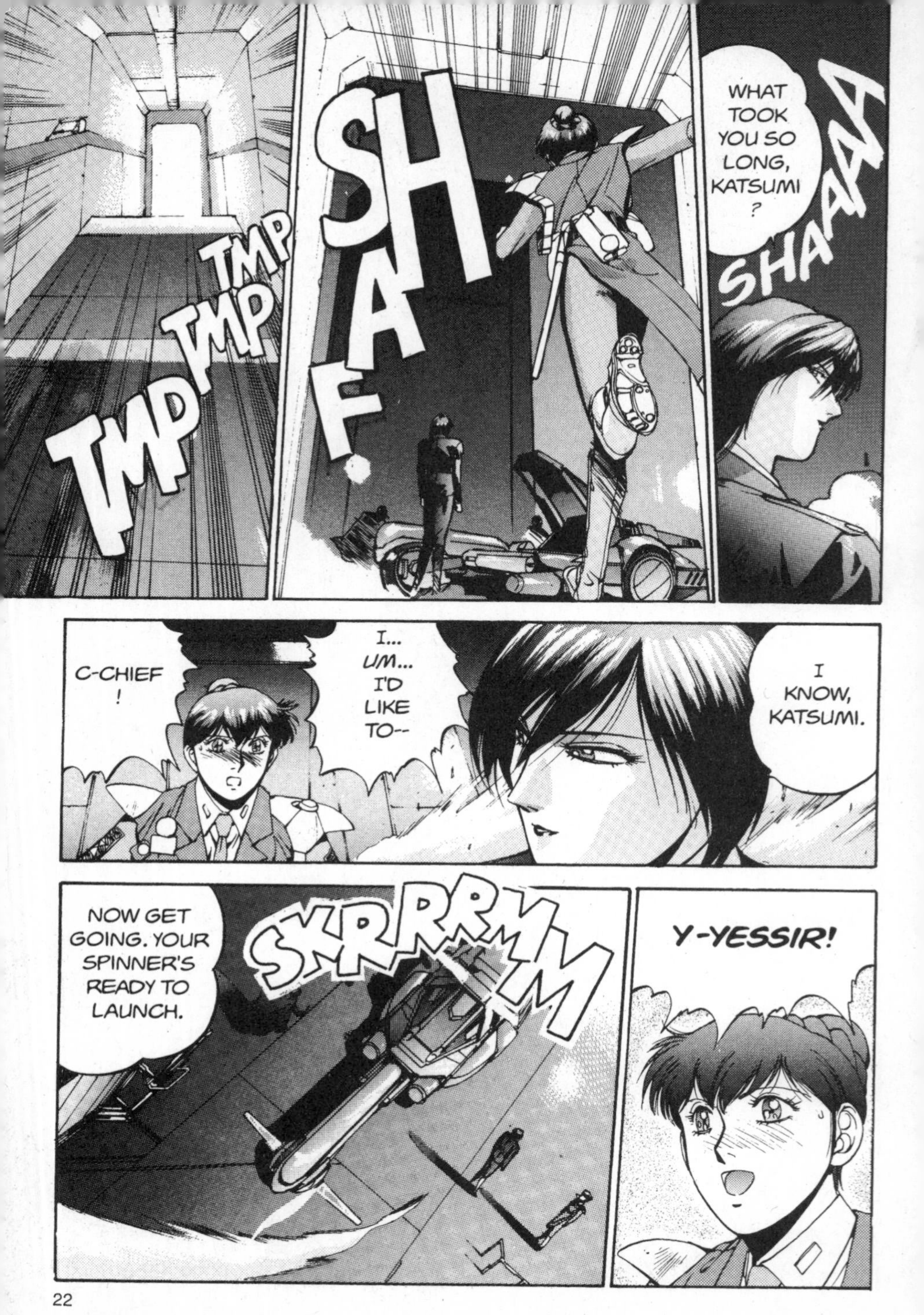
TMP TMP TMP TMP
SH A F
WHAT TOOK YOU SO LONG, KATSUMI ?
SHAAAA
C-CHIEF !
I... UM... I'D LIKE TO--
I KNOW, KATSUMI.
NOW GET GOING. YOUR SPINNER'S READY TO LAUNCH.
SKRRRMMM
Y-YESSIR!

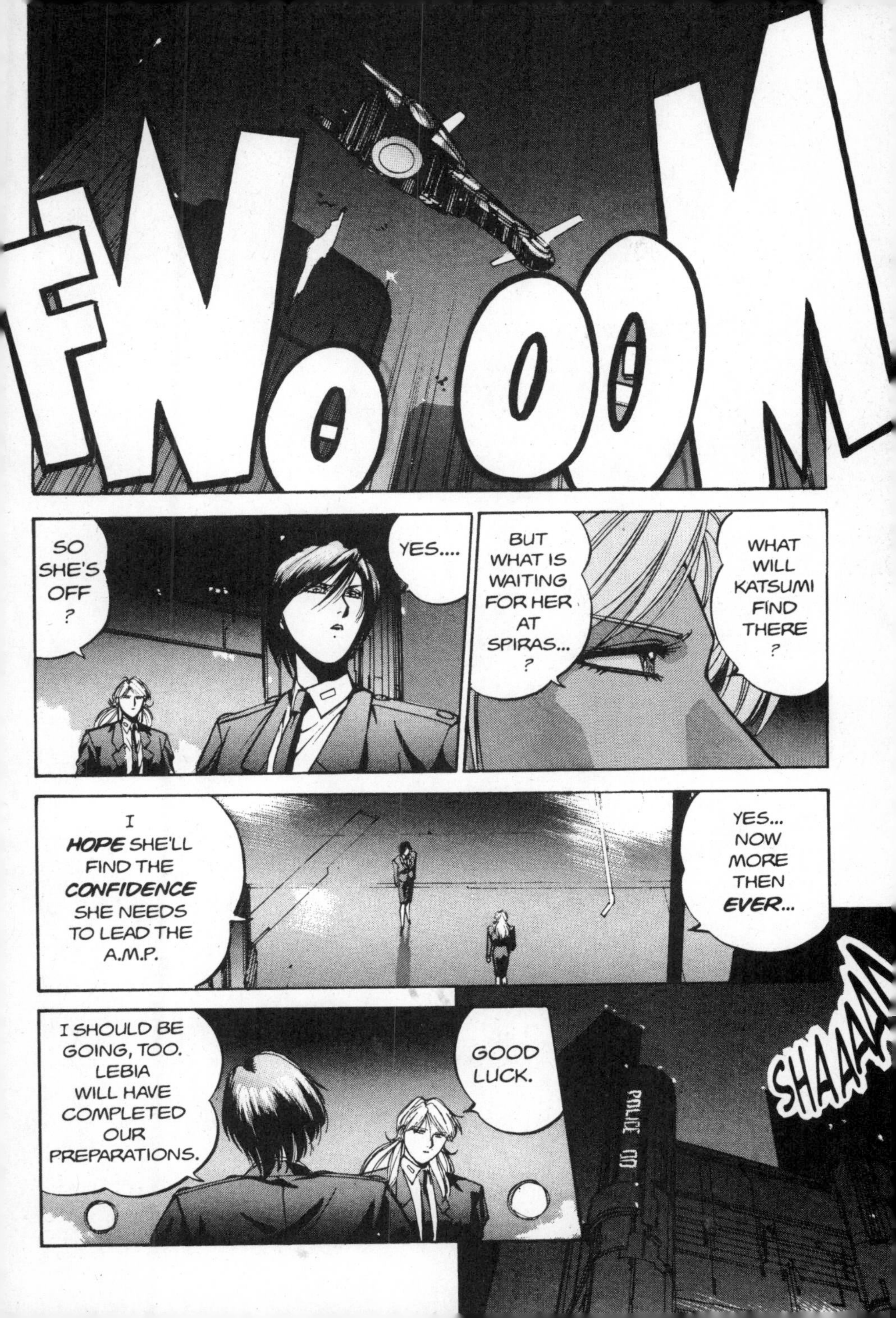
FWOOOM
SO SHE'S OFF?
YES....
BUT WHAT IS WAITING FOR HER AT SPIRAS...?
WHAT WILL KATSUMI FIND THERE?
I HOPE SHE'LL FIND THE CONFIDENCE SHE NEEDS TO LEAD THE A.M.P.
YES... NOW MORE THEN EVER...
I SHOULD BE GOING, TOO. LEBIA WILL HAVE COMPLETED OUR PREPARATIONS.
GOOD LUCK.
SHAAA
POLICE 00

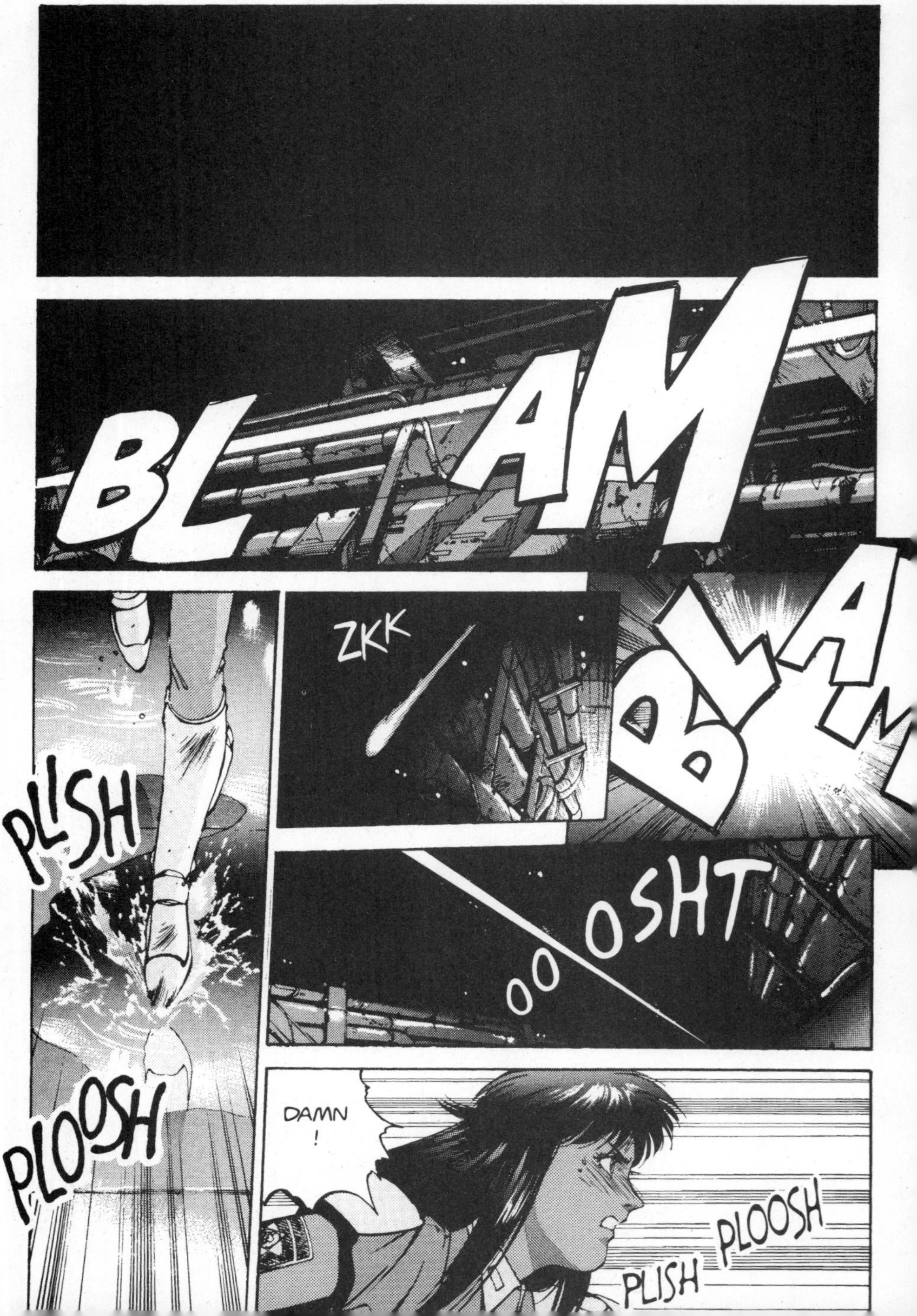
BLAM
PLISH
PLOOSH
ZKK
BLAM
OOOSHT
DAMN
!
PLISH
PLOOSH

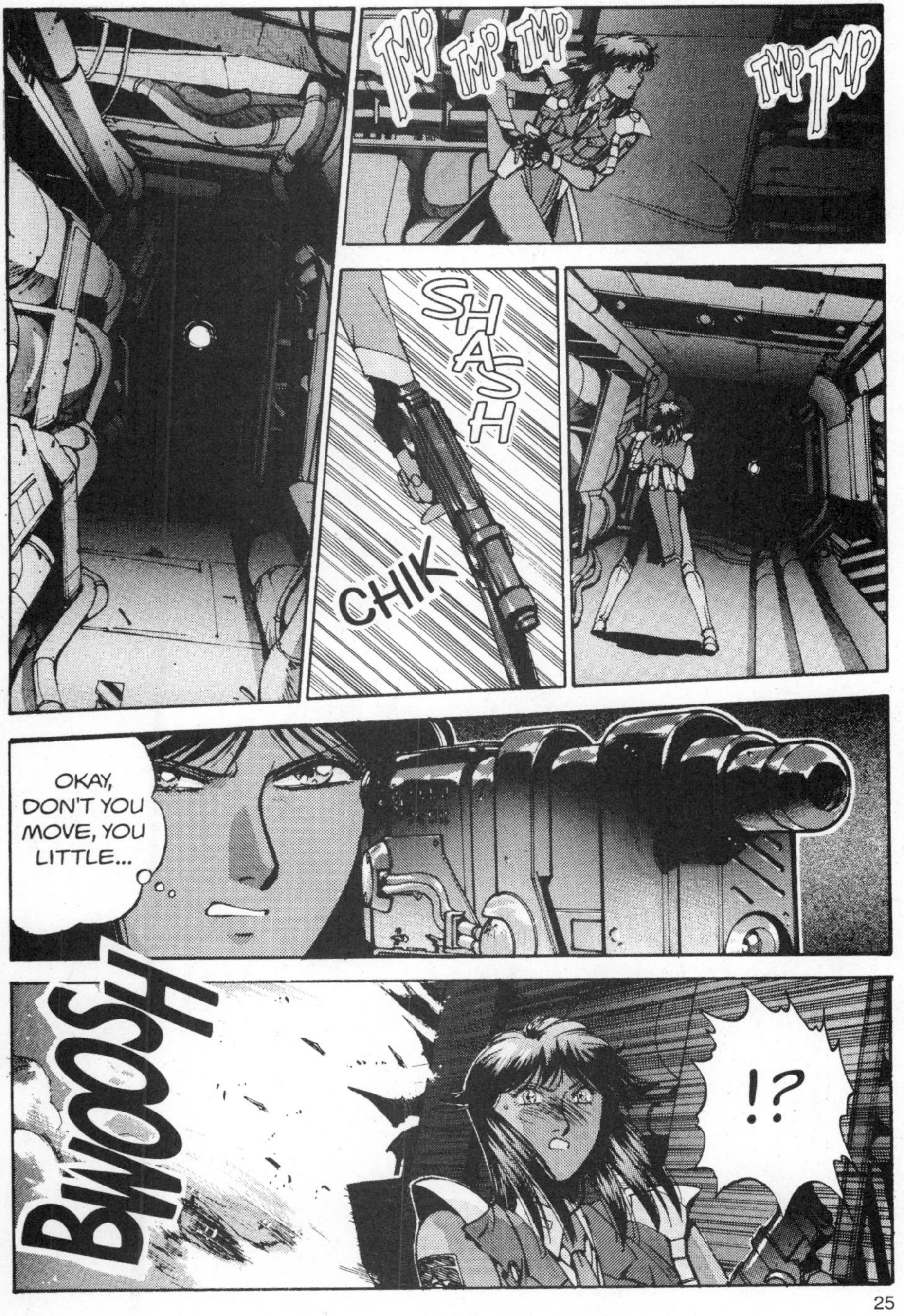
TMP TMP TMP
TMP TMP
SHA-SH
CHIK
OKAY, DON'T YOU MOVE, YOU LITTLE...
BWOOSH
!?

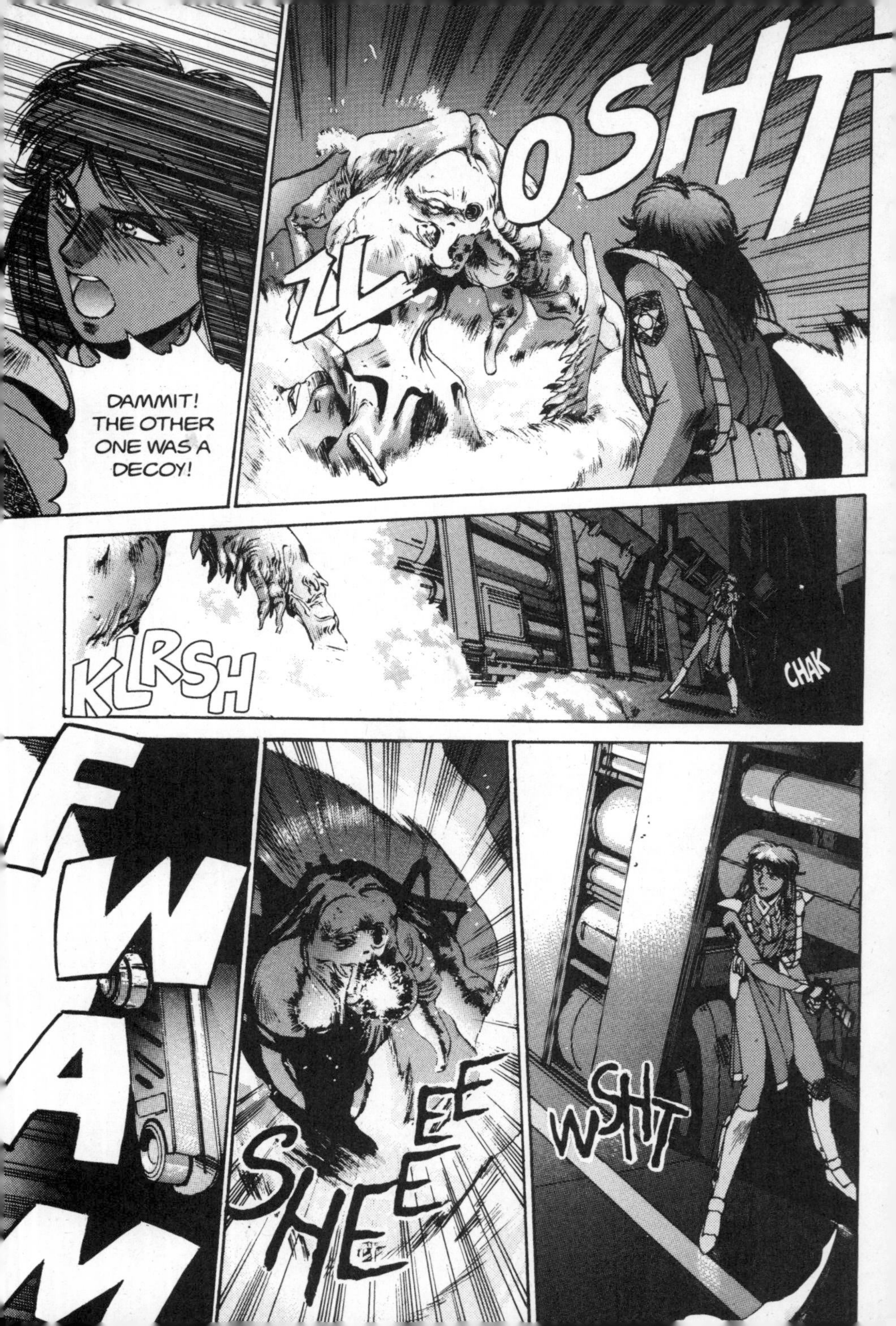
DAMMIT! THE OTHER ONE WAS A DECOY!
ZZ
OSHT
KLRSH
CHAK
FWAM
SHEEEE
WSHT

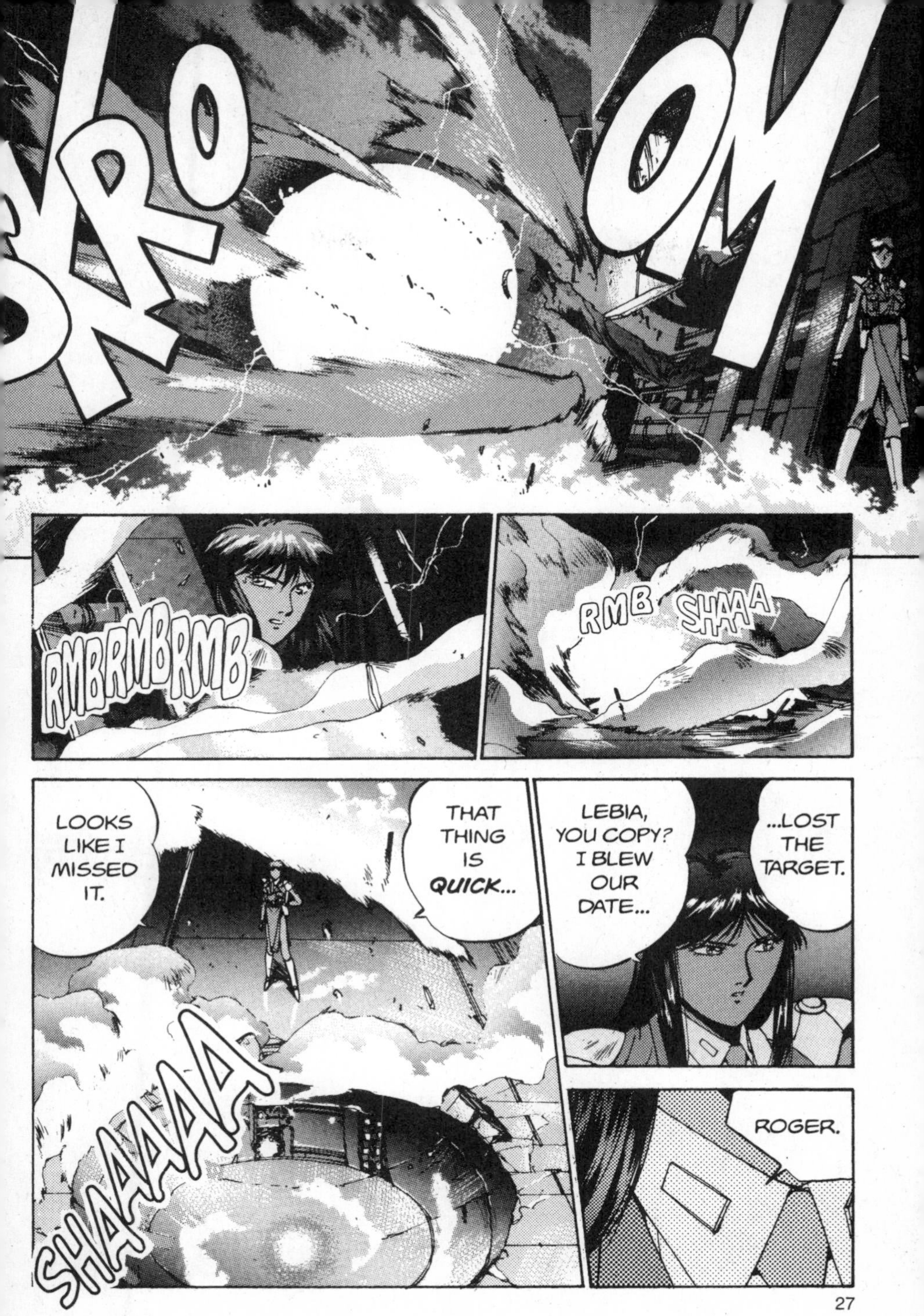
KRO
OM
RMBRMBRMB
RMB
SHAAA
LOOKS LIKE I MISSED IT.
THAT THING IS *QUICK*...
SHAAAAAA
LEBIA, YOU COPY? I BLEW OUR DATE...
...LOST THE TARGET.
ROGER.

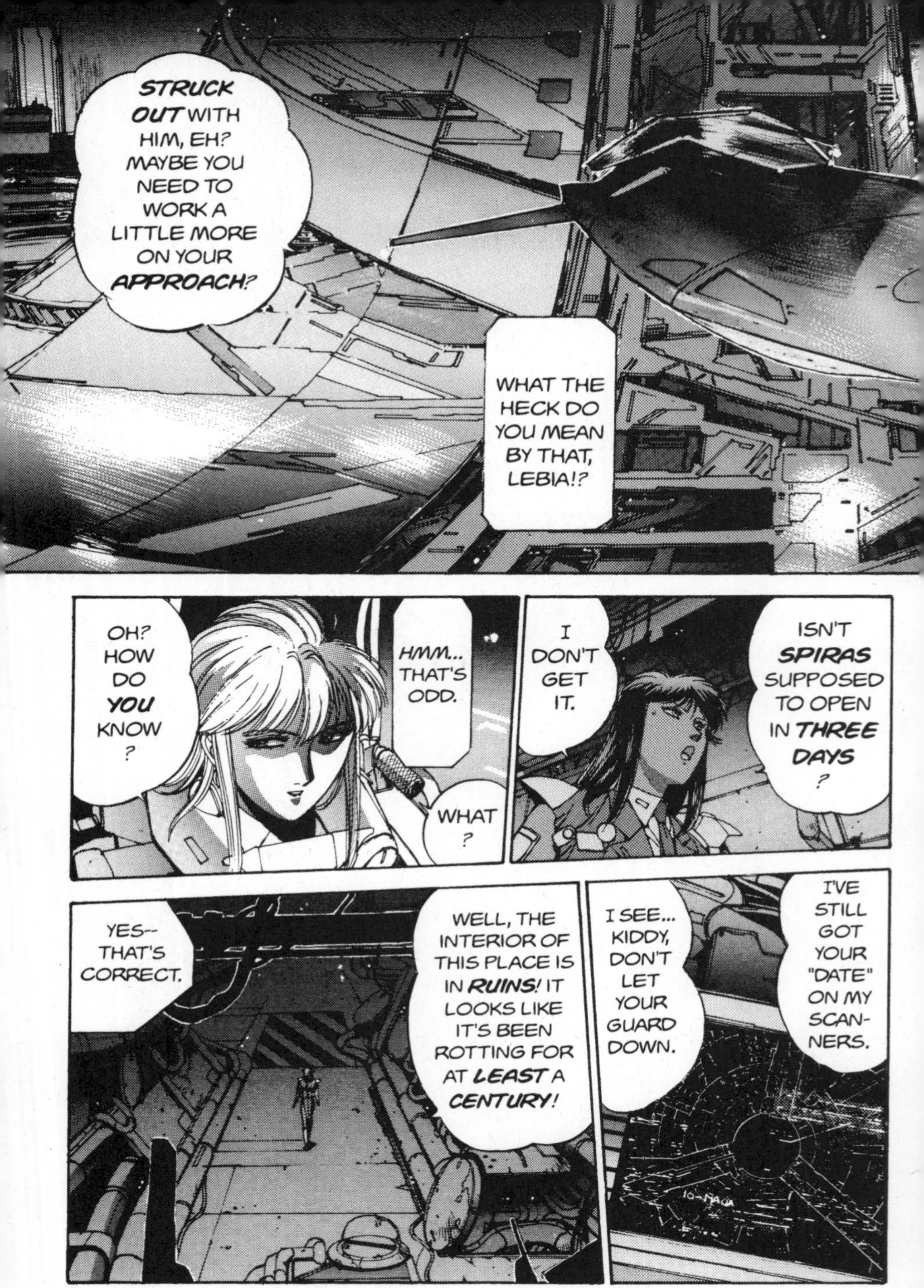
STRUCK OUT WITH HIM, EH? MAYBE YOU NEED TO WORK A LITTLE MORE ON YOUR APPROACH?
WHAT THE HECK DO YOU MEAN BY THAT, LEBIA!?
OH? HOW DO YOU KNOW ?
HMM... THAT'S ODD.
WHAT ?
I DON'T GET IT.
ISN'T SPIRAS SUPPOSED TO OPEN IN THREE DAYS ?
YES-- THAT'S CORRECT.
WELL, THE INTERIOR OF THIS PLACE IS IN RUINS! IT LOOKS LIKE IT'S BEEN ROTTING FOR AT LEAST A CENTURY!
I SEE... KIDDY, DON'T LET YOUR GUARD DOWN.
I'VE STILL GOT YOUR "DATE" ON MY SCAN-NERS.

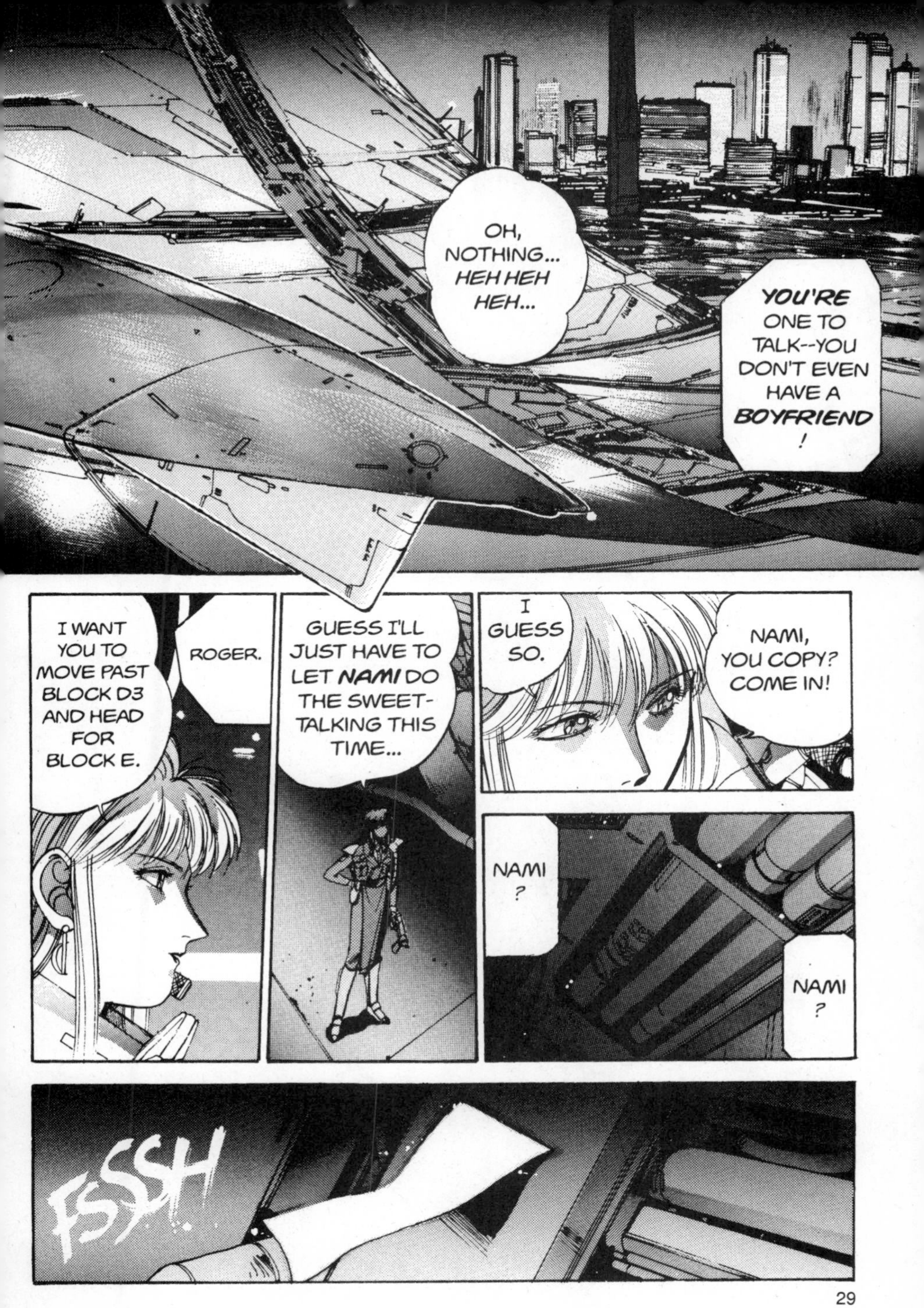
OH, NOTHING... HEH HEH HEH...
YOU'RE ONE TO TALK--YOU DON'T EVEN HAVE A BOYFRIEND!
I WANT YOU TO MOVE PAST BLOCK D3 AND HEAD FOR BLOCK E.
ROGER.
GUESS I'LL JUST HAVE TO LET NAMI DO THE SWEET-TALKING THIS TIME...
I GUESS SO.
NAMI, YOU COPY? COME IN!
NAMI?
NAMI?
FSSH

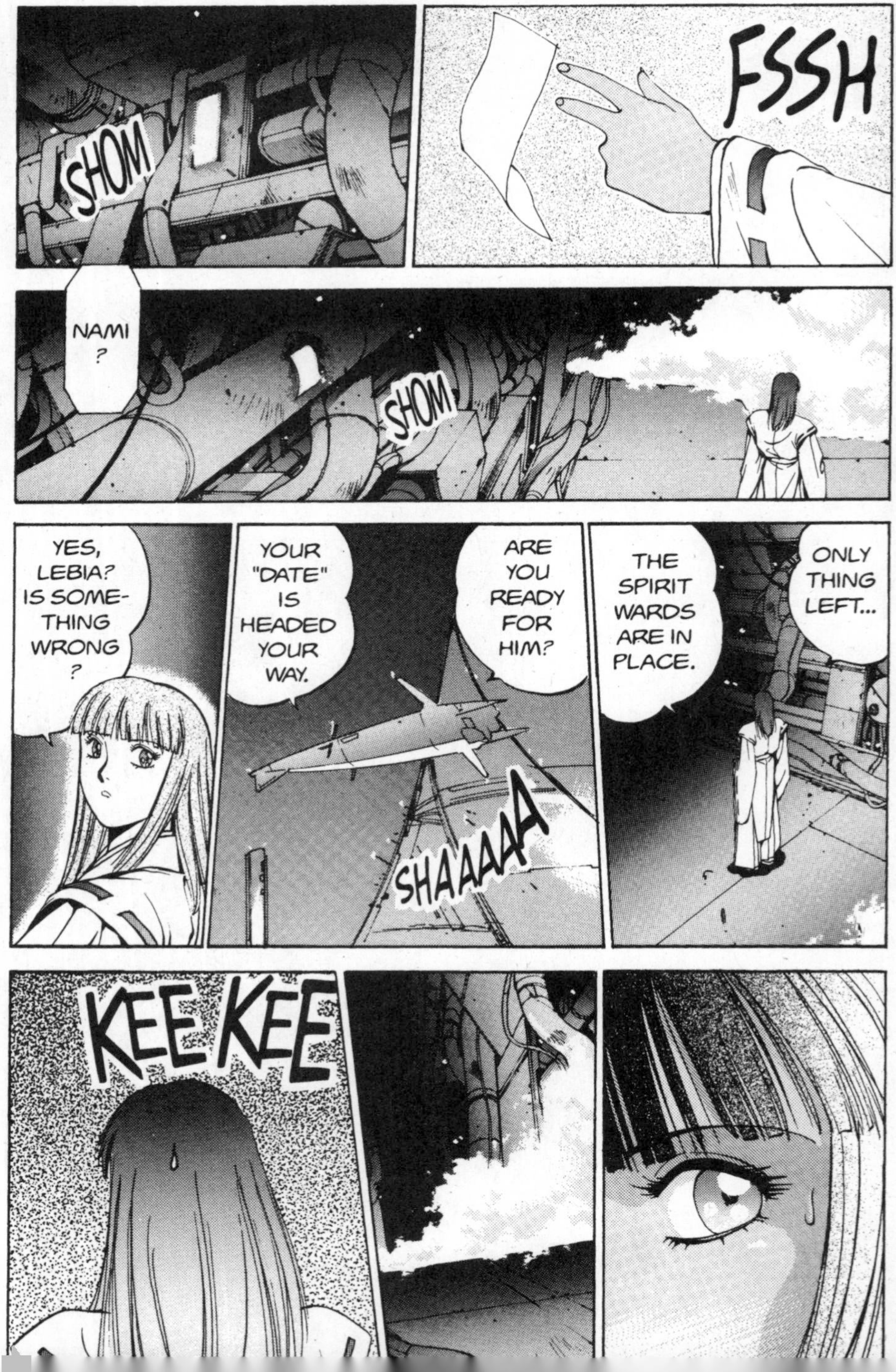
SHOM
FSSH
NAMI?
SHOM
YES, LEBIA? IS SOMETHING WRONG?
YOUR "DATE" IS HEADED YOUR WAY.
ARE YOU READY FOR HIM?
SHAAAAA
THE SPIRIT WARDS ARE IN PLACE.
ONLY THING LEFT...
KEE KEE

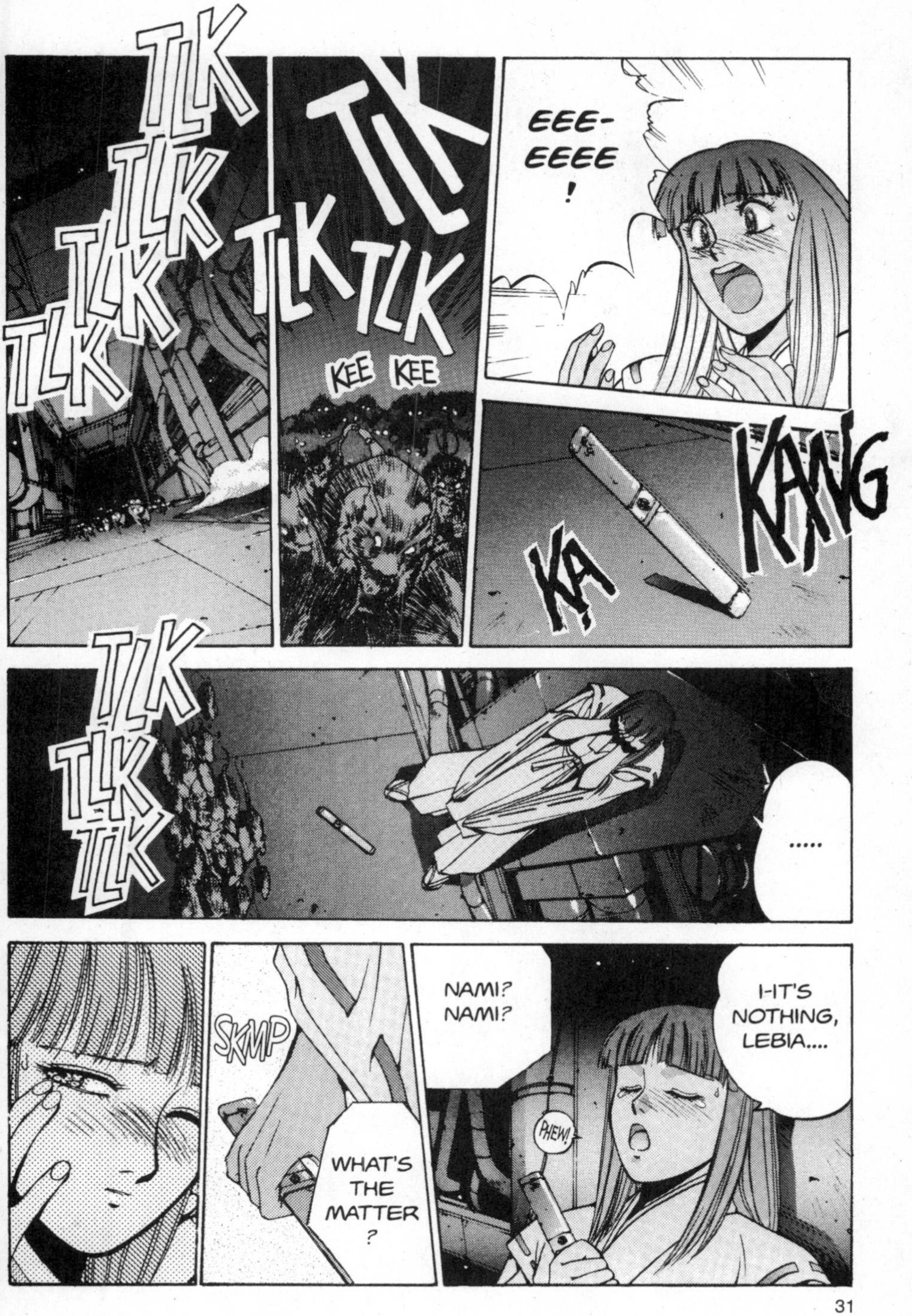
TLK
TLK
TLK
TLK
TLK
TIK
TLK TLK
KEE KEE
EEE-EEEE!
KA KANG
TLK
TLK
TLK
.....
SKMP
WHAT'S THE MATTER?
NAMI? NAMI?
PHEW!
I-IT'S NOTHING, LEBIA....

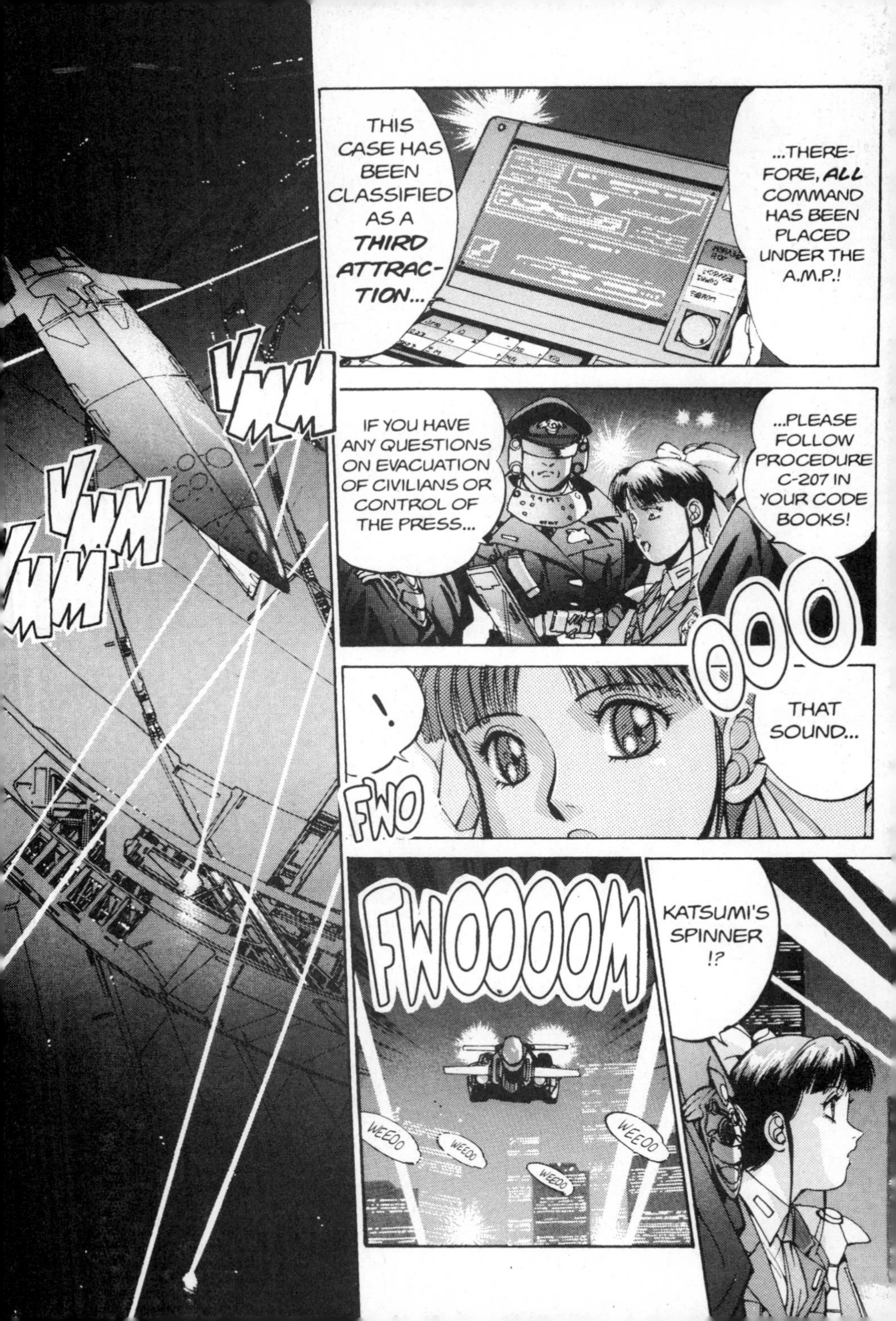
VMM
VMM
VMM
THIS CASE HAS BEEN CLASSIFIED AS A *THIRD ATTRACTION*...
...THEREFORE, *ALL* COMMAND HAS BEEN PLACED UNDER THE A.M.P.!
IF YOU HAVE ANY QUESTIONS ON EVACUATION OF CIVILIANS OR CONTROL OF THE PRESS...
...PLEASE FOLLOW PROCEDURE C-207 IN YOUR CODE BOOKS!
!
FWO
OOOO
THAT SOUND...
FWOOOOM
KATSUMI'S SPINNER !?
WEEOO
WEEOO
WEEOO
WEEOO

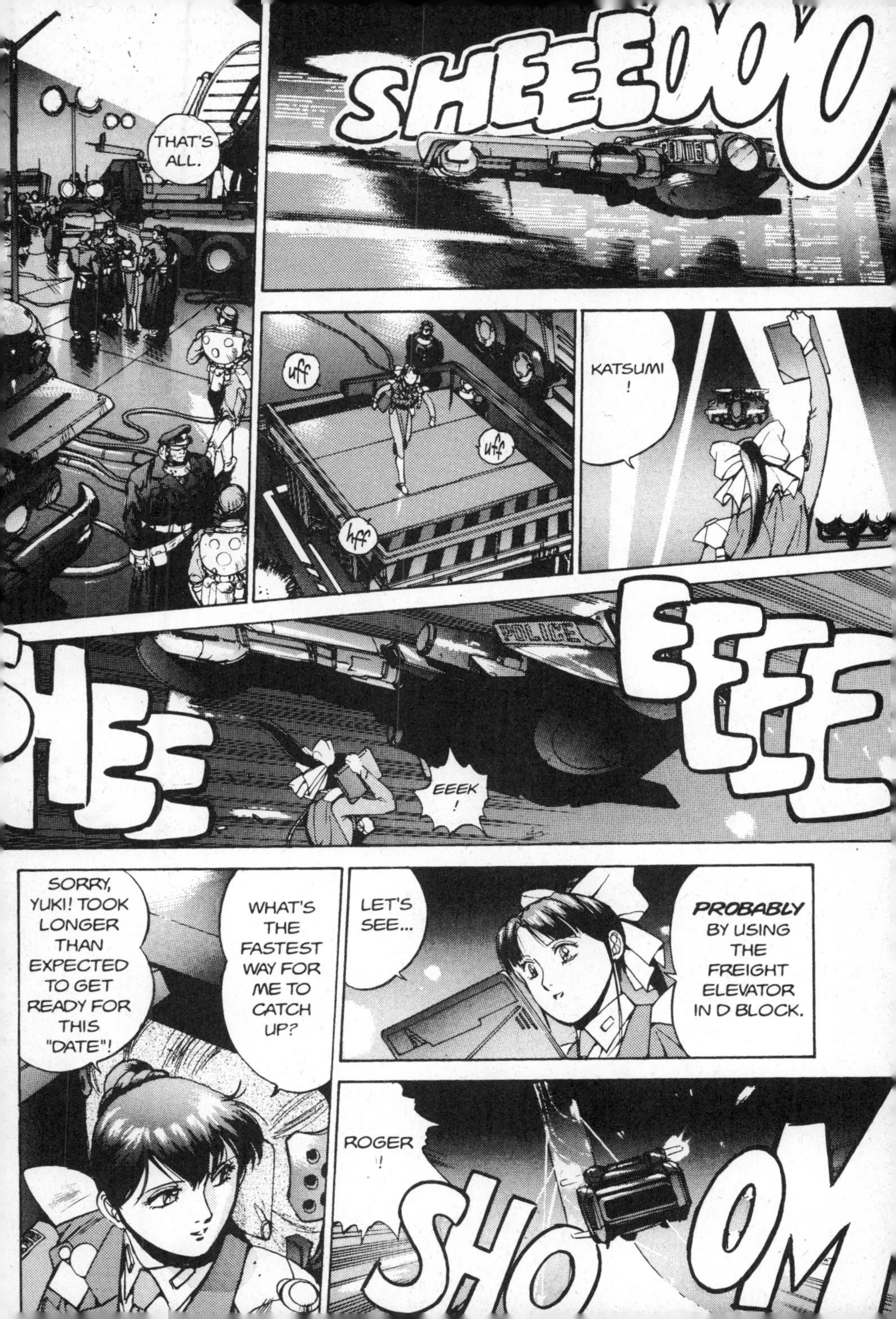
THAT'S ALL.
SHEEOOOO
uff
uff
huff
KATSUMI!
SHEE
EEEE
EEEK!
SORRY, YUKI! TOOK LONGER THAN EXPECTED TO GET READY FOR THIS "DATE"!
WHAT'S THE FASTEST WAY FOR ME TO CATCH UP?
LET'S SEE...
PROBABLY BY USING THE FREIGHT ELEVATOR IN D BLOCK.
ROGER!
SHO
OM

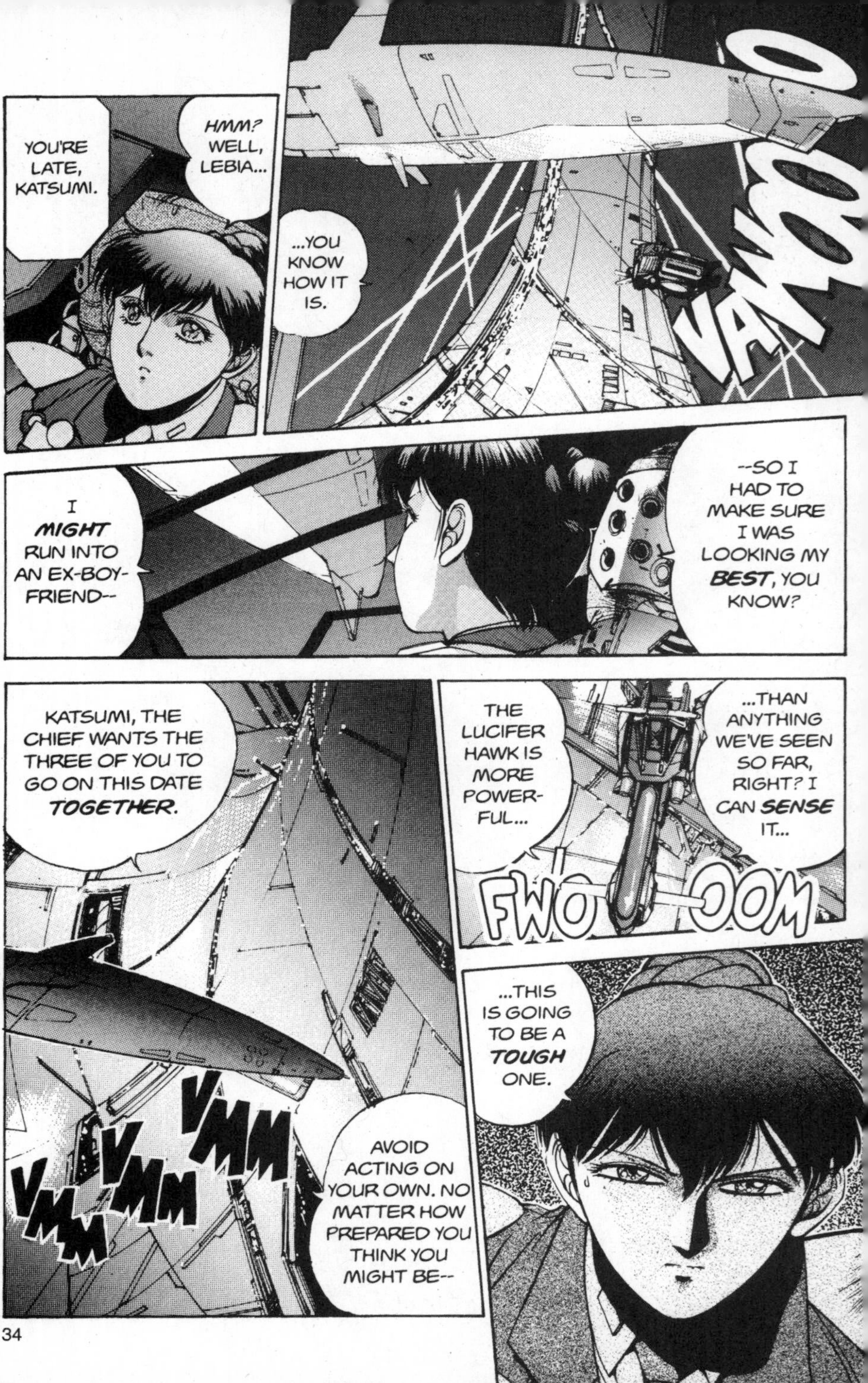
YOU'RE LATE, KATSUMI.
HMM? WELL, LEBIA...
...YOU KNOW HOW IT IS.
VAWOOO
I *MIGHT* RUN INTO AN EX-BOY-FRIEND--
--SO I HAD TO MAKE SURE I WAS LOOKING MY *BEST*, YOU KNOW?
KATSUMI, THE CHIEF WANTS THE THREE OF YOU TO GO ON THIS DATE *TOGETHER*.
VMM VMM VMM
AVOID ACTING ON YOUR OWN. NO MATTER HOW PREPARED YOU THINK YOU MIGHT BE--
THE LUCIFER HAWK IS MORE POWER-FUL...
...THAN ANYTHING WE'VE SEEN SO FAR, RIGHT? I CAN *SENSE* IT...
FWOOOM
...THIS IS GOING TO BE A *TOUGH* ONE.

SHEEEOOOMM

FWOOOOM

GROS-
POLINER,
DO *YOU*
THINK IT'S
THAT
POWERFUL
?

YES...
JUDGING
FROM THE
MASSIVE OUT-
PUT OF *KI*,
I WOULD
THINK SO.

THE
DATE
IS IN E
BLOCK...

VREEEN

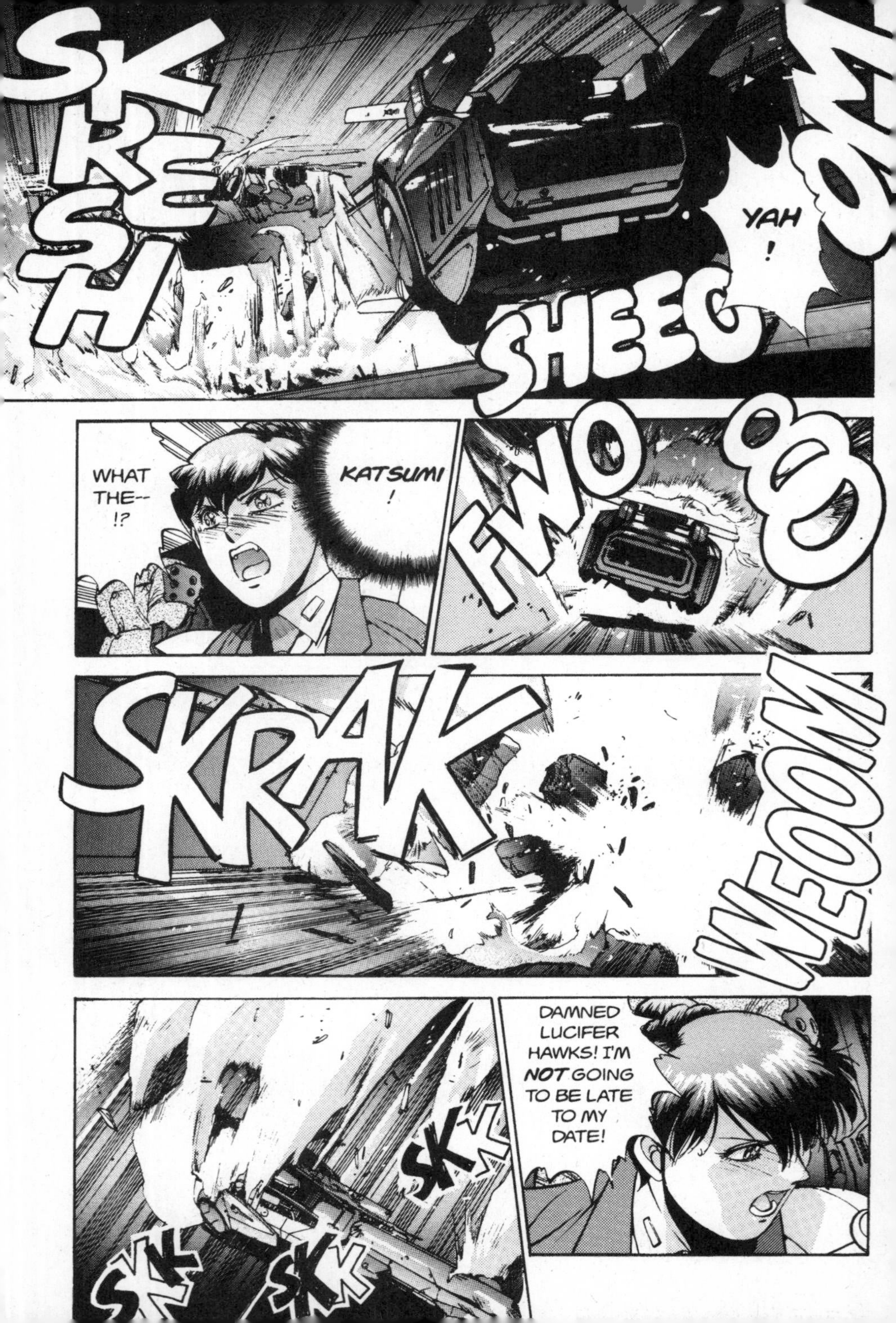
SKRESH
YAH!
SHEEG
WHAT THE--!?
KATSUMI!
FWOOM
SKRAK
WEOOM
SK
SK
SK
DAMNED LUCIFER HAWKS! I'M **NOT** GOING TO BE LATE TO MY DATE!

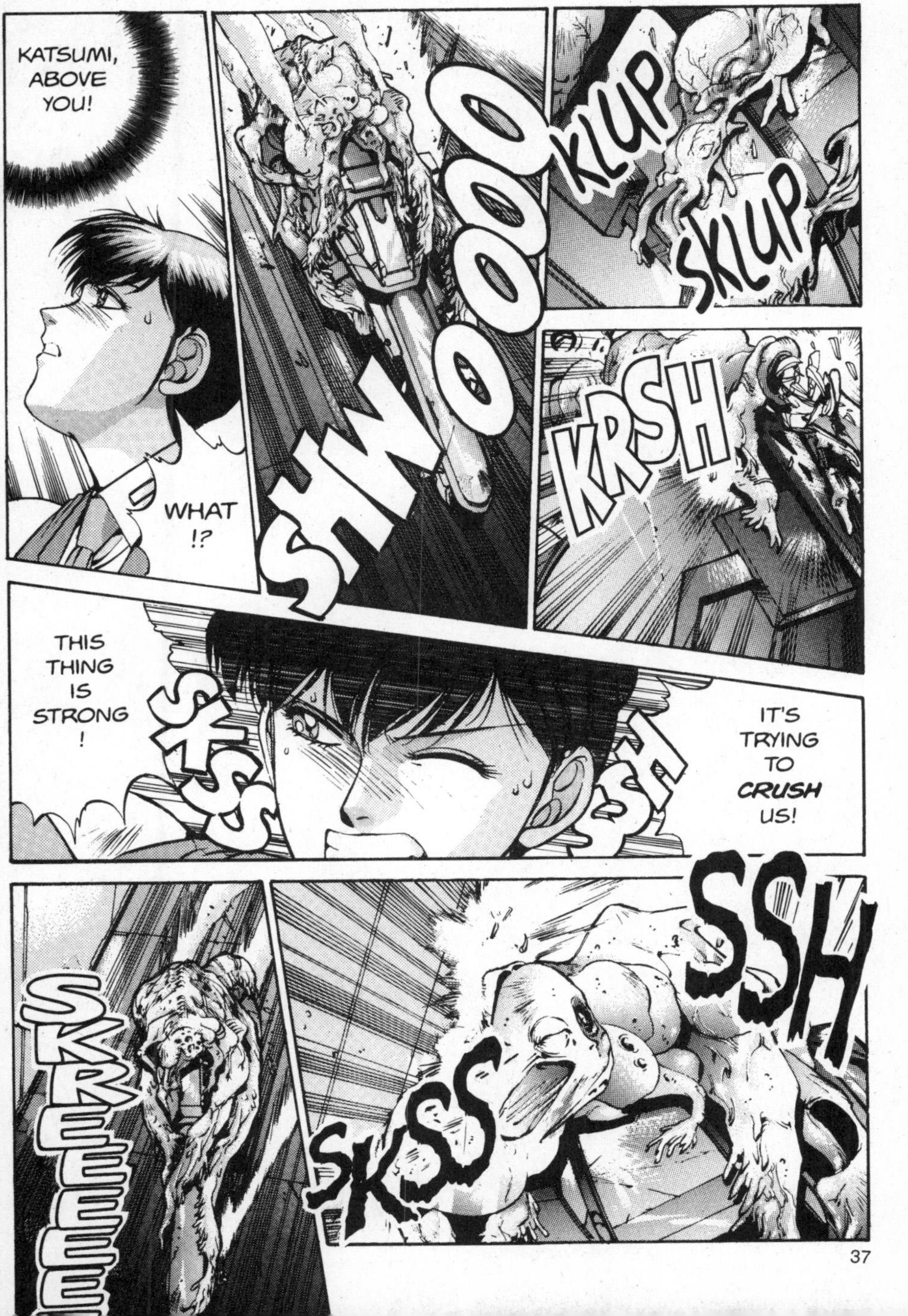
KATSUMI, ABOVE YOU!
WHAT !?
SHWOOOOO
KLUP
SKLUP
KRSH
THIS THING IS STRONG !
SKSS
IT'S TRYING TO **CRUSH** US!
SKREEEEE
SKSS
SSH

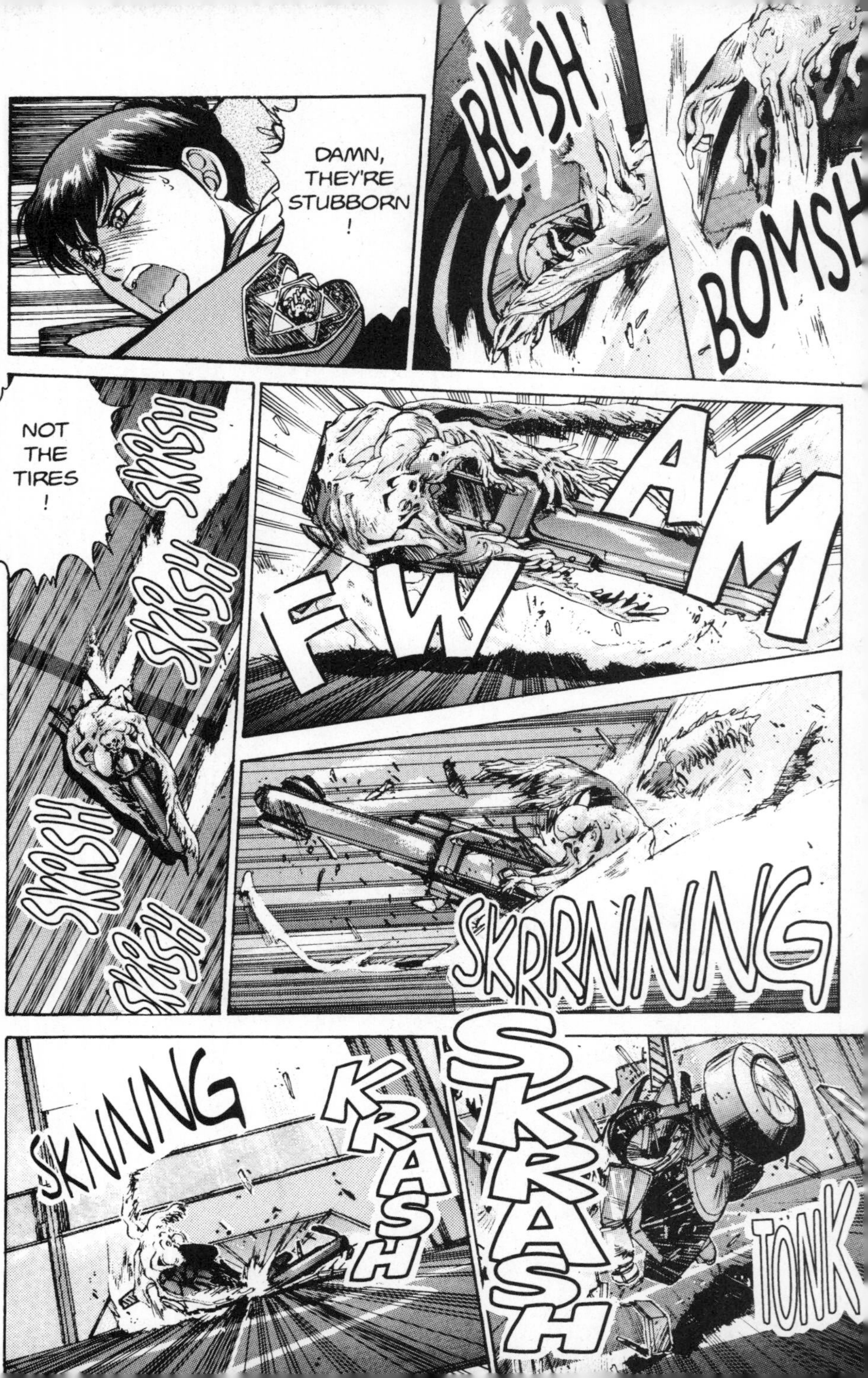
DAMN, THEY'RE STUBBORN !
BLMSH
BOMSH
NOT THE TIRES !
SKRSH SKRSH SKRSH
SKRSH SKRSH SKRSH
FWAM
SKRRNNNG
SKNNG
KRASH
SKRASH
TONK

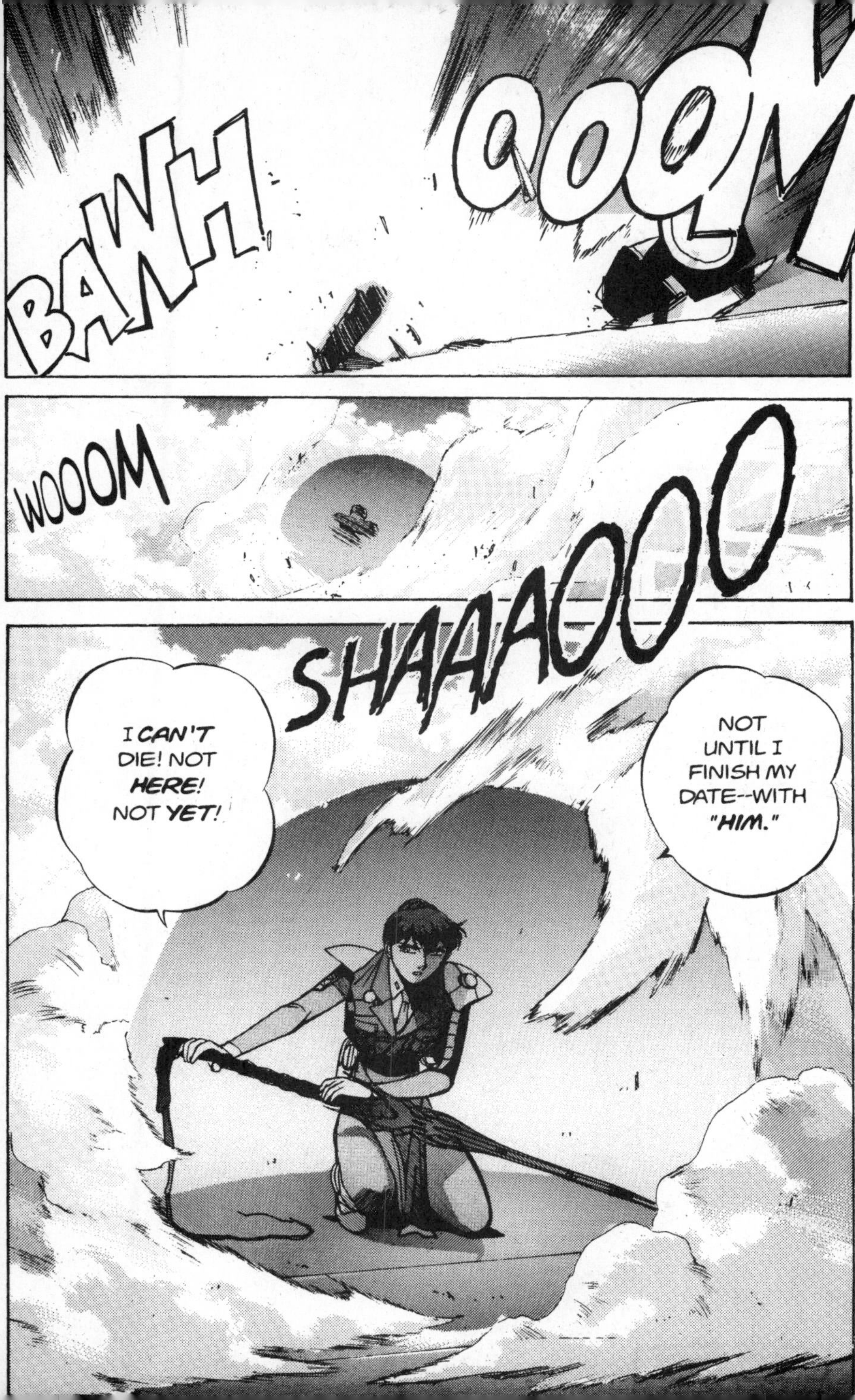
BAWH
OOOOM
WOOOM
SHAAAOOO
I CAN'T DIE! NOT HERE! NOT YET!
NOT UNTIL I FINISH MY DATE--WITH "HIM."

IT--IT **CAN'T** BE...

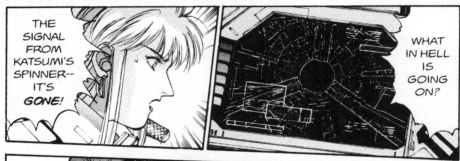

THE SIGNAL FROM KATSUMI'S SPINNER-- IT'S **GONE!**

WHAT IN HELL IS GOING ON?

KATSUMI, CAN YOU READ ME!?

KATSUMI !?

KATSUMI !?

LEBIA ?

KAT- SUMI !

CALM DOWN, LEBIA-- IT'S NOT LIKE YOU !

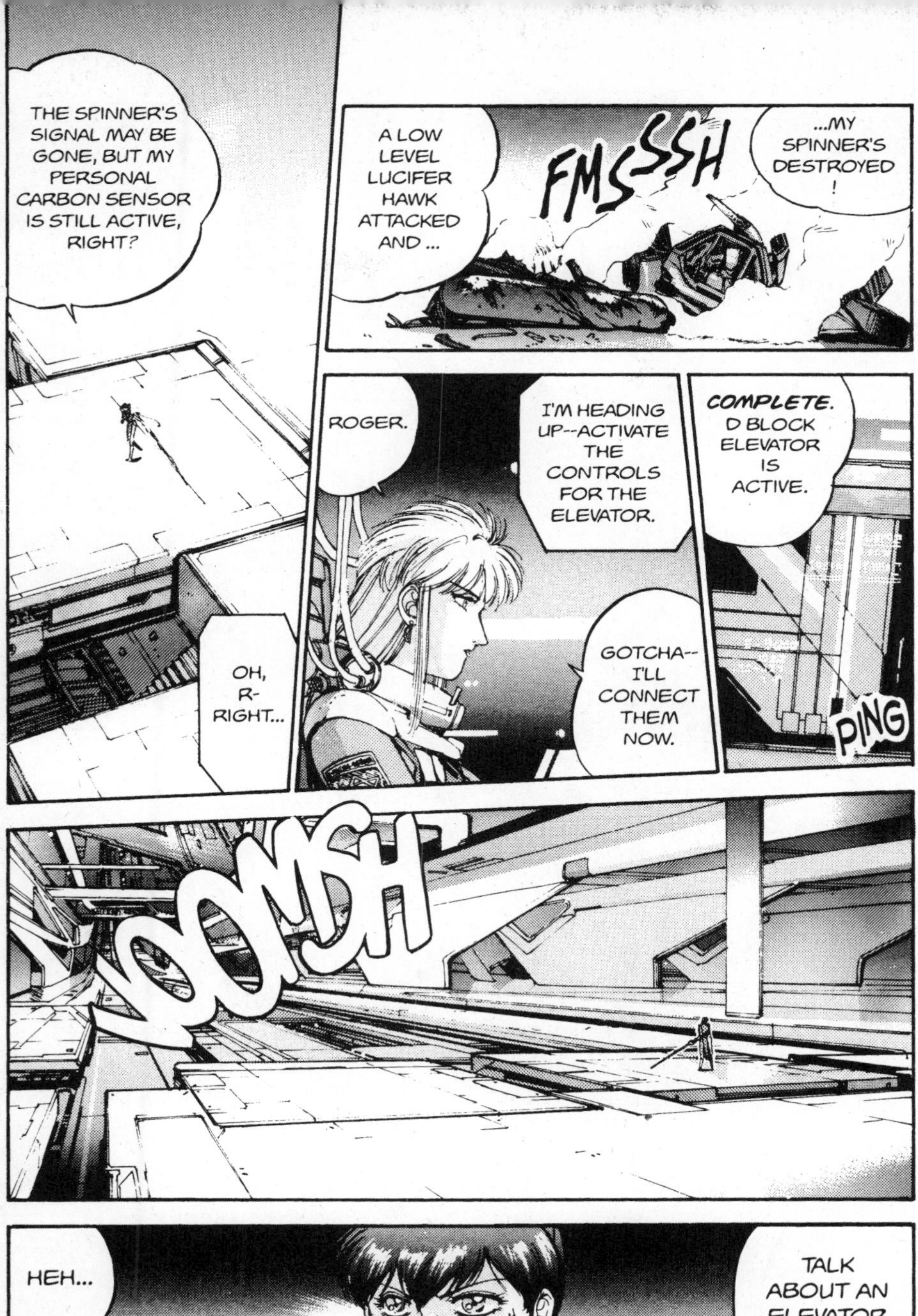
THE SPINNER'S SIGNAL MAY BE GONE, BUT MY PERSONAL CARBON SENSOR IS STILL ACTIVE, RIGHT?
OH, R-RIGHT...
A LOW LEVEL LUCIFER HAWK ATTACKED AND ...
FMSSSH
...MY SPINNER'S DESTROYED!
ROGER.
I'M HEADING UP--ACTIVATE THE CONTROLS FOR THE ELEVATOR.
GOTCHA-- I'LL CONNECT THEM NOW.
COMPLETE. D BLOCK ELEVATOR IS ACTIVE.
PING
VOOMSH
HEH...
TALK ABOUT AN ELEVATOR TO HELL...

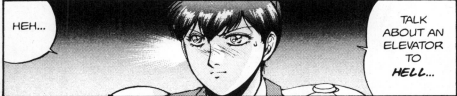

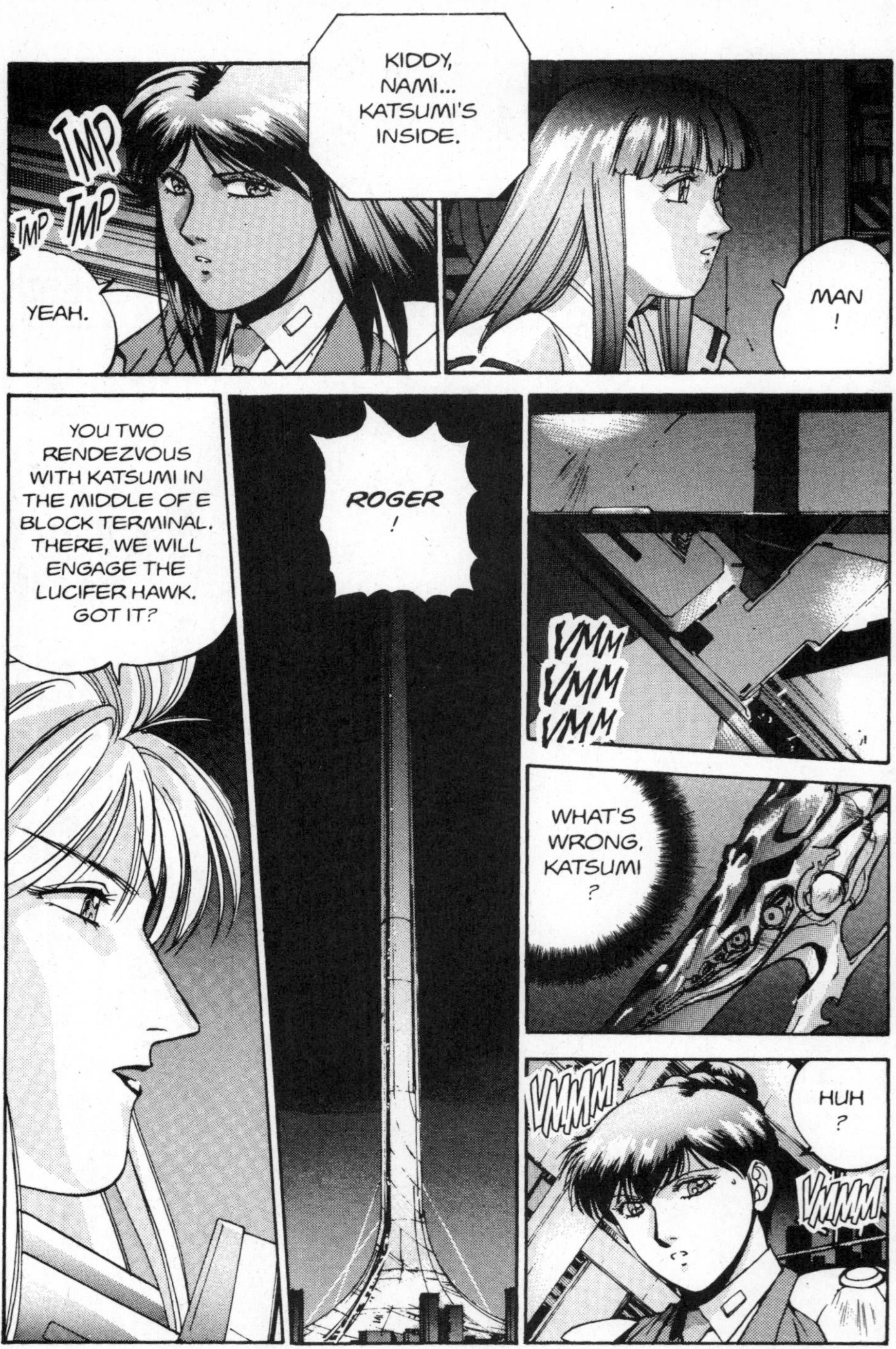

TMP TMP
TMP TMP
KIDDY, NAMI... KATSUMI'S INSIDE.
YEAH.
MAN!
YOU TWO RENDEZVOUS WITH KATSUMI IN THE MIDDLE OF E BLOCK TERMINAL. THERE, WE WILL ENGAGE THE LUCIFER HAWK. GOT IT?
ROGER!
VMM VMM VMM
WHAT'S WRONG, KATSUMI?
VMMM
HUH?
VMMM

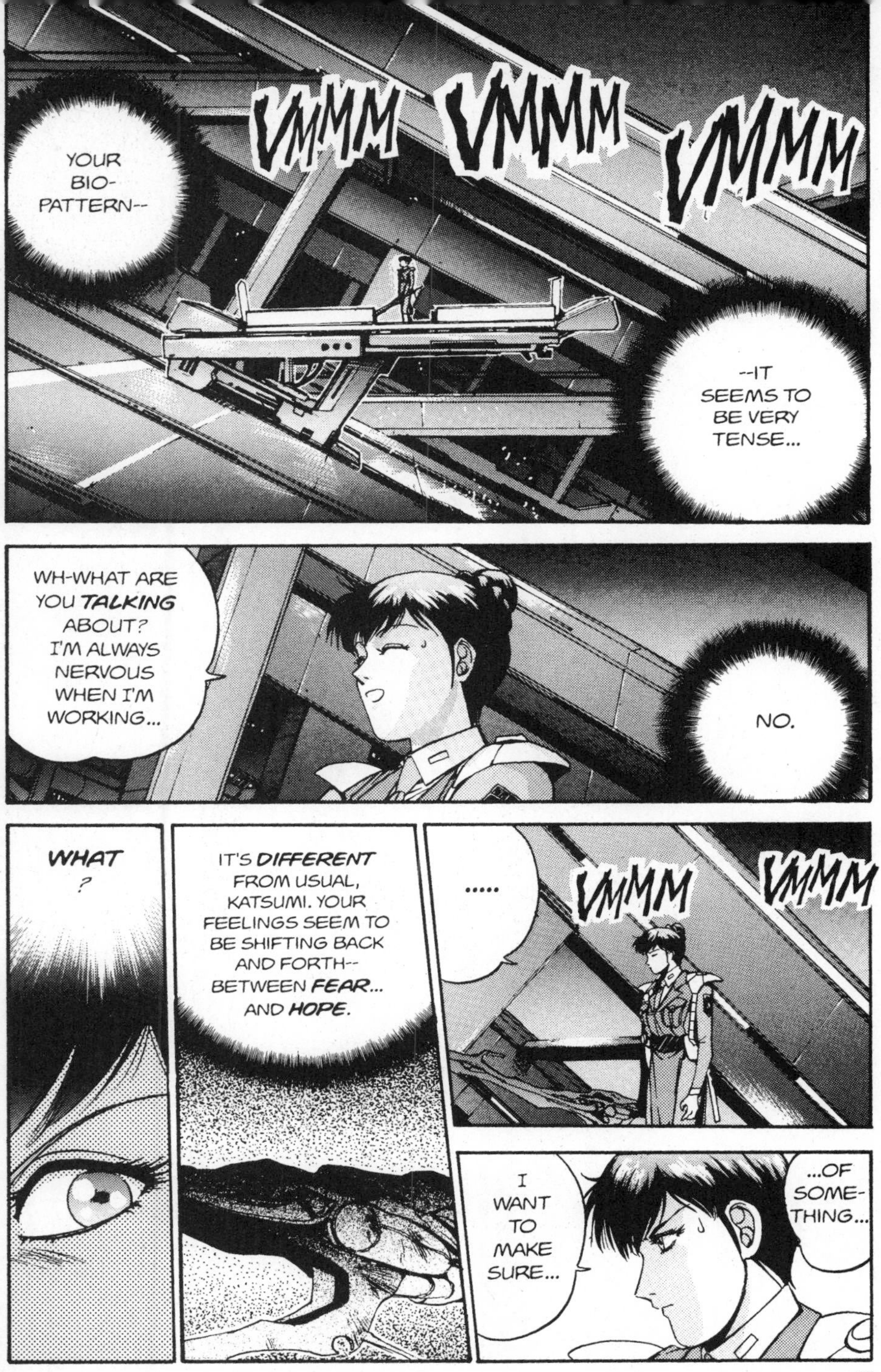
YOUR BIO-PATTERN--
VMMM VMMM VMMM
--IT SEEMS TO BE VERY TENSE...
WH-WHAT ARE YOU TALKING ABOUT? I'M ALWAYS NERVOUS WHEN I'M WORKING...
NO.
WHAT ?
IT'S DIFFERENT FROM USUAL, KATSUMI. YOUR FEELINGS SEEM TO BE SHIFTING BACK AND FORTH-- BETWEEN FEAR... AND HOPE.
.....
VMMM VMMM
I WANT TO MAKE SURE...
...OF SOMETHING...

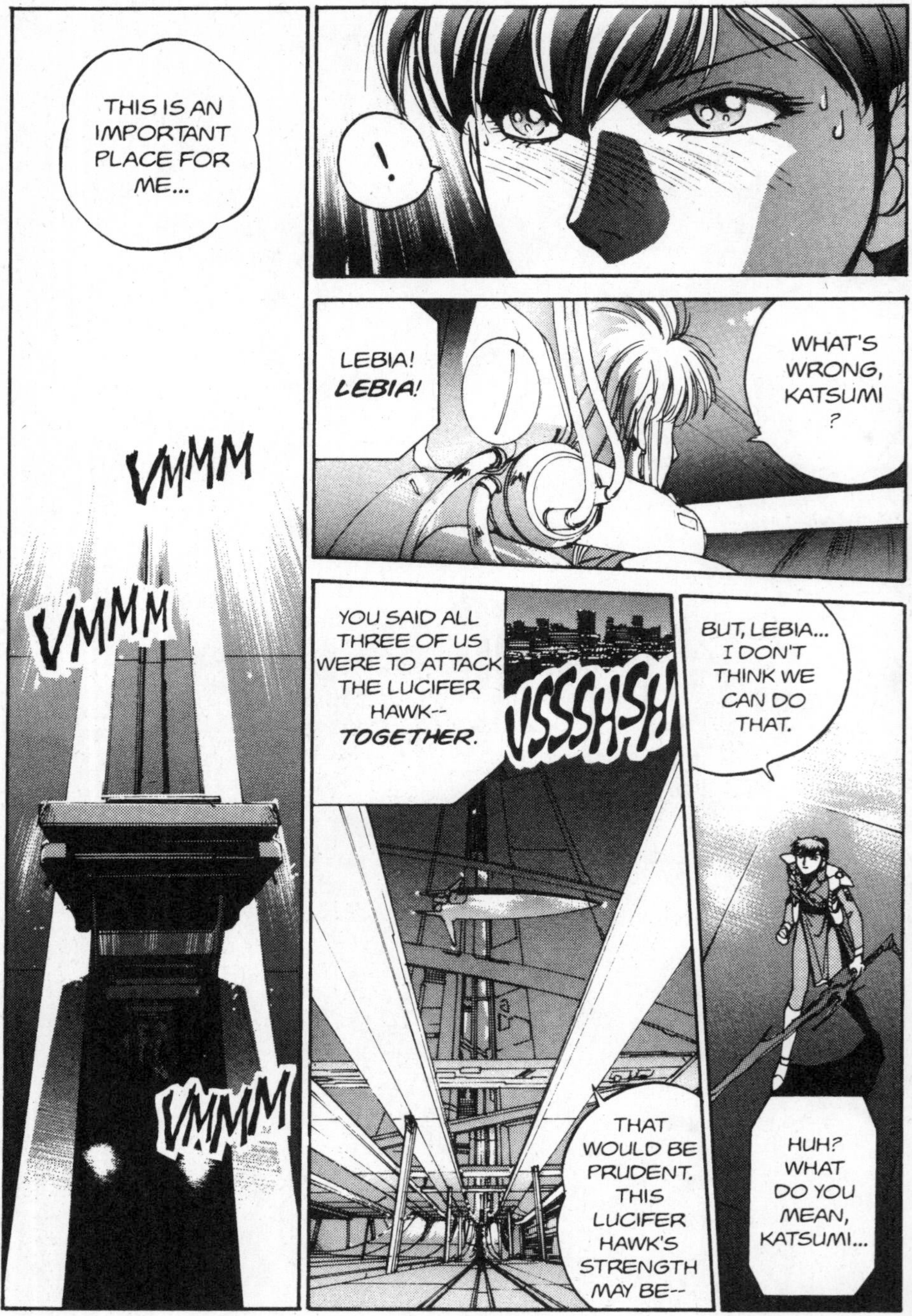
THIS IS AN IMPORTANT PLACE FOR ME...
VMMM
VMMM
VMMM
!
LEBIA! LEBIA!
WHAT'S WRONG, KATSUMI ?
YOU SAID ALL THREE OF US WERE TO ATTACK THE LUCIFER HAWK-- TOGETHER.
VSSSHSH
THAT WOULD BE PRUDENT. THIS LUCIFER HAWK'S STRENGTH MAY BE--
BUT, LEBIA... I DON'T THINK WE CAN DO THAT.
HUH? WHAT DO YOU MEAN, KATSUMI...

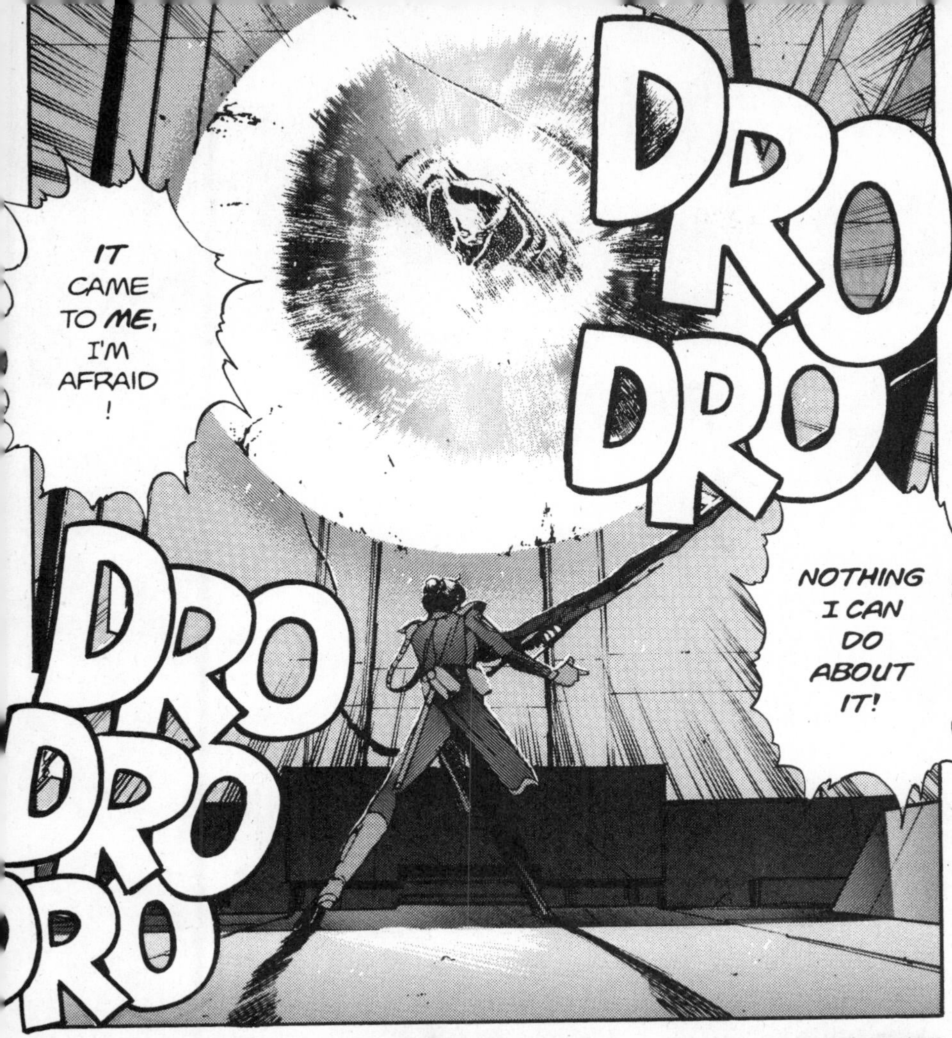
IT CAME TO ME, I'M AFRAID!
DRO DRO
DRO DRO DRO DRO
NOTHING I CAN DO ABOUT IT!
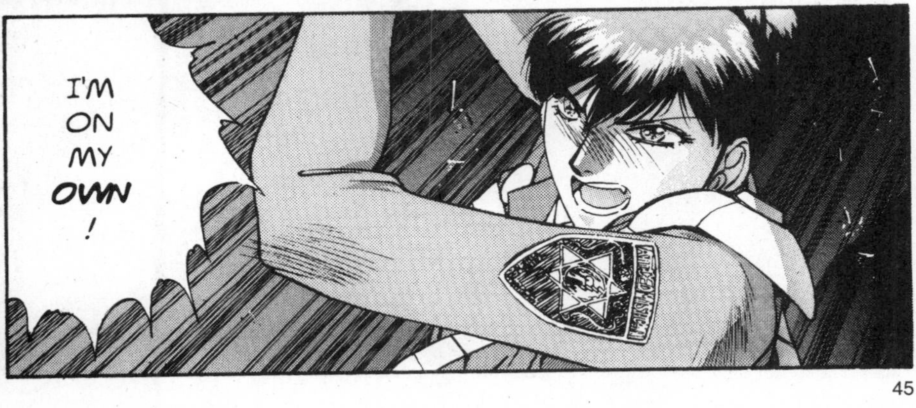
I'M ON MY OWN!

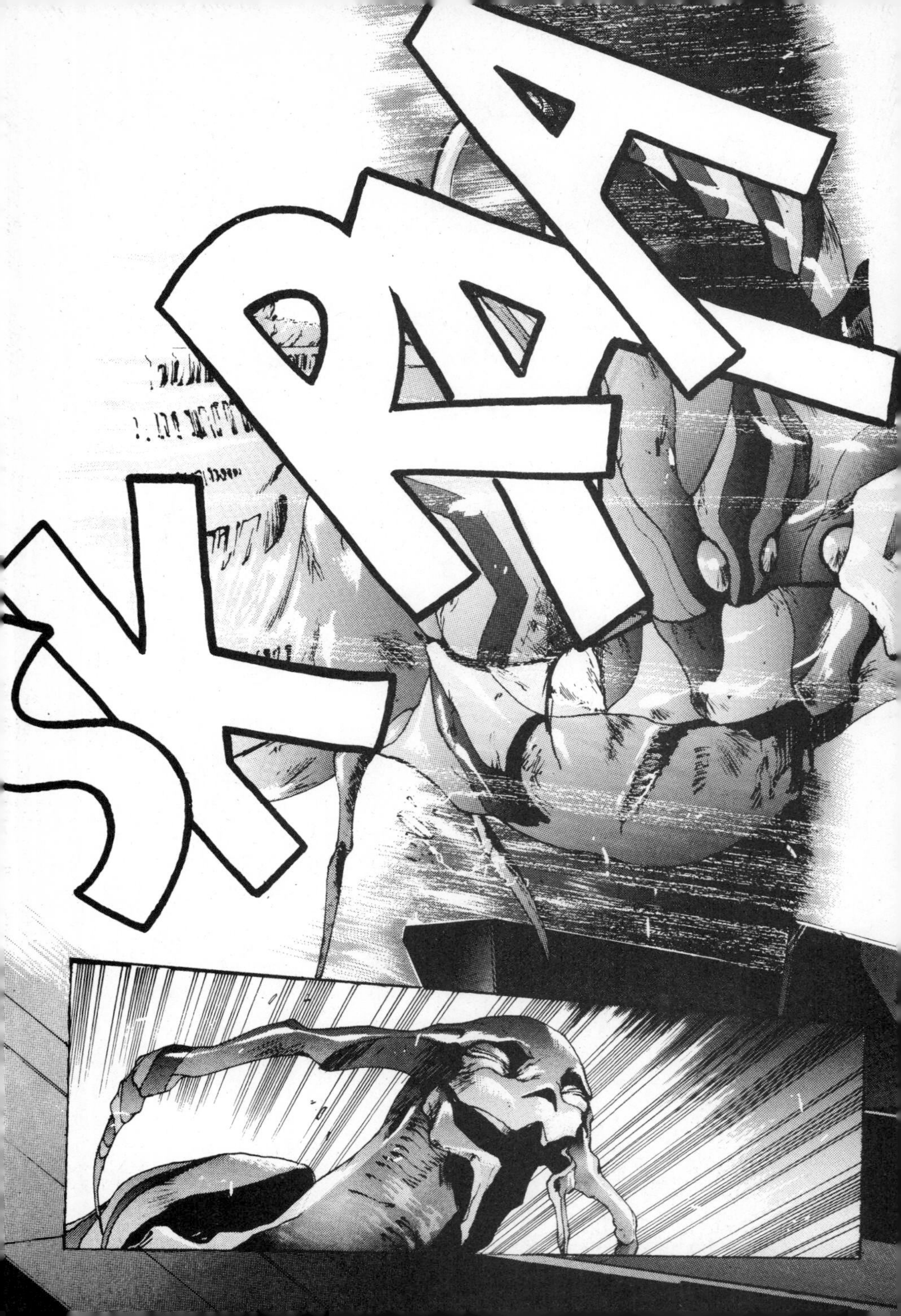

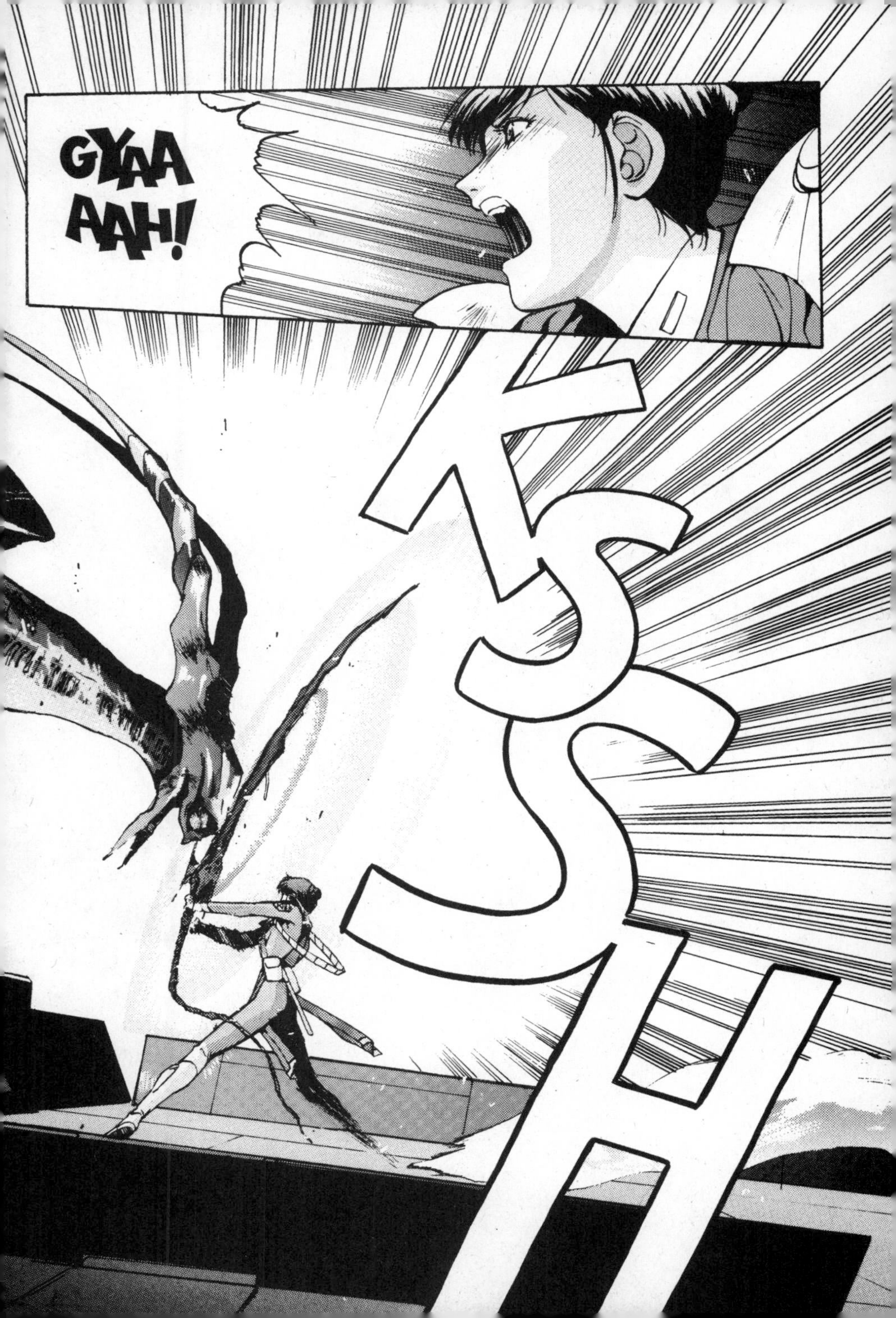
GYAA AAH!
TSSH

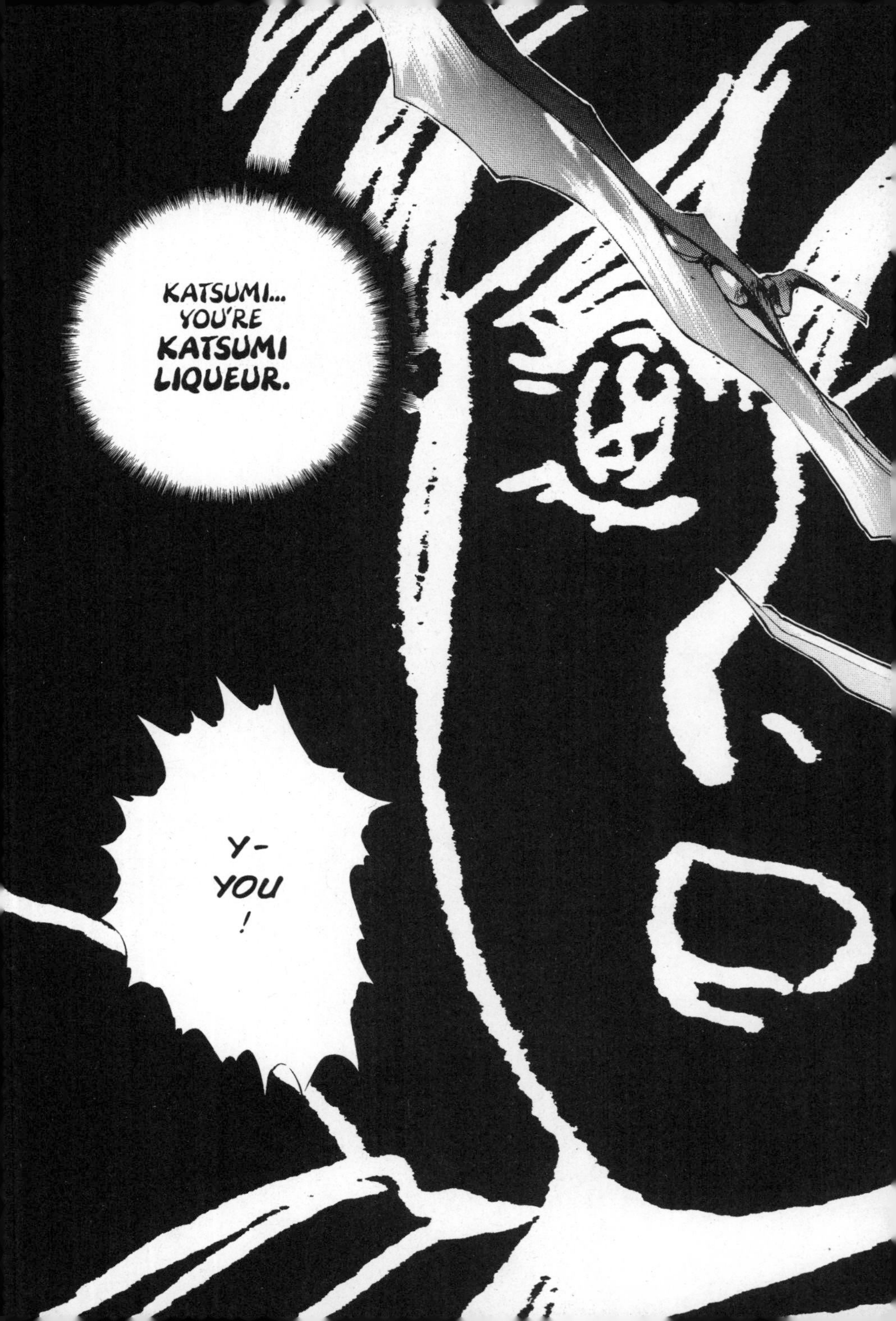
KATSUMI... YOU'RE KATSUMI LIQUEUR.
Y-YOU!

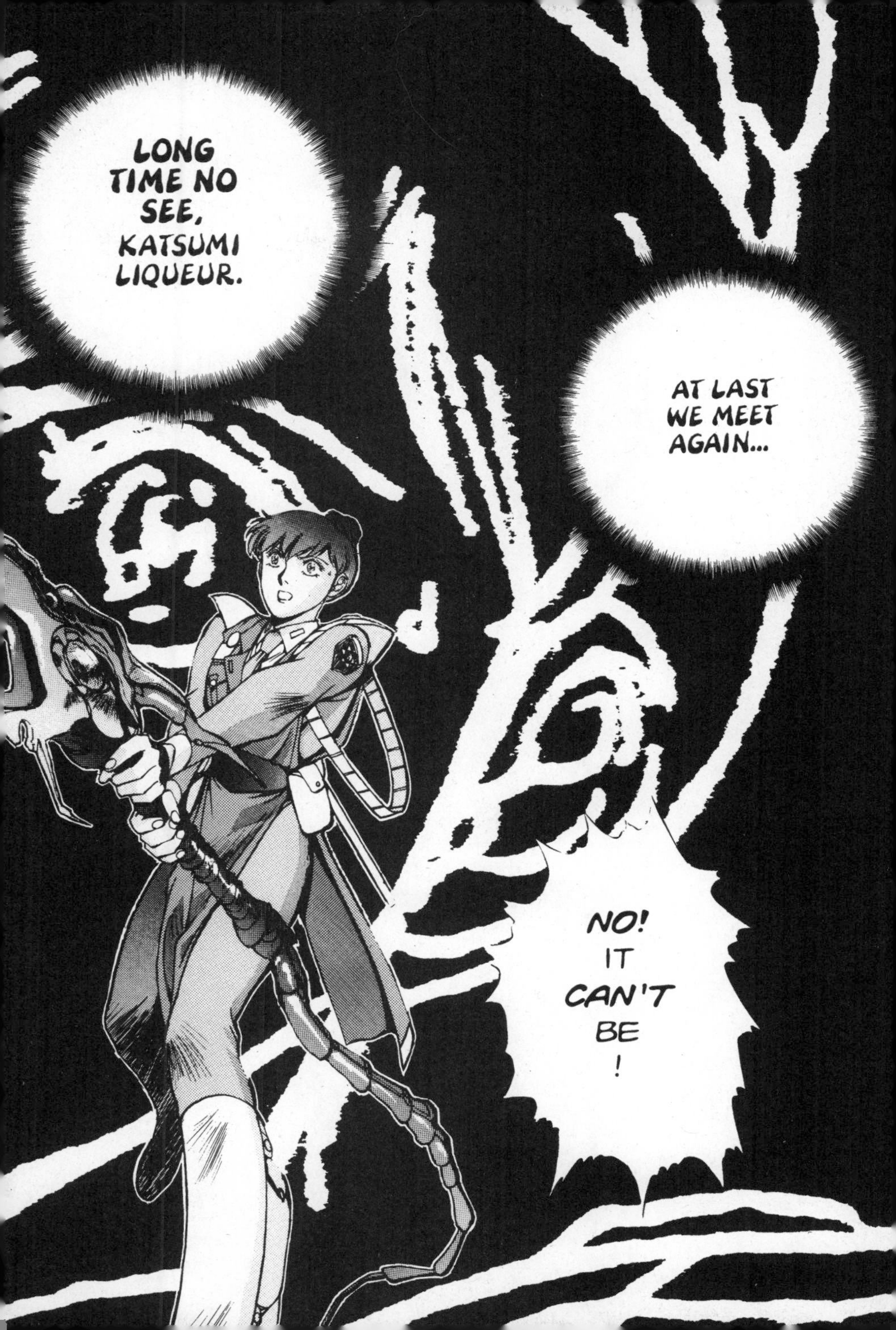
LONG TIME NO SEE, KATSUMI LIQUEUR.
AT LAST WE MEET AGAIN...
NO! IT CAN'T BE !

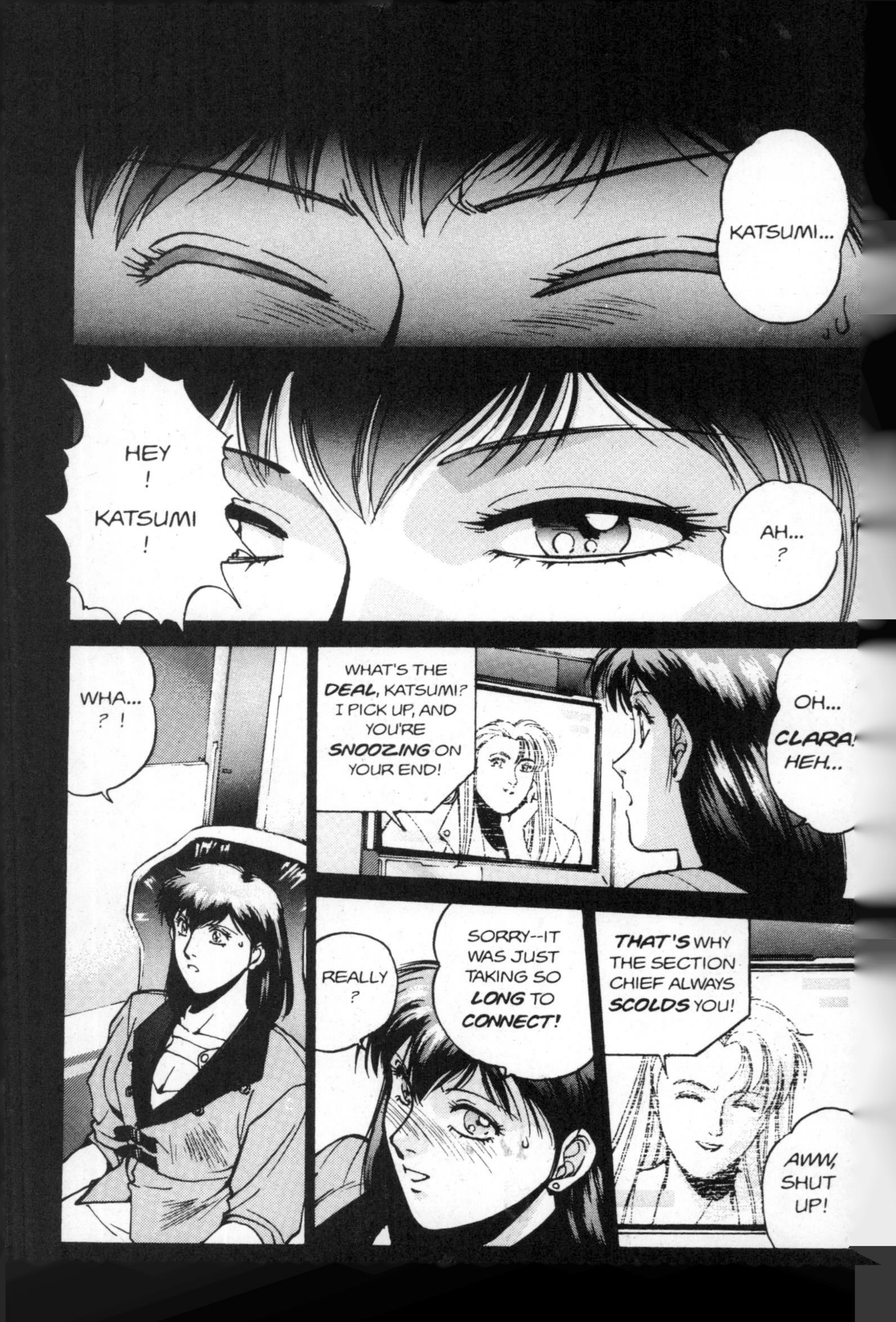
KATSUMI...
HEY! KATSUMI!
AH...?
WHA...?!
WHAT'S THE DEAL, KATSUMI? I PICK UP, AND YOU'RE SNOOZING ON YOUR END!
OH... CLARA! HEH...
REALLY?
SORRY--IT WAS JUST TAKING SO LONG TO CONNECT!
THAT'S WHY THE SECTION CHIEF ALWAYS SCOLDS YOU!
AWW, SHUT UP!

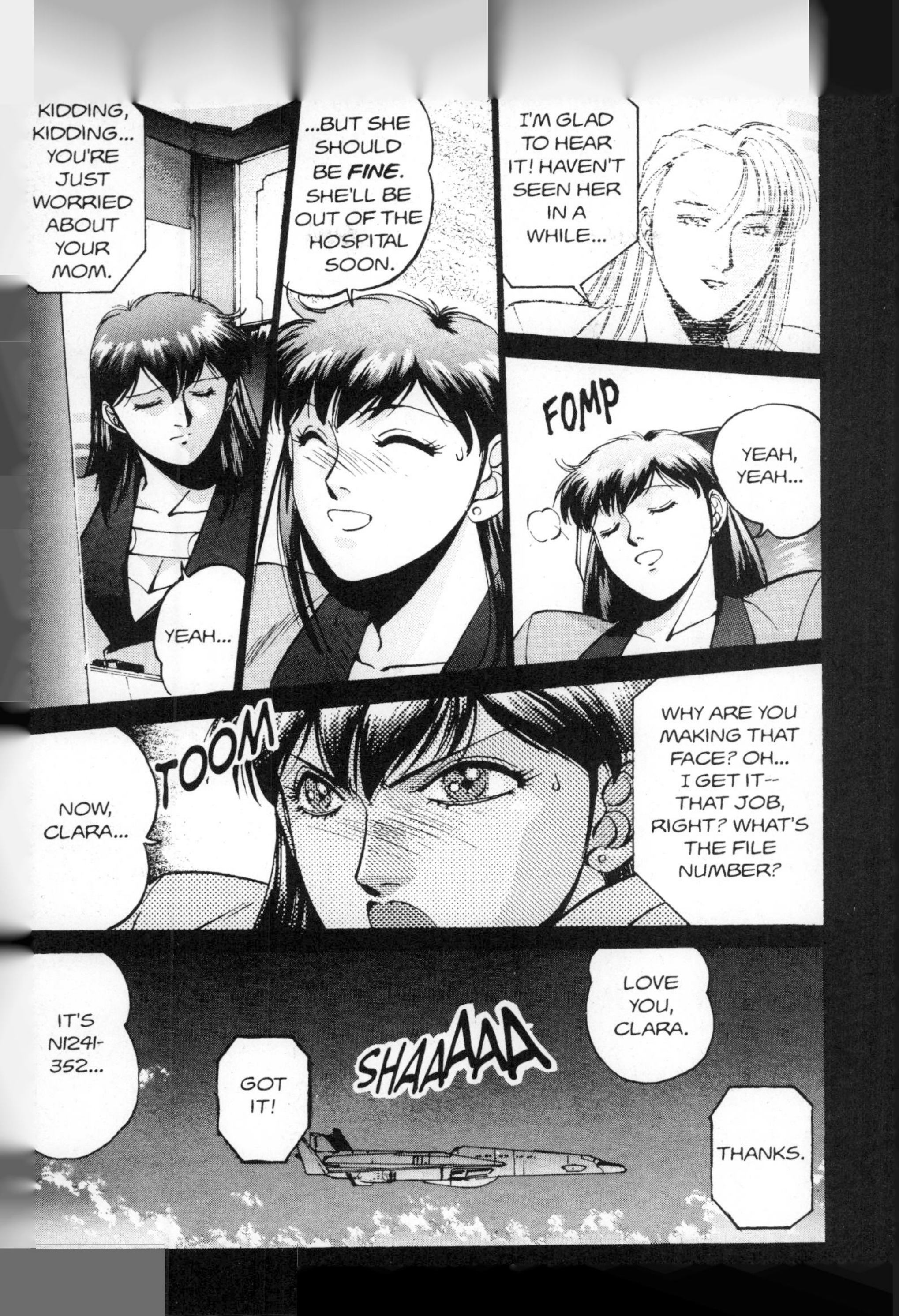
KIDDING, KIDDING... YOU'RE JUST WORRIED ABOUT YOUR MOM.
YEAH...
...BUT SHE SHOULD BE **FINE**. SHE'LL BE OUT OF THE HOSPITAL SOON.
I'M GLAD TO HEAR IT! HAVEN'T SEEN HER IN A WHILE...
FOMP
YEAH, YEAH...
NOW, CLARA...
TOOM
WHY ARE YOU MAKING THAT FACE? OH... I GET IT-- THAT JOB, RIGHT? WHAT'S THE FILE NUMBER?
IT'S N1241-352...
GOT IT!
SHAAAAA
LOVE YOU, CLARA.
THANKS.

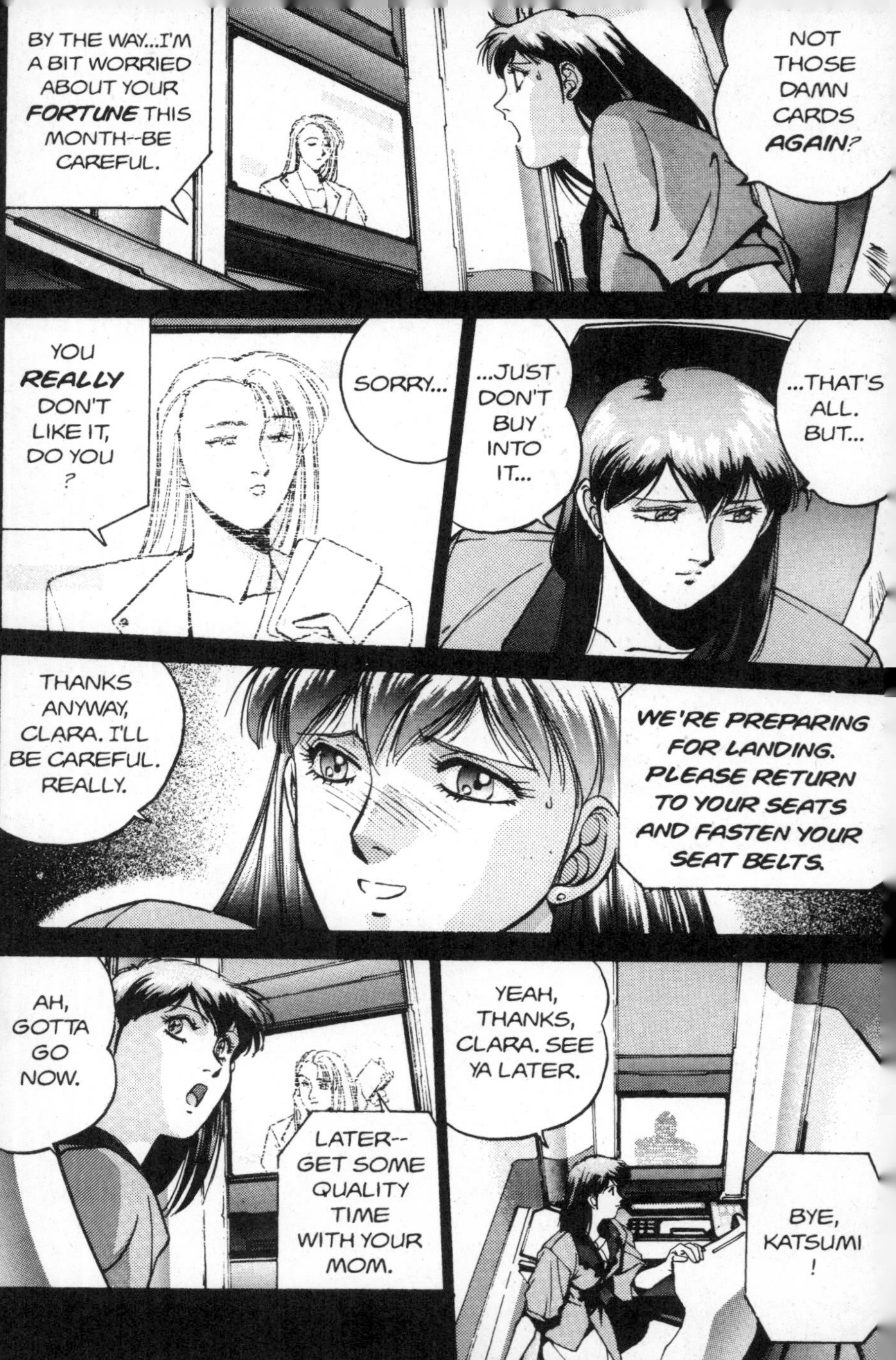
BY THE WAY...I'M A BIT WORRIED ABOUT YOUR FORTUNE THIS MONTH--BE CAREFUL.
NOT THOSE DAMN CARDS AGAIN?
YOU REALLY DON'T LIKE IT, DO YOU ?
SORRY...
...JUST DON'T BUY INTO IT...
...THAT'S ALL. BUT...
THANKS ANYWAY, CLARA. I'LL BE CAREFUL. REALLY.
WE'RE PREPARING FOR LANDING. PLEASE RETURN TO YOUR SEATS AND FASTEN YOUR SEAT BELTS.
AH, GOTTA GO NOW.
LATER--GET SOME QUALITY TIME WITH YOUR MOM.
YEAH, THANKS, CLARA. SEE YA LATER.
BYE, KATSUMI !

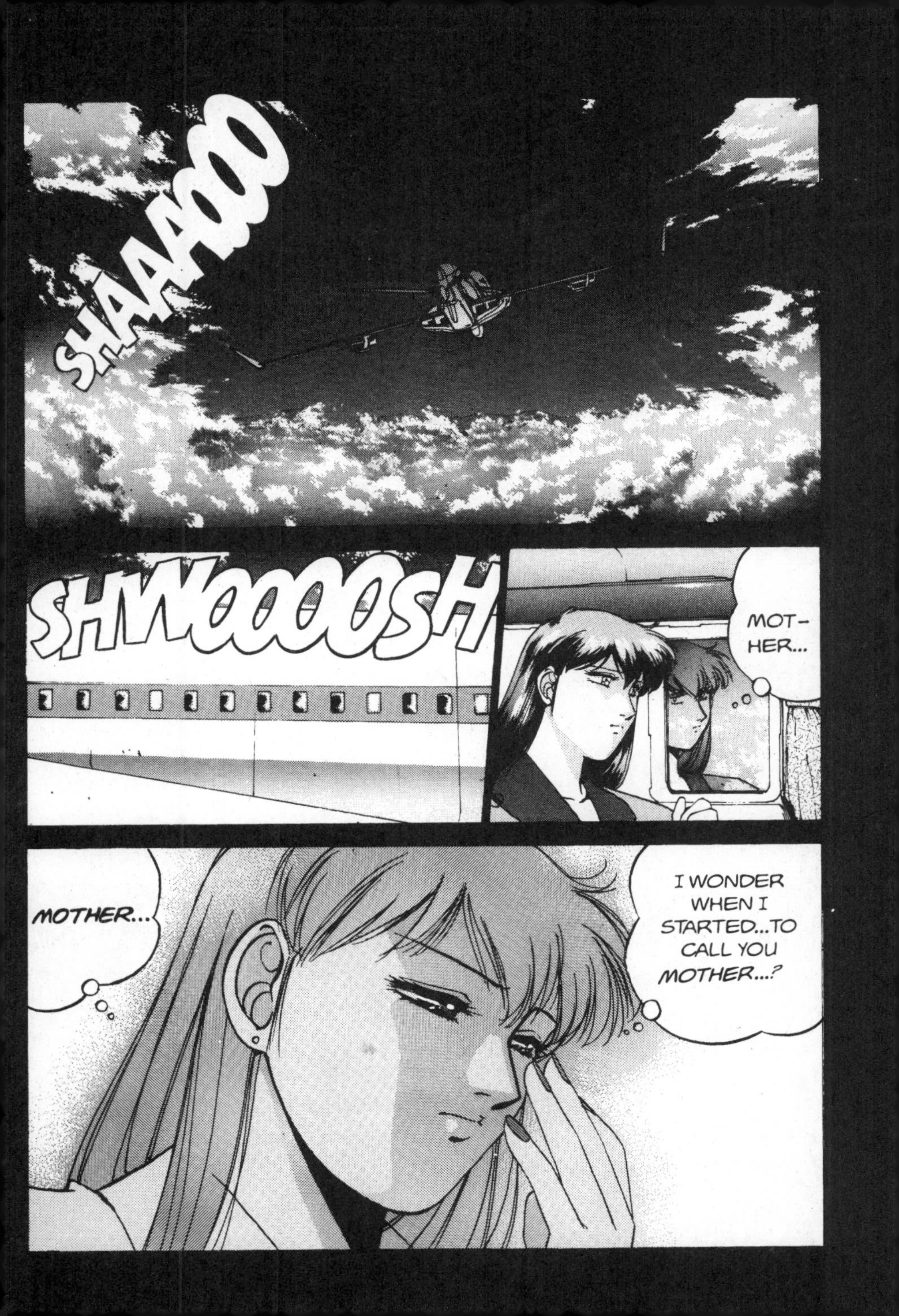
SHAAAOOO
SHWOOOOSH
MOT-HER...
MOTHER...
I WONDER WHEN I STARTED...TO CALL YOU MOTHER...?

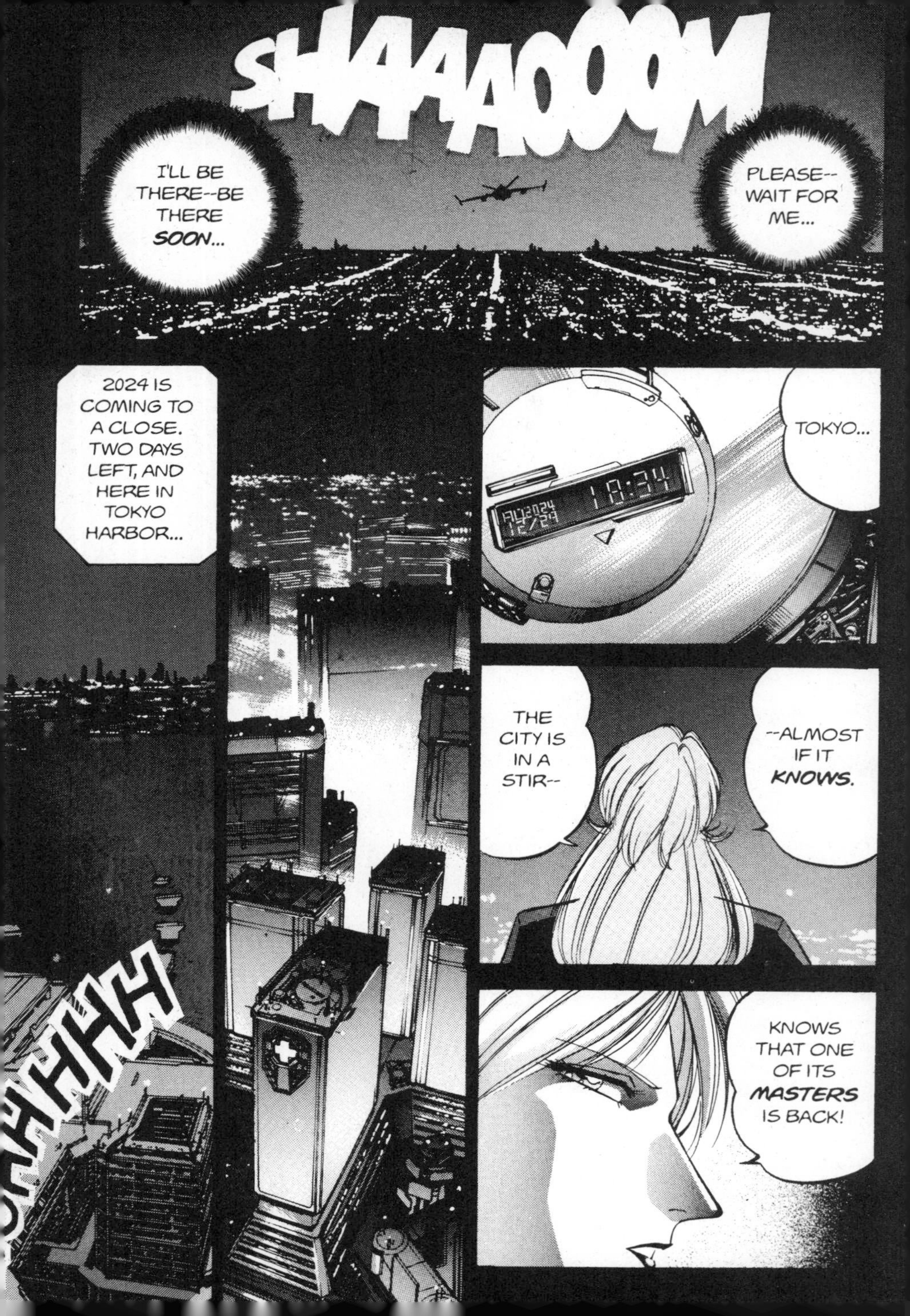
SHAAAOOOM
I'LL BE THERE--BE THERE *SOON*...
PLEASE-- WAIT FOR ME...
2024 IS COMING TO A CLOSE. TWO DAYS LEFT, AND HERE IN TOKYO HARBOR...
TOKYO...
10:34
THE CITY IS IN A STIR--
--ALMOST IF IT *KNOWS.*
KNOWS THAT ONE OF ITS *MASTERS* IS BACK!

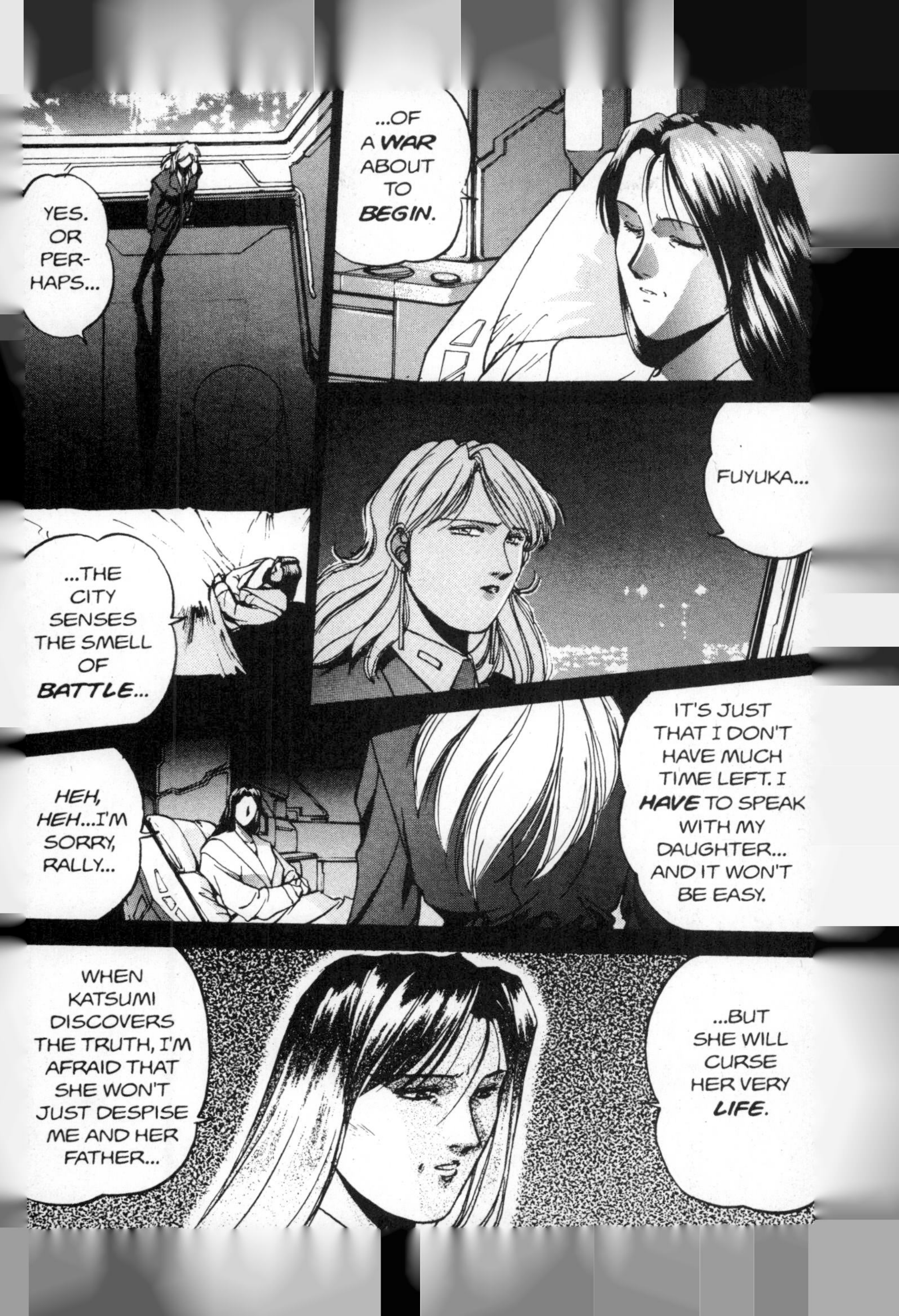
YES. OR PER-HAPS...
...THE CITY SENSES THE SMELL OF BATTLE...
...OF A WAR ABOUT TO BEGIN.
FUYUKA...
HEH, HEH...I'M SORRY, RALLY...
IT'S JUST THAT I DON'T HAVE MUCH TIME LEFT. I HAVE TO SPEAK WITH MY DAUGHTER... AND IT WON'T BE EASY.
WHEN KATSUMI DISCOVERS THE TRUTH, I'M AFRAID THAT SHE WON'T JUST DESPISE ME AND HER FATHER...
...BUT SHE WILL CURSE HER VERY LIFE.

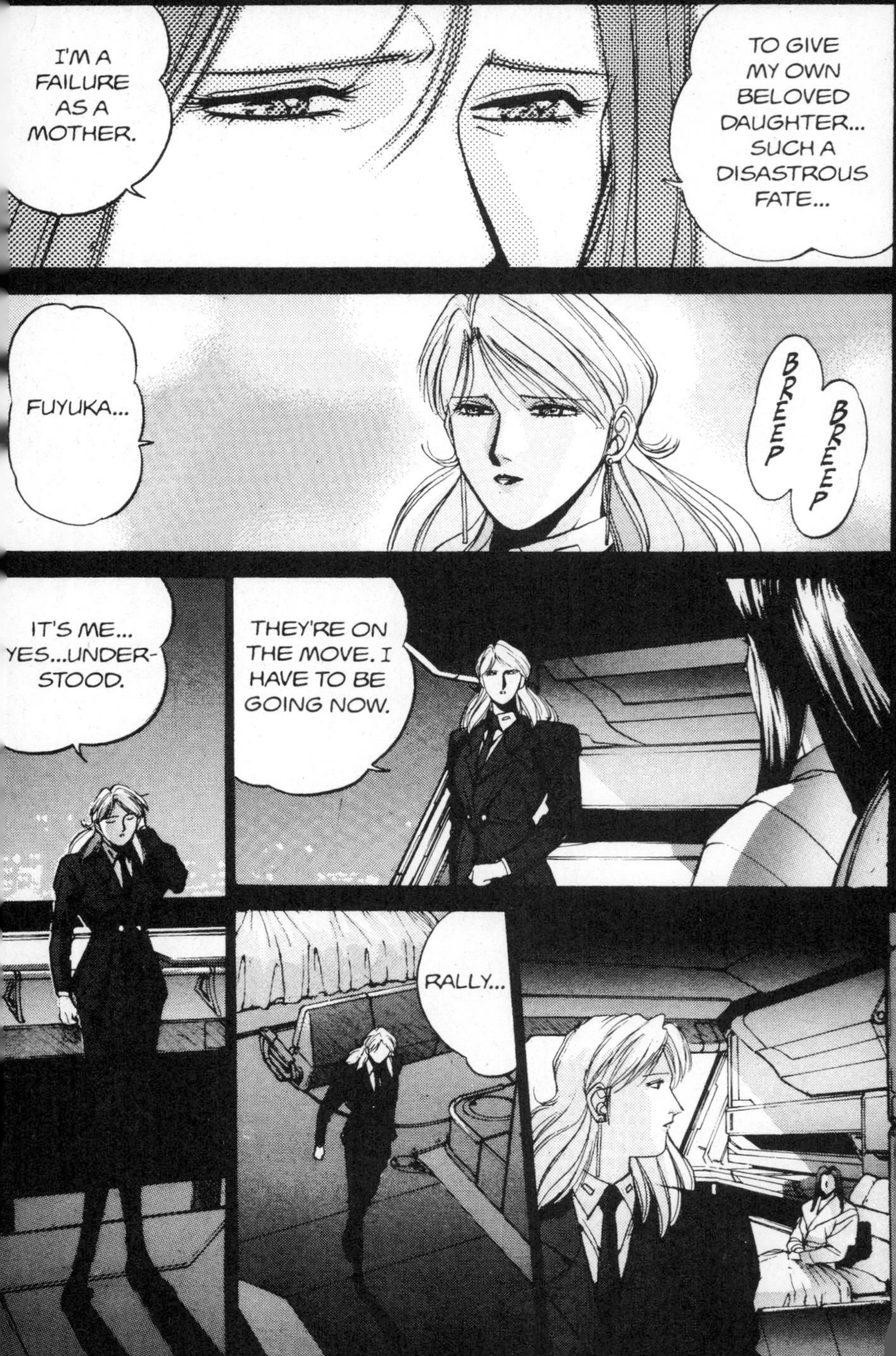
I'M A FAILURE AS A MOTHER.
TO GIVE MY OWN BELOVED DAUGHTER... SUCH A DISASTROUS FATE...
FUYUKA...
BREEP BREEP
IT'S ME... YES...UNDER-STOOD.
THEY'RE ON THE MOVE. I HAVE TO BE GOING NOW.
RALLY...

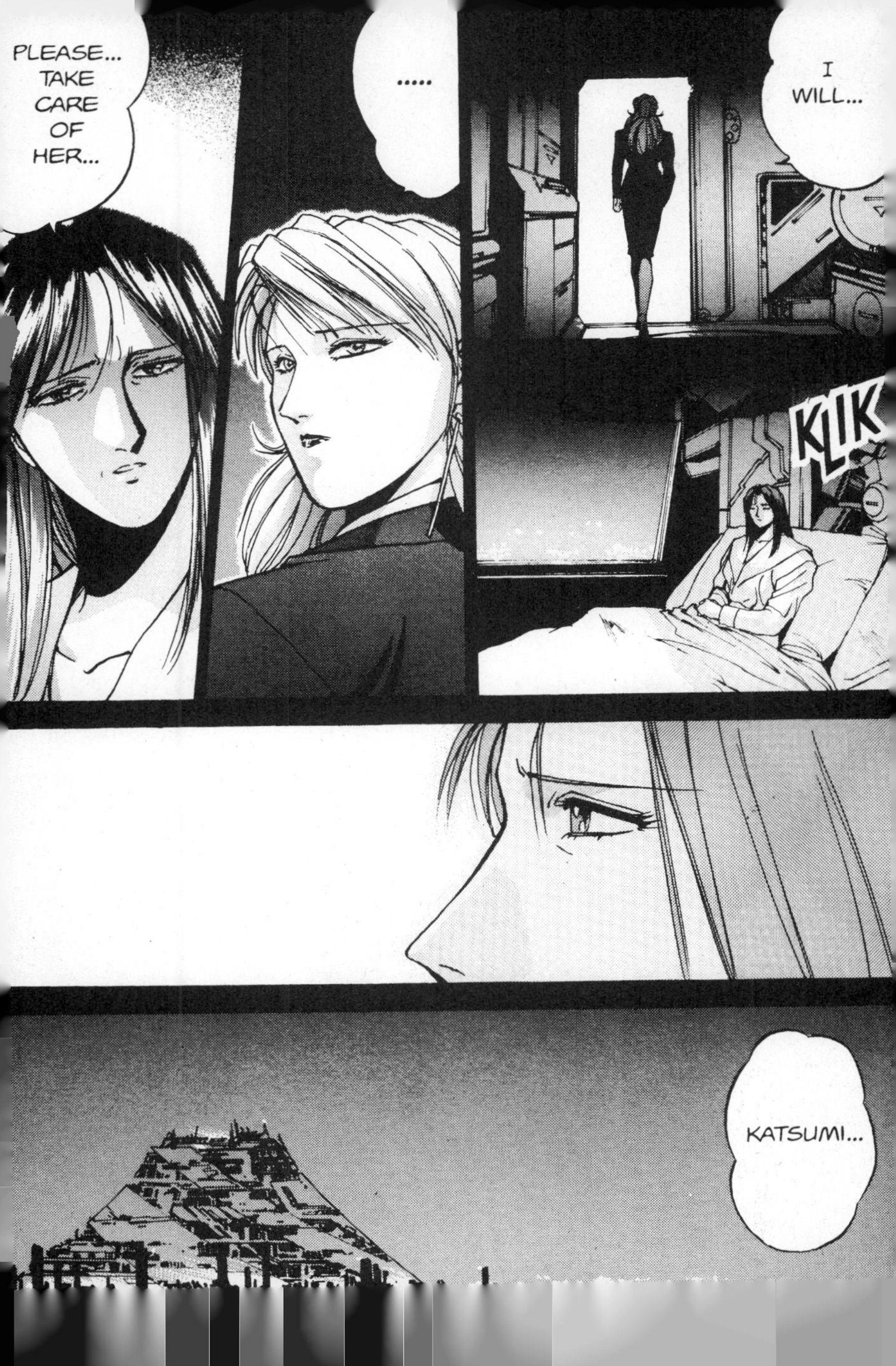
PLEASE... TAKE CARE OF HER...
.....
I WILL...
KLIK
KATSUMI...

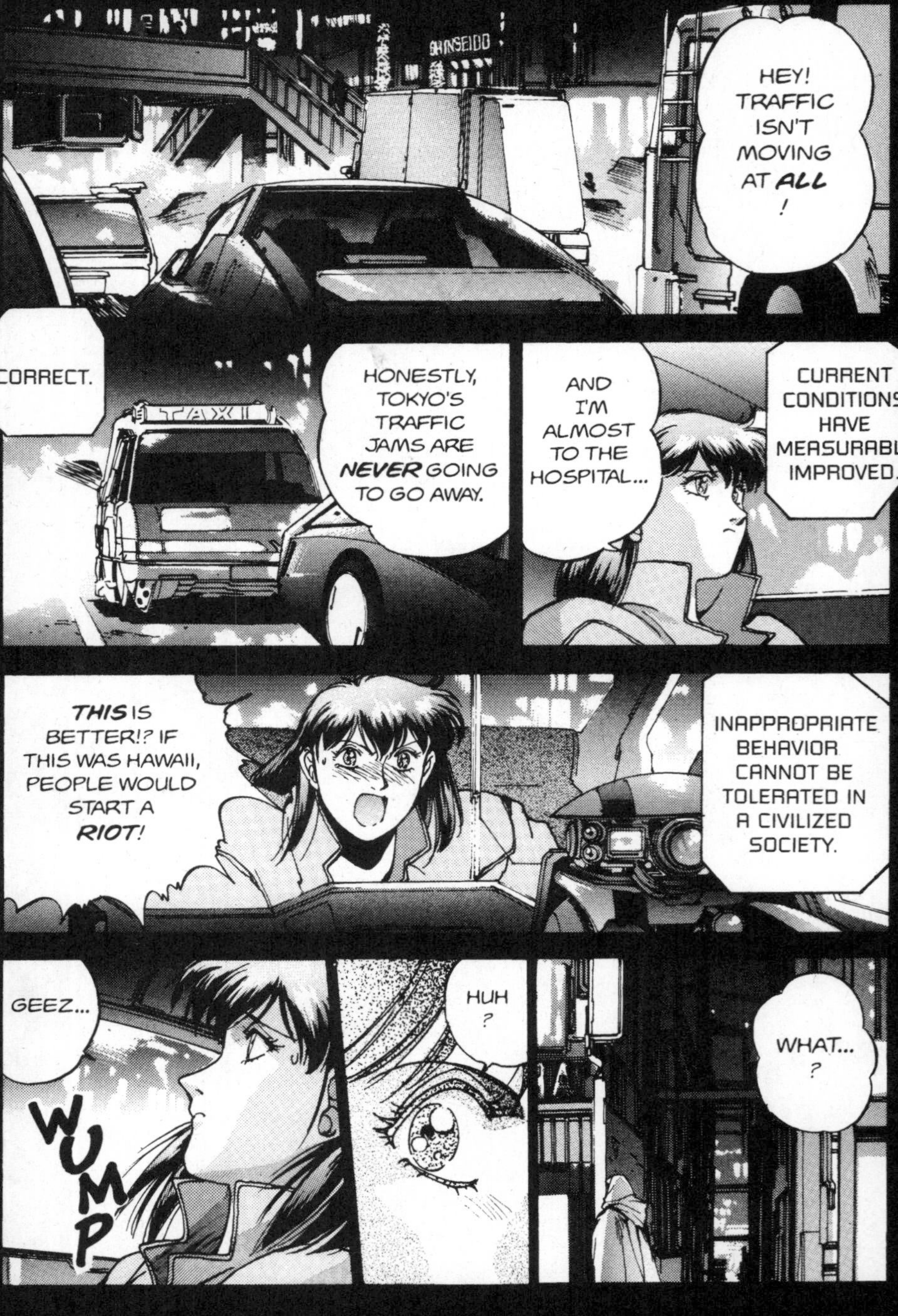

HEY! TRAFFIC ISN'T MOVING AT ALL!
CORRECT.
HONESTLY, TOKYO'S TRAFFIC JAMS ARE NEVER GOING TO GO AWAY.
AND I'M ALMOST TO THE HOSPITAL...
CURRENT CONDITIONS HAVE MEASURABLY IMPROVED.
THIS IS BETTER!? IF THIS WAS HAWAII, PEOPLE WOULD START A RIOT!
INAPPROPRIATE BEHAVIOR CANNOT BE TOLERATED IN A CIVILIZED SOCIETY.
GEEZ...
WUMP
HUH?
WHAT...?

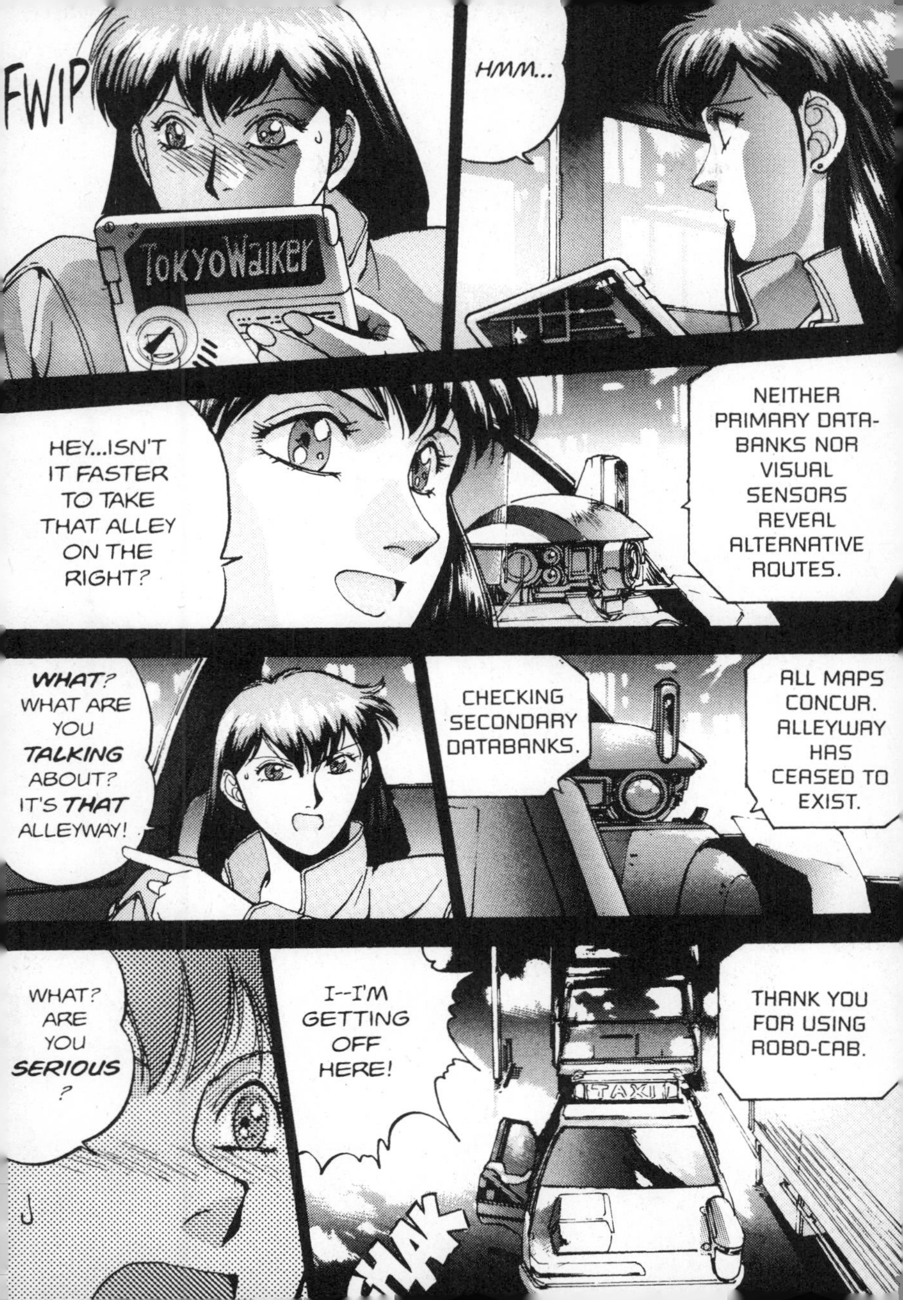
FWIP
TokyoWalker
HMM...
HEY...ISN'T IT FASTER TO TAKE THAT ALLEY ON THE RIGHT?
NEITHER PRIMARY DATA-BANKS NOR VISUAL SENSORS REVEAL ALTERNATIVE ROUTES.
WHAT? WHAT ARE YOU TALKING ABOUT? IT'S THAT ALLEYWAY!
CHECKING SECONDARY DATABANKS.
ALL MAPS CONCUR. ALLEYWAY HAS CEASED TO EXIST.
WHAT? ARE YOU SERIOUS?
I--I'M GETTING OFF HERE!
THANK YOU FOR USING ROBO-CAB.
TAXI
CHAK

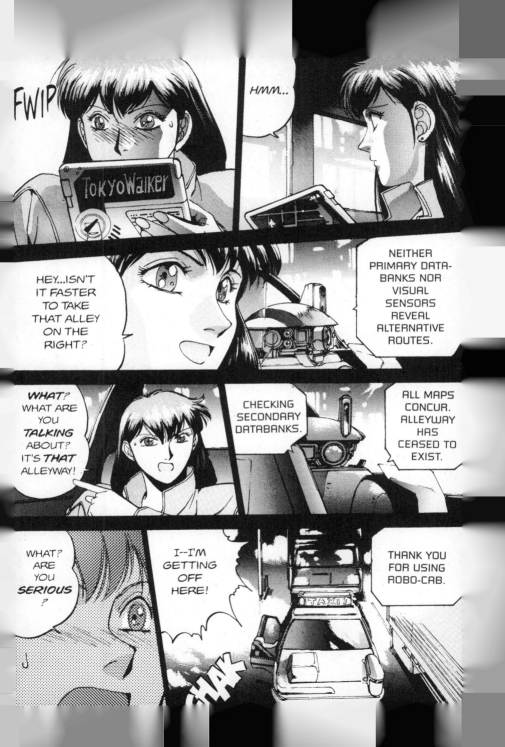

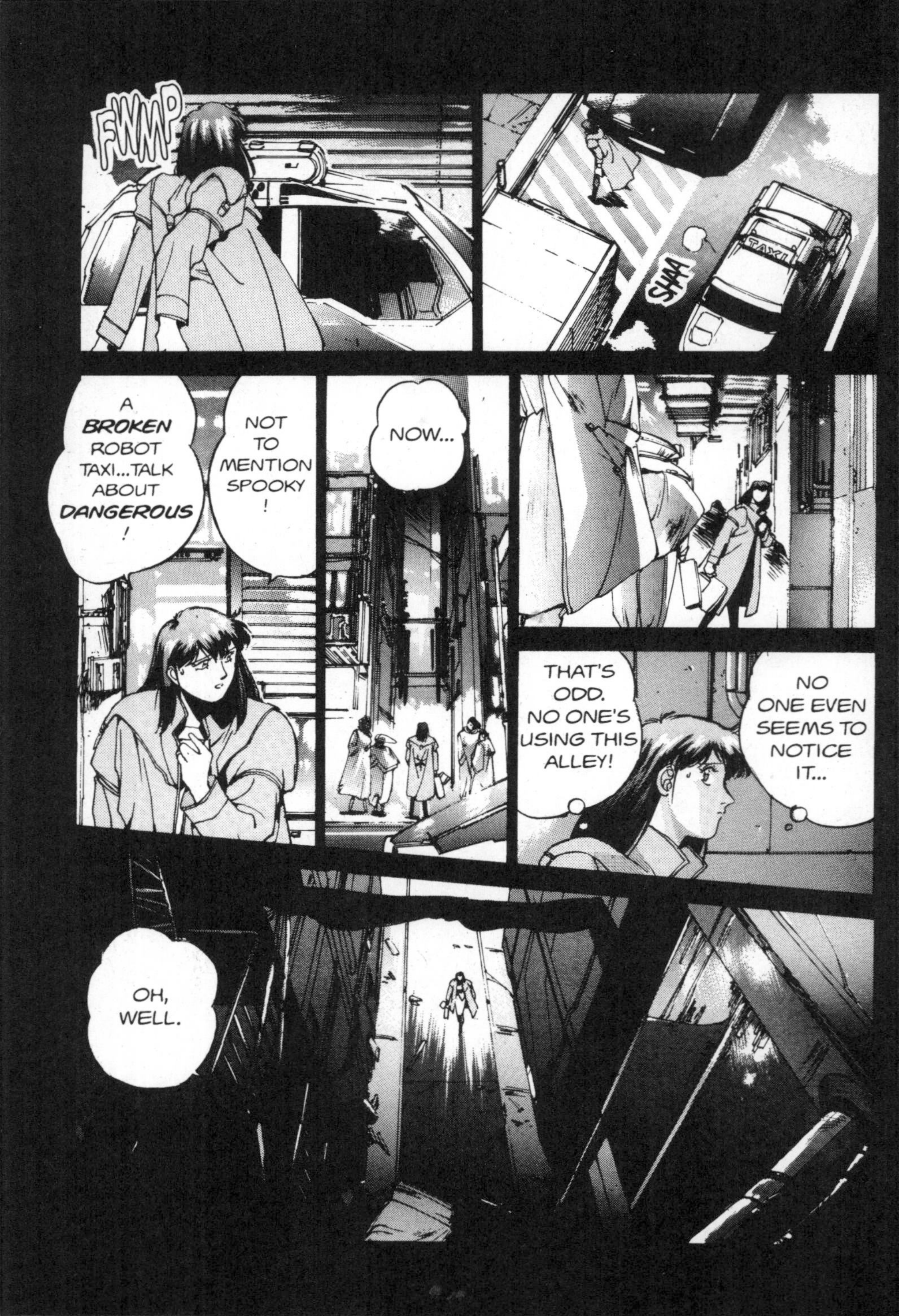
FWMP
SHAA
TAXI
A BROKEN ROBOT TAXI...TALK ABOUT DANGEROUS!
NOT TO MENTION SPOOKY!
NOW...
THAT'S ODD. NO ONE'S USING THIS ALLEY!
NO ONE EVEN SEEMS TO NOTICE IT...
OH, WELL.

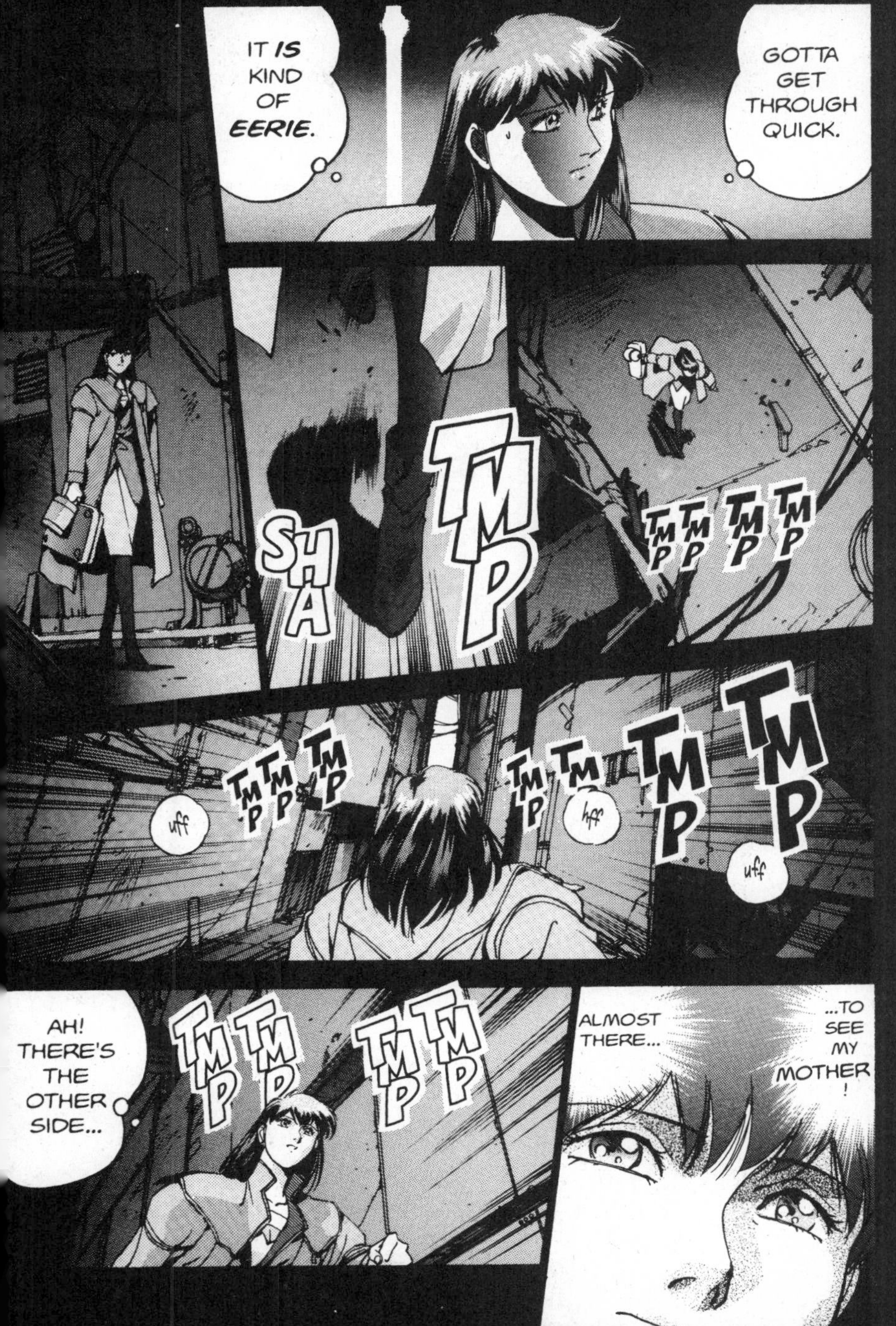

IT IS KIND OF EERIE.
GOTTA GET THROUGH QUICK.
SHA
TMP
TMP TMP TMP TMP
uff
TMP TMP TMP
TMP TMP
hff
TMP
TMP
uff
AH! THERE'S THE OTHER SIDE...
TMP TMP TMP TMP
ALMOST THERE...
...TO SEE MY MOTHER!

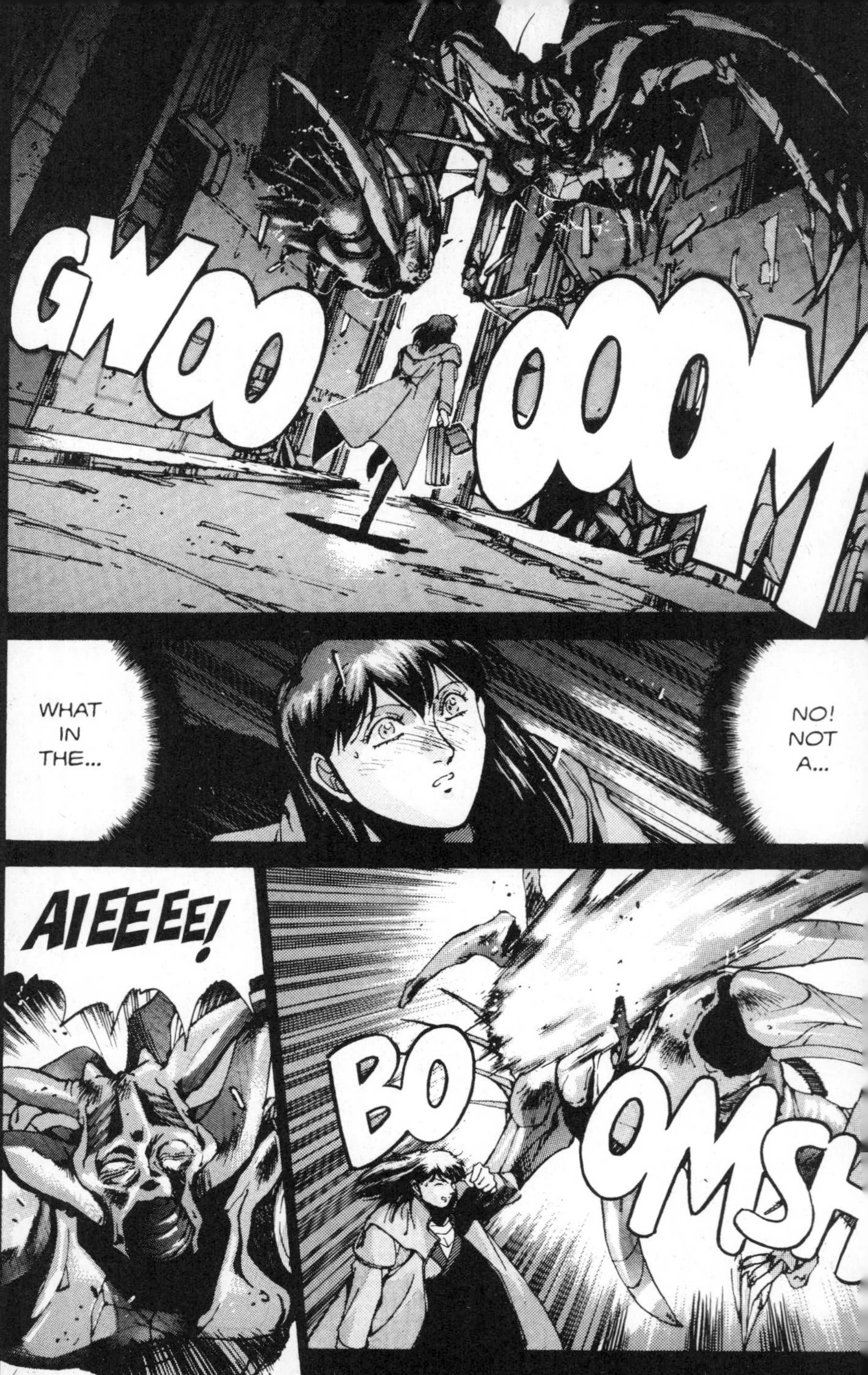
GWOOOOOM
WHAT IN THE...
NO! NOT A...
AIEEEEE!
BOOMSH

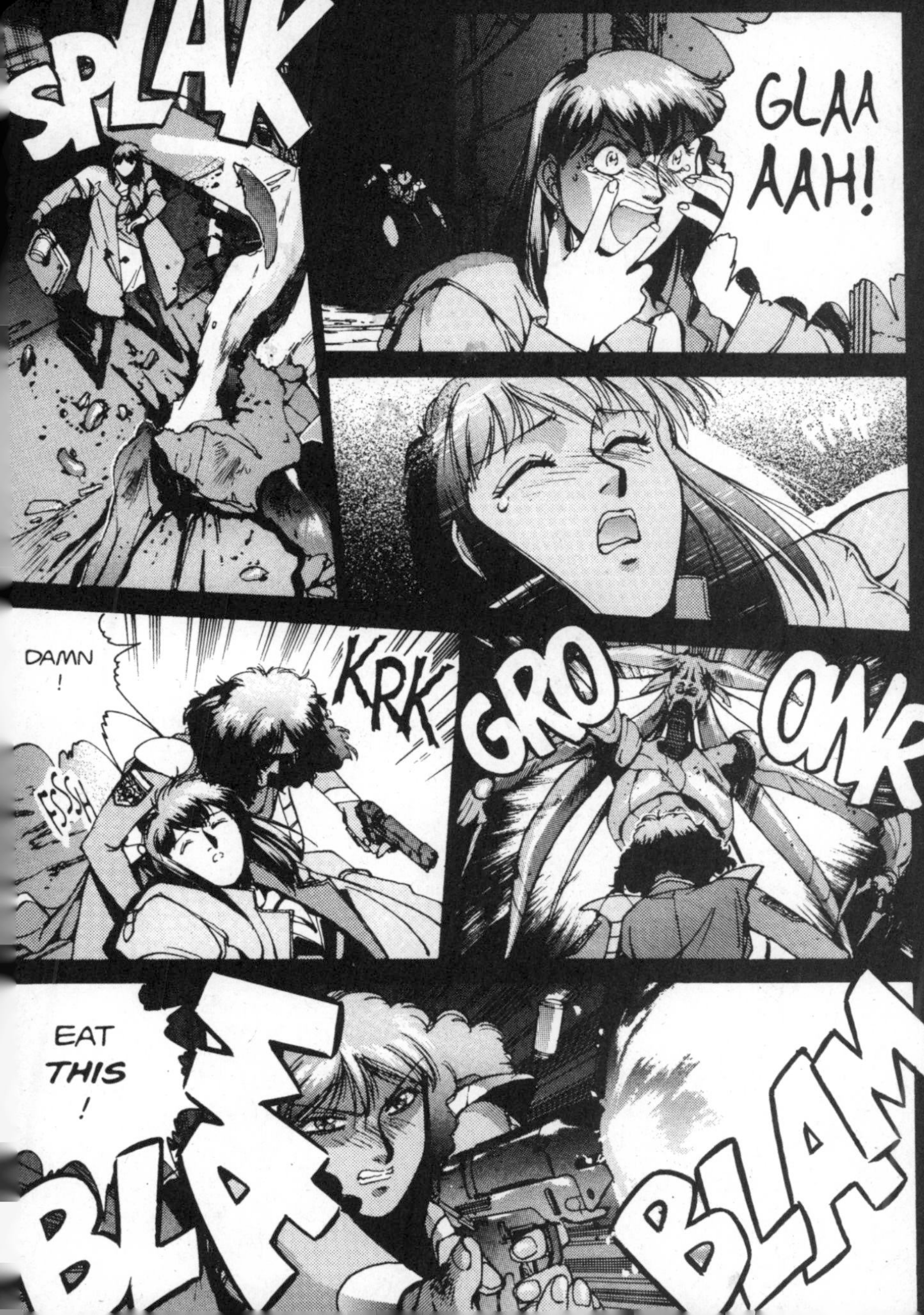
SPLAK
GLAA AAH!
DAMN!
FSSSH
KRK
GRO ONR
EAT THIS!
BLAT
BLAM

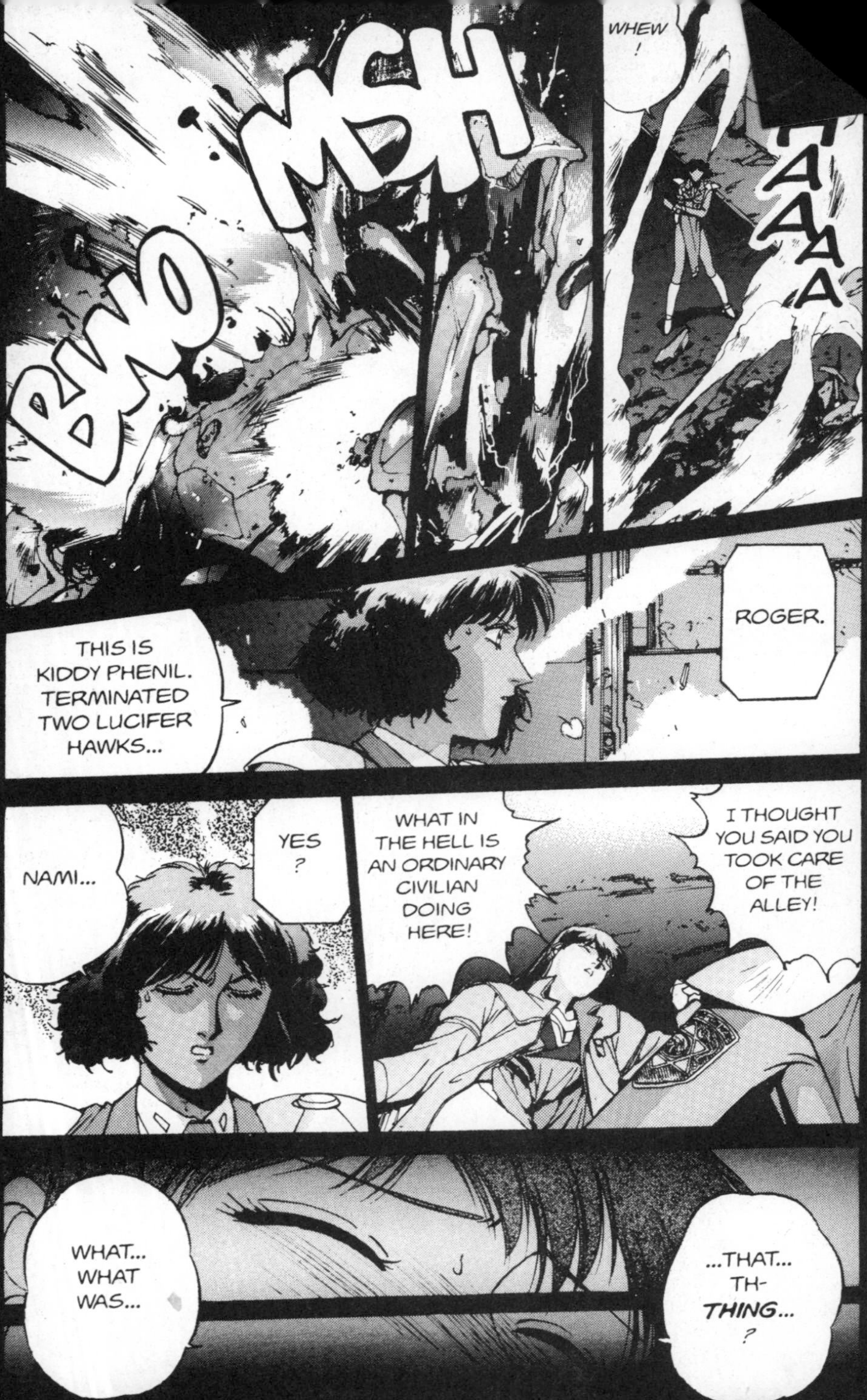
BWOMSH
WHEW!
HAAAAA
THIS IS KIDDY PHENIL. TERMINATED TWO LUCIFER HAWKS...
ROGER.
NAMI...
YES?
WHAT IN THE HELL IS AN ORDINARY CIVILIAN DOING HERE!
I THOUGHT YOU SAID YOU TOOK CARE OF THE ALLEY!
WHAT... WHAT WAS...
...THAT... TH- THING...?

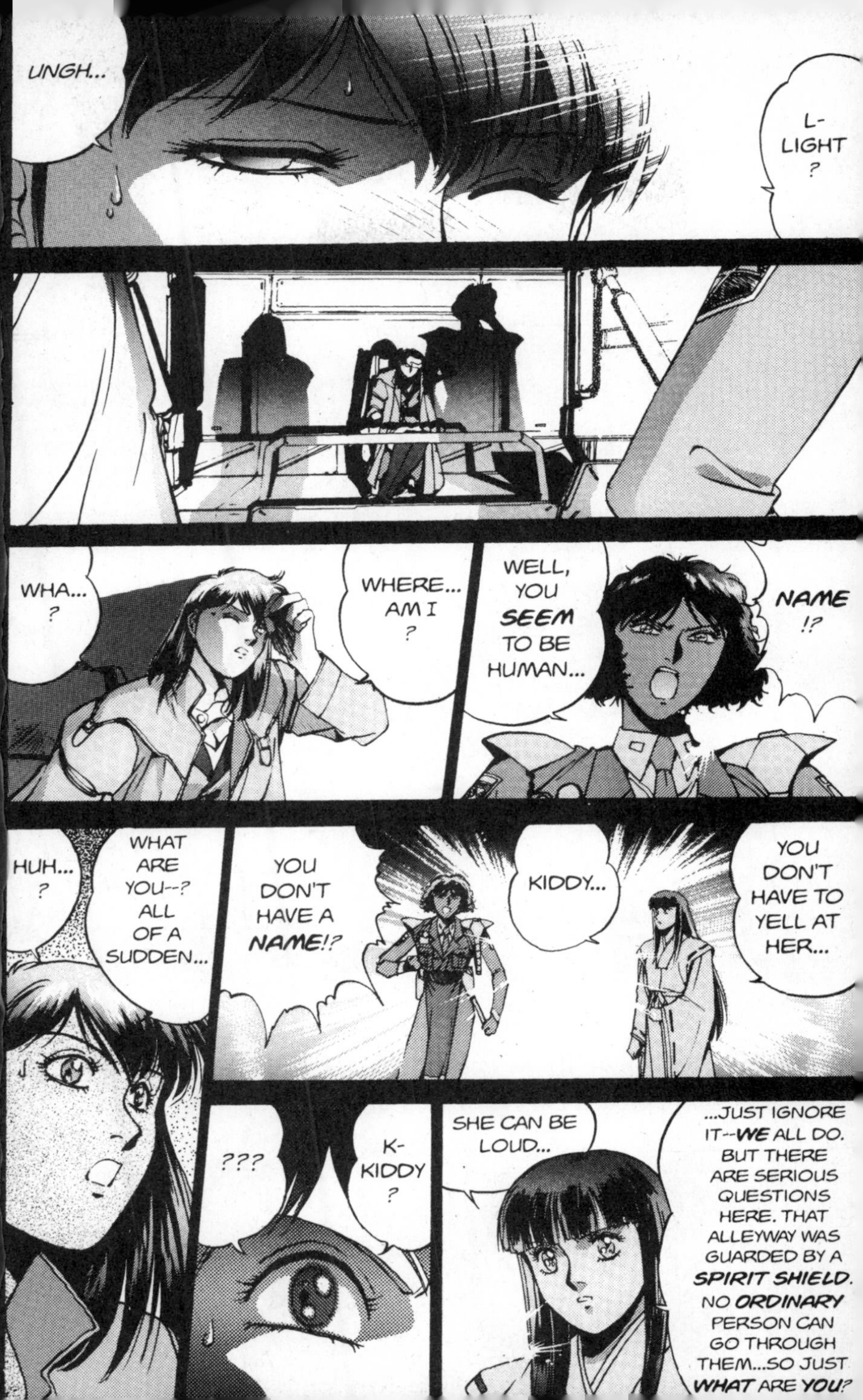
UNGH...
L-LIGHT?
WHA...?
WHERE... AM I?
WELL, YOU SEEM TO BE HUMAN...
NAME!?
HUH...?
WHAT ARE YOU--? ALL OF A SUDDEN...
YOU DON'T HAVE A NAME!?
KIDDY...
YOU DON'T HAVE TO YELL AT HER...
???
K-KIDDY?
SHE CAN BE LOUD...
...JUST IGNORE IT--WE ALL DO. BUT THERE ARE SERIOUS QUESTIONS HERE. THAT ALLEYWAY WAS GUARDED BY A SPIRIT SHIELD. NO ORDINARY PERSON CAN GO THROUGH THEM...SO JUST WHAT ARE YOU?

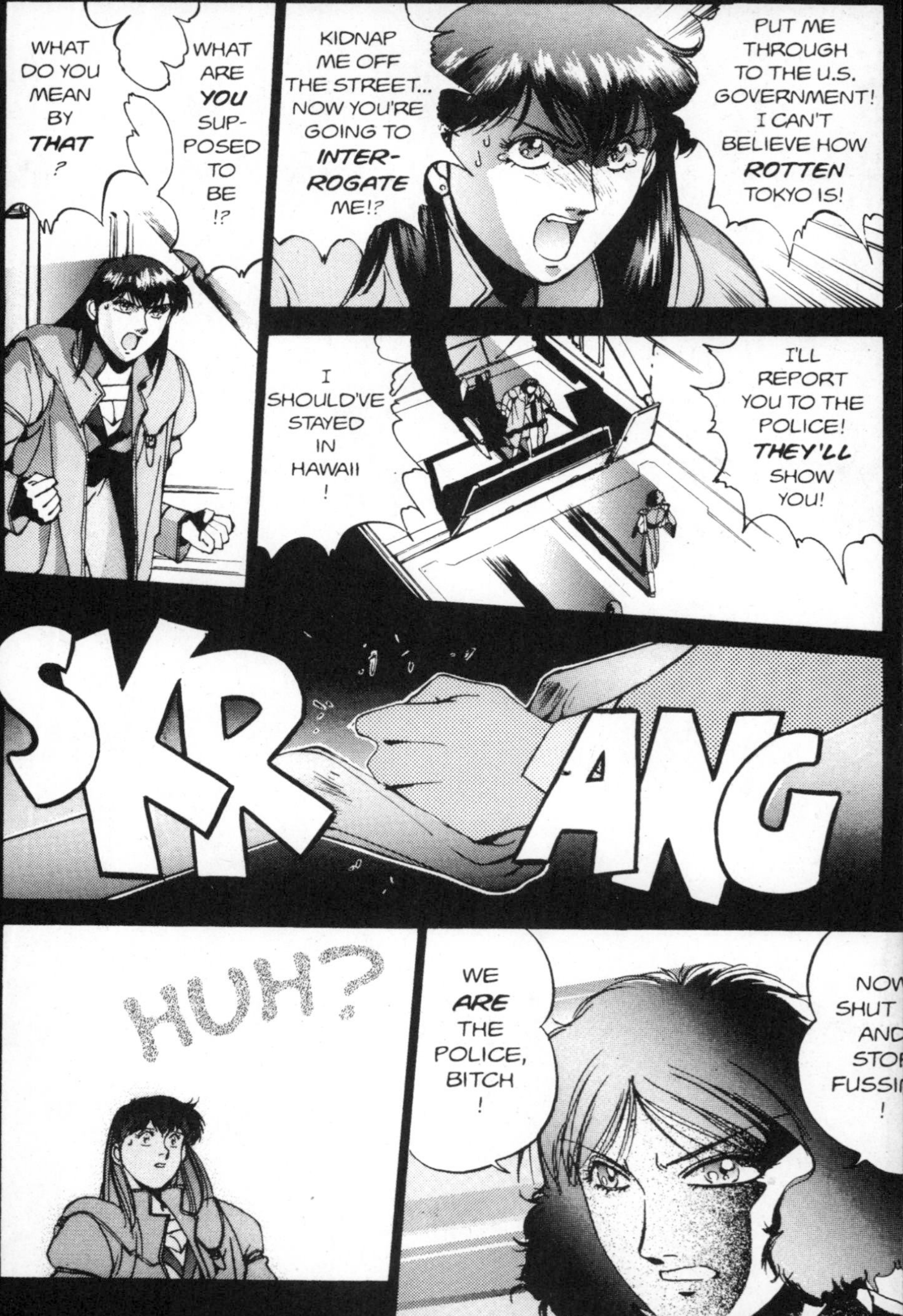
WHAT DO YOU MEAN BY THAT ?
WHAT ARE YOU SUPPOSED TO BE !?
KIDNAP ME OFF THE STREET... NOW YOU'RE GOING TO INTERROGATE ME!?
PUT ME THROUGH TO THE U.S. GOVERNMENT! I CAN'T BELIEVE HOW ROTTEN TOKYO IS!
I SHOULD'VE STAYED IN HAWAII !
I'LL REPORT YOU TO THE POLICE! THEY'LL SHOW YOU!
SKRANG
HUH?
WE ARE THE POLICE, BITCH !
NOW SHUT AND STOP FUSSIN !

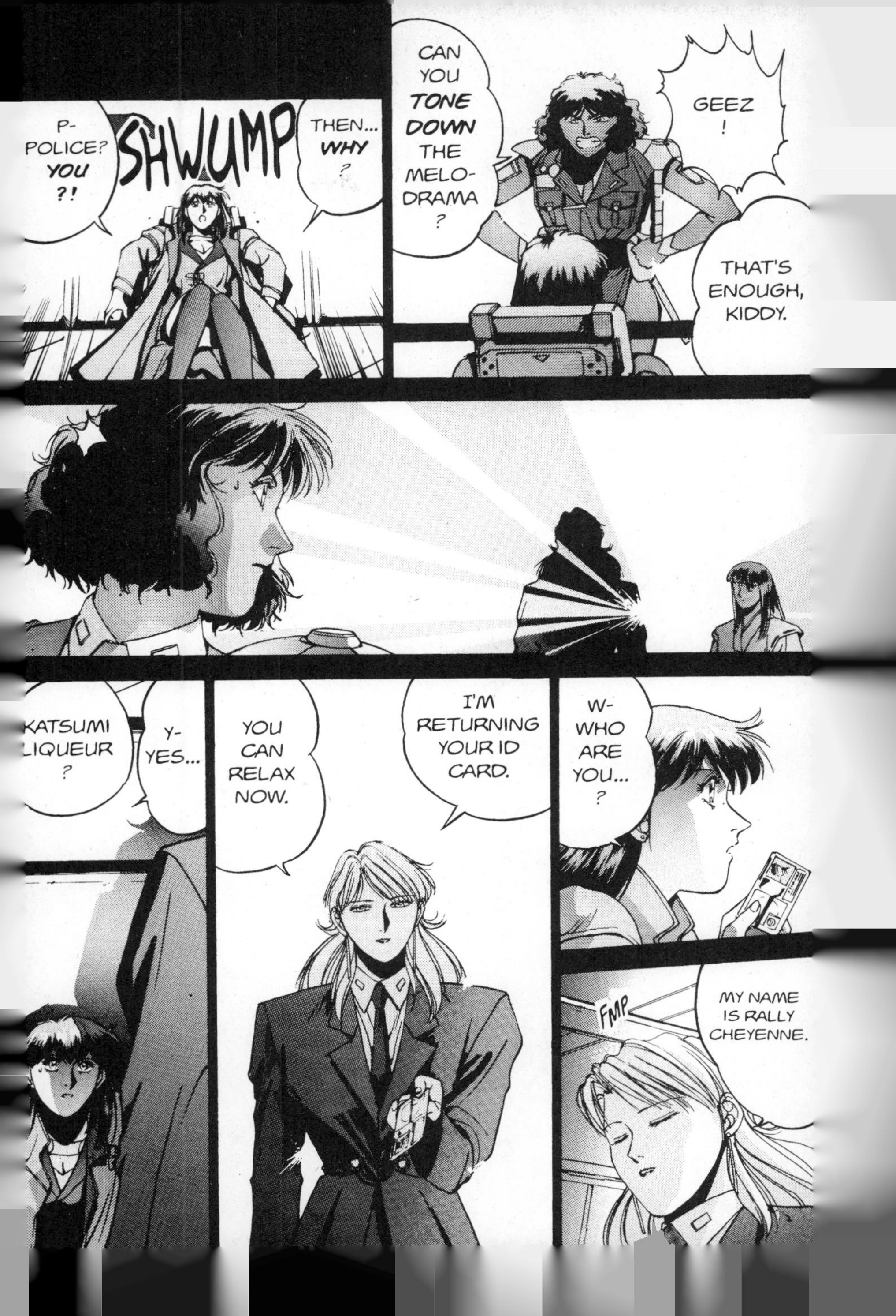
P-POLICE? YOU?!
SHWUMP
THEN... WHY?
CAN YOU TONE DOWN THE MELO-DRAMA?
GEEZ!
THAT'S ENOUGH, KIDDY.
KATSUMI LIQUEUR?
Y-YES...
YOU CAN RELAX NOW.
I'M RETURNING YOUR ID CARD.
W-WHO ARE YOU...?
FMP
MY NAME IS RALLY CHEYENNE.

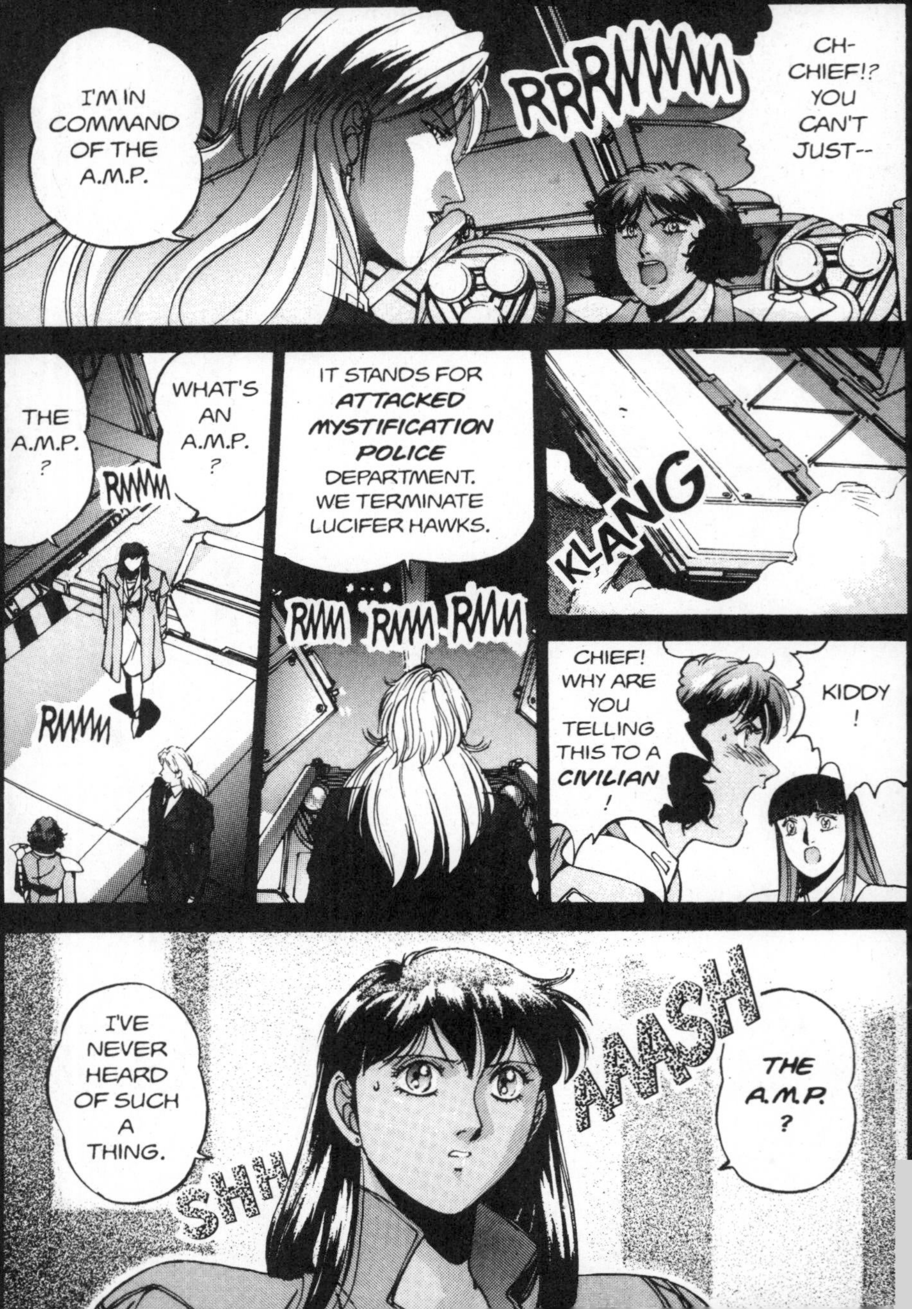
I'M IN COMMAND OF THE A.M.P.
RRRMMMM
CH- CHIEF!? YOU CAN'T JUST--
THE A.M.P. ?
WHAT'S AN A.M.P. ?
RMMM
RMMM
IT STANDS FOR ATTACKED MYSTIFICATION POLICE DEPARTMENT. WE TERMINATE LUCIFER HAWKS.
RMM RMM RMM
KLANG
CHIEF! WHY ARE YOU TELLING THIS TO A CIVILIAN !
KIDDY !
I'VE NEVER HEARD OF SUCH A THING.
SHH
AAASH
THE A.M.P. ?

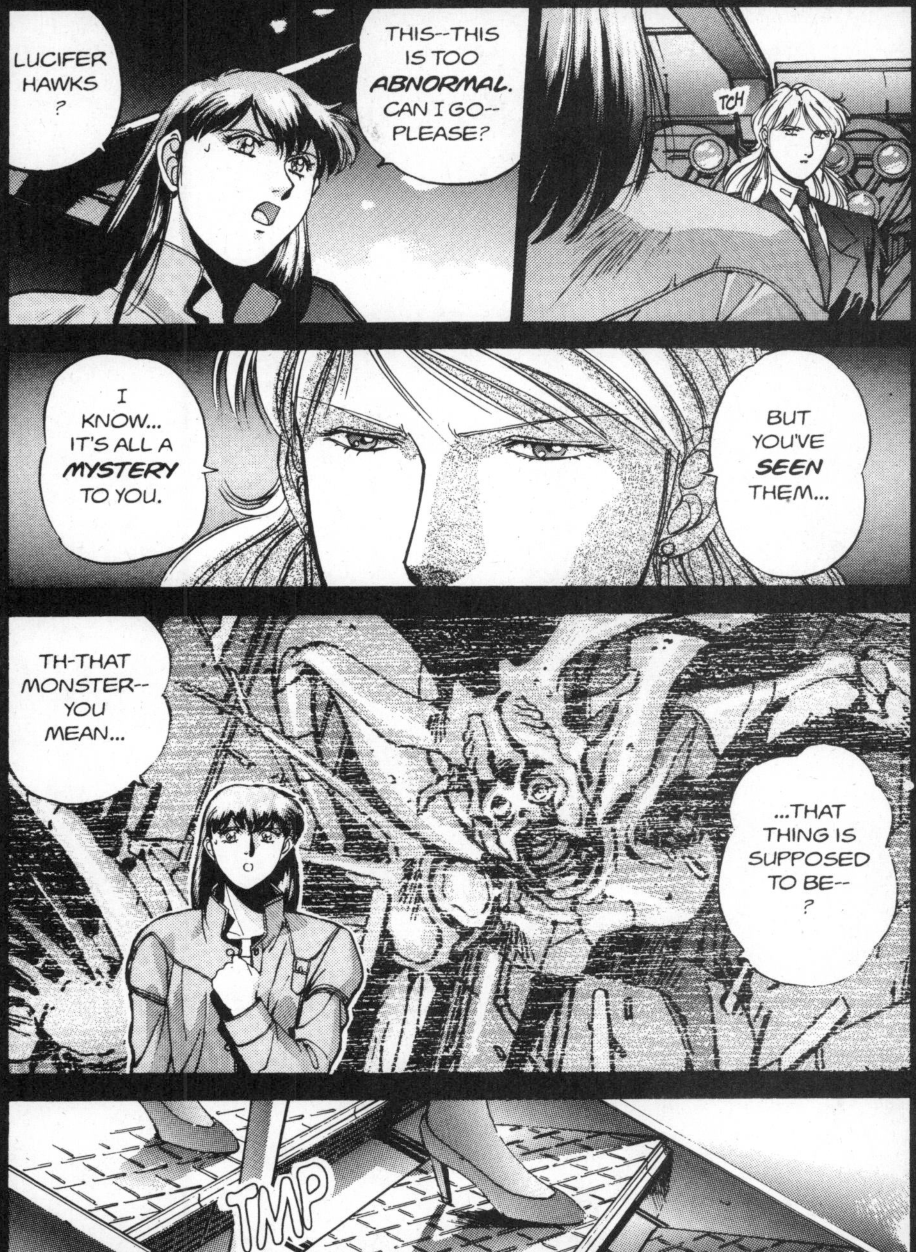
LUCIFER HAWKS ?
THIS--THIS IS TOO ABNORMAL. CAN I GO-- PLEASE?
TCH
I KNOW... IT'S ALL A MYSTERY TO YOU.
BUT YOU'VE SEEN THEM...
TH-THAT MONSTER-- YOU MEAN...
...THAT THING IS SUPPOSED TO BE-- ?
TMP

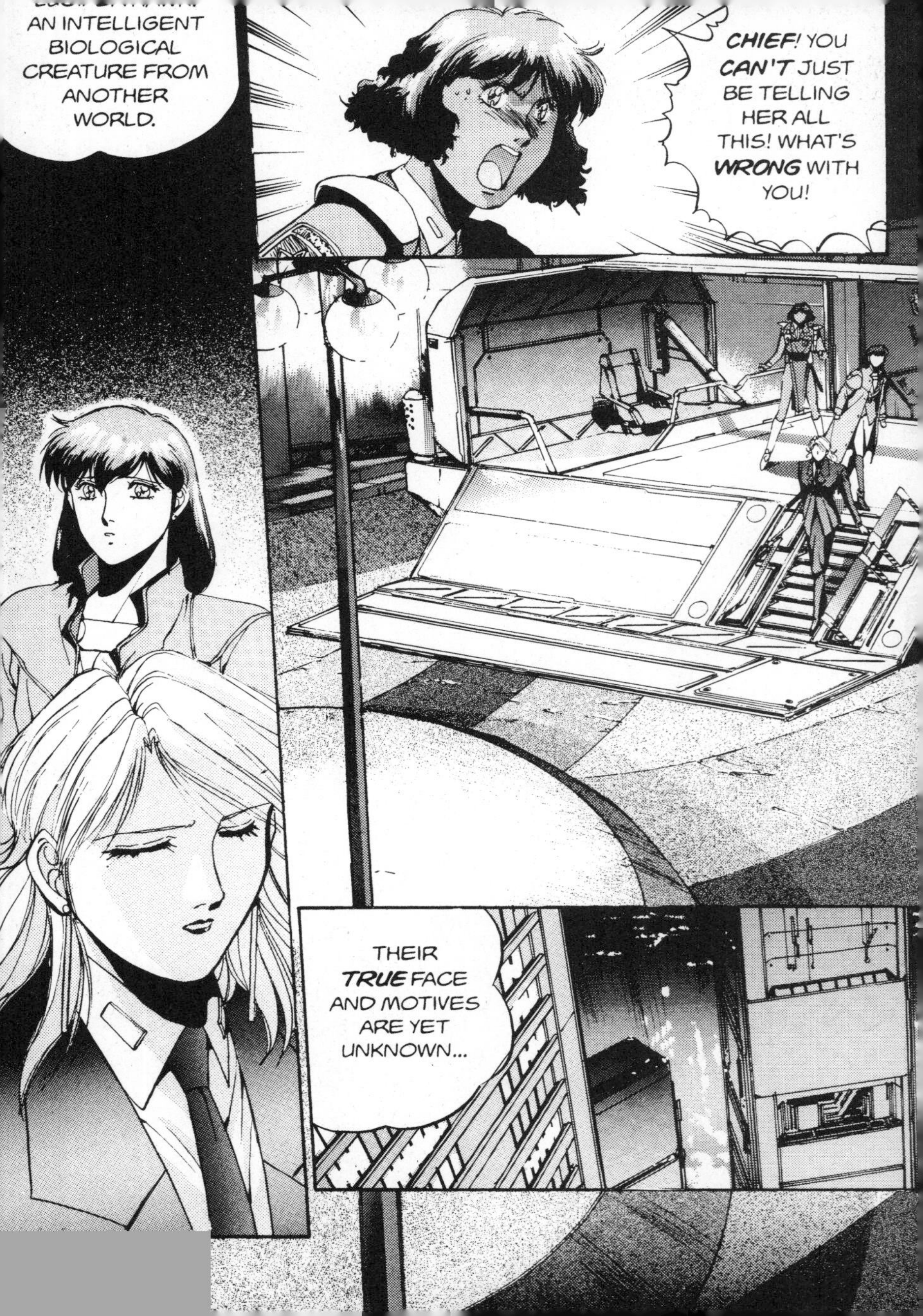
AN INTELLIGENT BIOLOGICAL CREATURE FROM ANOTHER WORLD.
CHIEF! YOU CAN'T JUST BE TELLING HER ALL THIS! WHAT'S WRONG WITH YOU!
THEIR TRUE FACE AND MOTIVES ARE YET UNKNOWN...

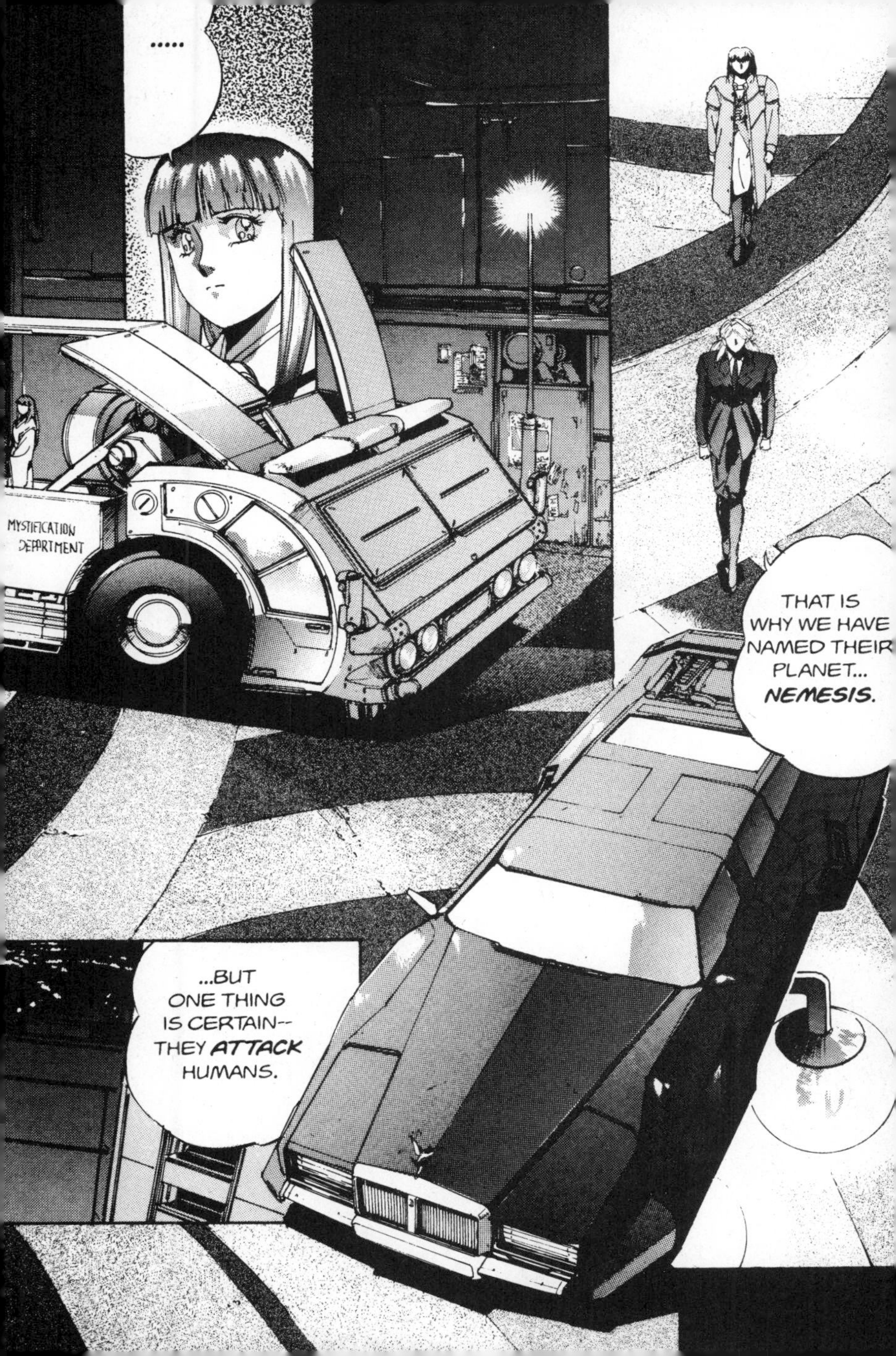
.....
MYSTIFICATION DEPARTMENT
THAT IS WHY WE HAVE NAMED THEIR PLANET... NEMESIS.
...BUT ONE THING IS CERTAIN-- THEY ATTACK HUMANS.

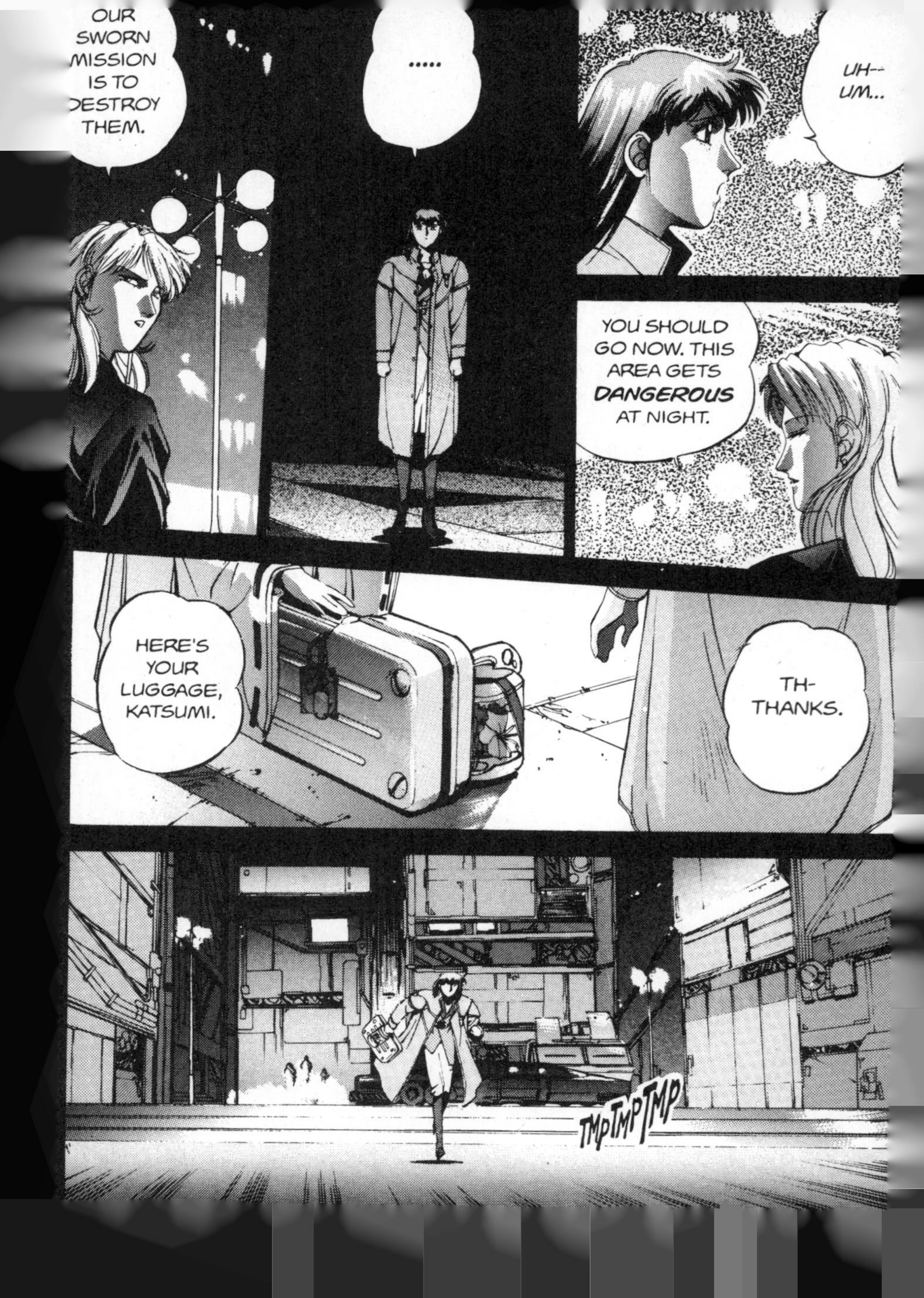
OUR SWORN MISSION IS TO DESTROY THEM.
.....
UH-- UM...
YOU SHOULD GO NOW. THIS AREA GETS **DANGEROUS** AT NIGHT.
HERE'S YOUR LUGGAGE, KATSUMI.
TH- THANKS.
TMP TMP TMP

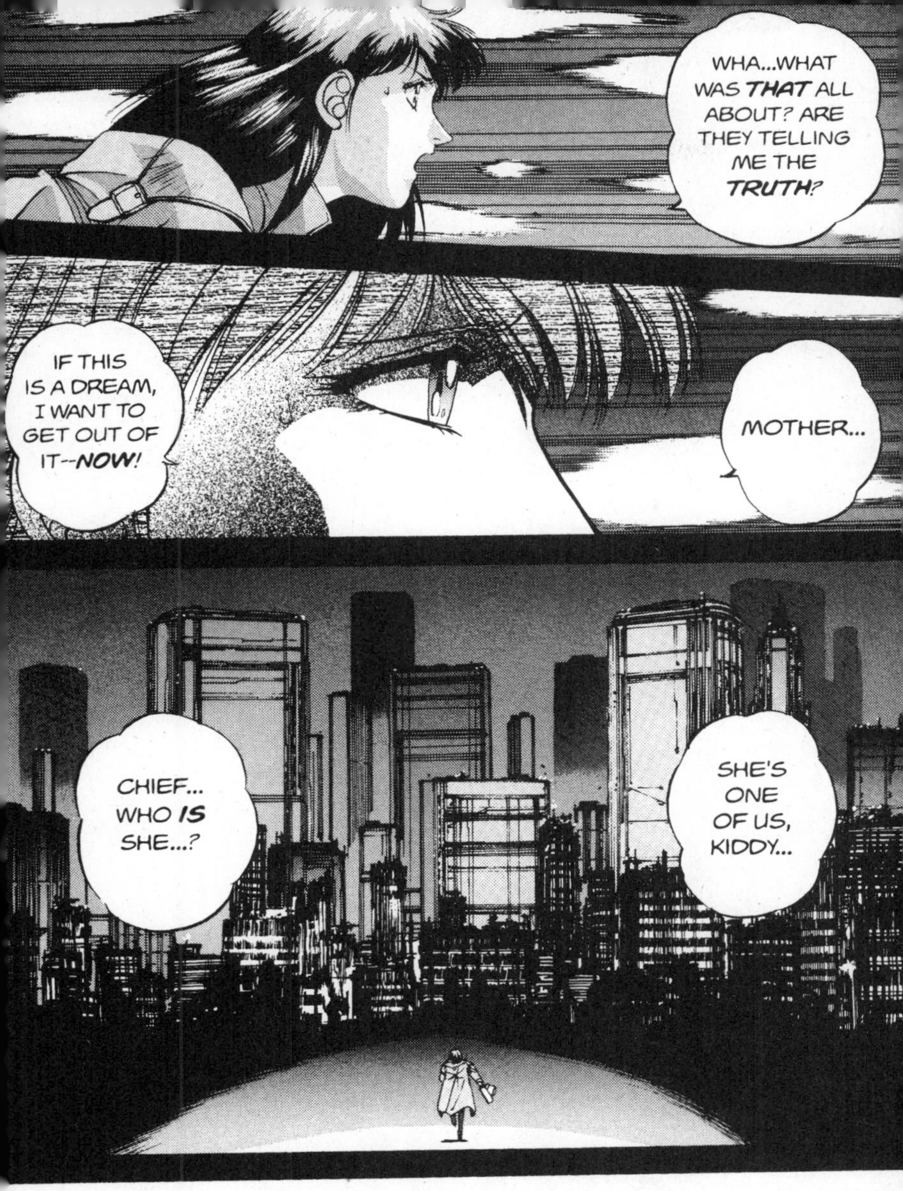
WHA...WHAT WAS THAT ALL ABOUT? ARE THEY TELLING ME THE TRUTH?
IF THIS IS A DREAM, I WANT TO GET OUT OF IT--NOW!
MOTHER...
CHIEF... WHO IS SHE...?
SHE'S ONE OF US, KIDDY...

EITHER OUR GREATEST ***CHAMPION...***
OR OUR GREATEST ***ENEMY...***

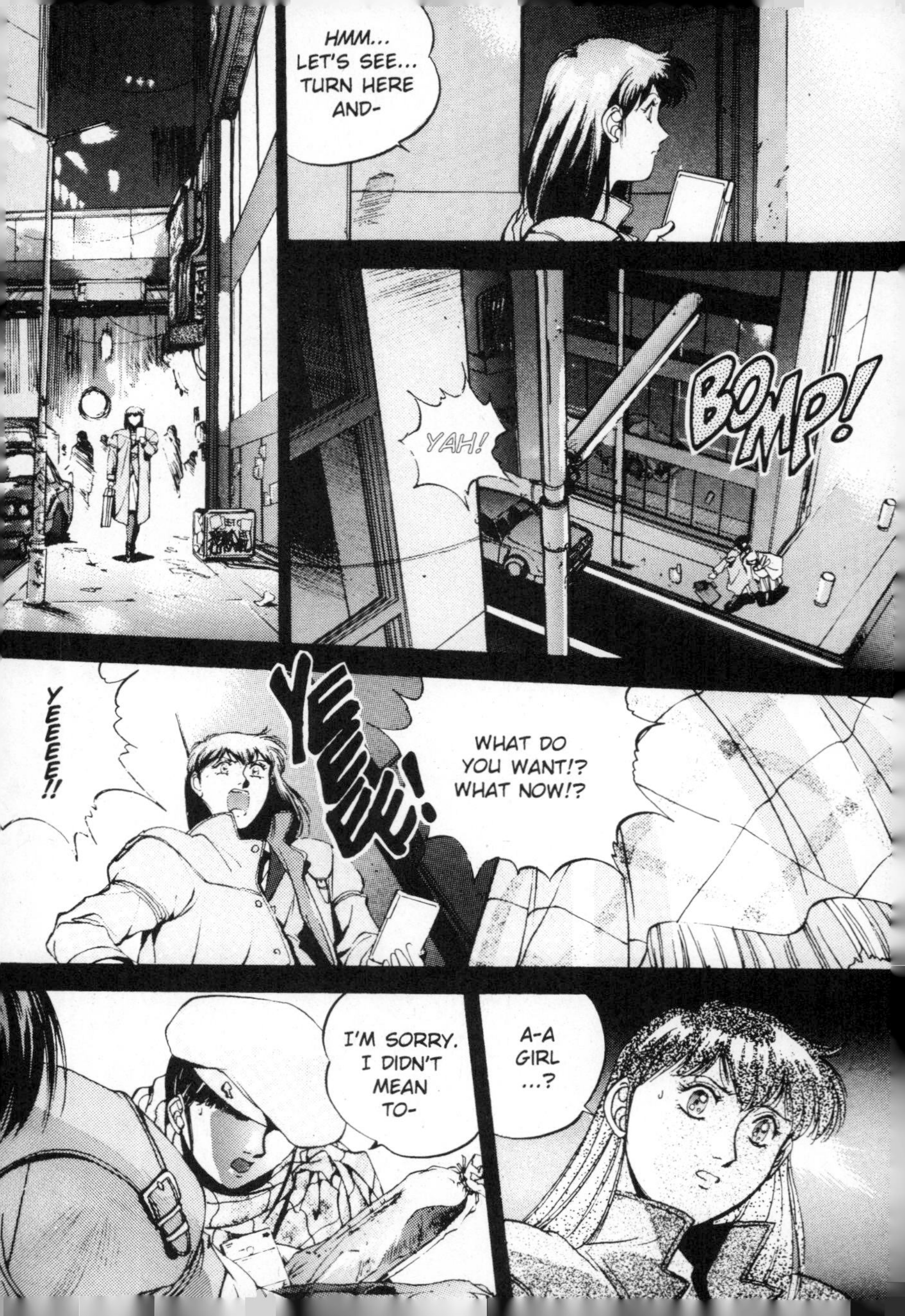
HMM... LET'S SEE... TURN HERE AND-
BOMP!
YAH!
WHAT DO YOU WANT!? WHAT NOW!?
YEEEEE!!
A-A GIRL ...?
I'M SORRY. I DIDN'T MEAN TO-

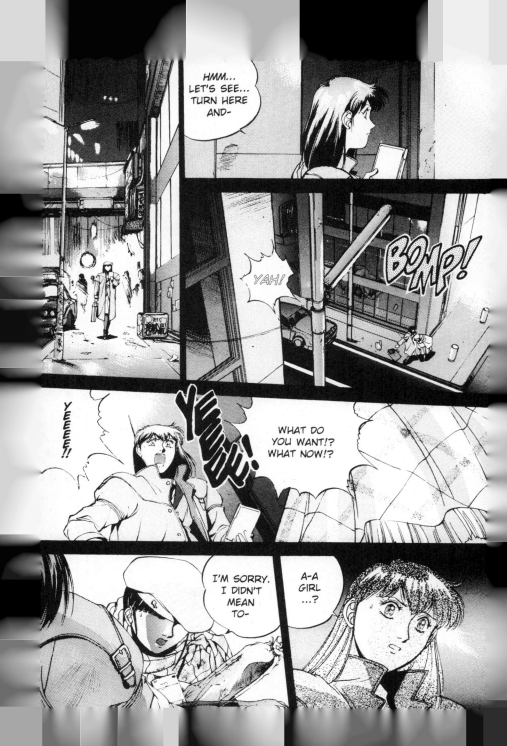

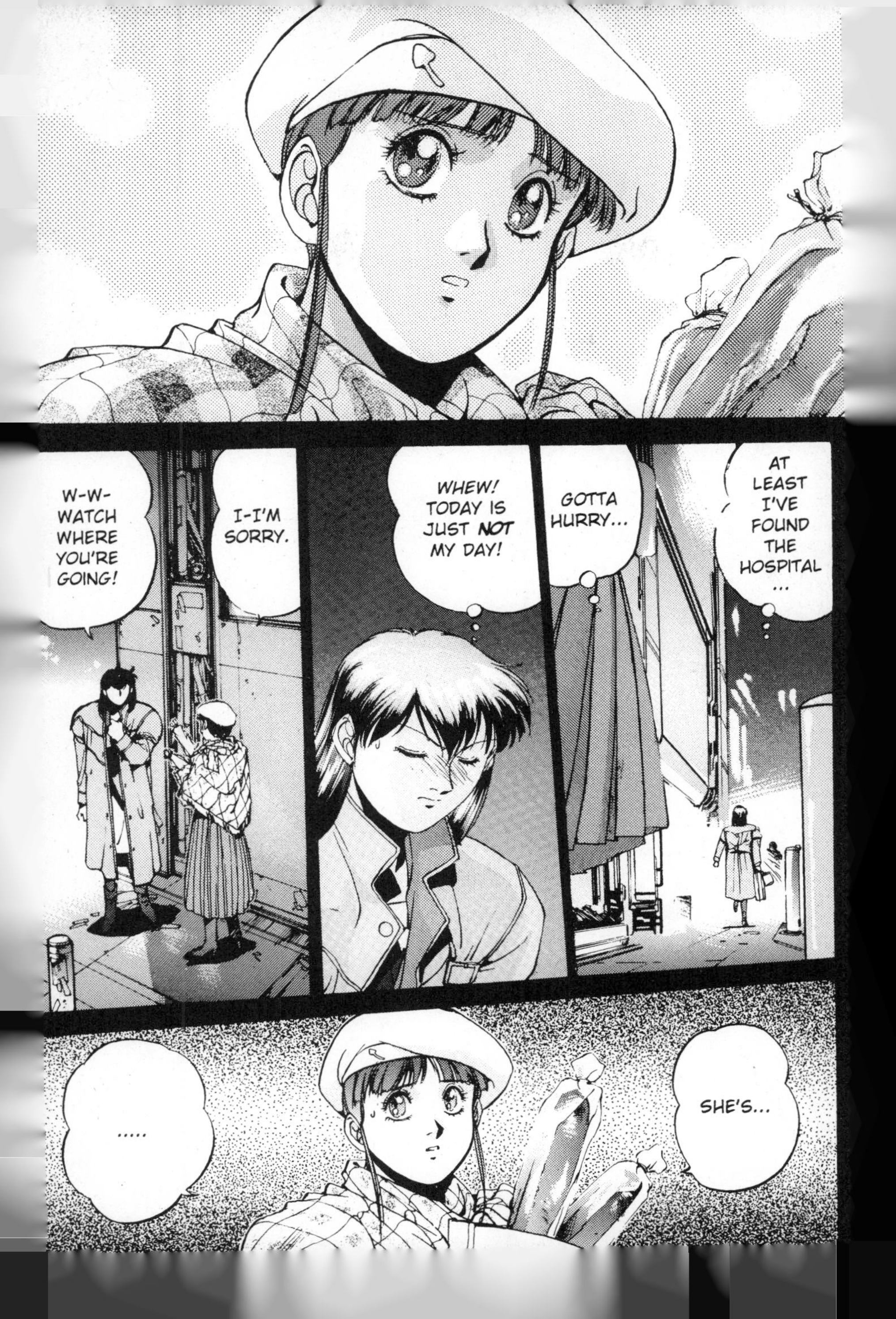

W-W-WATCH WHERE YOU'RE GOING!
I-I'M SORRY.
WHEW! TODAY IS JUST NOT MY DAY!
GOTTA HURRY...
AT LEAST I'VE FOUND THE HOSPITAL ...
.....
SHE'S...

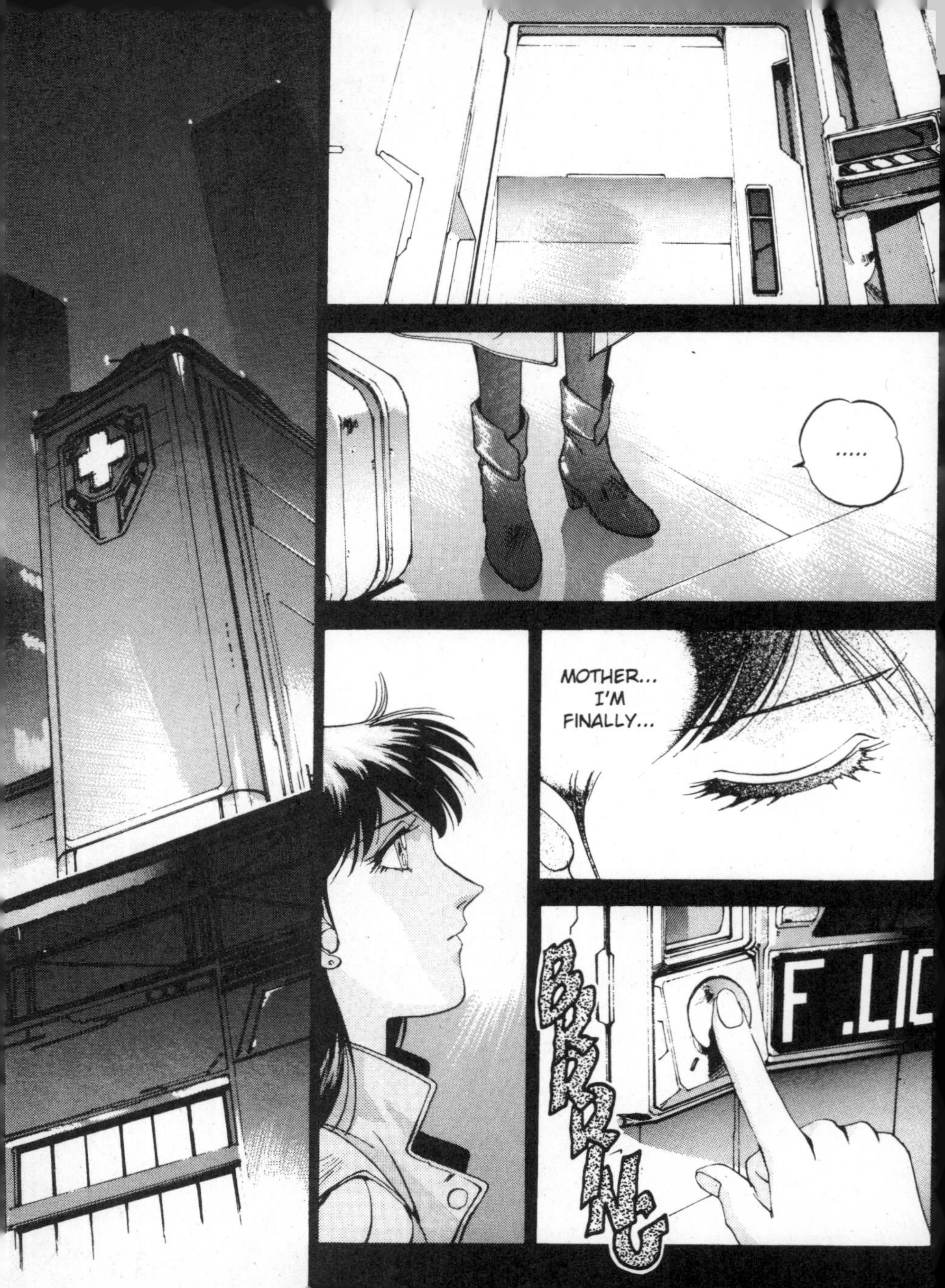
.....
MOTHER... I'M FINALLY...
BZZZING
F. LIC

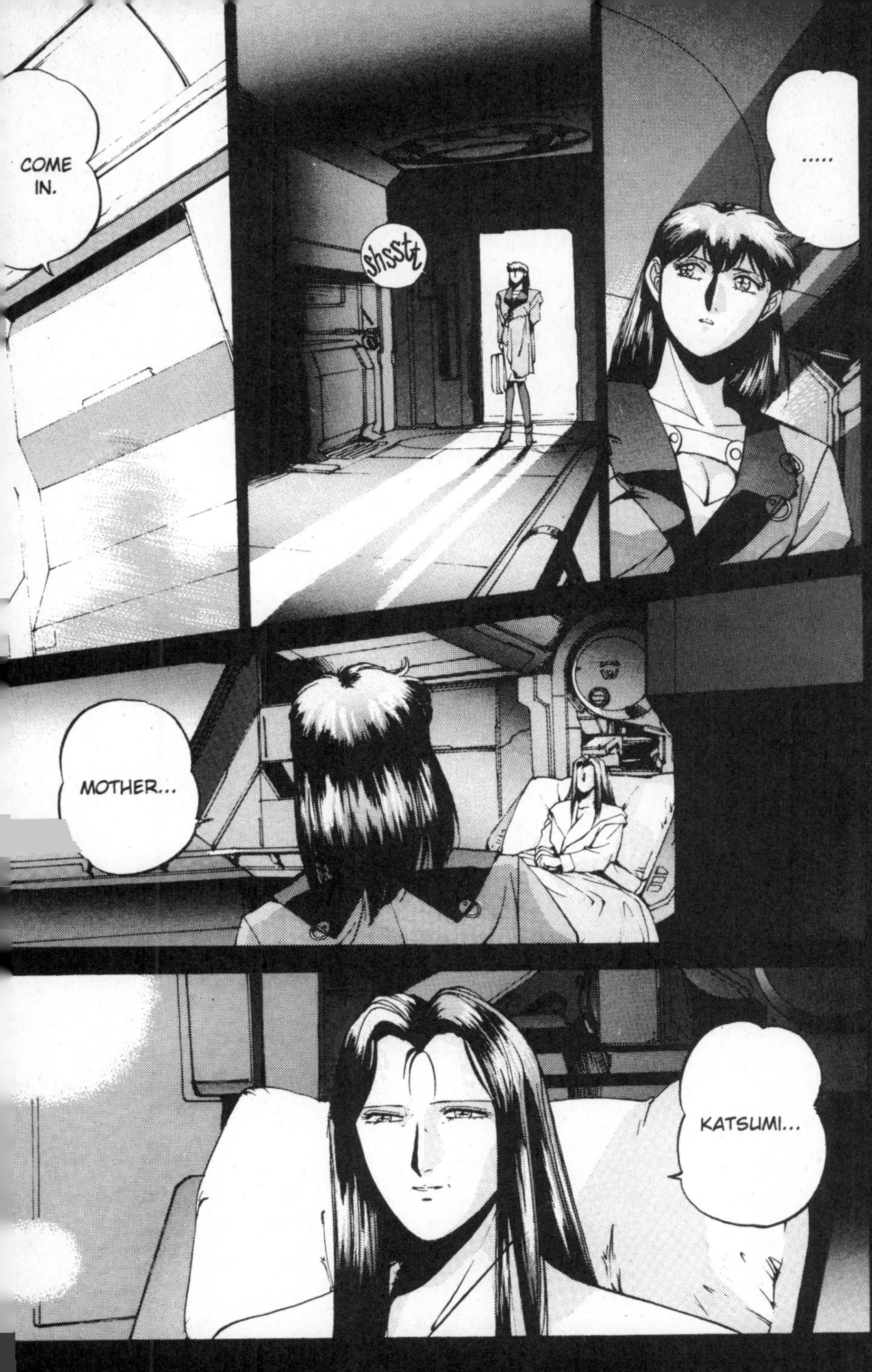
COME IN.
shsstt
.....
MOTHER...
KATSUMI...

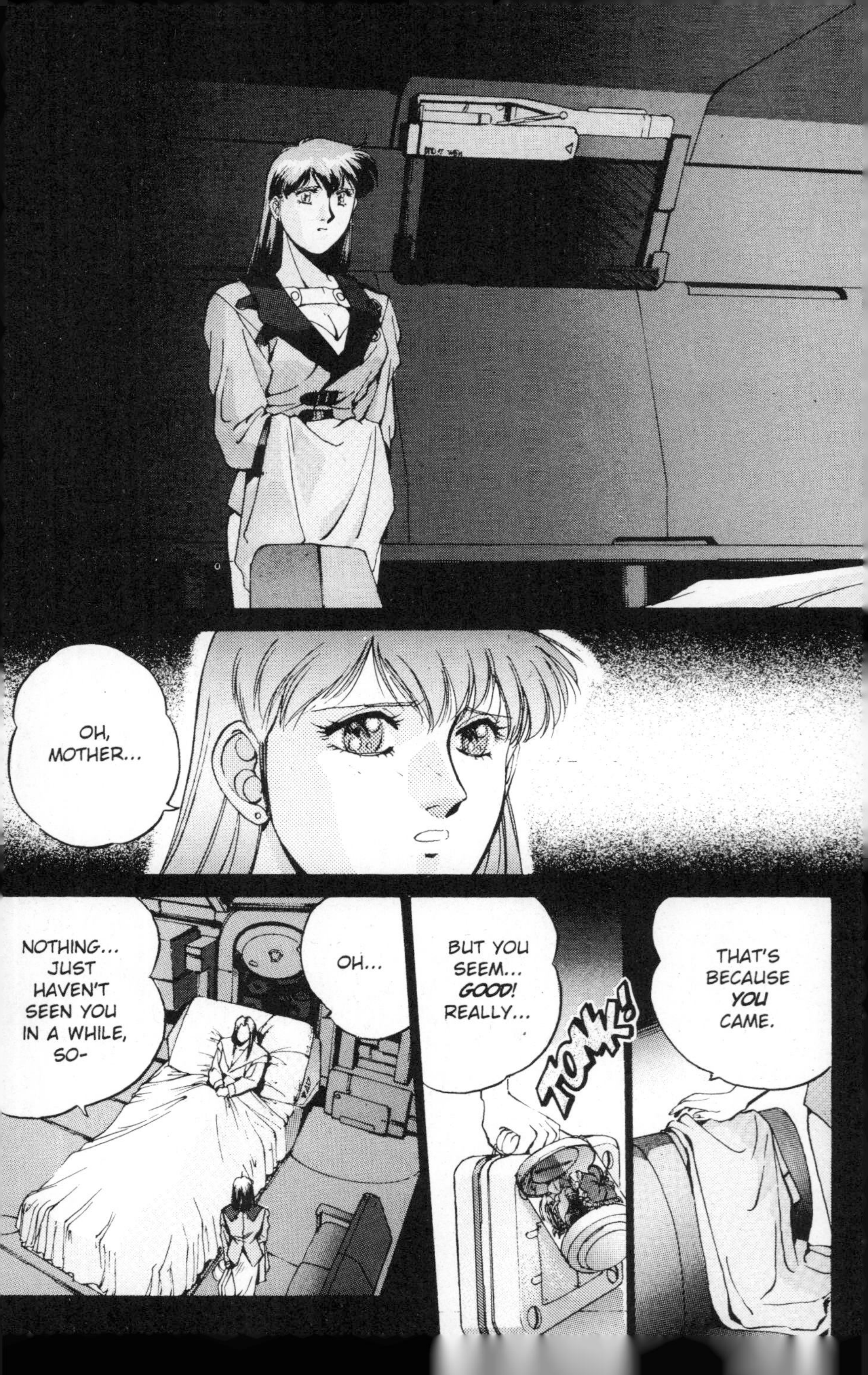
OH, MOTHER...
NOTHING... JUST HAVEN'T SEEN YOU IN A WHILE, SO-
OH...
BUT YOU SEEM... GOOD! REALLY...
TONK!
THAT'S BECAUSE YOU CAME.

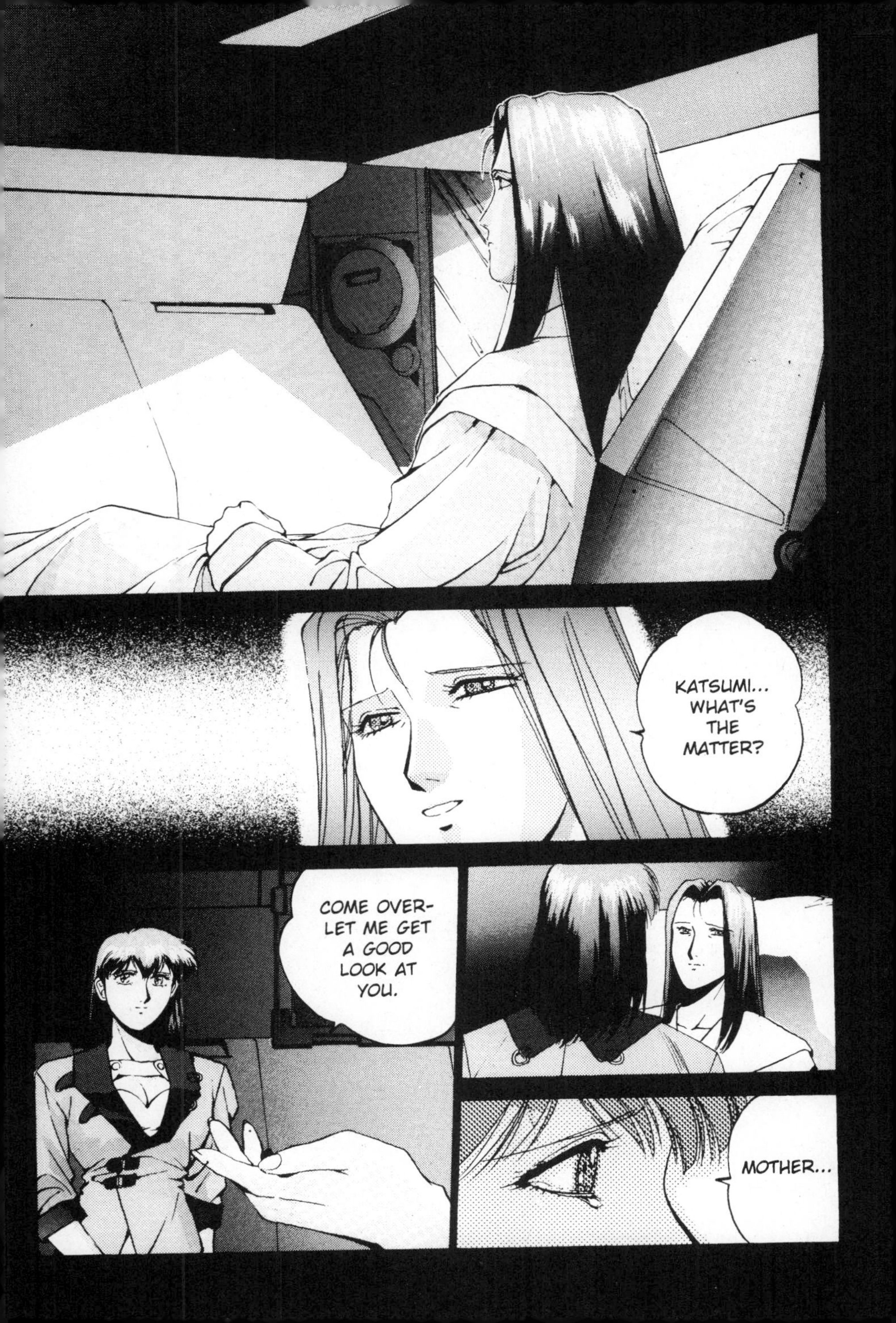
KATSUMI... WHAT'S THE MATTER?
COME OVER- LET ME GET A GOOD LOOK AT YOU.
MOTHER...

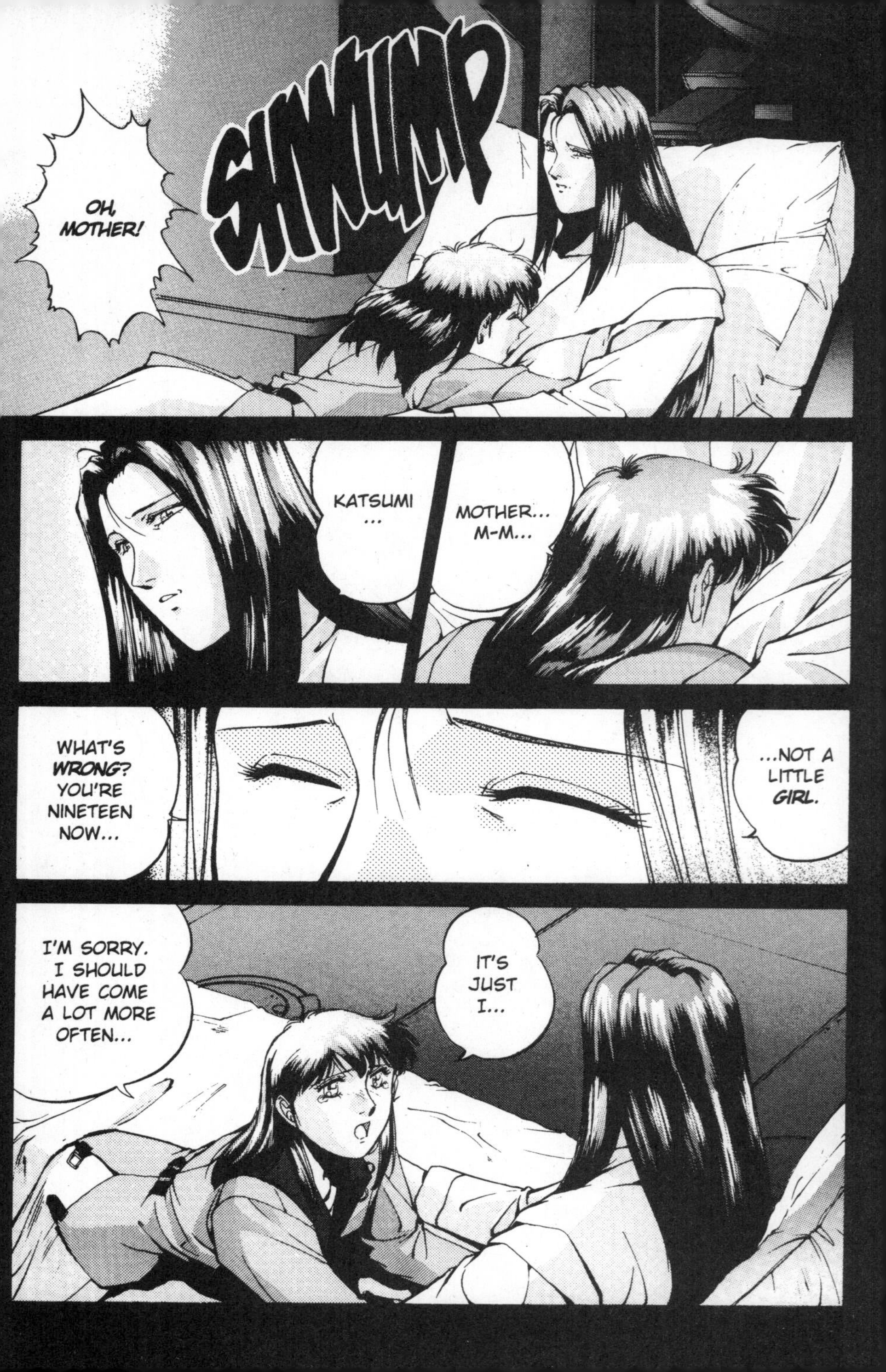
OH, MOTHER!
SHWUMP
KATSUMI ...
MOTHER... M-M...
WHAT'S WRONG? YOU'RE NINETEEN NOW...
...NOT A LITTLE GIRL.
I'M SORRY. I SHOULD HAVE COME A LOT MORE OFTEN...
IT'S JUST I...

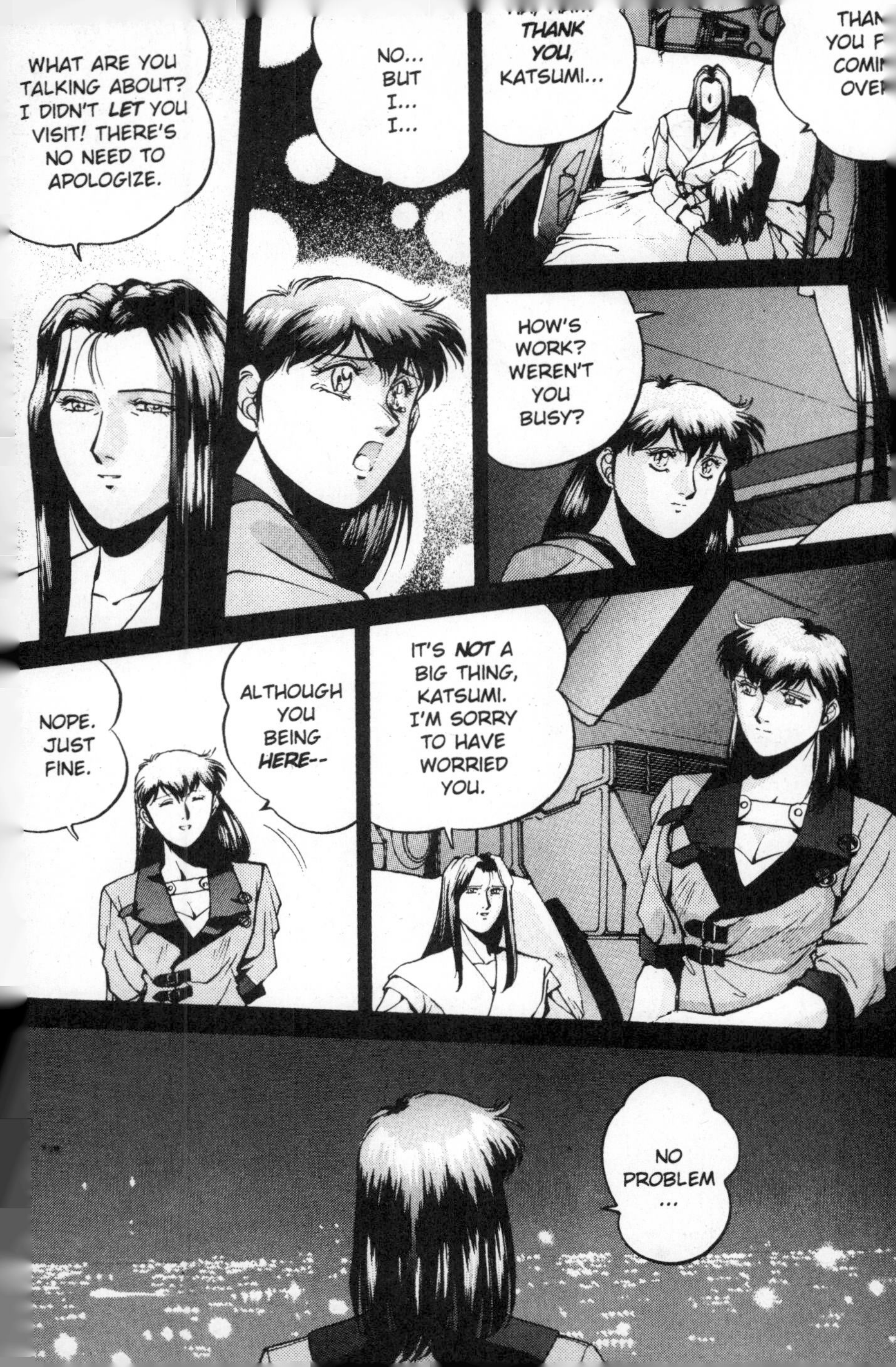
WHAT ARE YOU TALKING ABOUT? I DIDN'T *LET* YOU VISIT! THERE'S NO NEED TO APOLOGIZE.
NO... BUT I... I...
THANK YOU, KATSUMI...
THAN YOU F COMI OVE
HOW'S WORK? WEREN'T YOU BUSY?
NOPE. JUST FINE.
ALTHOUGH YOU BEING *HERE*--
IT'S *NOT* A BIG THING, KATSUMI. I'M SORRY TO HAVE WORRIED YOU.
NO PROBLEM ...

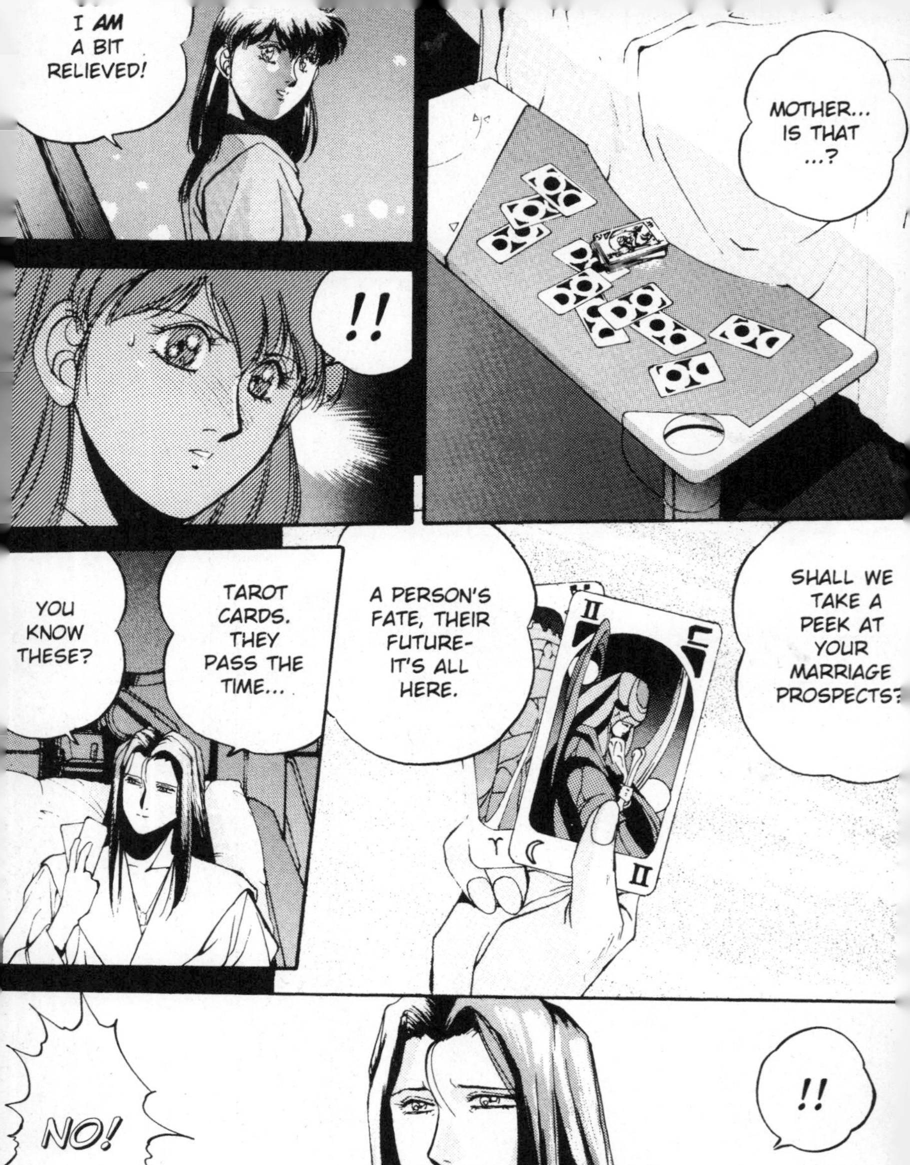
I AM A BIT RELIEVED!
!!
MOTHER... IS THAT ...?
YOU KNOW THESE?
TAROT CARDS. THEY PASS THE TIME...
A PERSON'S FATE, THEIR FUTURE-IT'S ALL HERE.
SHALL WE TAKE A PEEK AT YOUR MARRIAGE PROSPECTS?
NO!
!!

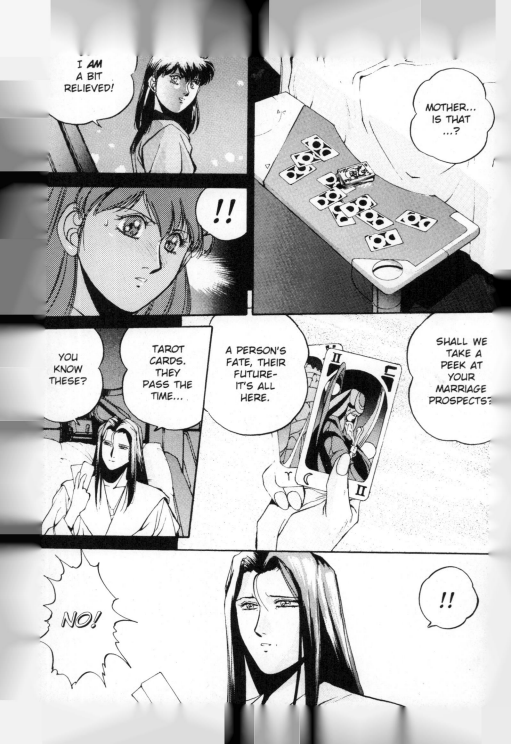

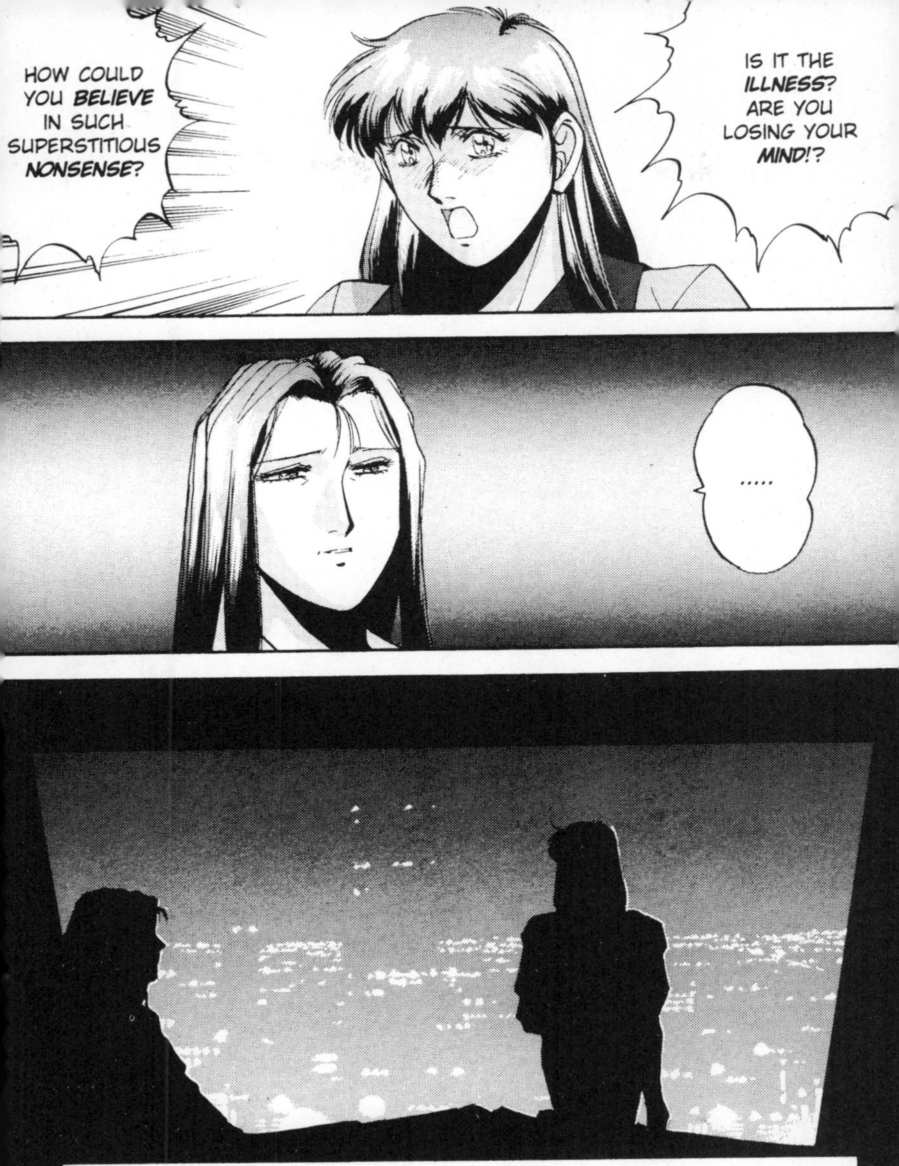
HOW COULD YOU **BELIEVE** IN SUCH SUPERSTITIOUS **NONSENSE?**
IS IT THE **ILLNESS?** ARE YOU LOSING YOUR **MIND!?**
.....
.....

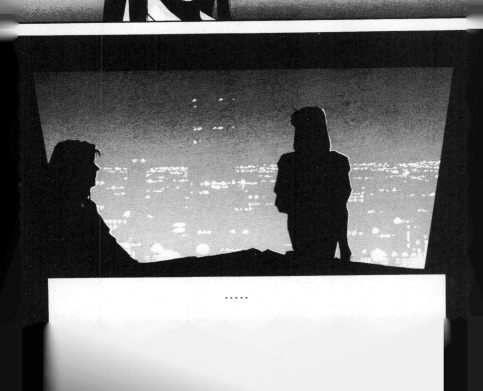

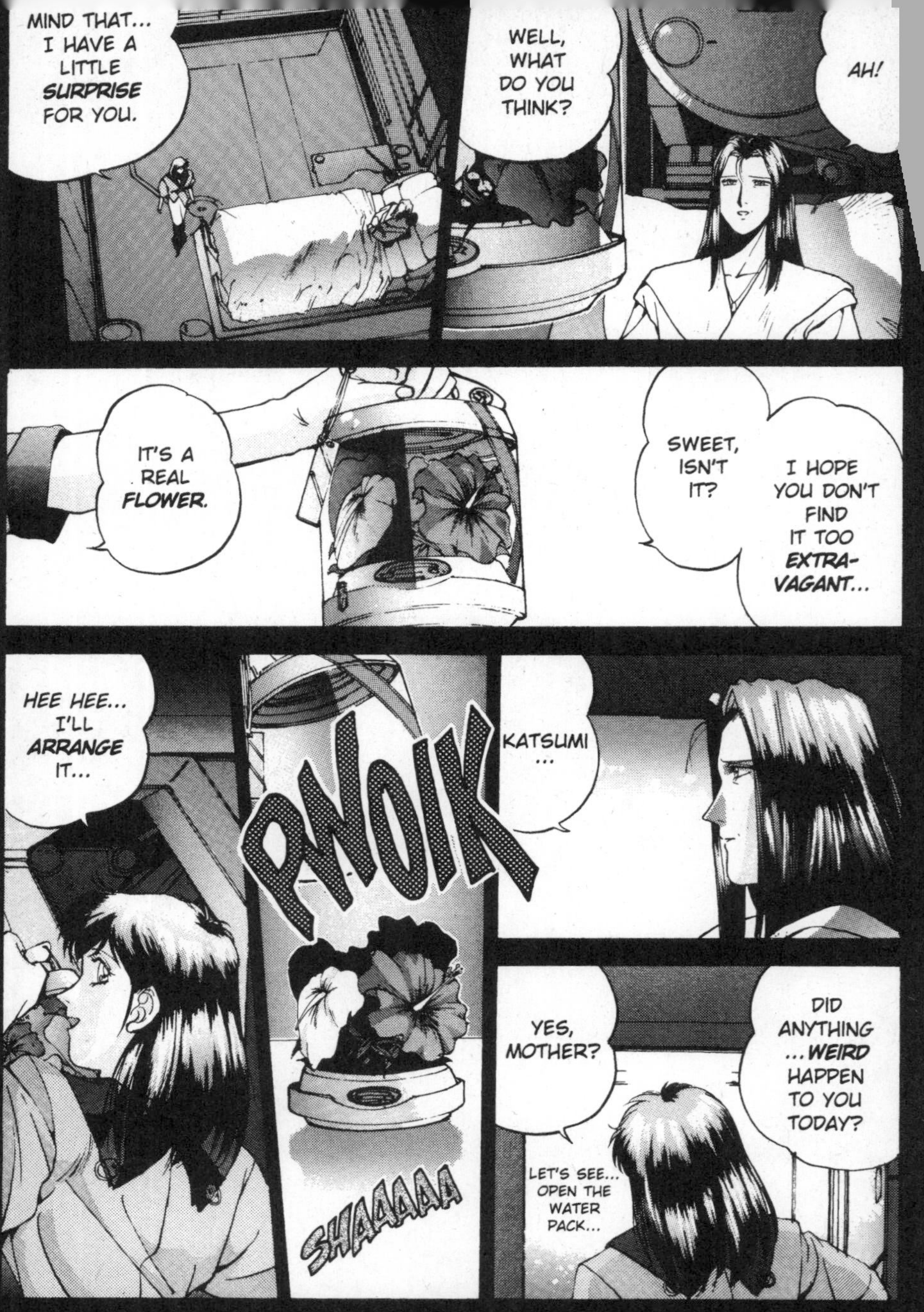
MIND THAT... I HAVE A LITTLE SURPRISE FOR YOU.
WELL, WHAT DO YOU THINK?
AH!
IT'S A REAL FLOWER.
SWEET, ISN'T IT?
I HOPE YOU DON'T FIND IT TOO EXTRA-VAGANT...
HEE HEE... I'LL ARRANGE IT...
PWOIK
SHAAAAA
KATSUMI...
YES, MOTHER?
DID ANYTHING ...WEIRD HAPPEN TO YOU TODAY?
LET'S SEE... OPEN THE WATER PACK...

SOME-
THING
WEIRD?

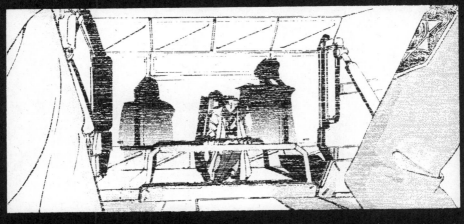

NO...
NOTHING
UNUSUAL,
IF THAT'S
WHAT YOU
MEAN...

IS
THAT
SO...?

FINISHED!

AHH...
IT'S SO
BEAUTIFUL!

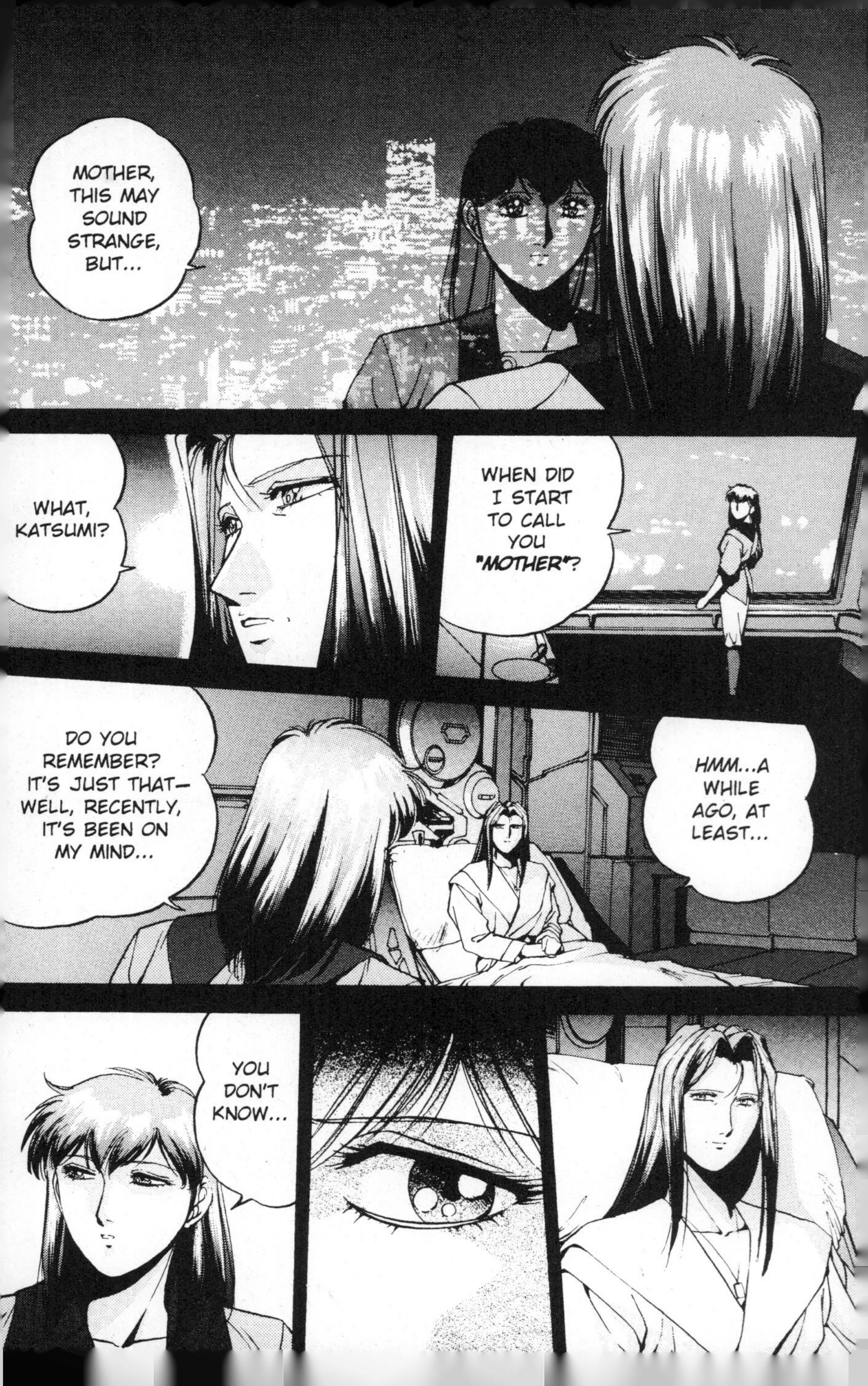
MOTHER, THIS MAY SOUND STRANGE, BUT...
WHAT, KATSUMI?
WHEN DID I START TO CALL YOU *"MOTHER"*?
DO YOU REMEMBER? IT'S JUST THAT— WELL, RECENTLY, IT'S BEEN ON MY MIND...
*HMM...*A WHILE AGO, AT LEAST...
YOU DON'T KNOW...

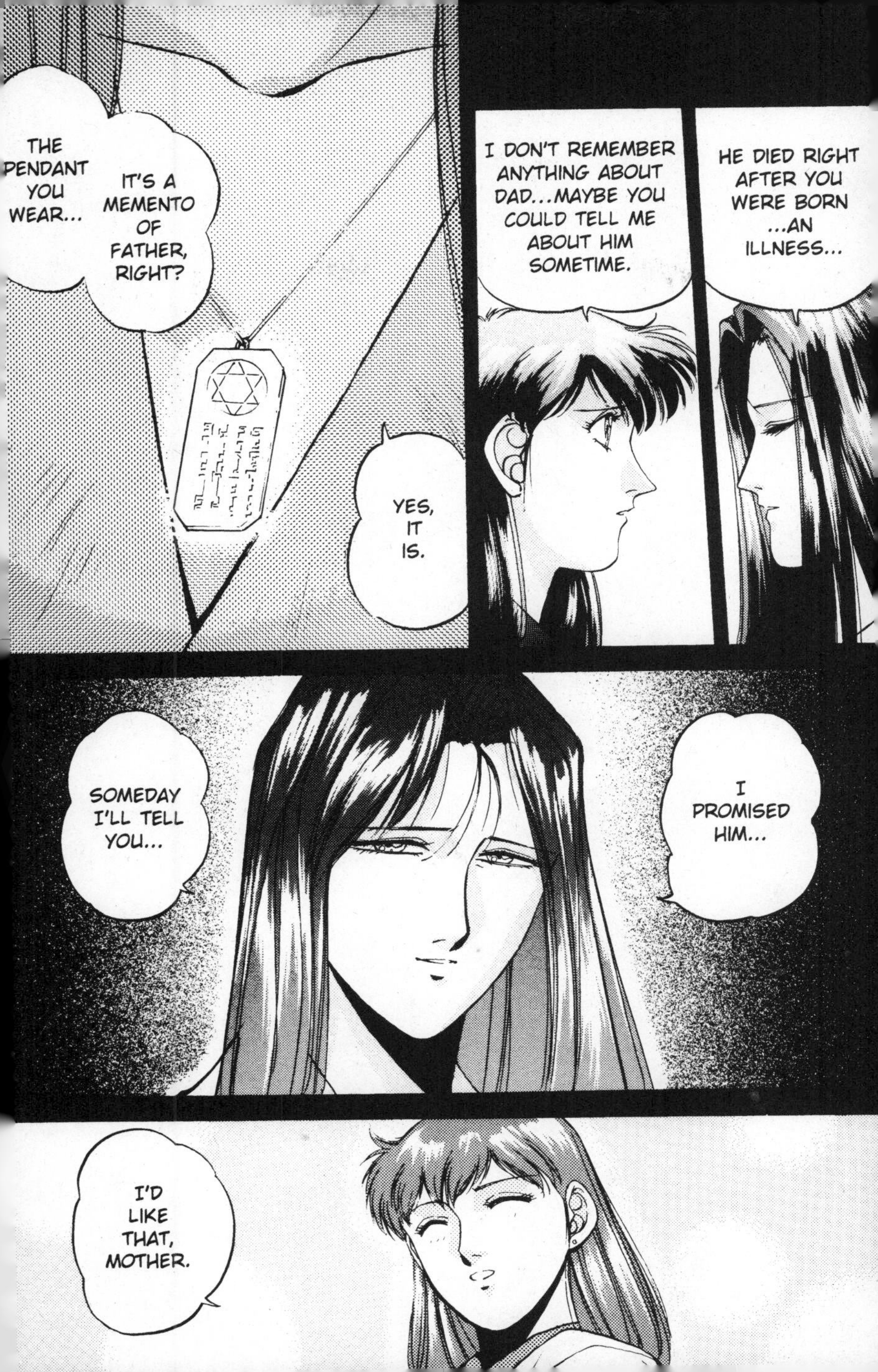
THE PENDANT YOU WEAR...
IT'S A MEMENTO OF FATHER, RIGHT?
YES, IT IS.
I DON'T REMEMBER ANYTHING ABOUT DAD...MAYBE YOU COULD TELL ME ABOUT HIM SOMETIME.
HE DIED RIGHT AFTER YOU WERE BORN ...AN ILLNESS...
SOMEDAY I'LL TELL YOU...
I PROMISED HIM...
I'D LIKE THAT, MOTHER.

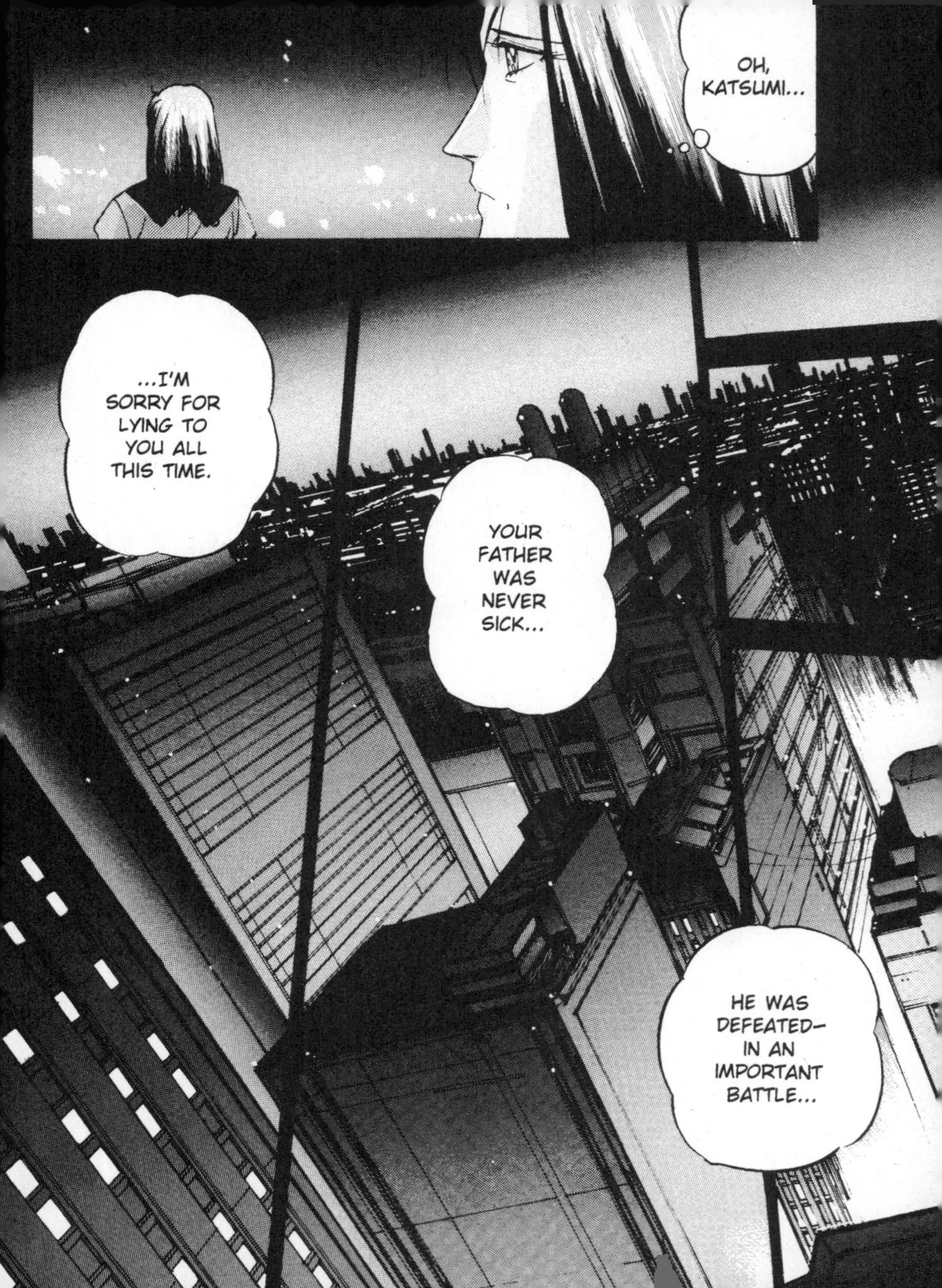
OH, KATSUMI...
...I'M SORRY FOR LYING TO YOU ALL THIS TIME.
YOUR FATHER WAS NEVER SICK...
HE WAS DEFEATED— IN AN IMPORTANT BATTLE...

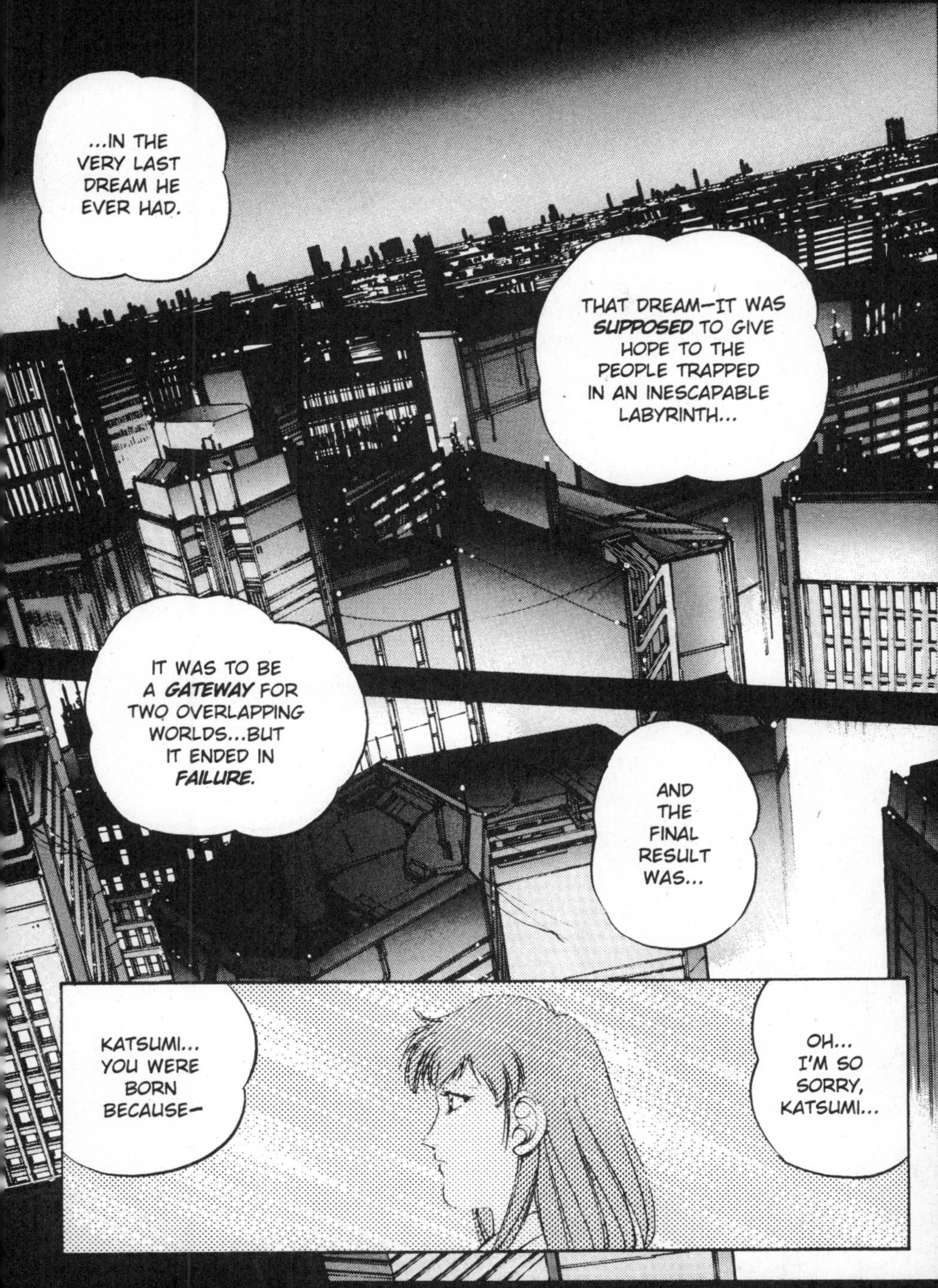
...IN THE VERY LAST DREAM HE EVER HAD.
THAT DREAM—IT WAS *SUPPOSED* TO GIVE HOPE TO THE PEOPLE TRAPPED IN AN INESCAPABLE LABYRINTH...
IT WAS TO BE A *GATEWAY* FOR TWO OVERLAPPING WORLDS...BUT IT ENDED IN *FAILURE.*
AND THE FINAL RESULT WAS...
KATSUMI... YOU WERE BORN BECAUSE—
OH... I'M SO SORRY, KATSUMI...

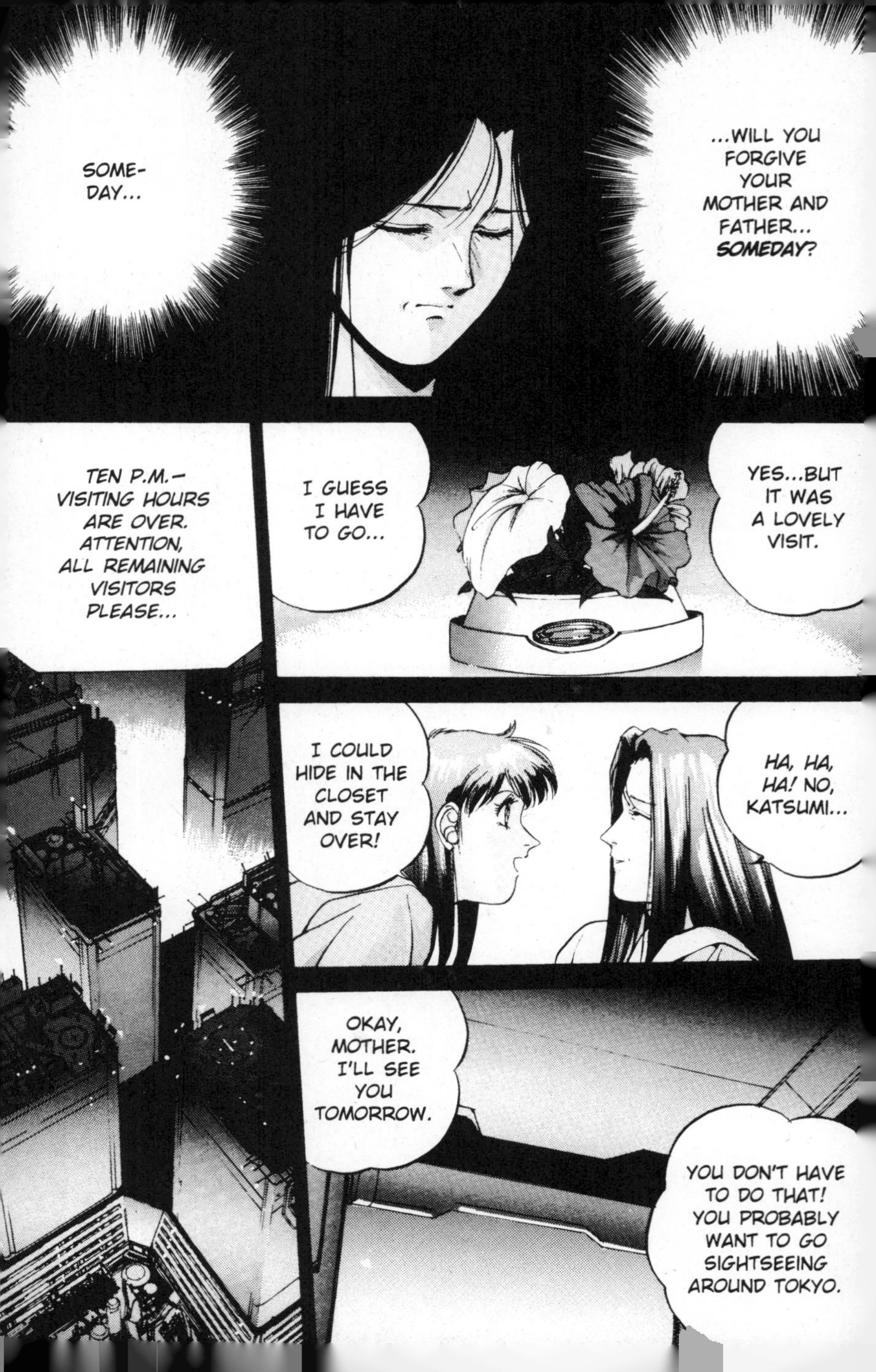
SOME-DAY...
...WILL YOU FORGIVE YOUR MOTHER AND FATHER... SOMEDAY?
TEN P.M.—VISITING HOURS ARE OVER. ATTENTION, ALL REMAINING VISITORS PLEASE...
I GUESS I HAVE TO GO...
YES...BUT IT WAS A LOVELY VISIT.
I COULD HIDE IN THE CLOSET AND STAY OVER!
HA, HA, HA! NO, KATSUMI...
OKAY, MOTHER. I'LL SEE YOU TOMORROW.
YOU DON'T HAVE TO DO THAT! YOU PROBABLY WANT TO GO SIGHTSEEING AROUND TOKYO.

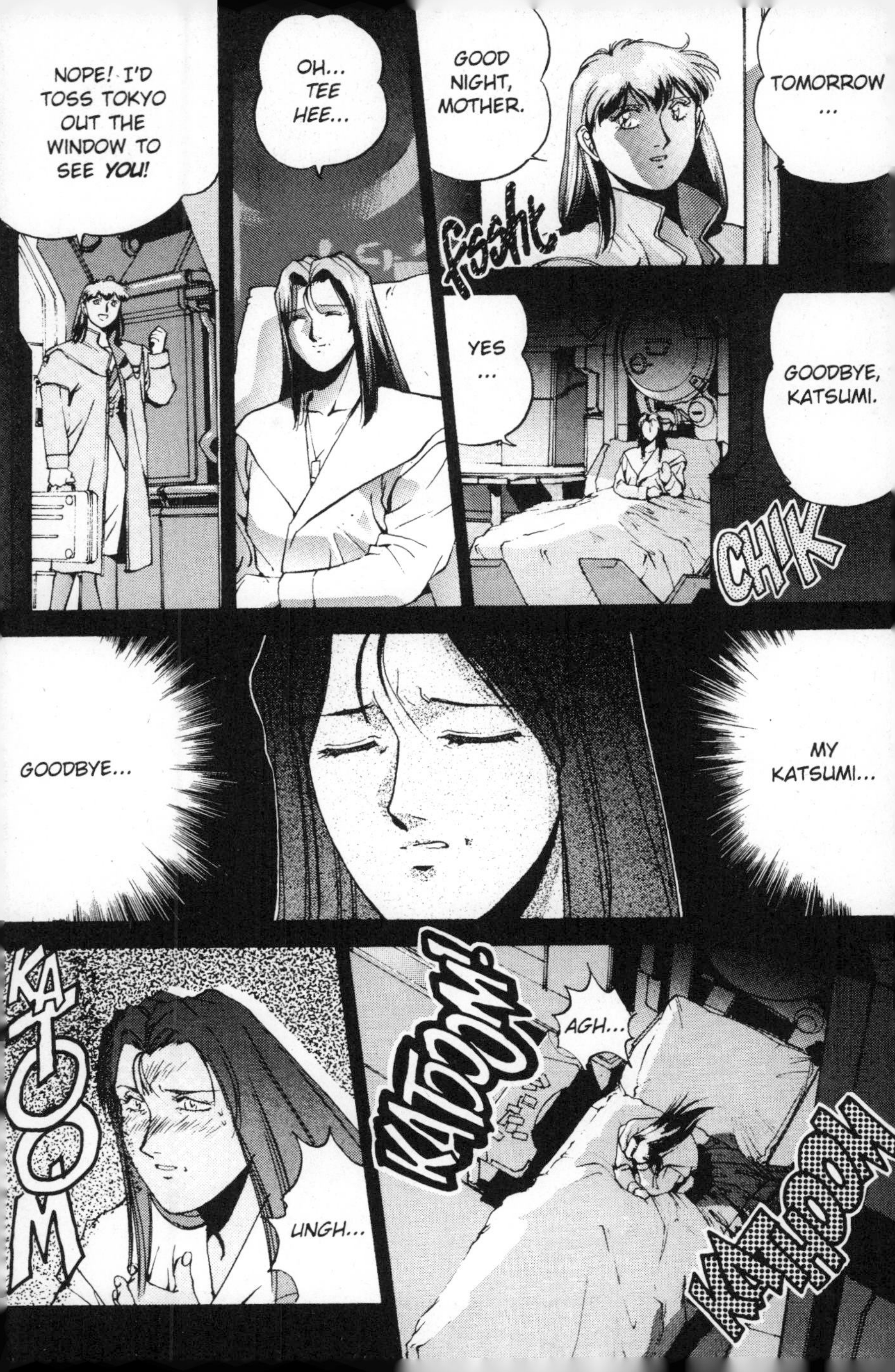
NOPE! I'D TOSS TOKYO OUT THE WINDOW TO SEE *YOU!*
OH... TEE HEE...
GOOD NIGHT, MOTHER.
fssht
TOMORROW ...
YES ...
GOODBYE, KATSUMI.
CHIK
GOODBYE...
MY KATSUMI...
KATOOM
UNGH...
KATOOM!
AGH...
KATHOOM

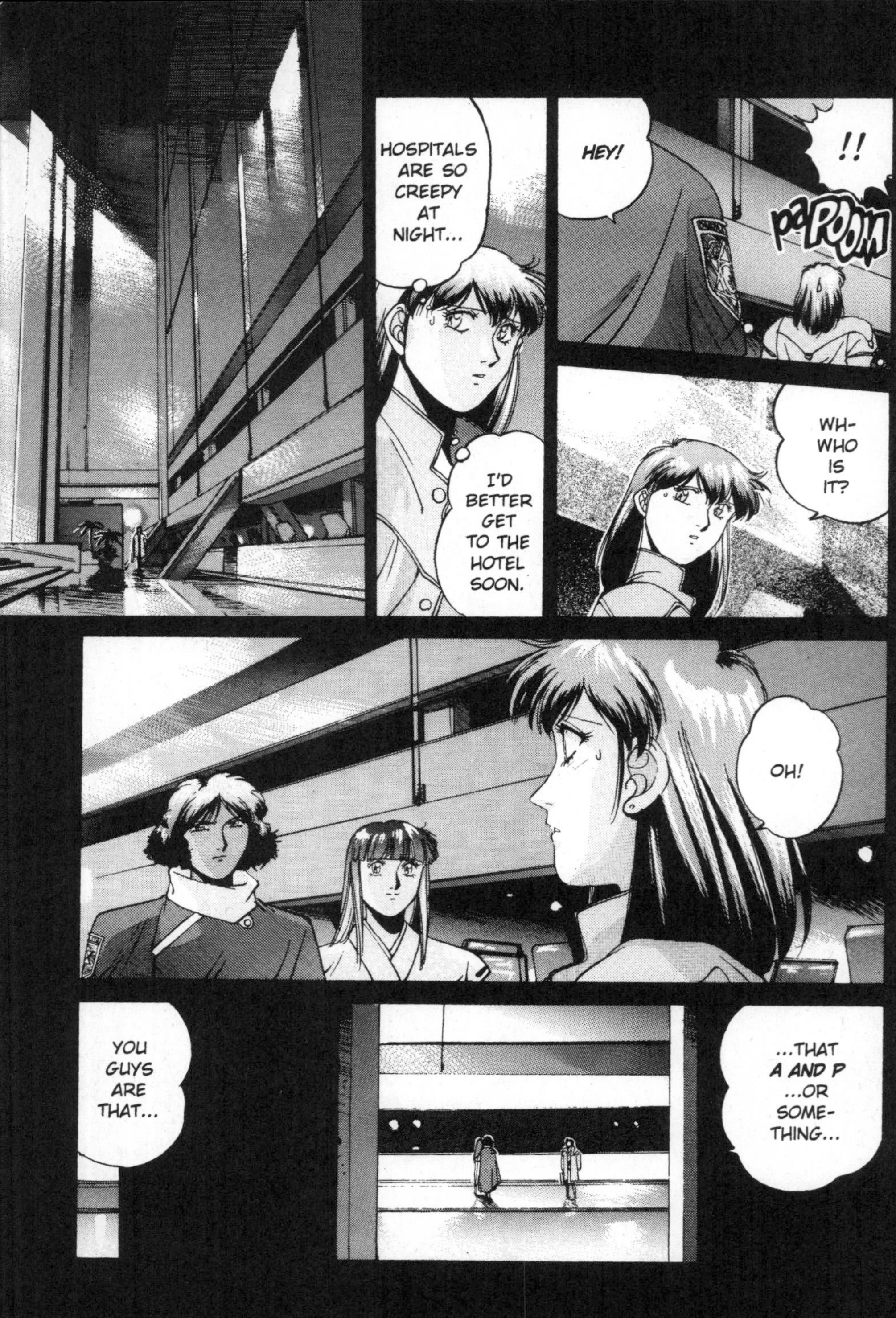
HOSPITALS ARE SO CREEPY AT NIGHT...
I'D BETTER GET TO THE HOTEL SOON.
HEY!
!!
PAPOOM
WH-WHO IS IT?
OH!
YOU GUYS ARE THAT...
...THAT A AND P ...OR SOMETHING...

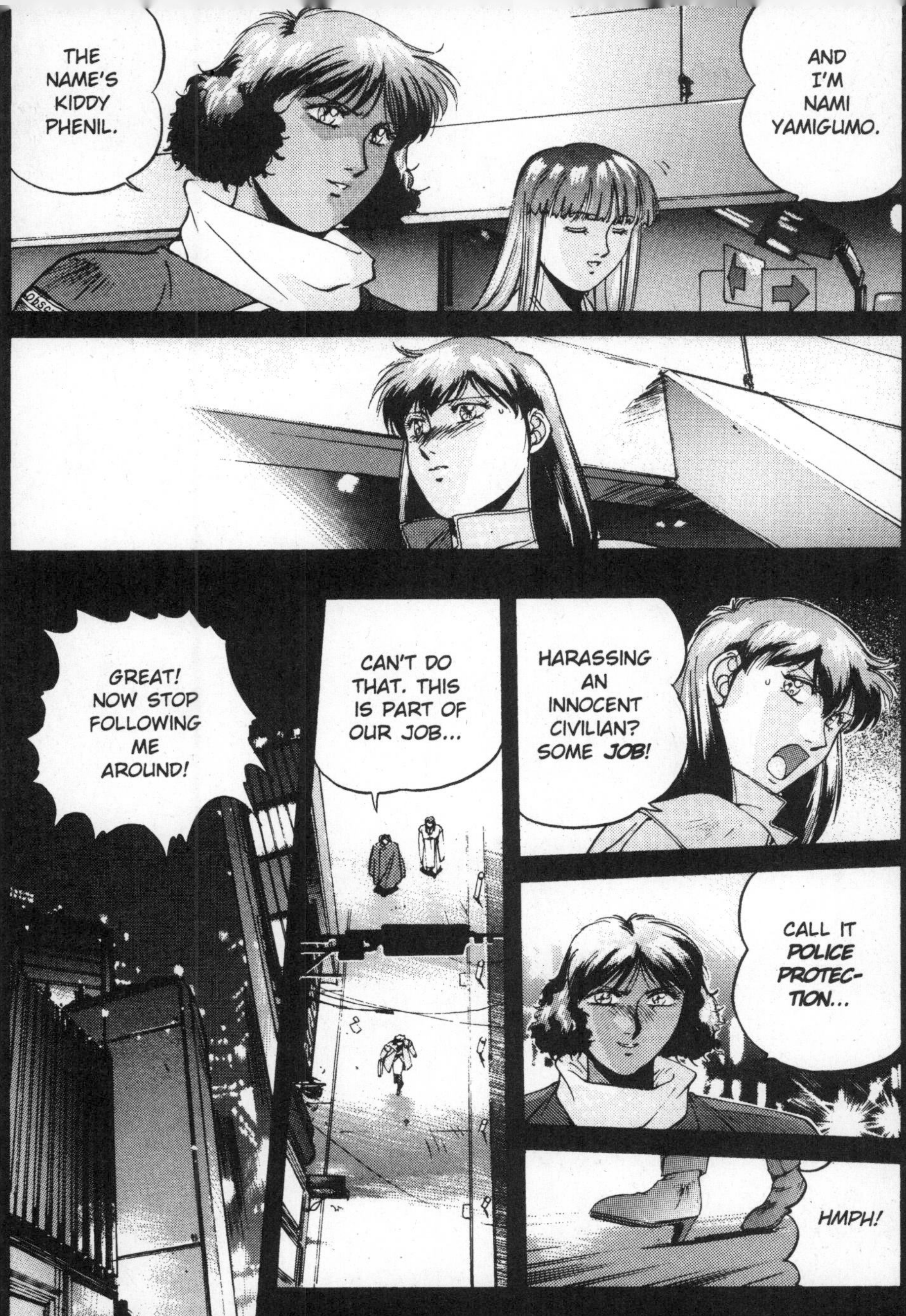
THE NAME'S KIDDY PHENIL.
AND I'M NAMI YAMIGUMO.
GREAT! NOW STOP FOLLOWING ME AROUND!
CAN'T DO THAT. THIS IS PART OF OUR JOB...
HARASSING AN INNOCENT CIVILIAN? SOME **JOB**!
CALL IT **POLICE PROTEC-TION**...
HMPH!

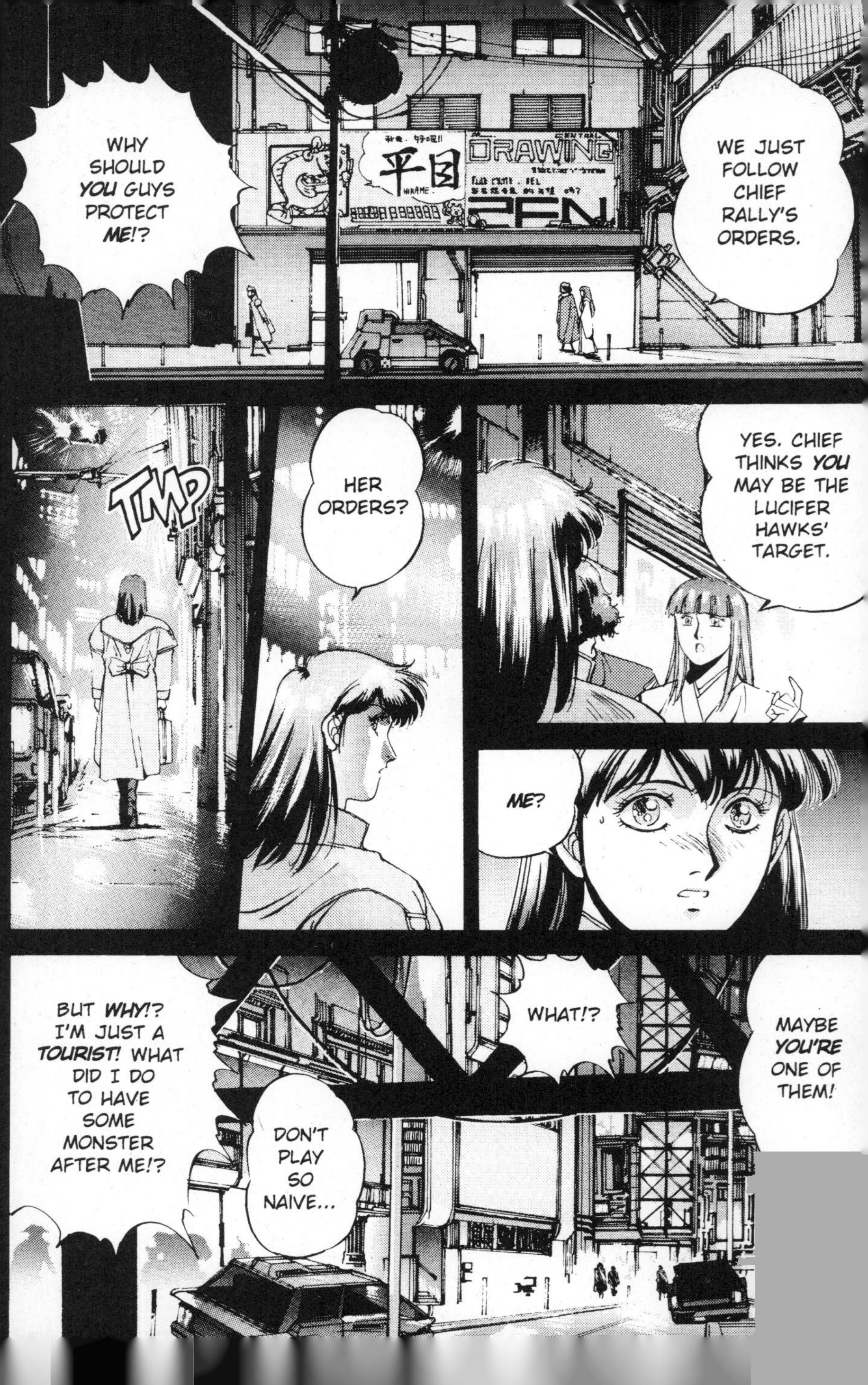
WHY SHOULD *YOU* GUYS PROTECT *ME!?*
平目
HIRAME
DRAWING
WE JUST FOLLOW CHIEF RALLY'S ORDERS.
TMP
HER ORDERS?
YES. CHIEF THINKS *YOU* MAY BE THE LUCIFER HAWKS' TARGET.
ME?
BUT *WHY!?* I'M JUST A *TOURIST!* WHAT DID I DO TO HAVE SOME MONSTER AFTER ME!?
DON'T PLAY SO NAIVE...
MAYBE *YOU'RE* ONE OF THEM!
WHAT!?

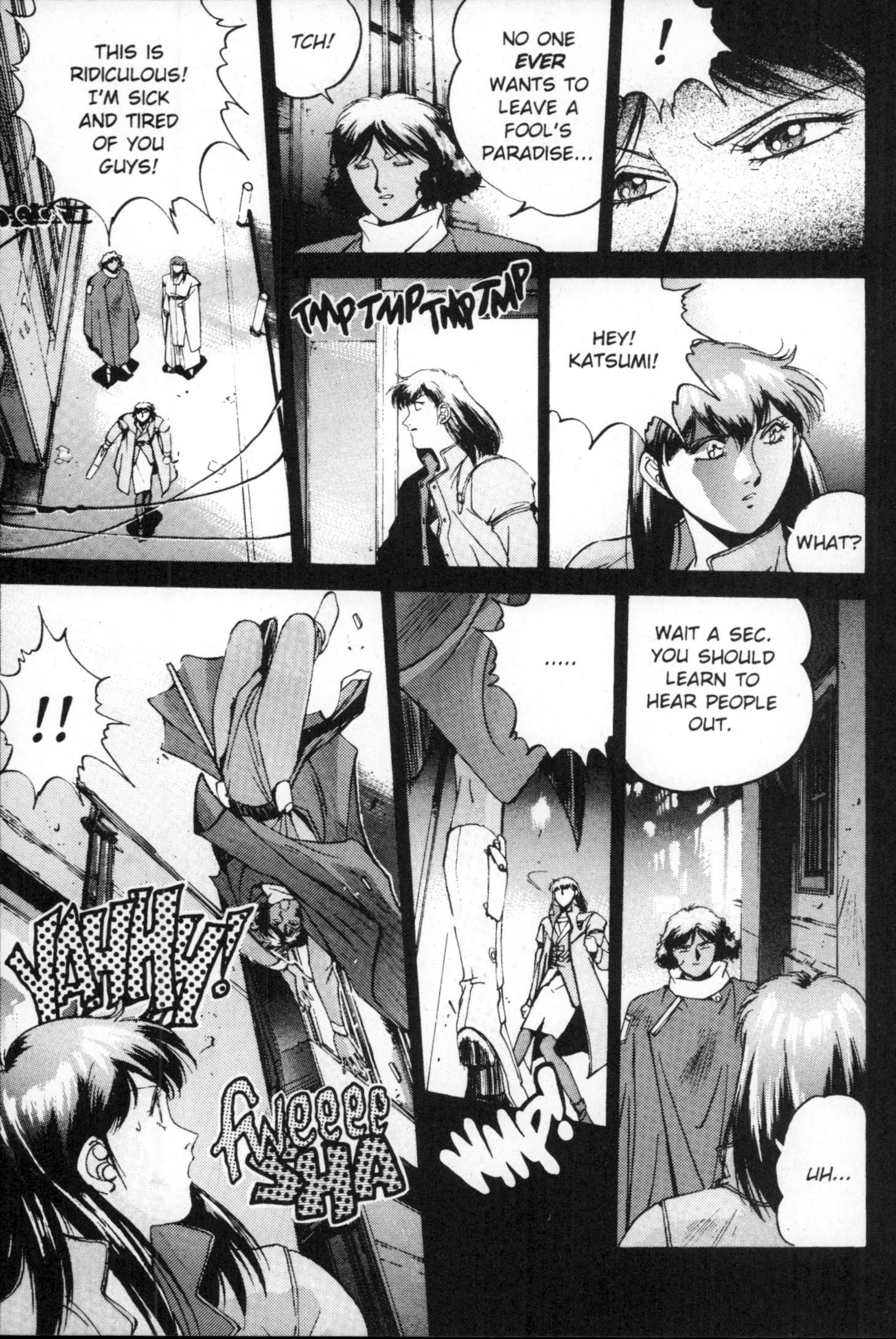
THIS IS RIDICULOUS! I'M SICK AND TIRED OF YOU GUYS!
TCH!
NO ONE EVER WANTS TO LEAVE A FOOL'S PARADISE...
!
TMP TMP TMP TMP
HEY! KATSUMI!
WHAT?
!!
YAHH!
FWEEEE SHA
WHP!
.....
WAIT A SEC. YOU SHOULD LEARN TO HEAR PEOPLE OUT.
UH...

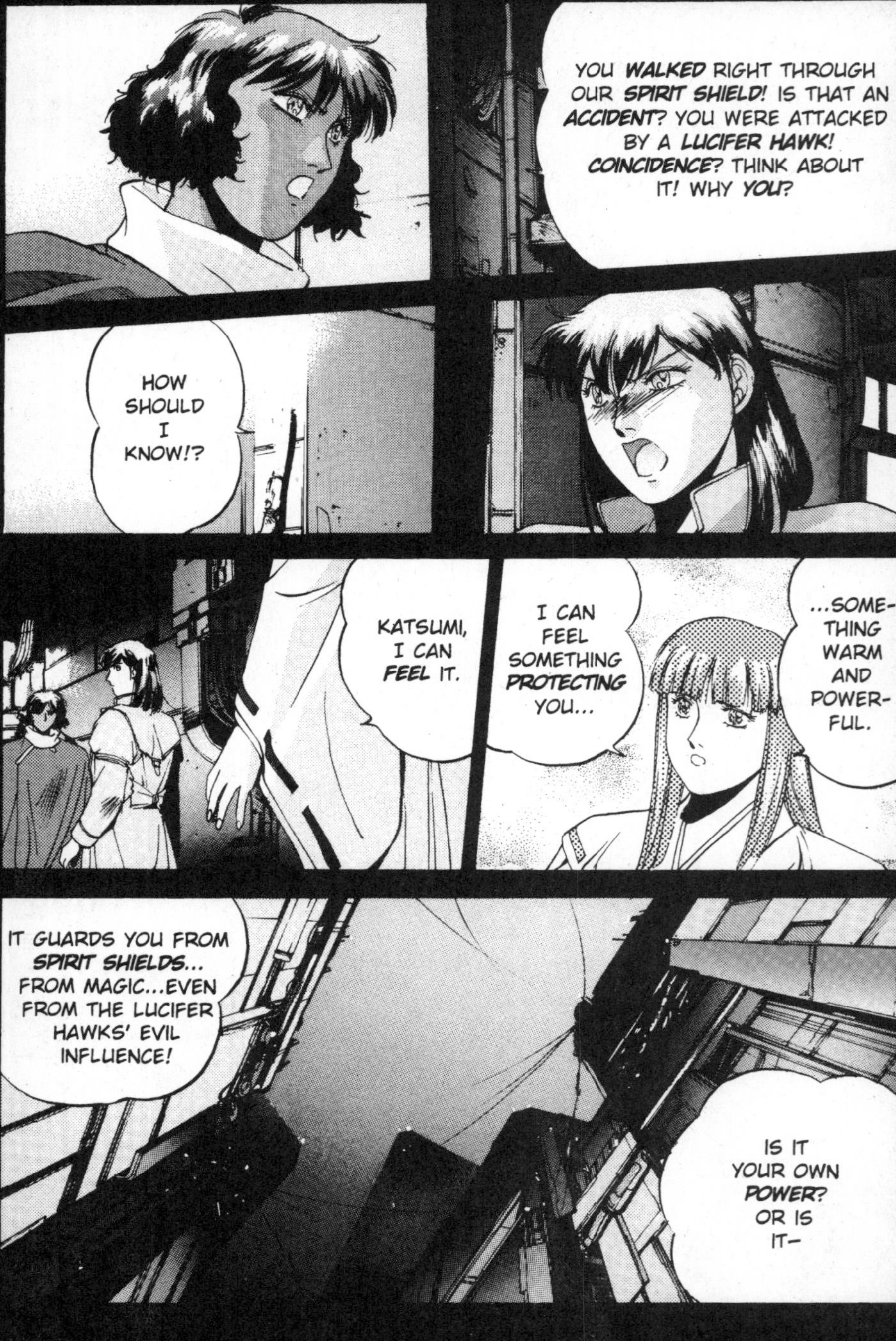
YOU **WALKED** RIGHT THROUGH OUR **SPIRIT SHIELD!** IS THAT AN **ACCIDENT**? YOU WERE ATTACKED BY A **LUCIFER HAWK!** **COINCIDENCE**? THINK ABOUT IT! WHY **YOU**?
HOW SHOULD I KNOW!?
KATSUMI, I CAN **FEEL** IT.
I CAN FEEL SOMETHING **PROTECTING** YOU...
...SOMETHING WARM AND POWERFUL.
IT GUARDS YOU FROM **SPIRIT SHIELDS**... FROM MAGIC...EVEN FROM THE LUCIFER HAWKS' EVIL INFLUENCE!
IS IT YOUR OWN **POWER**? OR IS IT—

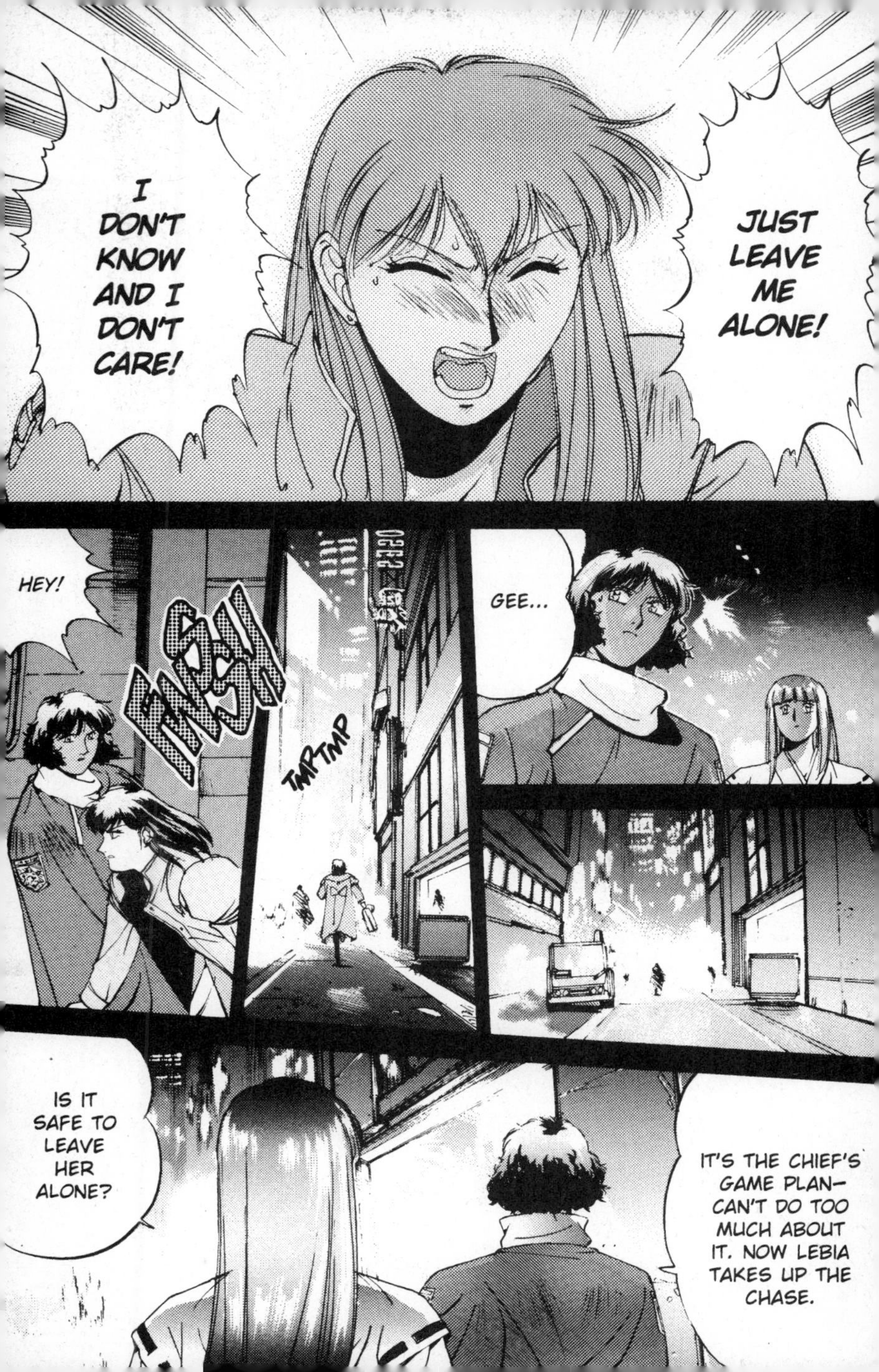
I DON'T KNOW AND I DON'T CARE!
JUST LEAVE ME ALONE!
HEY!
SWISH!
TMP TMP
GEE...
IS IT SAFE TO LEAVE HER ALONE?
IT'S THE CHIEF'S GAME PLAN— CAN'T DO TOO MUCH ABOUT IT. NOW LEBIA TAKES UP THE CHASE.

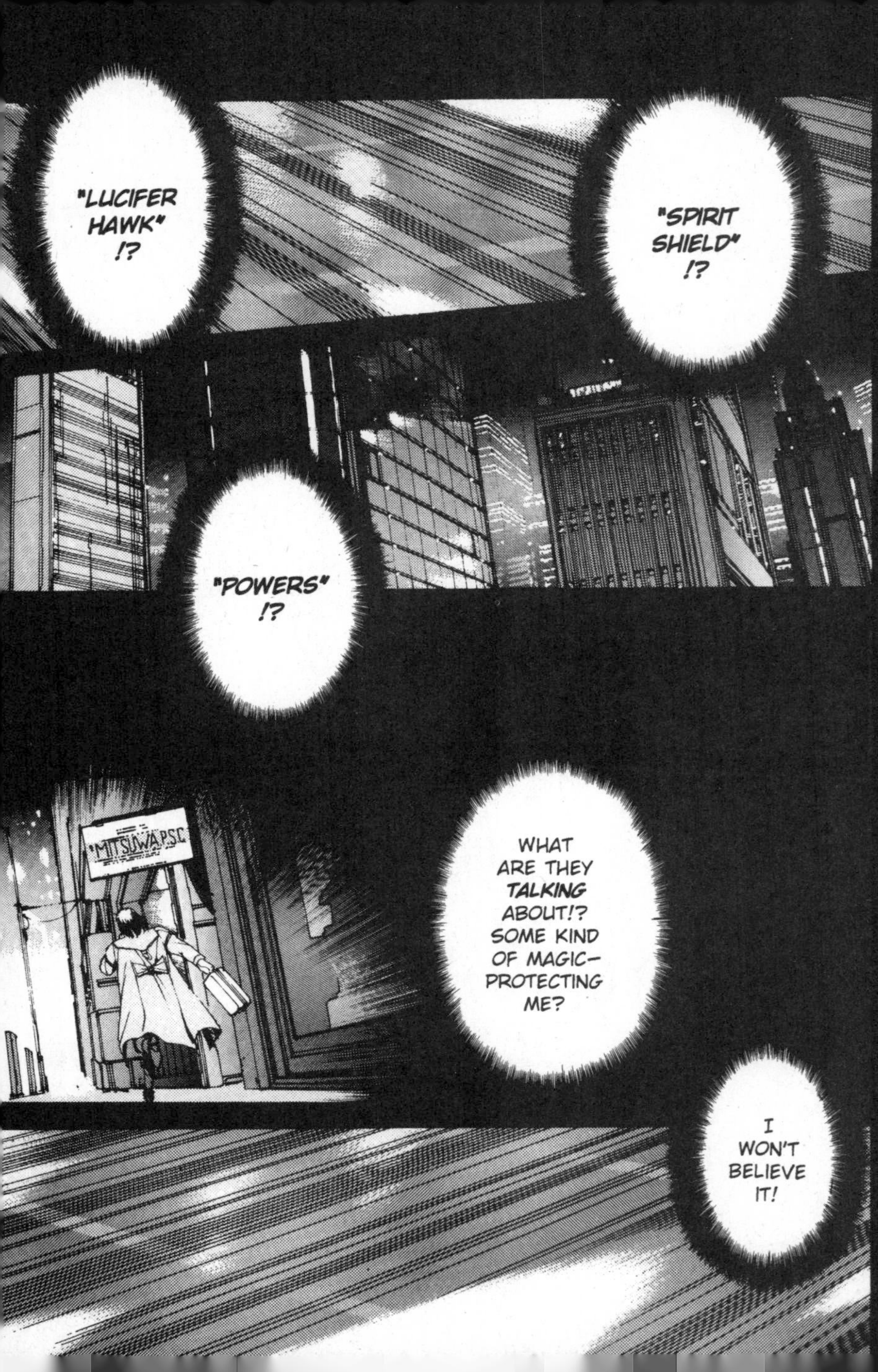
"LUCIFER HAWK" !?
"SPIRIT SHIELD" !?
"POWERS" !?
MITSUWA P.S.C
WHAT ARE THEY *TALKING* ABOUT!? SOME KIND OF MAGIC-PROTECTING ME?
I WON'T BELIEVE IT!

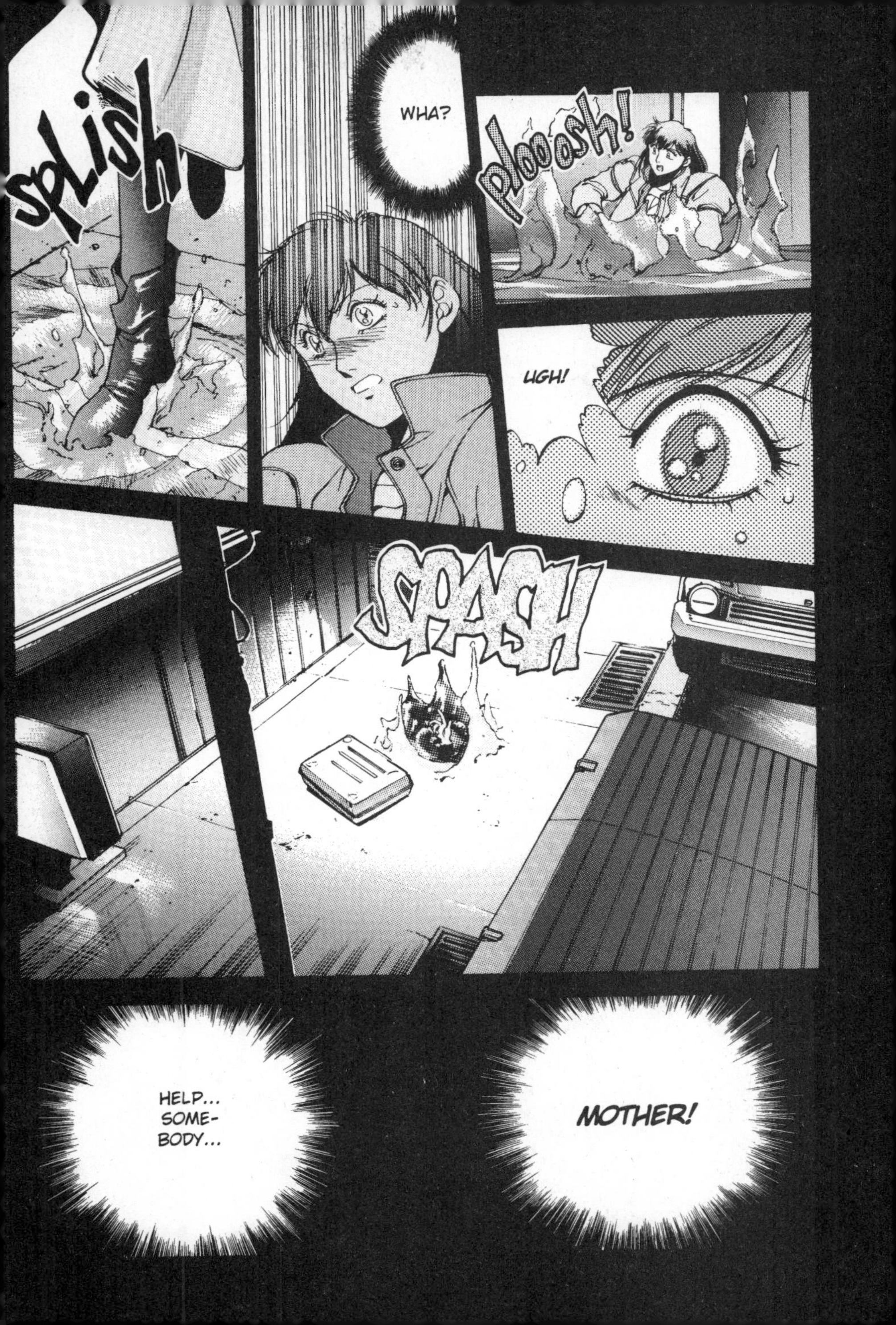
splish
WHA?
plooosh!
UGH!
SPASH
HELP... SOME-BODY...
MOTHER!

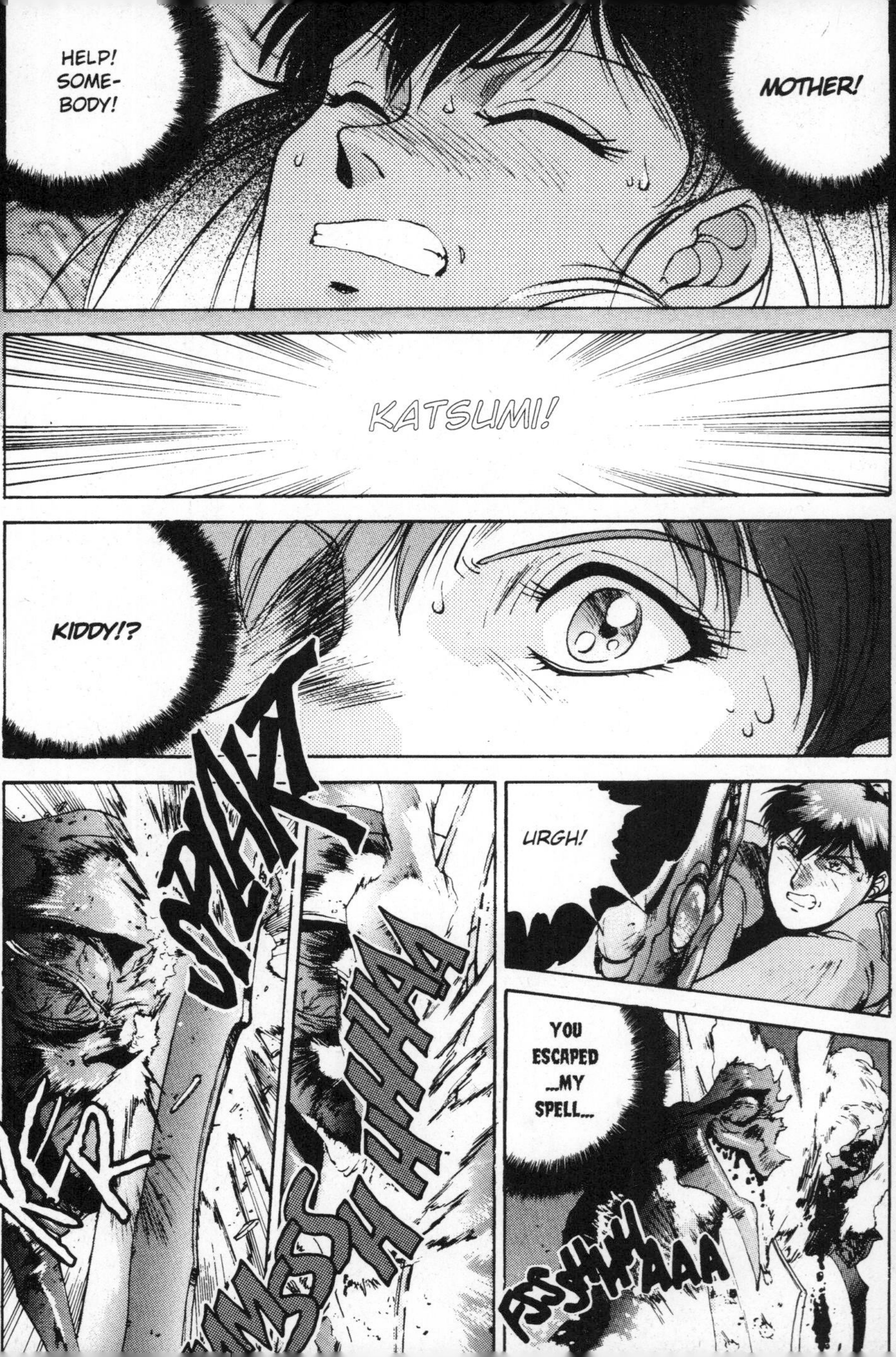
HELP! SOME-BODY!
MOTHER!
KATSUMI!
KIDDY!?
URGH!
YOU ESCAPED ...MY SPELL...

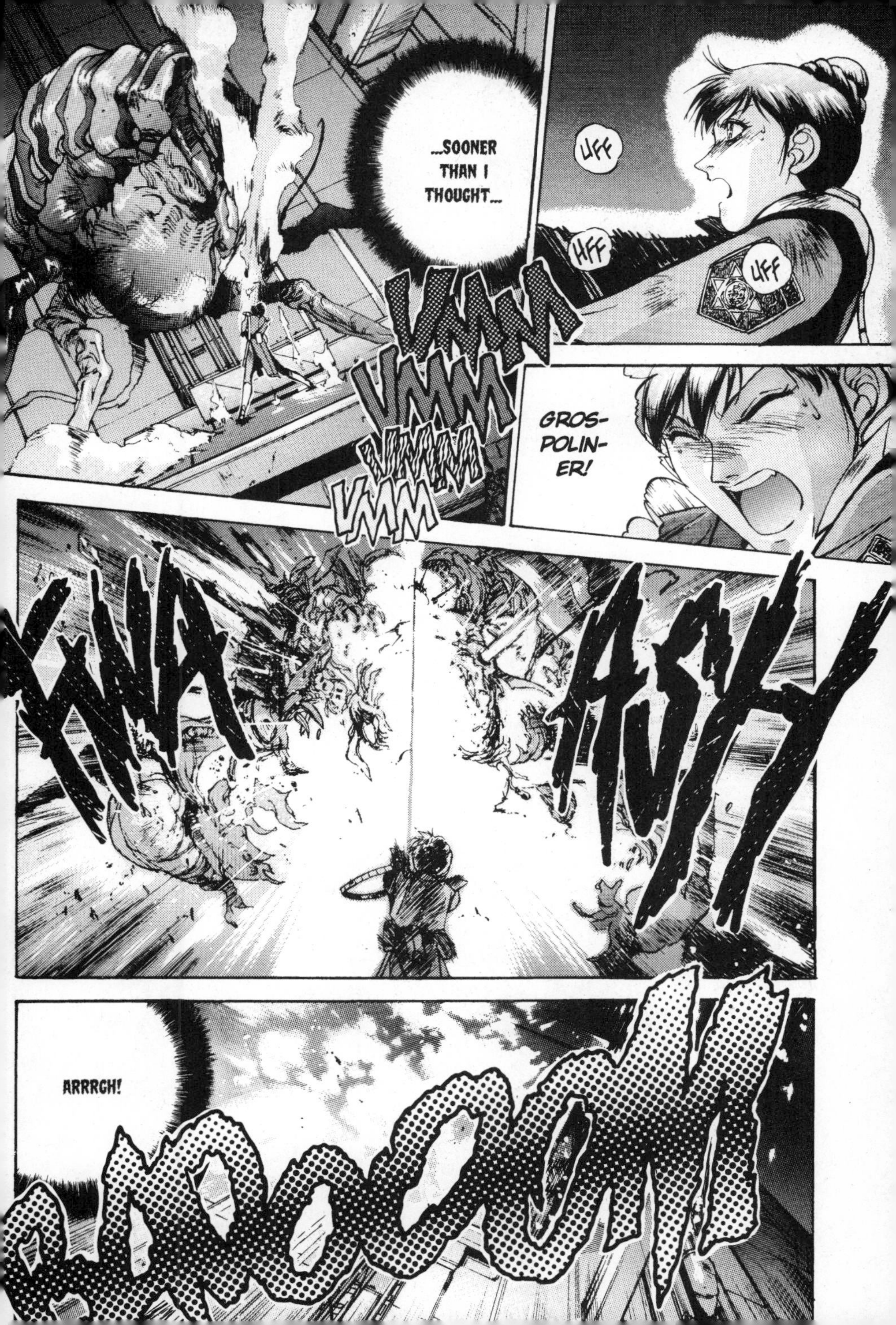
...SOONER THAN I THOUGHT...
VMM
VMM
VMM
UFF
HFF
UFF
GROS-POLINER!
FWA
ASH
ARRRGH!

VMM VMM M M M M M M M M M M M M

BWOOOOM

VMM VMM MM M M

!?

KATSUMI ...!?

OOM OOM OOM OOM OOM

UNGH...

KATSUMI!? ARE YOU ALL RIGHT?

KAT-SUMI ...

THAT WAS CLOSE, KATSUMI. YOU AL-MOST FELL UNDER HIS SPELL.

NO "ALMOST" ABOUT IT. I DID.

PHEW ...

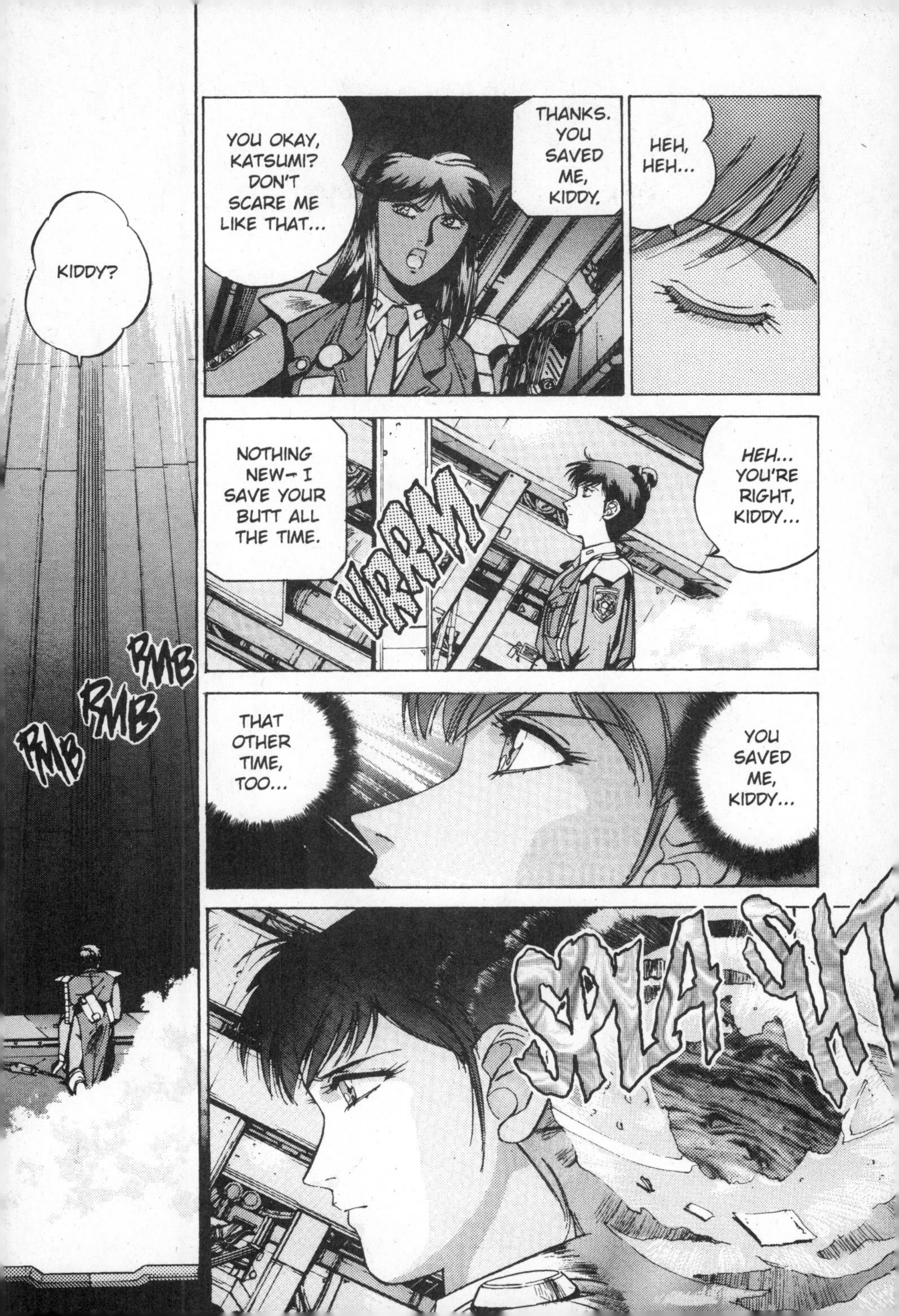
KIDDY?
RMB RMB RMB
YOU OKAY, KATSUMI? DON'T SCARE ME LIKE THAT...
THANKS. YOU SAVED ME, KIDDY.
HEH, HEH...
NOTHING NEW— I SAVE YOUR BUTT ALL THE TIME.
VRRM
HEH... YOU'RE RIGHT, KIDDY...
THAT OTHER TIME, TOO...
YOU SAVED ME, KIDDY...
SPLASH

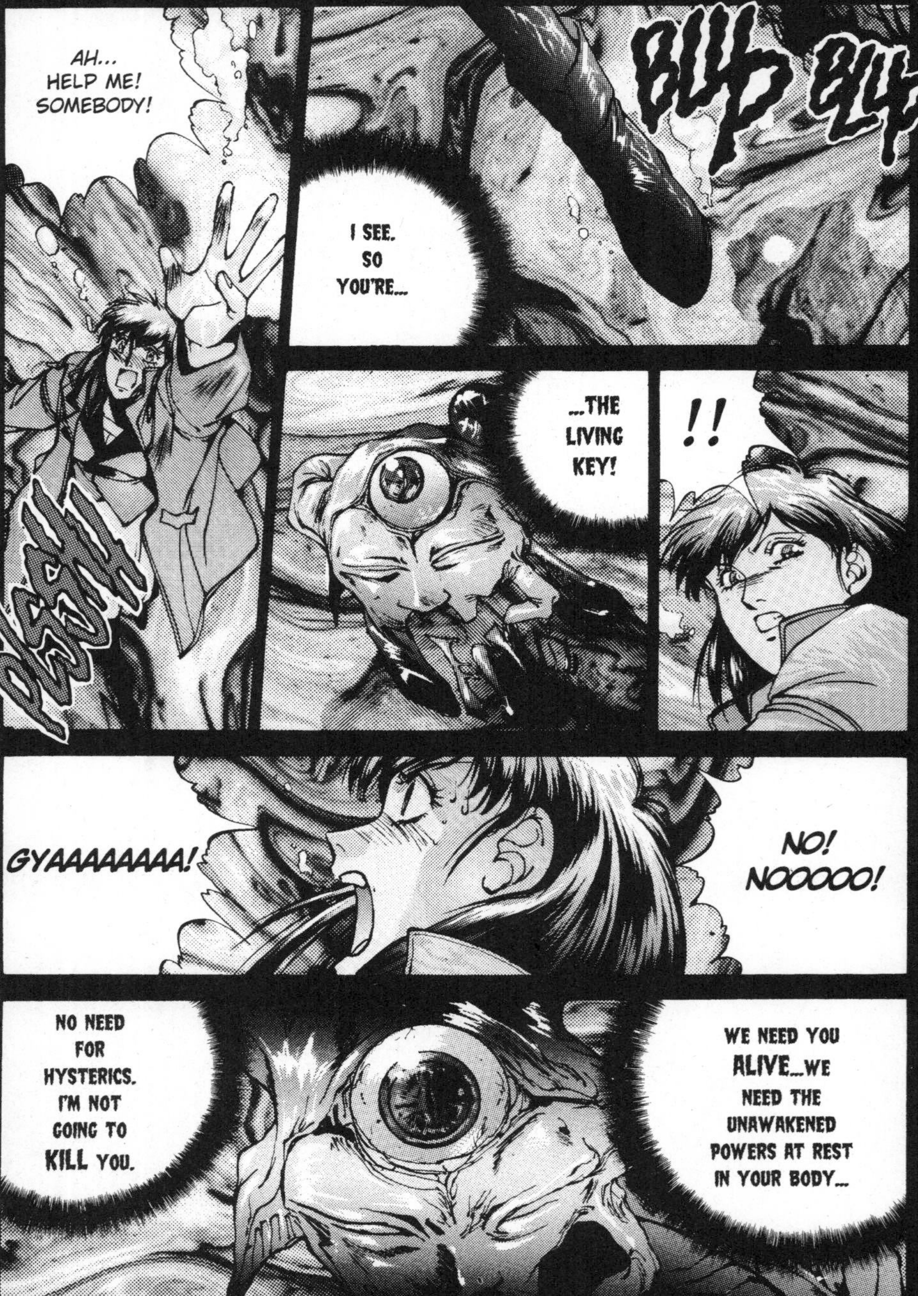
AH...
HELP ME!
SOMEBODY!
PSSSH
I SEE.
SO
YOU'RE...
BLUP BLUP
...THE
LIVING
KEY!
!!
GYAAAAAAAA!
NO!
NOOOOO!
NO NEED
FOR
HYSTERICS.
I'M NOT
GOING TO
KILL YOU.
WE NEED YOU
ALIVE...WE
NEED THE
UNAWAKENED
POWERS AT REST
IN YOUR BODY...

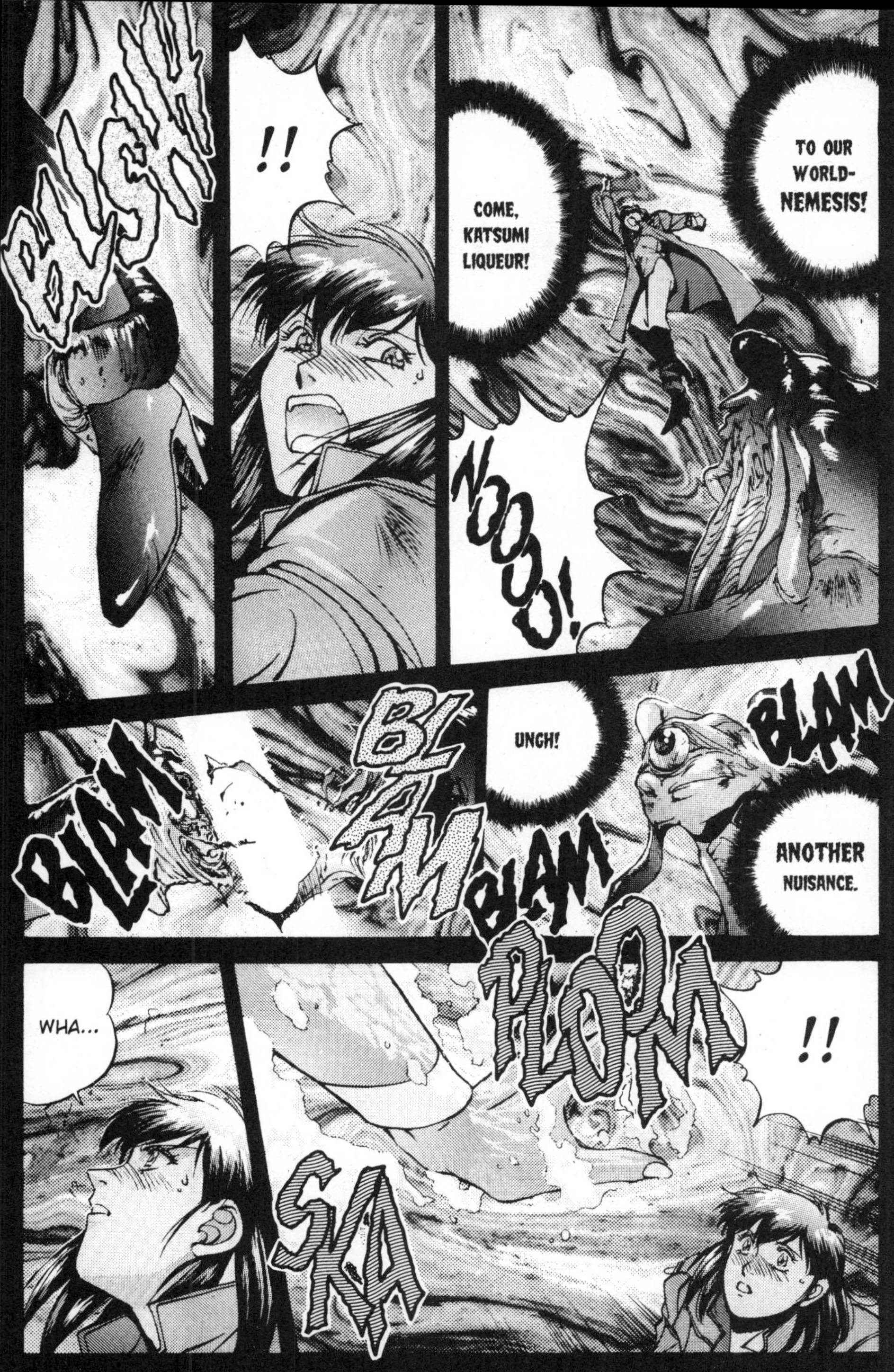
BLGSHH!!
!!
COME, KATSUMI LIQUEUR!
TO OUR WORLD-NEMESIS!
NOOOOO!
BLAM
BLAM
UNGH!
BLAM
BLAM
ANOTHER NUISANCE.
WHA...
PLOOM
!!
SKA

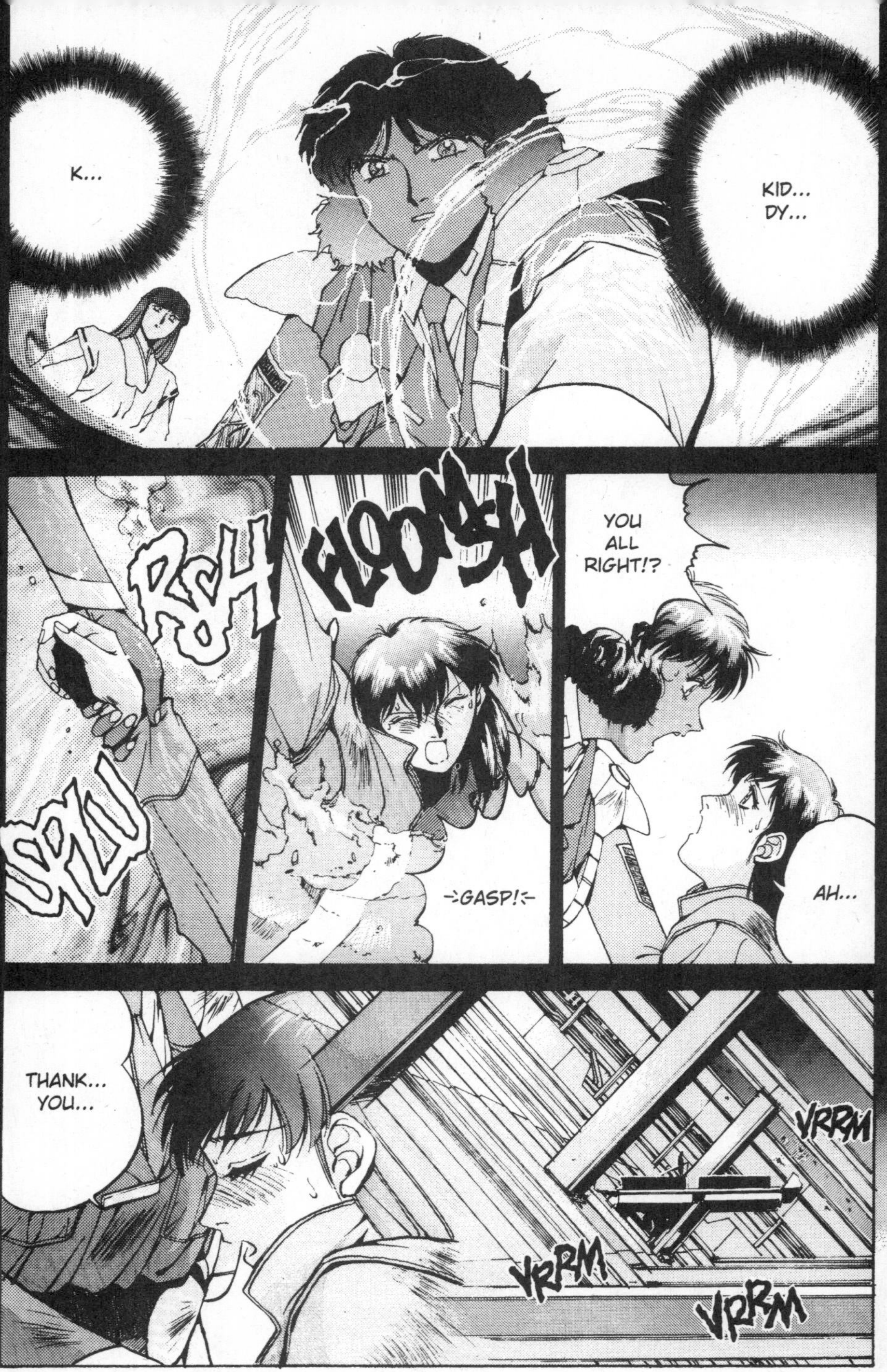
K...
KID...
DY...
YOU
ALL
RIGHT!?
GASP!
AH...
THANK...
YOU...
VRRM
VRRM
VRRM

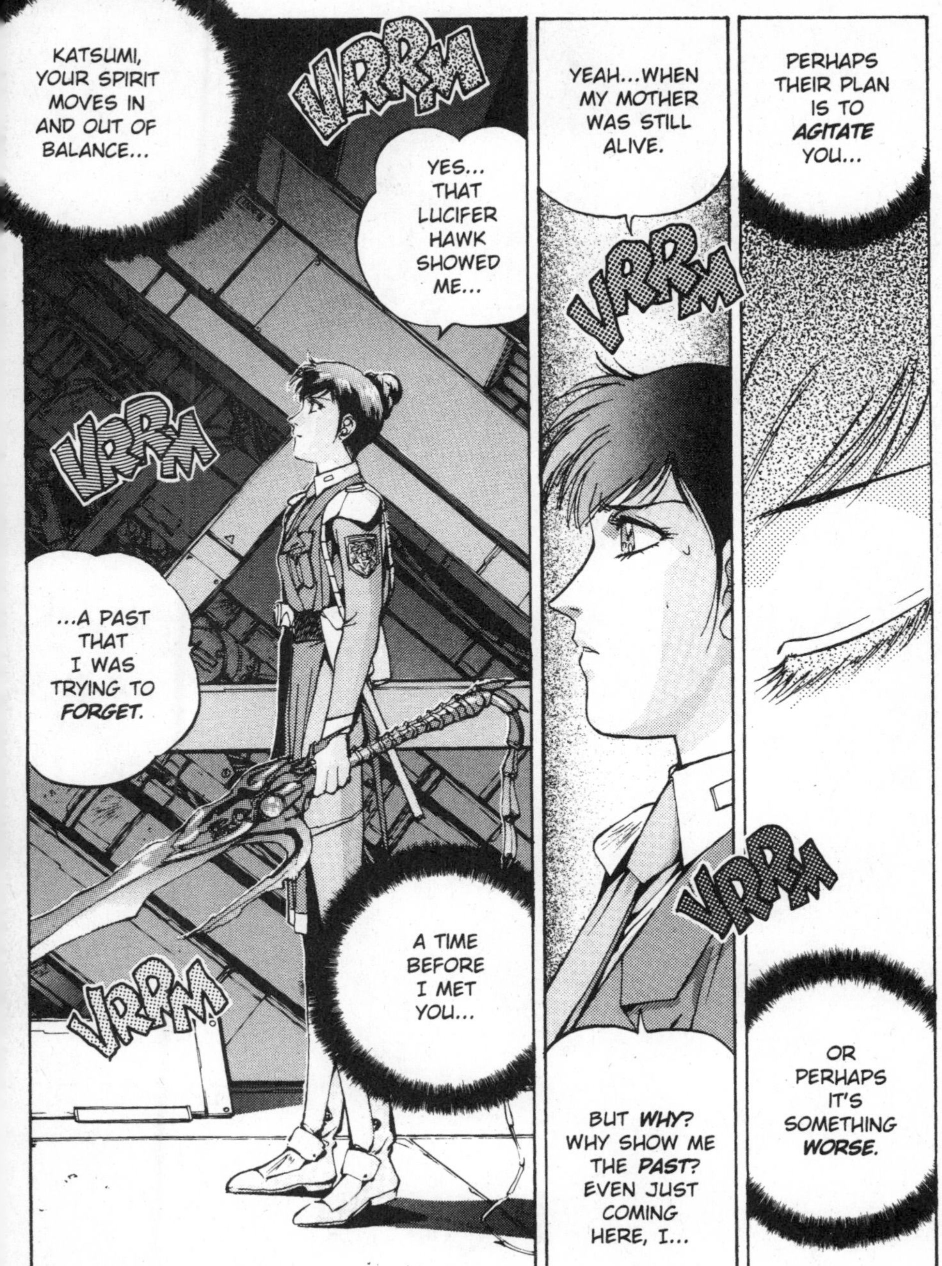
KATSUMI, YOUR SPIRIT MOVES IN AND OUT OF BALANCE...
VRRM
YES... THAT LUCIFER HAWK SHOWED ME...
VRRM
...A PAST THAT I WAS TRYING TO FORGET.
A TIME BEFORE I MET YOU...
VRRM
YEAH...WHEN MY MOTHER WAS STILL ALIVE.
VRRM
VRRM
BUT WHY? WHY SHOW ME THE PAST? EVEN JUST COMING HERE, I...
PERHAPS THEIR PLAN IS TO AGITATE YOU...
OR PERHAPS IT'S SOMETHING WORSE.

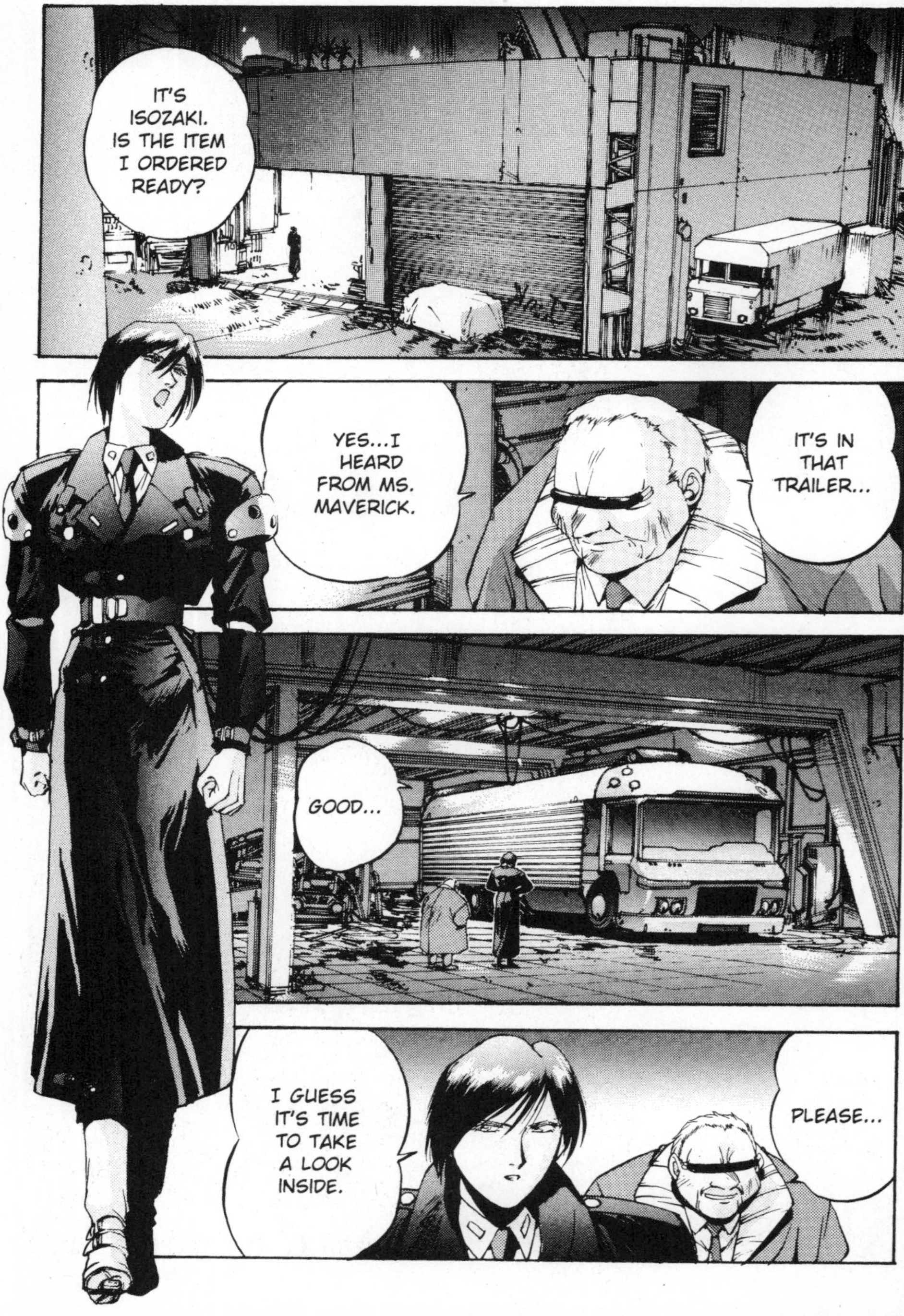

IT'S ISOZAKI. IS THE ITEM I ORDERED READY?
YES...I HEARD FROM MS. MAVERICK.
IT'S IN THAT TRAILER...
GOOD...
I GUESS IT'S TIME TO TAKE A LOOK INSIDE.
PLEASE...

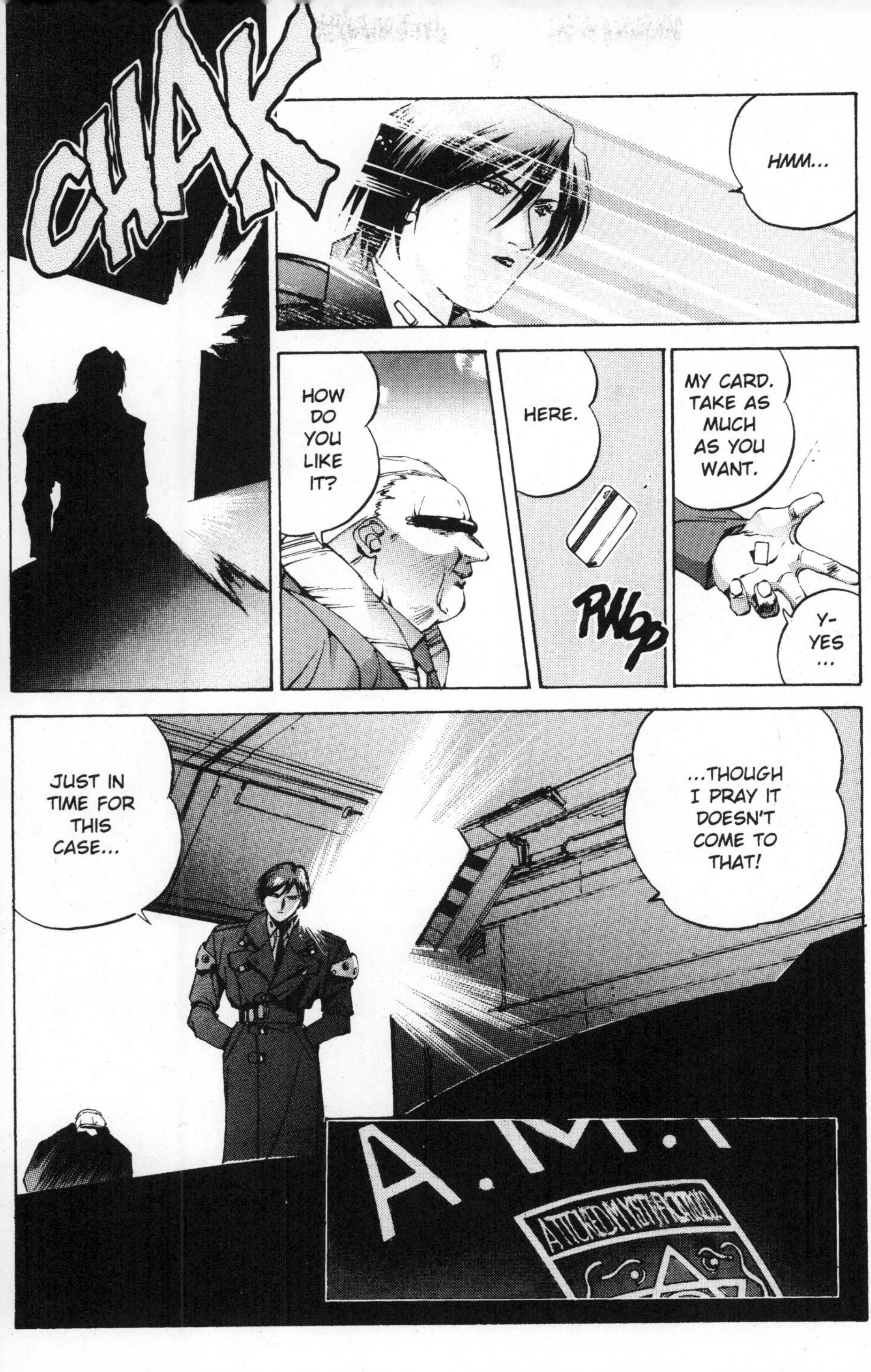
CHAK
HMM...
HOW DO YOU LIKE IT?
HERE.
MY CARD. TAKE AS MUCH AS YOU WANT.
PWOP
Y-YES...
JUST IN TIME FOR THIS CASE...
...THOUGH I PRAY IT DOESN'T COME TO THAT!
A.M.I

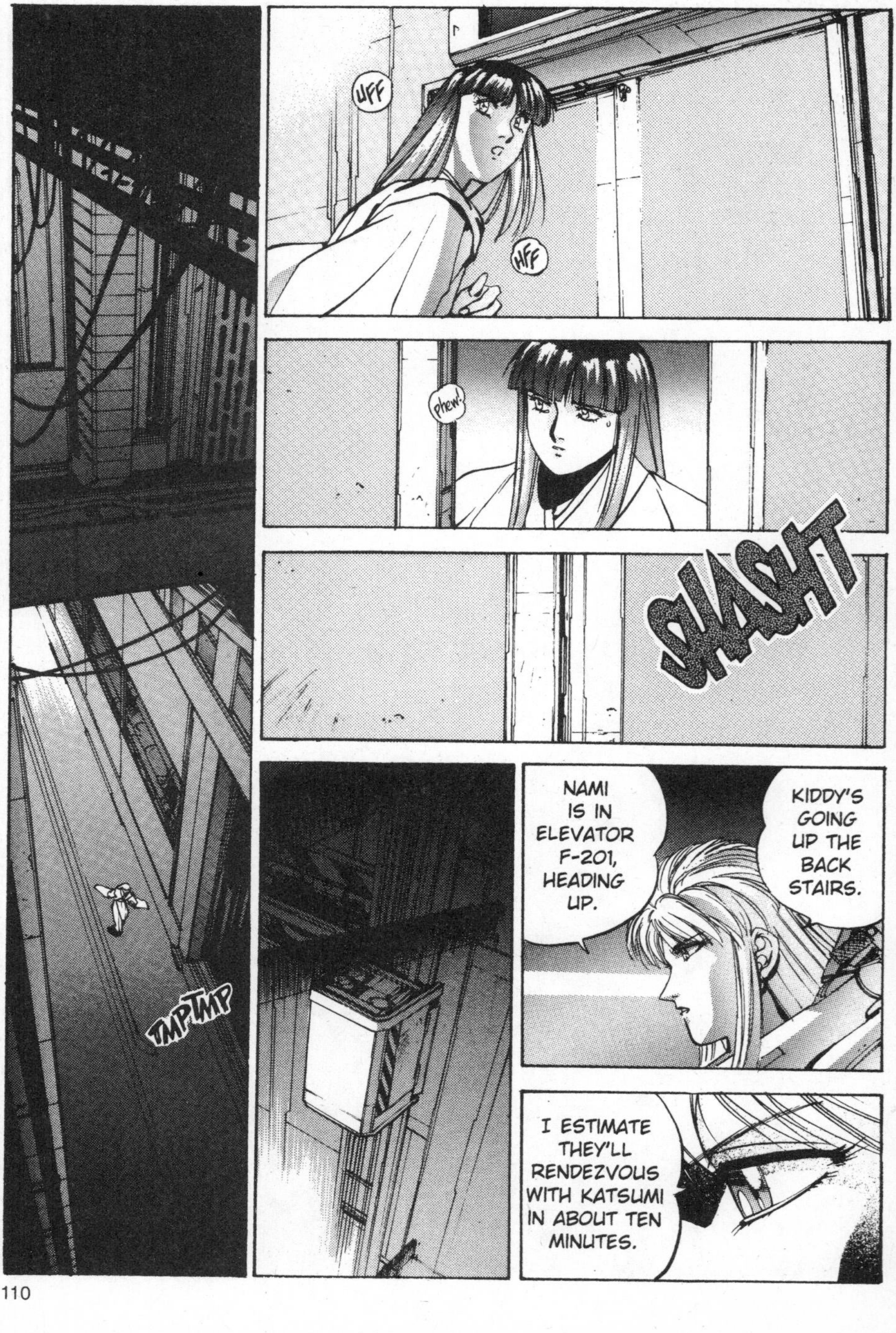
TMPTMP
UFF
HFF
phew!
SHASHT
NAMI IS IN ELEVATOR F-201, HEADING UP.
KIDDY'S GOING UP THE BACK STAIRS.
I ESTIMATE THEY'LL RENDEZVOUS WITH KATSUMI IN ABOUT TEN MINUTES.

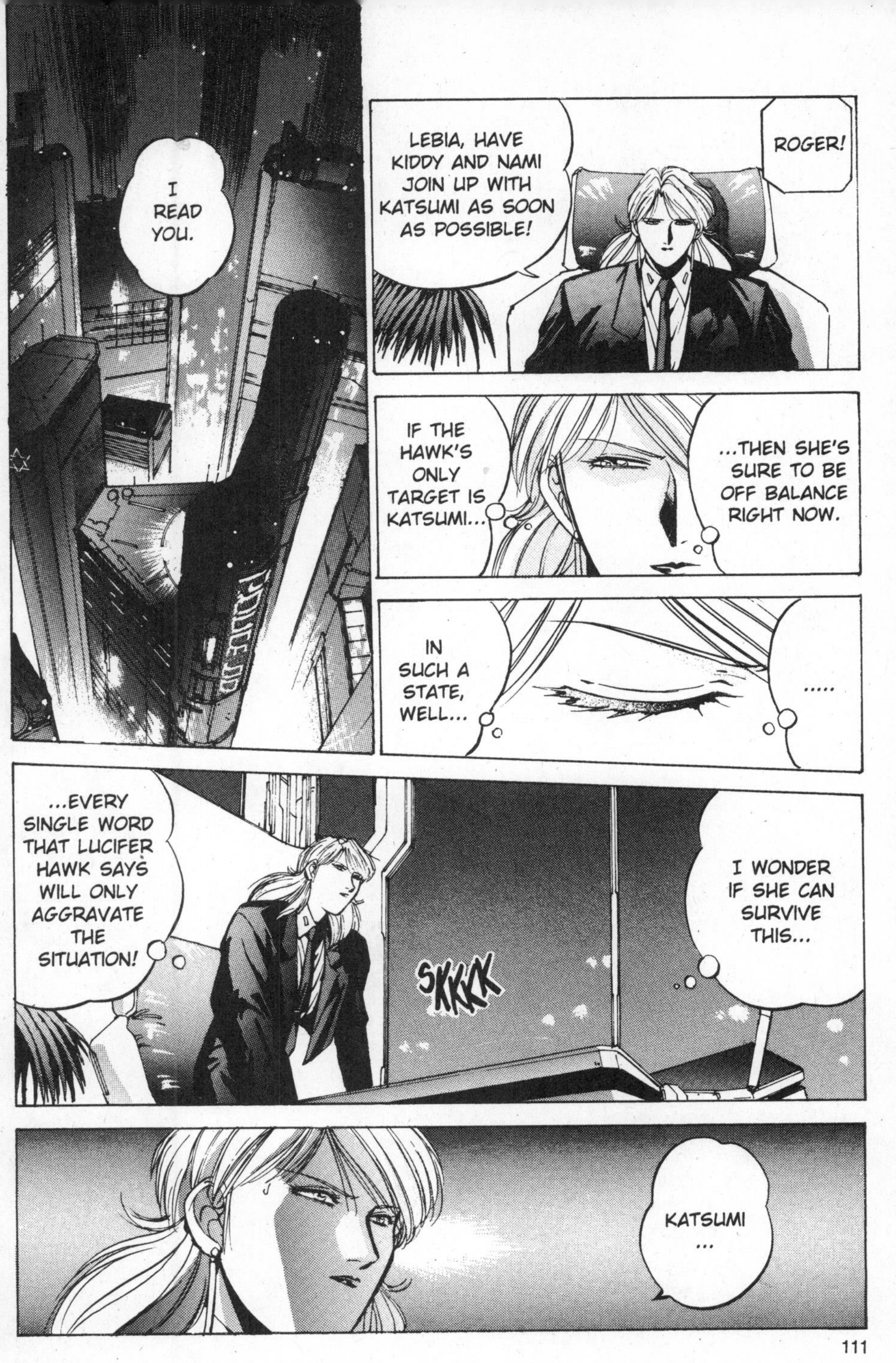
I READ YOU.
LEBIA, HAVE KIDDY AND NAMI JOIN UP WITH KATSUMI AS SOON AS POSSIBLE!
ROGER!
IF THE HAWK'S ONLY TARGET IS KATSUMI...
...THEN SHE'S SURE TO BE OFF BALANCE RIGHT NOW.
IN SUCH A STATE, WELL...
.....
...EVERY SINGLE WORD THAT LUCIFER HAWK SAYS WILL ONLY AGGRAVATE THE SITUATION!
SKKKK
I WONDER IF SHE CAN SURVIVE THIS...
KATSUMI ...

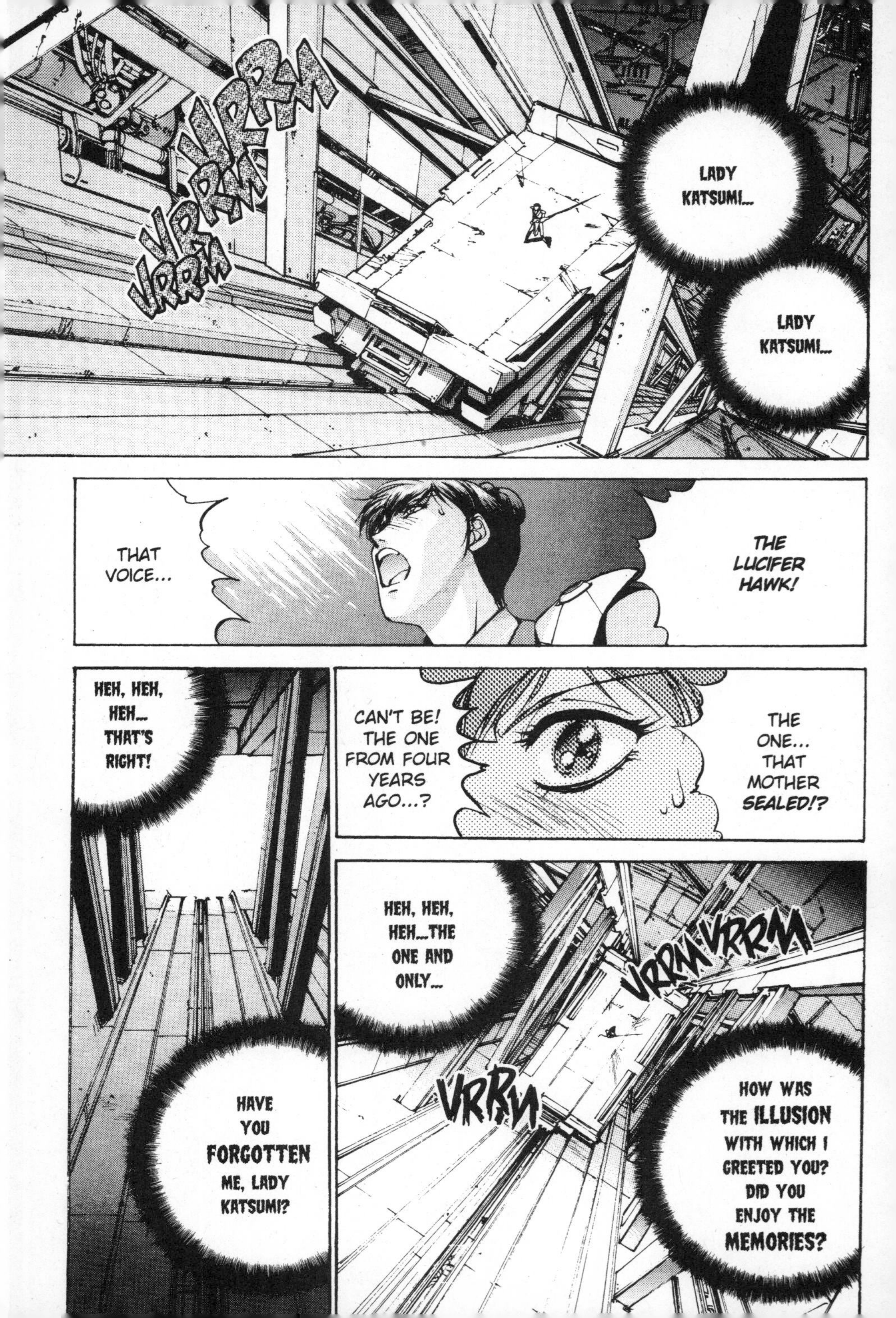
LADY KATSUMI...
LADY KATSUMI...
THAT VOICE...
THE LUCIFER HAWK!
HEH, HEH, HEH... THAT'S RIGHT!
HAVE YOU FORGOTTEN ME, LADY KATSUMI?
CAN'T BE! THE ONE FROM FOUR YEARS AGO...?
THE ONE... THAT MOTHER SEALED!?
HEH, HEH, HEH...THE ONE AND ONLY...
VRRM VRRM
VRRN
HOW WAS THE ILLUSION WITH WHICH I GREETED YOU? DID YOU ENJOY THE MEMORIES?

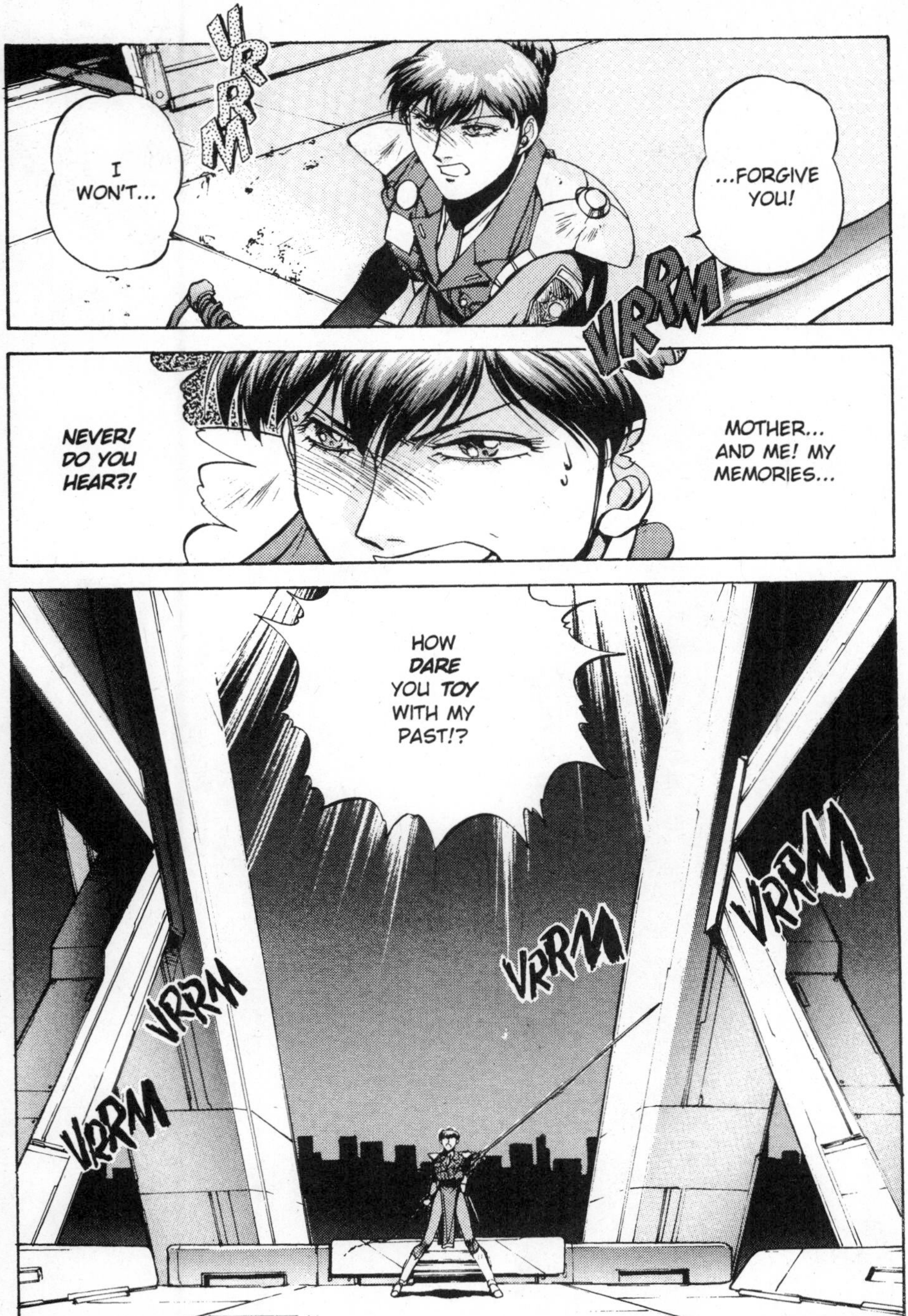
VRRM
I WON'T...
...FORGIVE YOU!
VRRM
NEVER! DO YOU HEAR?!
MOTHER... AND ME! MY MEMORIES...
HOW *DARE* YOU *TOY* WITH MY PAST!?
VRRM
VRRM
VRRM
VRRM
VRRM

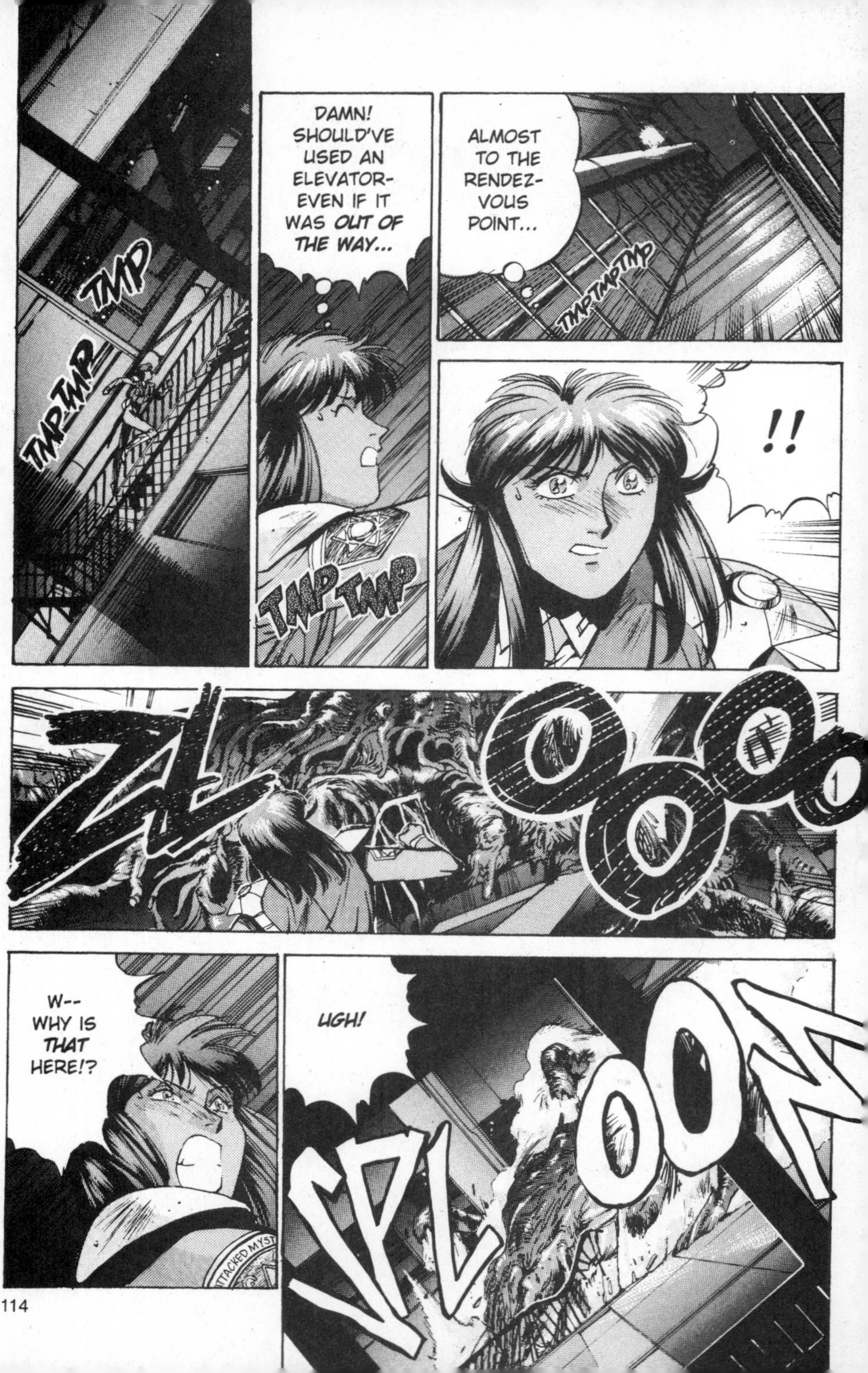
TMP
TMP-TMP
DAMN! SHOULD'VE USED AN ELEVATOR- EVEN IF IT WAS OUT OF THE WAY...
TMP TMP
ALMOST TO THE RENDEZ-VOUS POINT...
TMP TMP TMP
!!
ZL
OOOOO
W-- WHY IS THAT HERE!?
UGH!
SPLOOOM

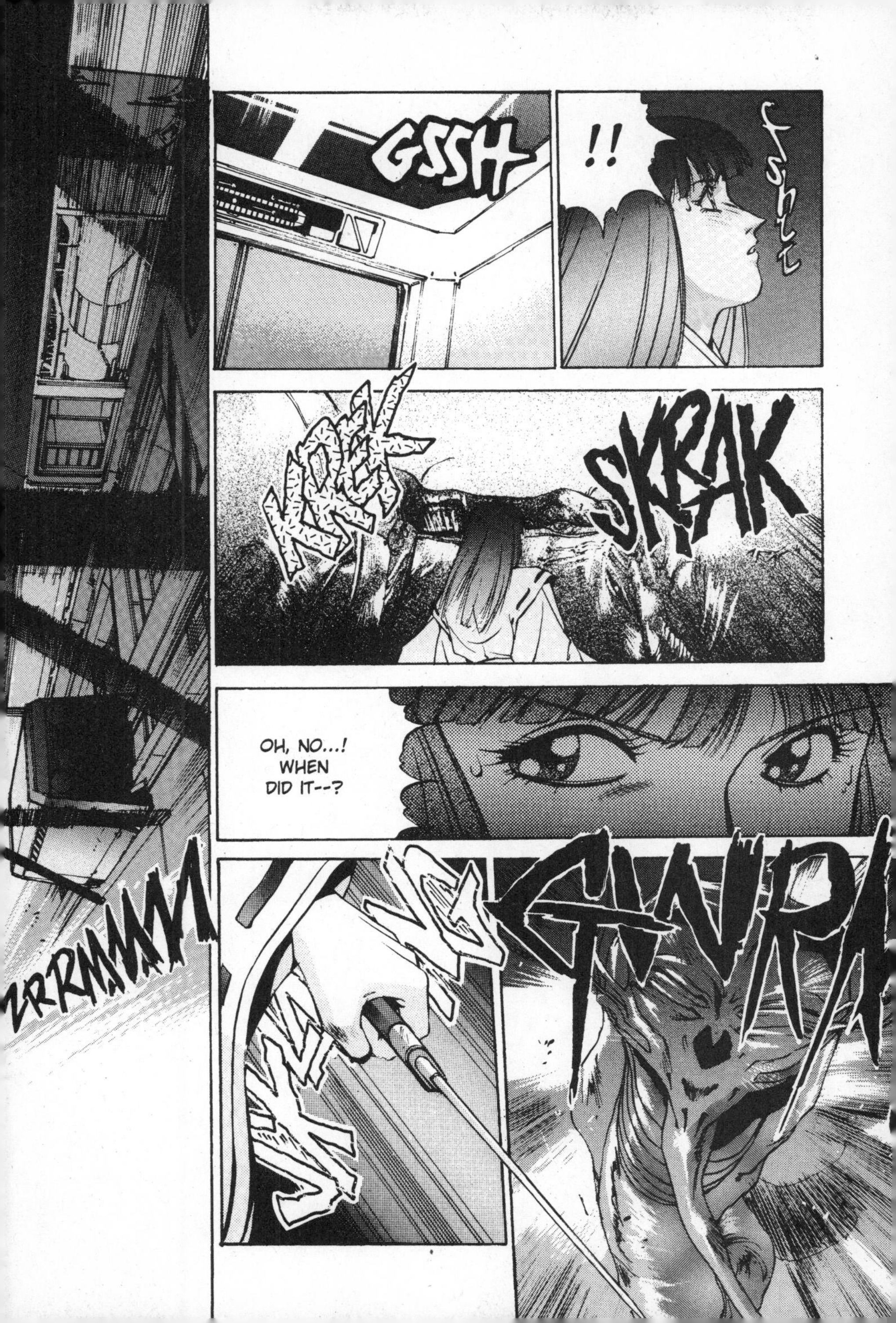
GSSH
!!
SKRAK
OH, NO...!
WHEN
DID IT--?

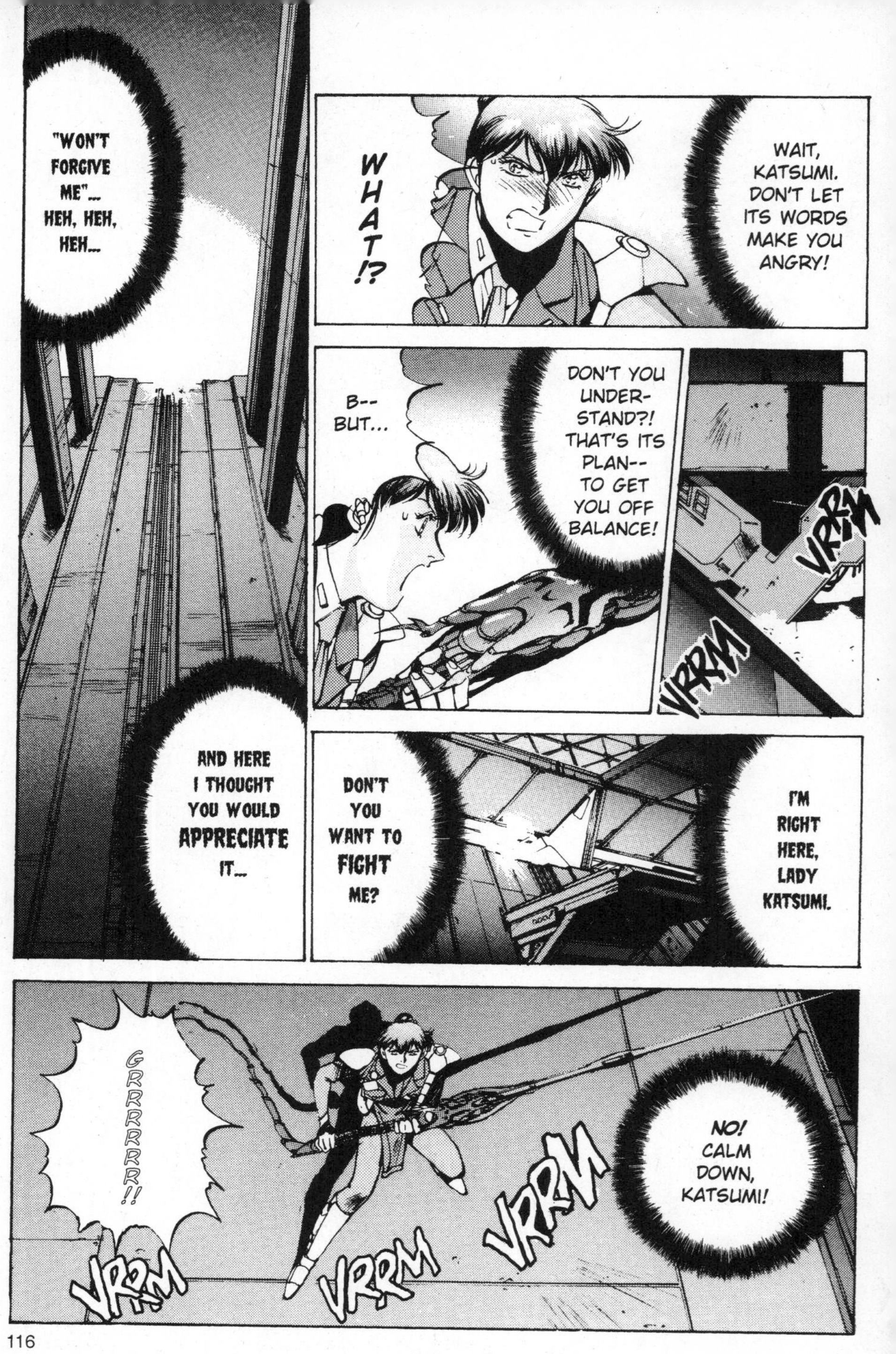
"WON'T FORGIVE ME"... HEH, HEH, HEH...
AND HERE I THOUGHT YOU WOULD APPRECIATE IT...
WHAT!?
WAIT, KATSUMI. DON'T LET ITS WORDS MAKE YOU ANGRY!
B-- BUT...
DON'T YOU UNDER-STAND?! THAT'S ITS PLAN-- TO GET YOU OFF BALANCE!
VRRM
VRRM
DON'T YOU WANT TO FIGHT ME?
I'M RIGHT HERE, LADY KATSUMI.
GRRRRRRR!!
VRRM
VRRM
VRRM
NO! CALM DOWN, KATSUMI!

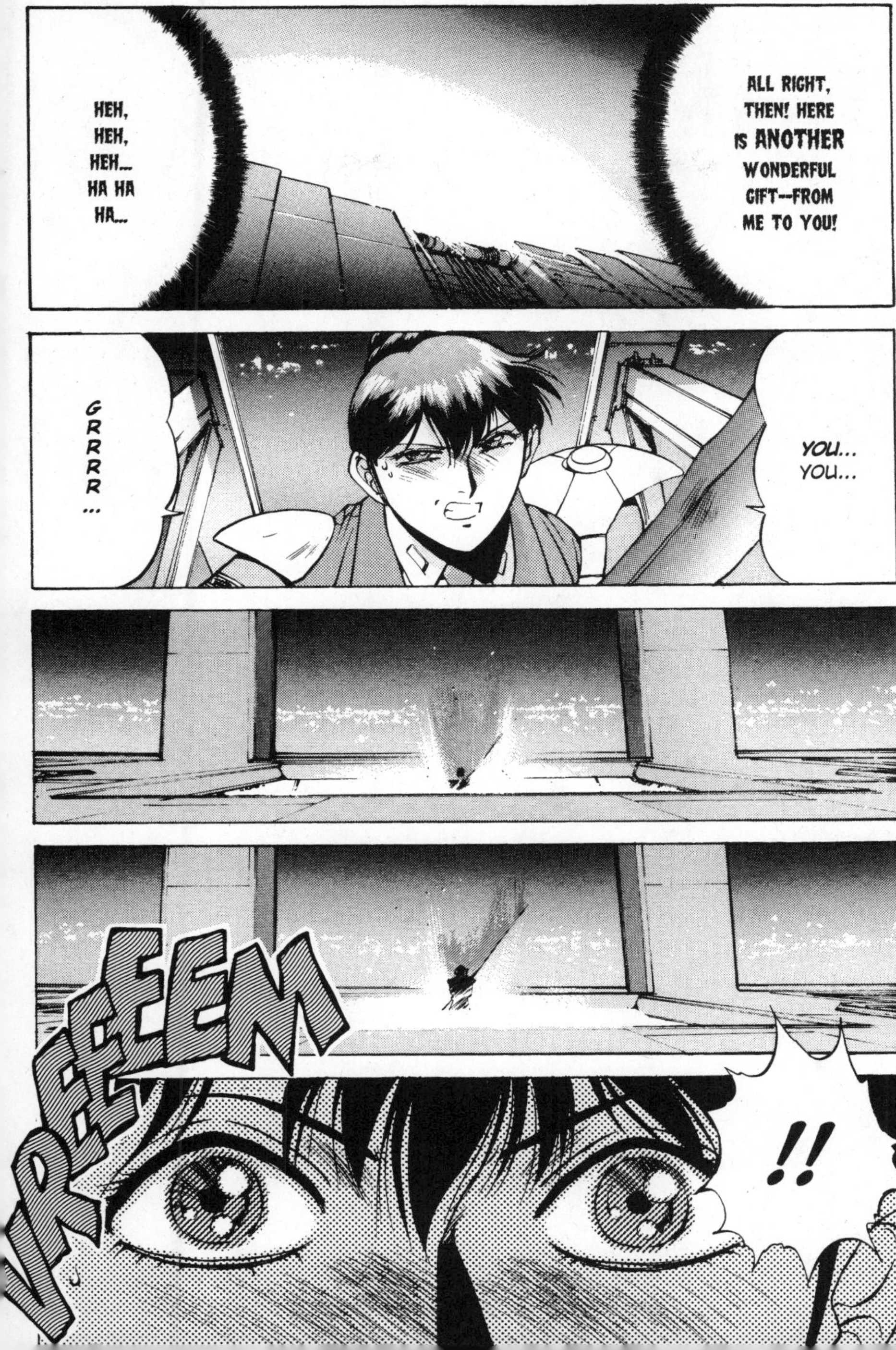
HEH, HEH, HEH... HA HA HA...
ALL RIGHT, THEN! HERE IS ANOTHER WONDERFUL GIFT--FROM ME TO YOU!
GRRRR...
YOU... YOU...
VREEEEM
!!

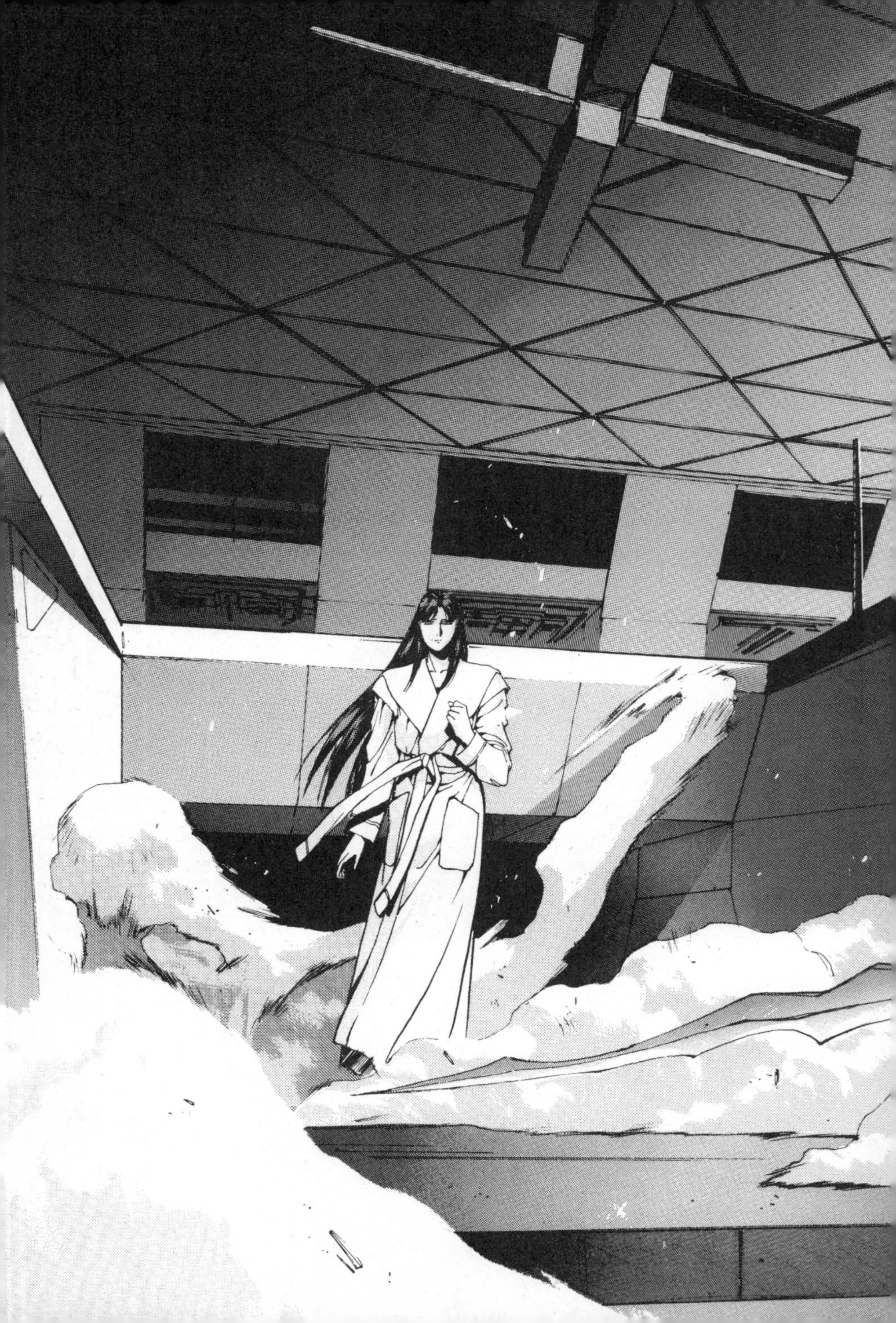

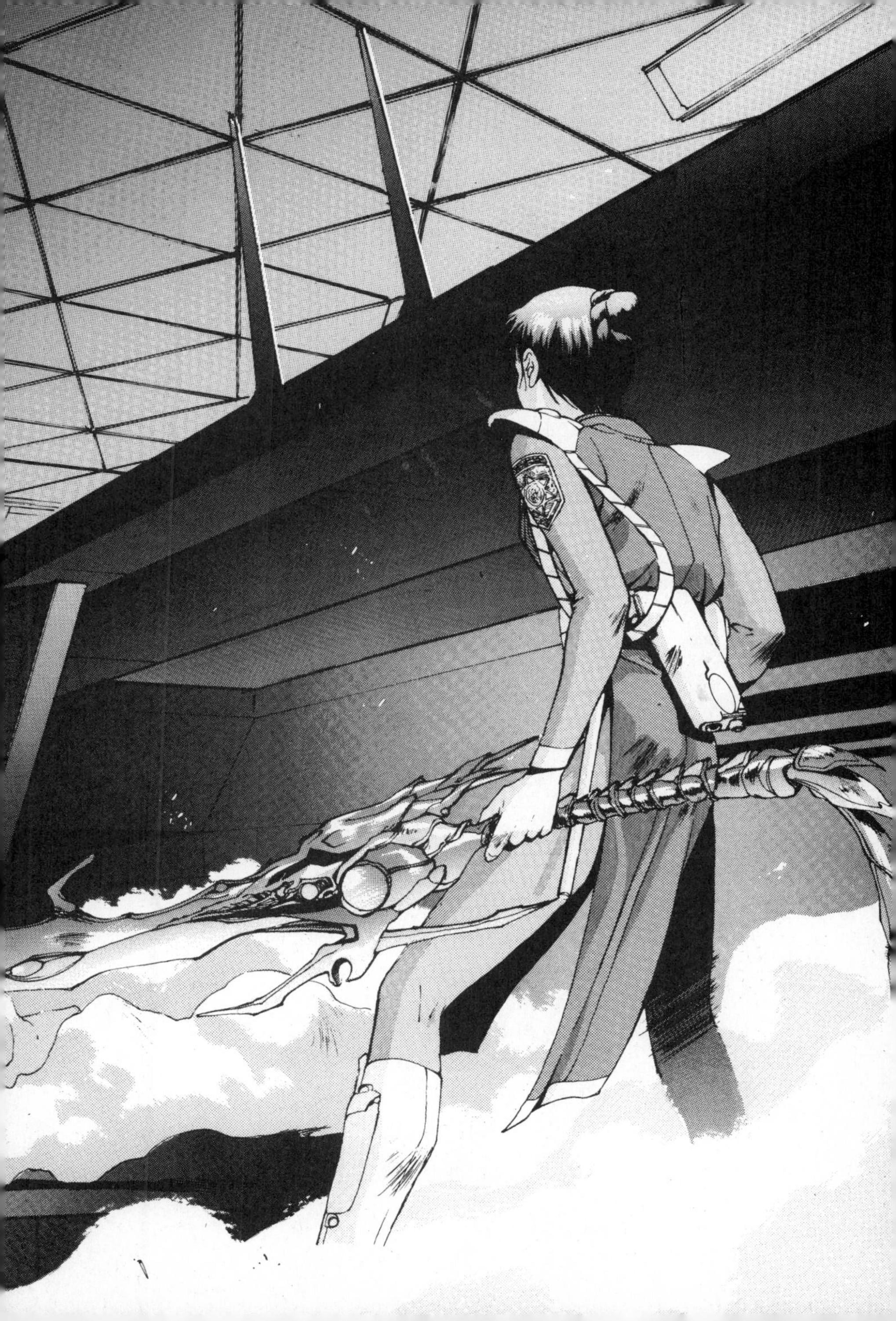

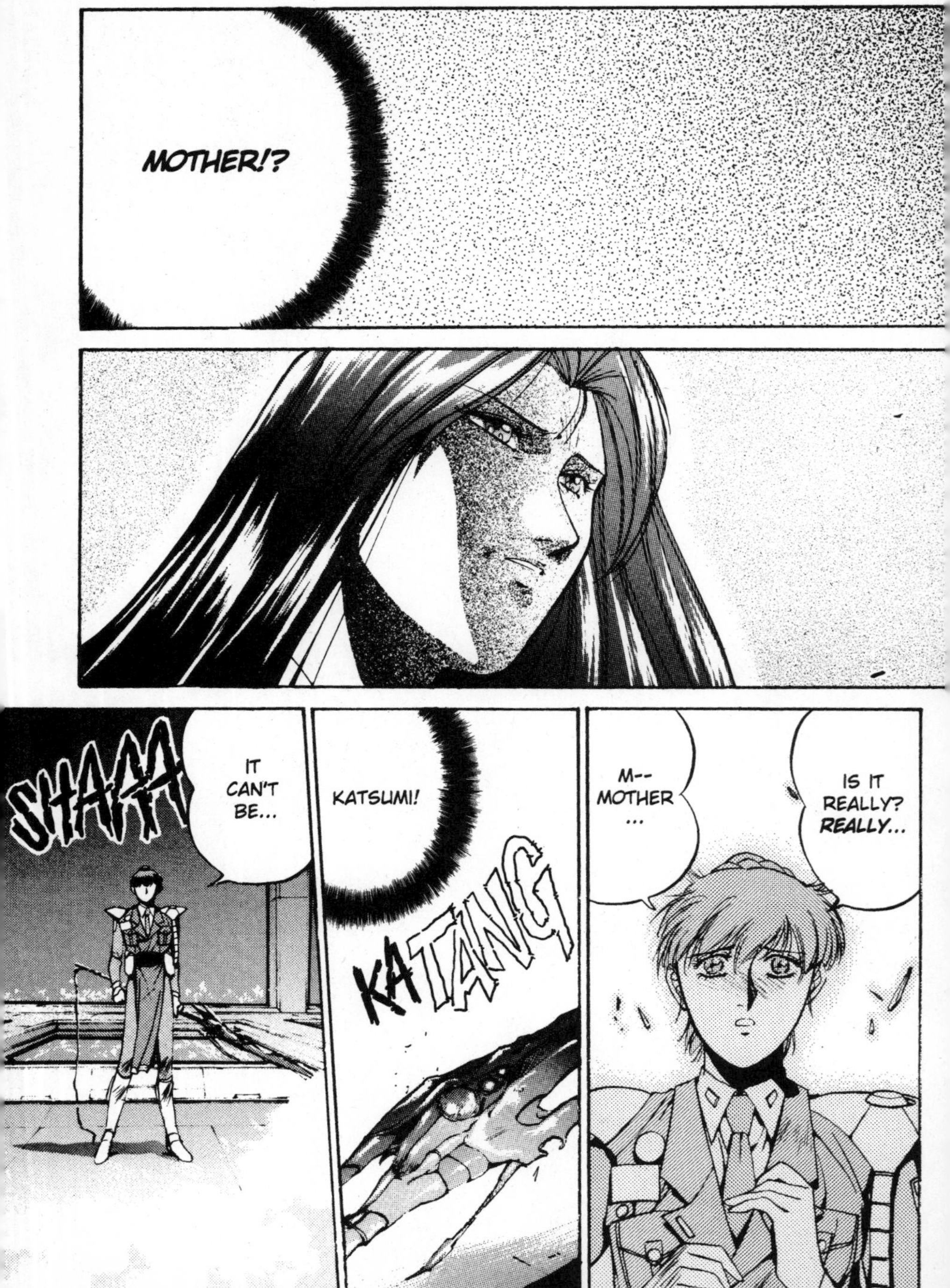
MOTHER!?
SHAAA
IT CAN'T BE...
KATSUMI!
KATANG
M-- MOTHER ...
IS IT REALLY? REALLY...

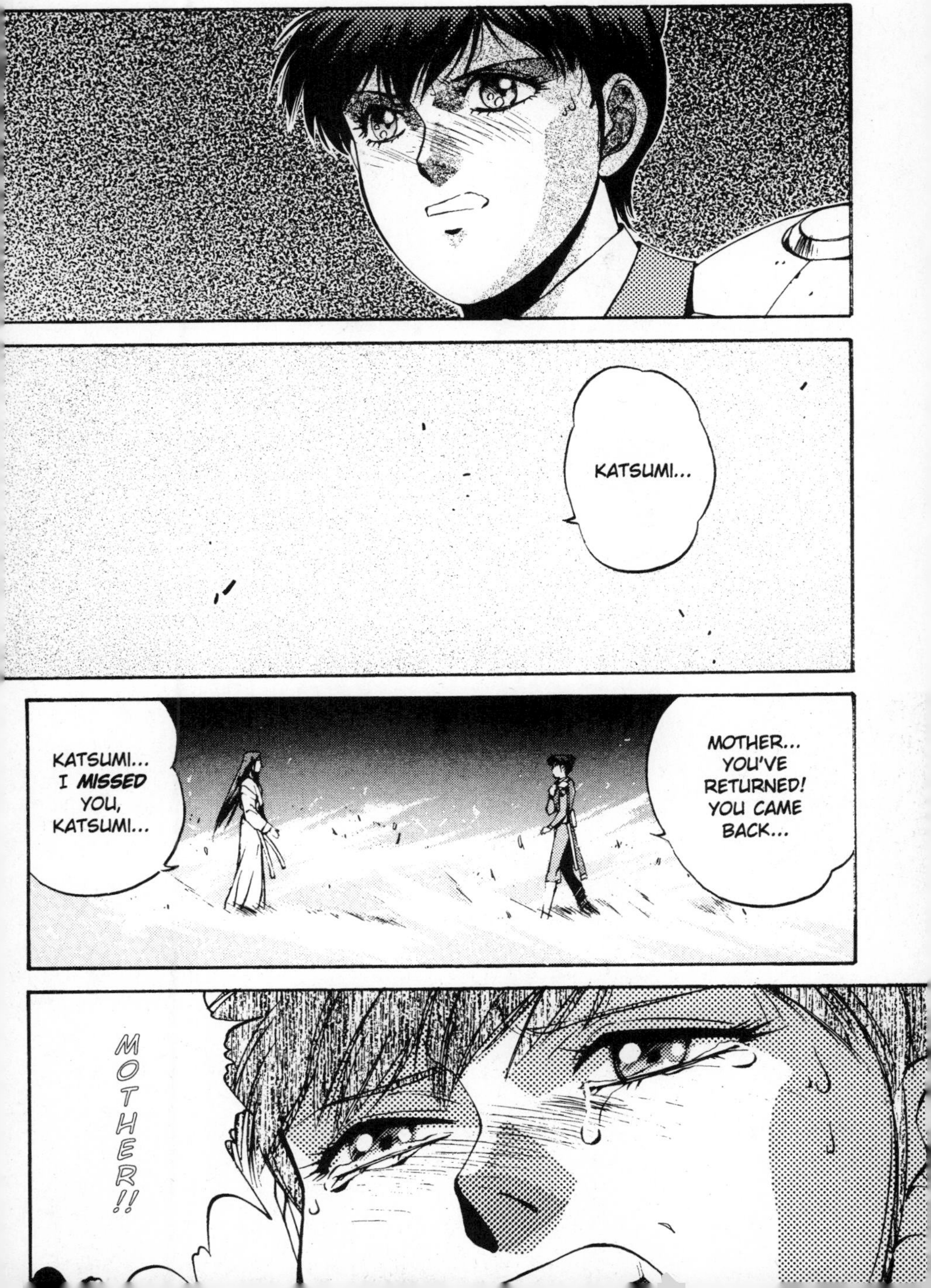
KATSUMI...
KATSUMI... I MISSED YOU, KATSUMI...
MOTHER... YOU'VE RETURNED! YOU CAME BACK...
MOTHER!!

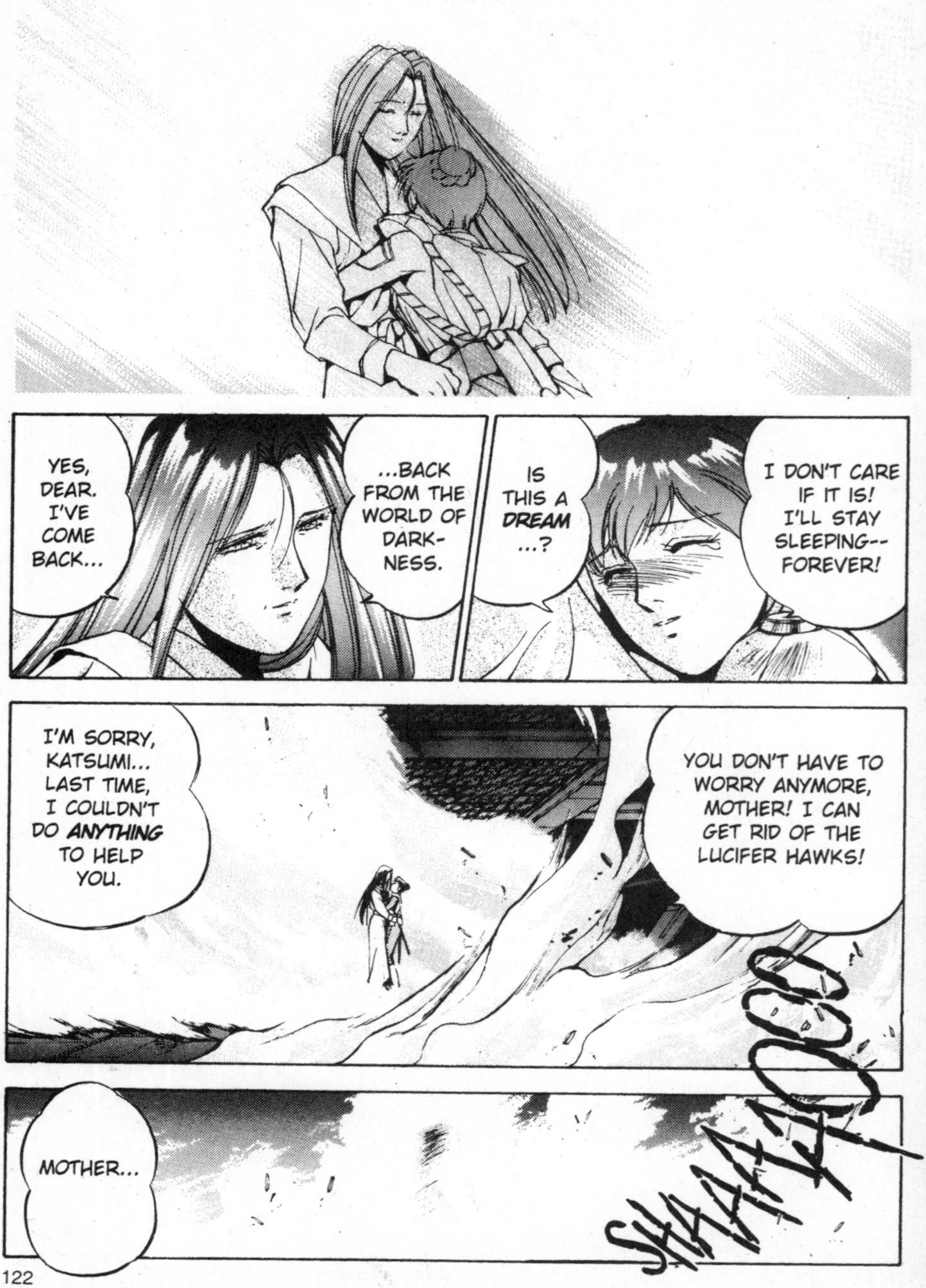
YES, DEAR. I'VE COME BACK...
...BACK FROM THE WORLD OF DARK- NESS.
IS THIS A **DREAM** ...?
I DON'T CARE IF IT IS! I'LL STAY SLEEPING-- FOREVER!
I'M SORRY, KATSUMI... LAST TIME, I COULDN'T DO **ANYTHING** TO HELP YOU.
YOU DON'T HAVE TO WORRY ANYMORE, MOTHER! I CAN GET RID OF THE LUCIFER HAWKS!
MOTHER...
SHAAAOOO

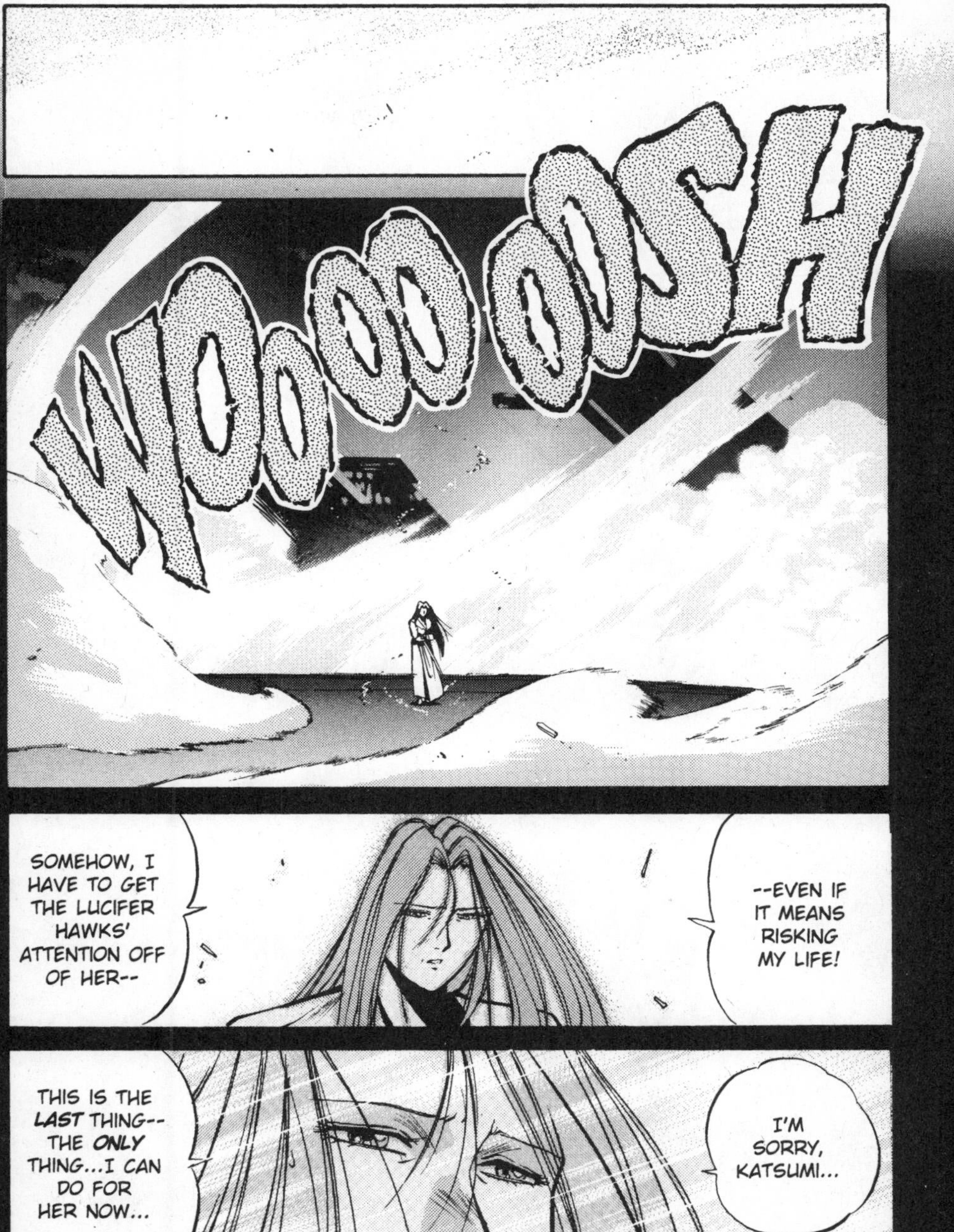
WOOOOOOSH
SOMEHOW, I HAVE TO GET THE LUCIFER HAWKS' ATTENTION OFF OF HER--
--EVEN IF IT MEANS RISKING MY LIFE!
THIS IS THE LAST THING-- THE ONLY THING...I CAN DO FOR HER NOW...
I'M SORRY, KATSUMI...

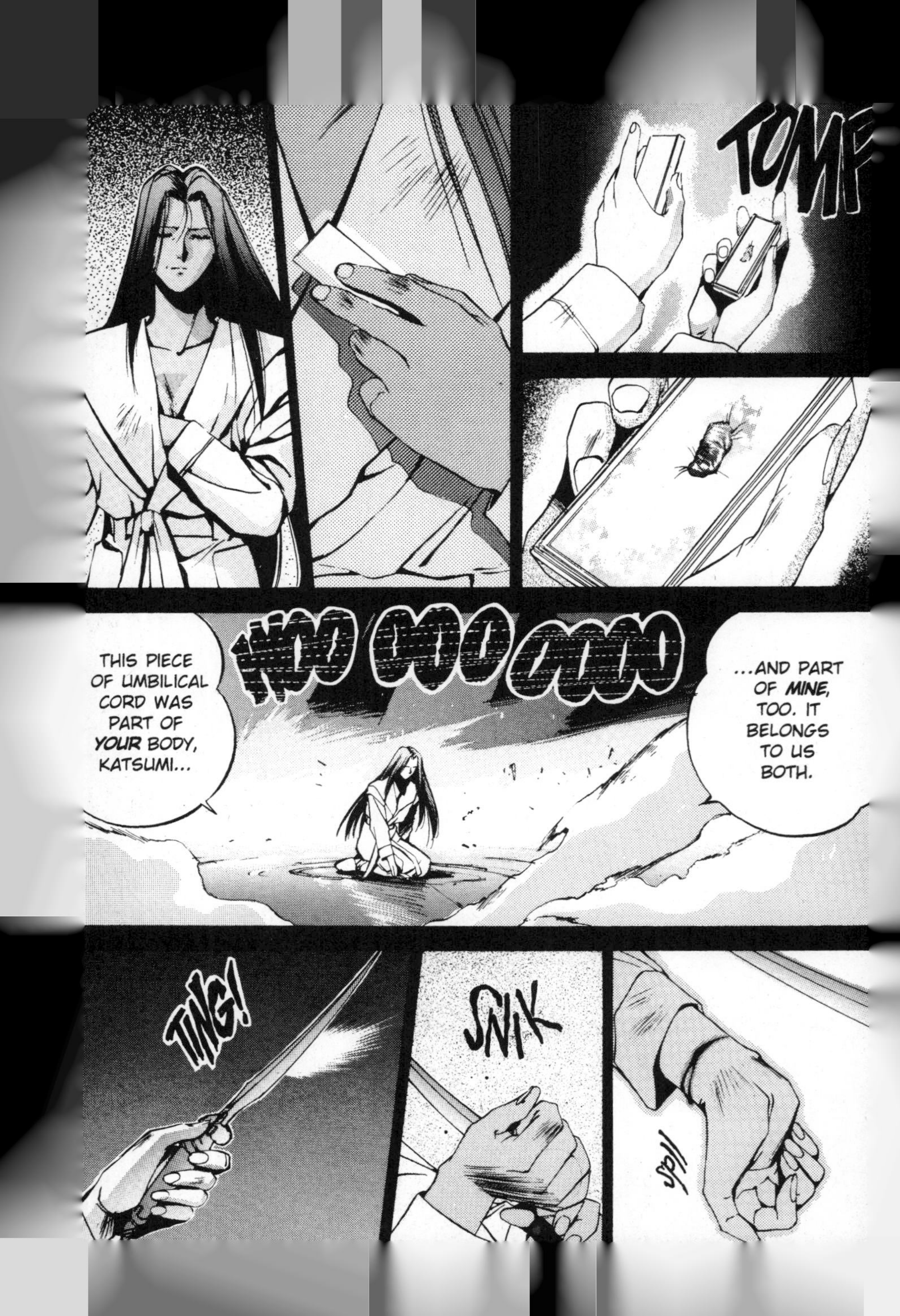
TOMF
THIS PIECE OF UMBILICAL CORD WAS PART OF YOUR BODY, KATSUMI...
WOO OOO OOOO
...AND PART OF MINE, TOO. IT BELONGS TO US BOTH.
TING!
SNIK

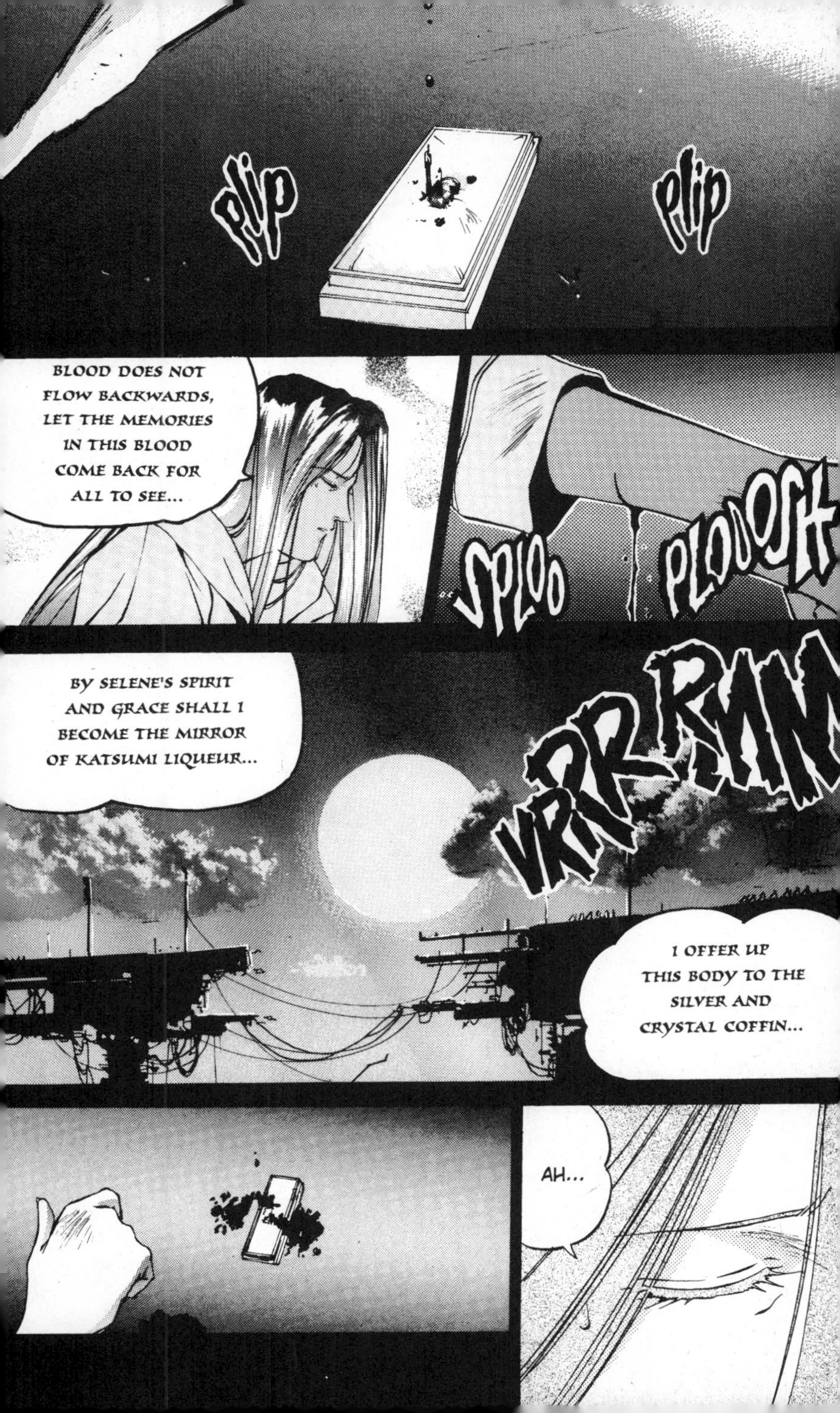
plip
plip
BLOOD DOES NOT FLOW BACKWARDS, LET THE MEMORIES IN THIS BLOOD COME BACK FOR ALL TO SEE...
SPLOO
PLOOOSH
BY SELENE'S SPIRIT AND GRACE SHALL I BECOME THE MIRROR OF KATSUMI LIQUEUR...
VRRRRMM
I OFFER UP THIS BODY TO THE SILVER AND CRYSTAL COFFIN...
AH...

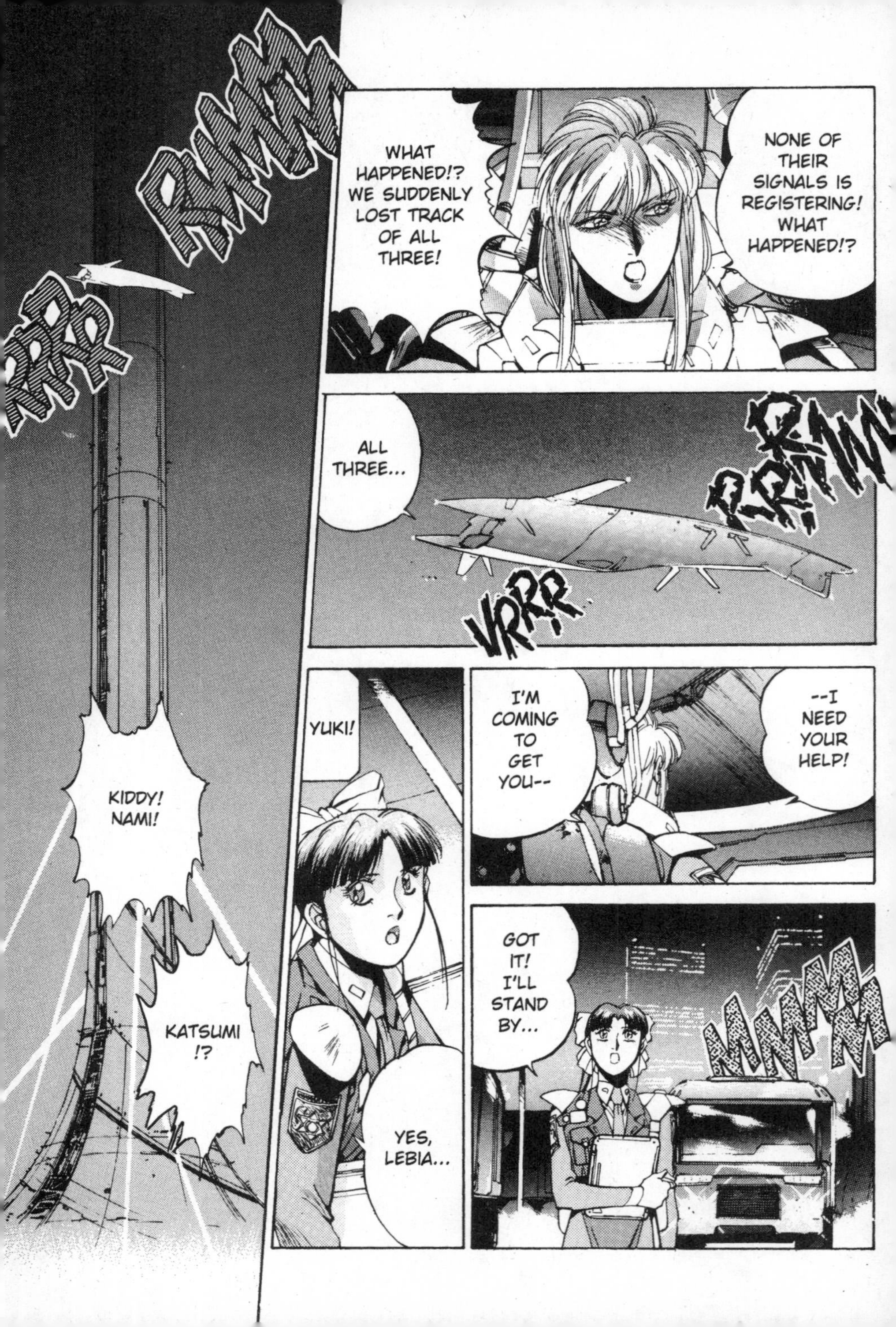
RRRR
KIDDY! NAMI!
KATSUMI !?
WHAT HAPPENED!? WE SUDDENLY LOST TRACK OF ALL THREE!
NONE OF THEIR SIGNALS IS REGISTERING! WHAT HAPPENED!?
ALL THREE...
VRRR
YUKI!
YES, LEBIA...
I'M COMING TO GET YOU--
--I NEED YOUR HELP!
GOT IT! I'LL STAND BY...

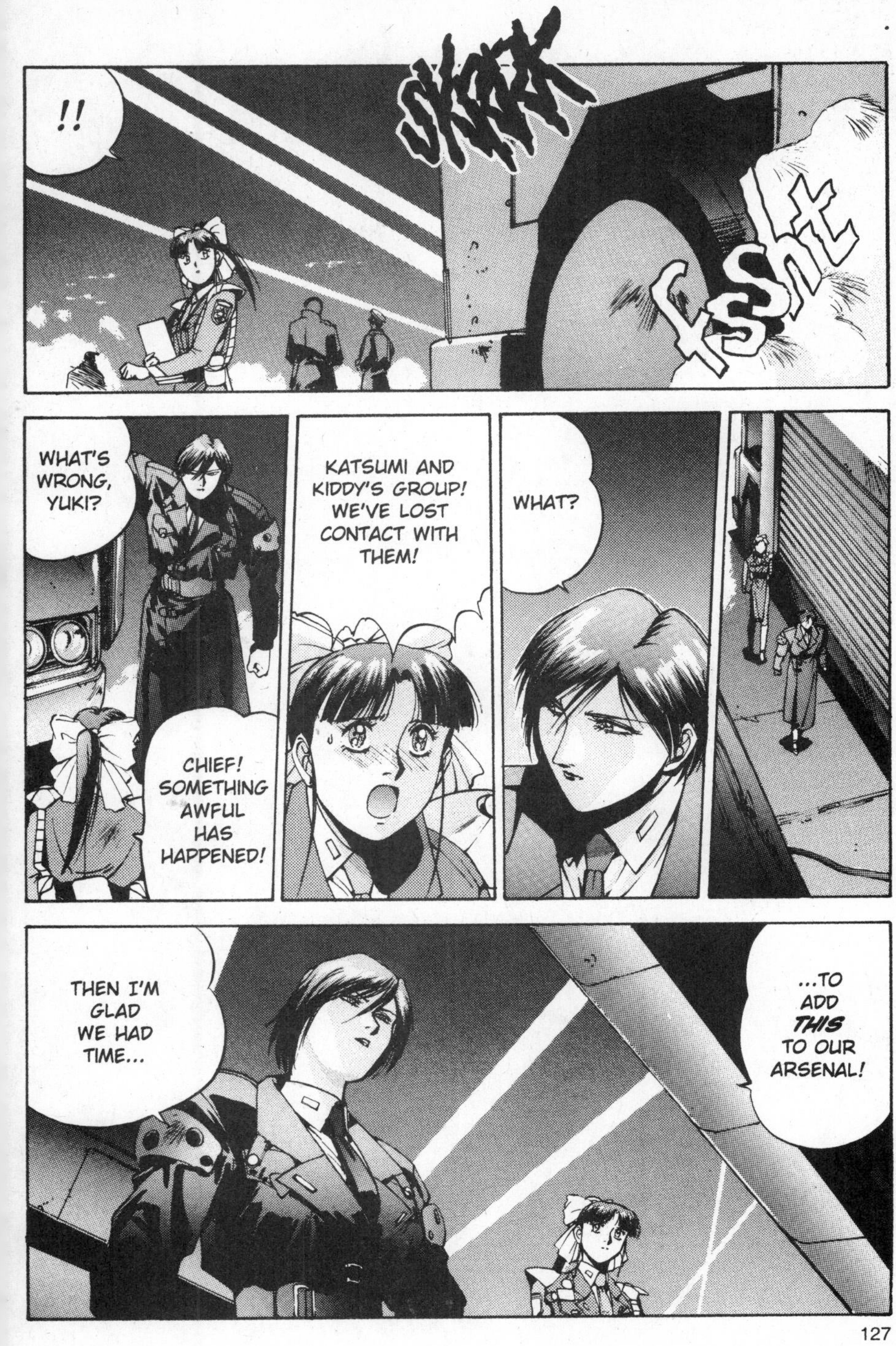
!!
FSSHT
WHAT'S WRONG, YUKI?
CHIEF! SOMETHING AWFUL HAS HAPPENED!
KATSUMI AND KIDDY'S GROUP! WE'VE LOST CONTACT WITH THEM!
WHAT?
THEN I'M GLAD WE HAD TIME...
...TO ADD ***THIS*** TO OUR ARSENAL!

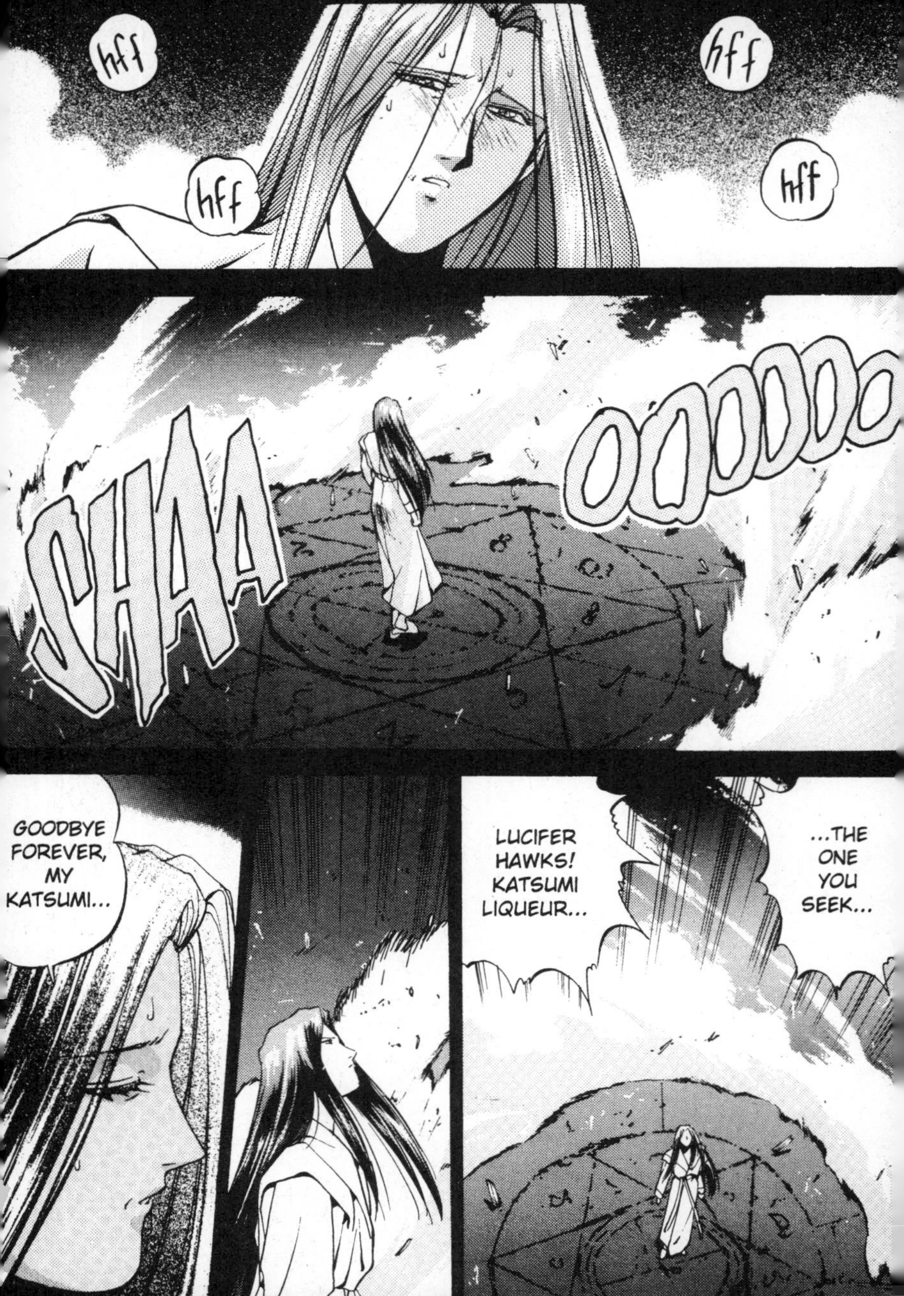
hff
hff
hff
hff
SHAA
OOOOOOO
GOODBYE FOREVER, MY KATSUMI...
LUCIFER HAWKS! KATSUMI LIQUEUR...
...THE ONE YOU SEEK...

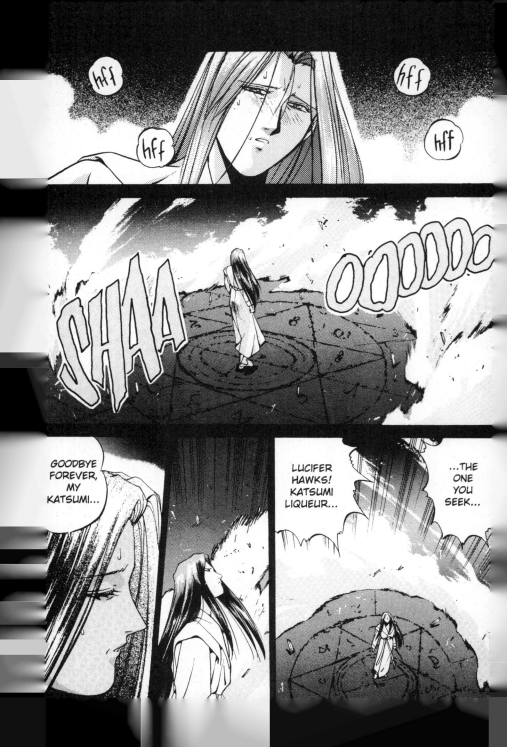

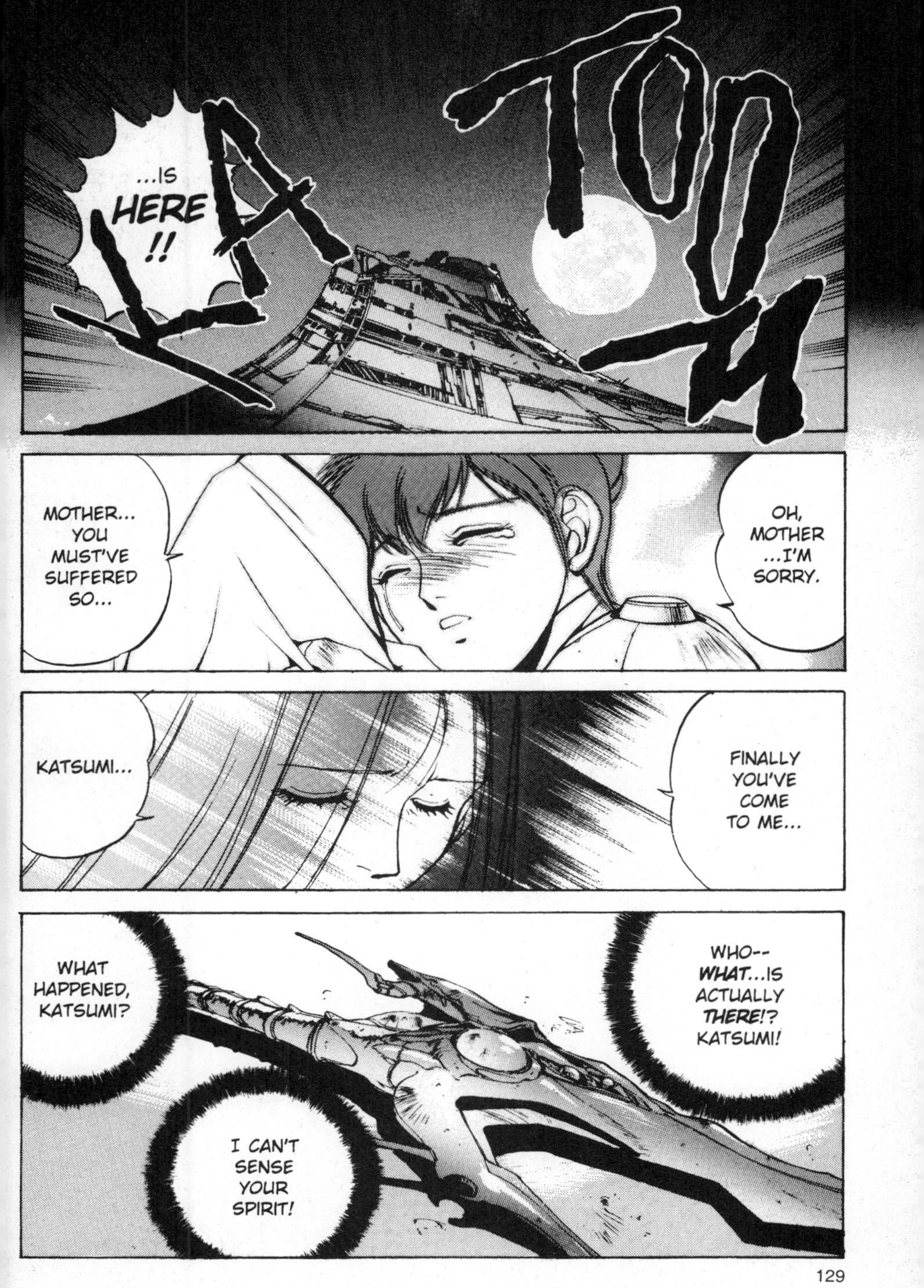
...IS HERE!!
KATOOM
MOTHER... YOU MUST'VE SUFFERED SO...
OH, MOTHER ...I'M SORRY.
KATSUMI...
FINALLY YOU'VE COME TO ME...
WHAT HAPPENED, KATSUMI?
WHO--WHAT...IS ACTUALLY THERE!? KATSUMI!
I CAN'T SENSE YOUR SPIRIT!

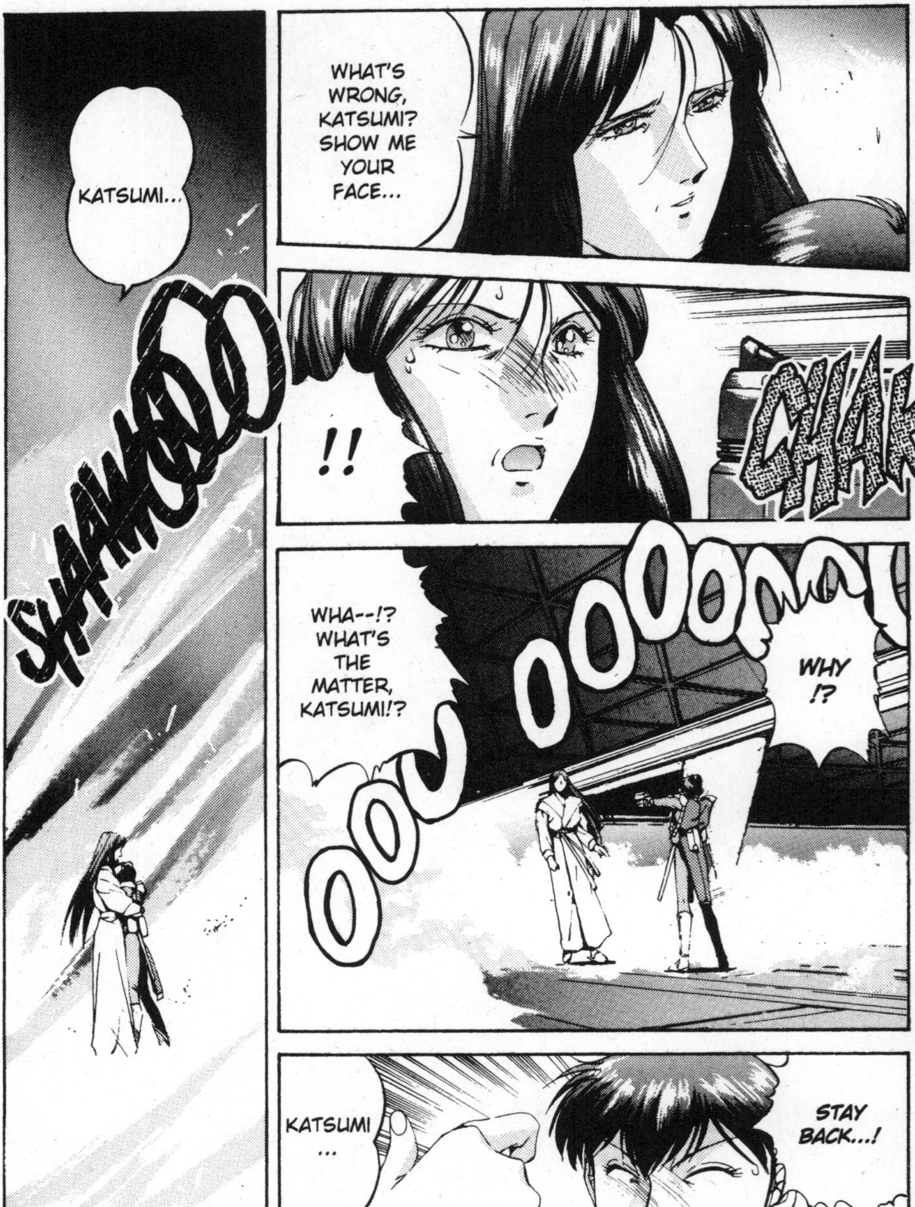
KATSUMI...
SHAAWOOO
WHAT'S WRONG, KATSUMI? SHOW ME YOUR FACE...
!!
CHAK
WHA--!? WHAT'S THE MATTER, KATSUMI!?
WHY !?
KATSUMI ...
STAY BACK...!

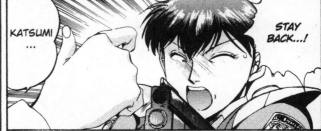

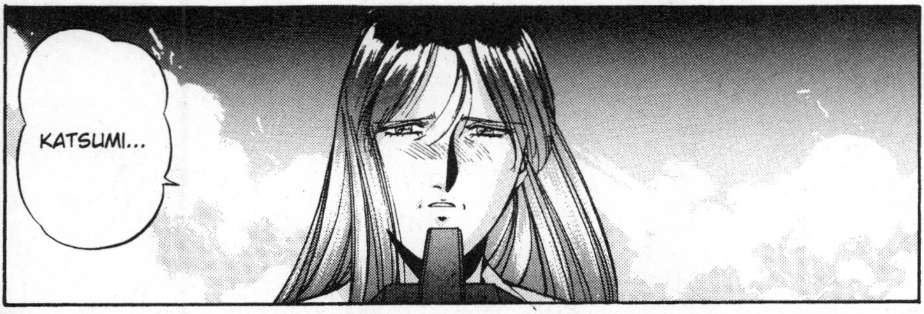
KATSUMI...

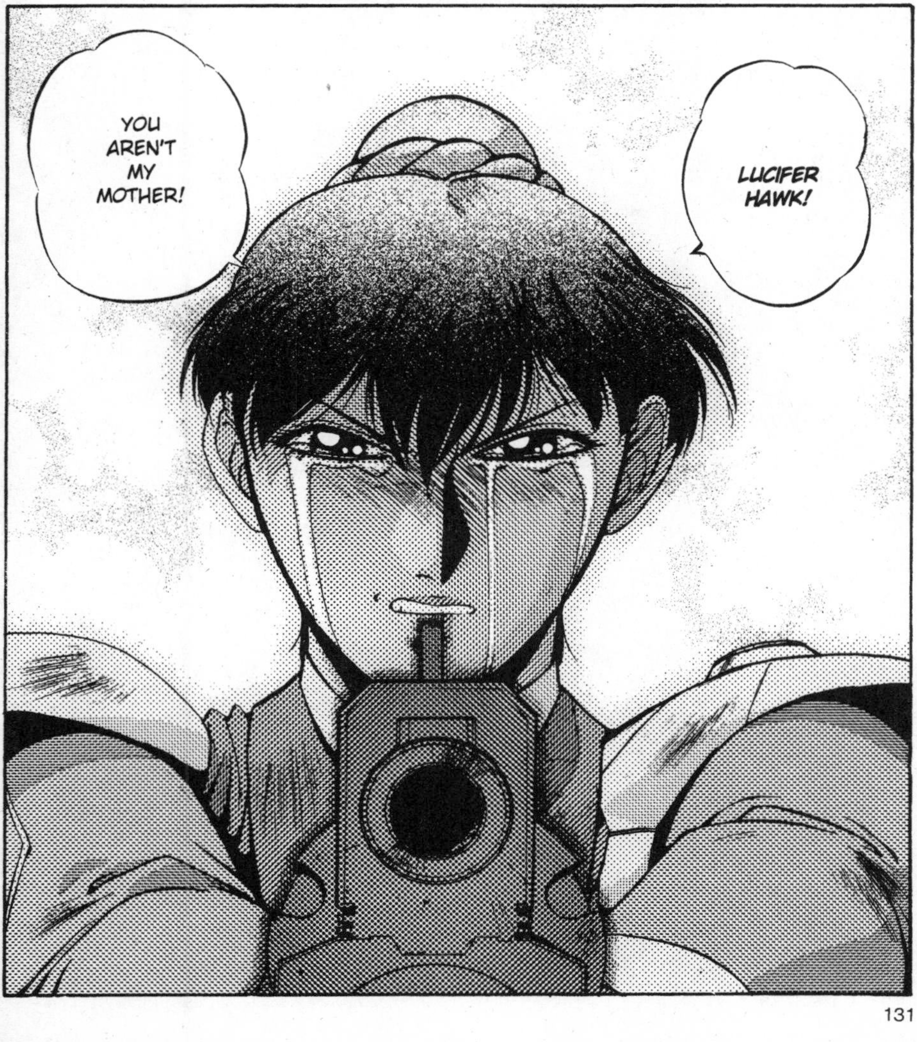
YOU AREN'T MY MOTHER!
LUCIFER HAWK!

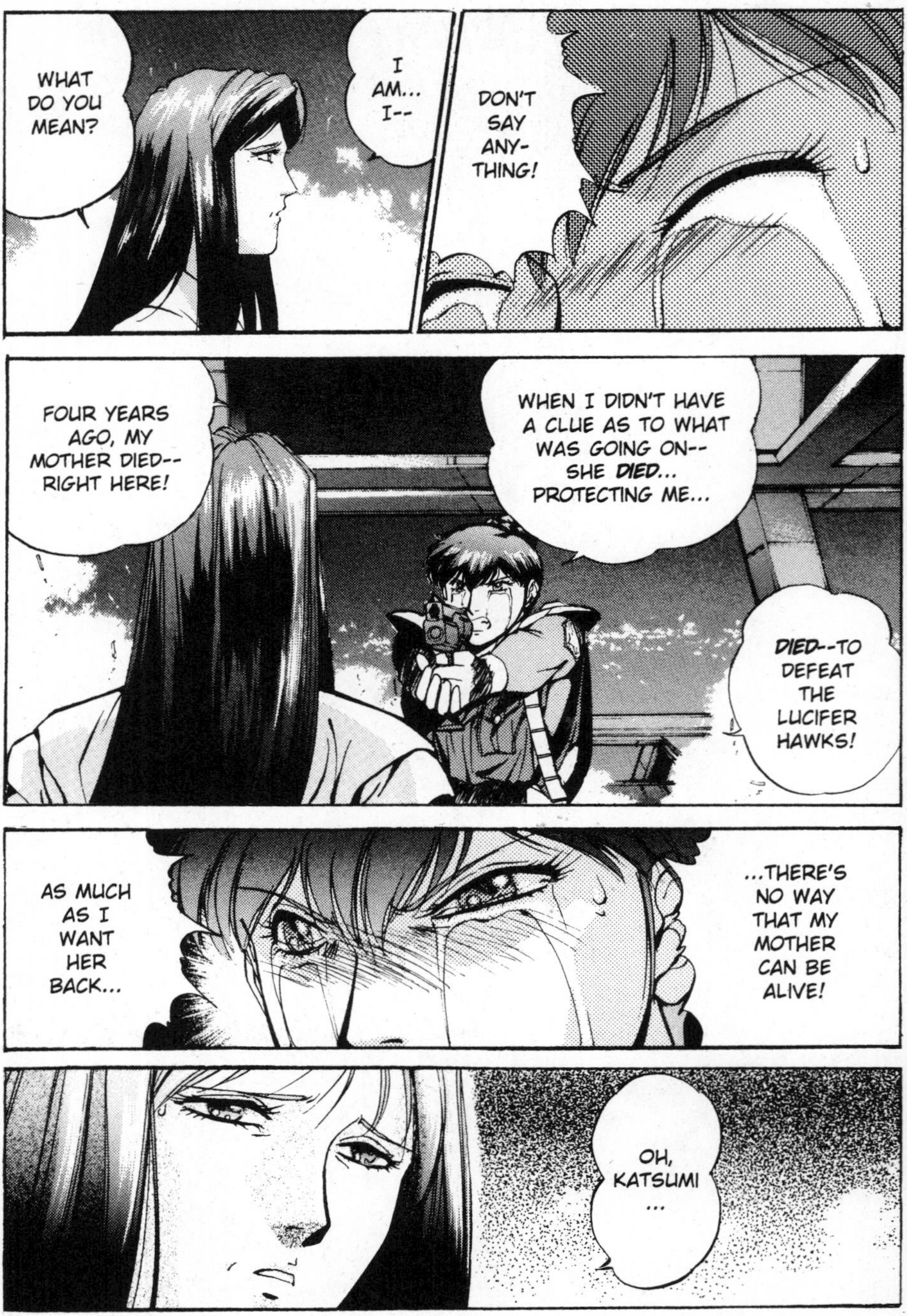

WHAT DO YOU MEAN?
I AM... I--
DON'T SAY ANY-THING!
FOUR YEARS AGO, MY MOTHER DIED-- RIGHT HERE!
WHEN I DIDN'T HAVE A CLUE AS TO WHAT WAS GOING ON-- SHE **DIED**... PROTECTING ME...
DIED--TO DEFEAT THE LUCIFER HAWKS!
AS MUCH AS I WANT HER BACK...
...THERE'S NO WAY THAT MY MOTHER CAN BE ALIVE!
OH, KATSUMI ...

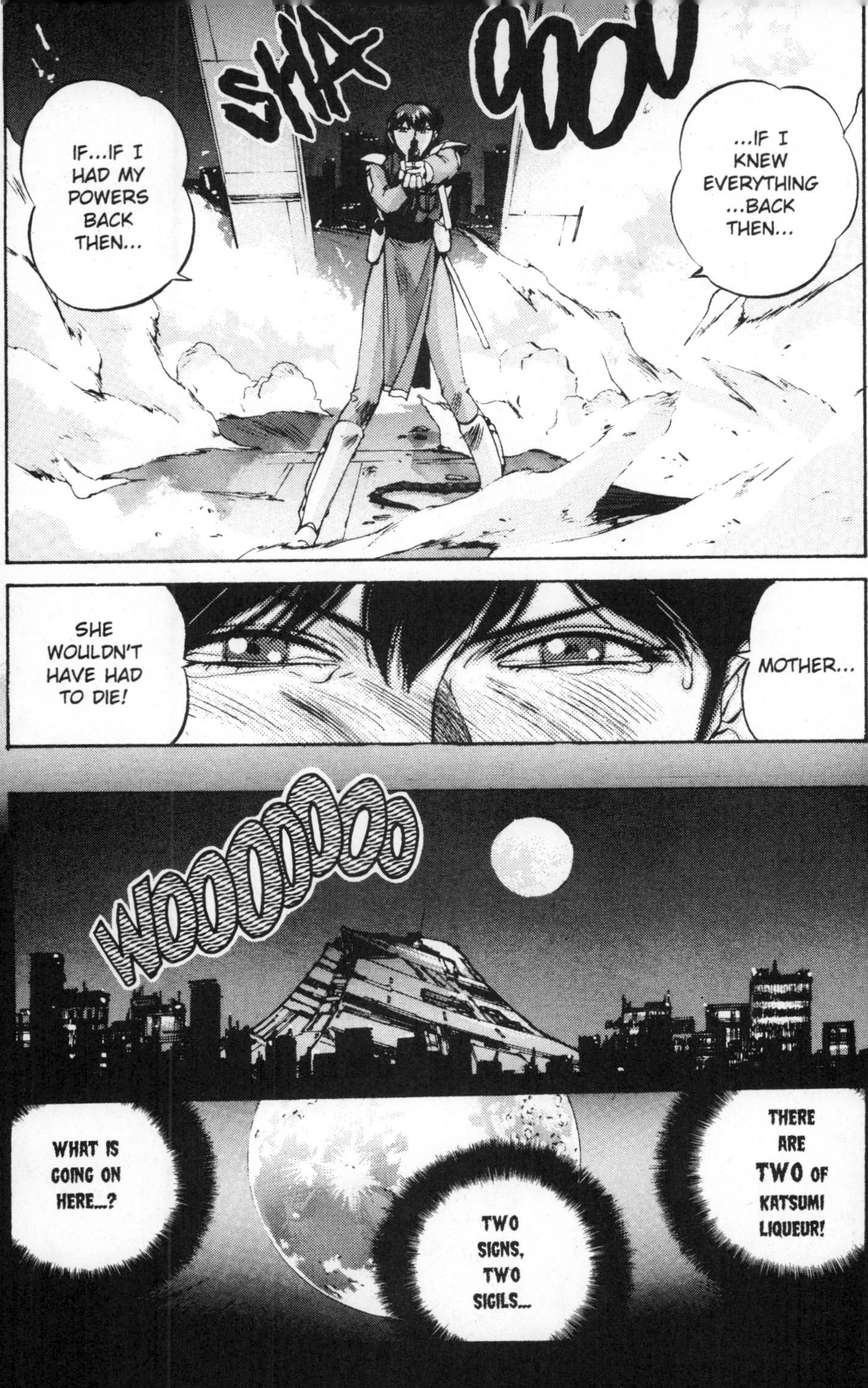
SHA
OOOV
IF...IF I HAD MY POWERS BACK THEN...
...IF I KNEW EVERYTHING ...BACK THEN...
SHE WOULDN'T HAVE HAD TO DIE!
MOTHER...
WOOOOOOOO
WHAT IS GOING ON HERE...?
TWO SIGNS, TWO SIGILS...
THERE ARE TWO OF KATSUMI LIQUEUR!

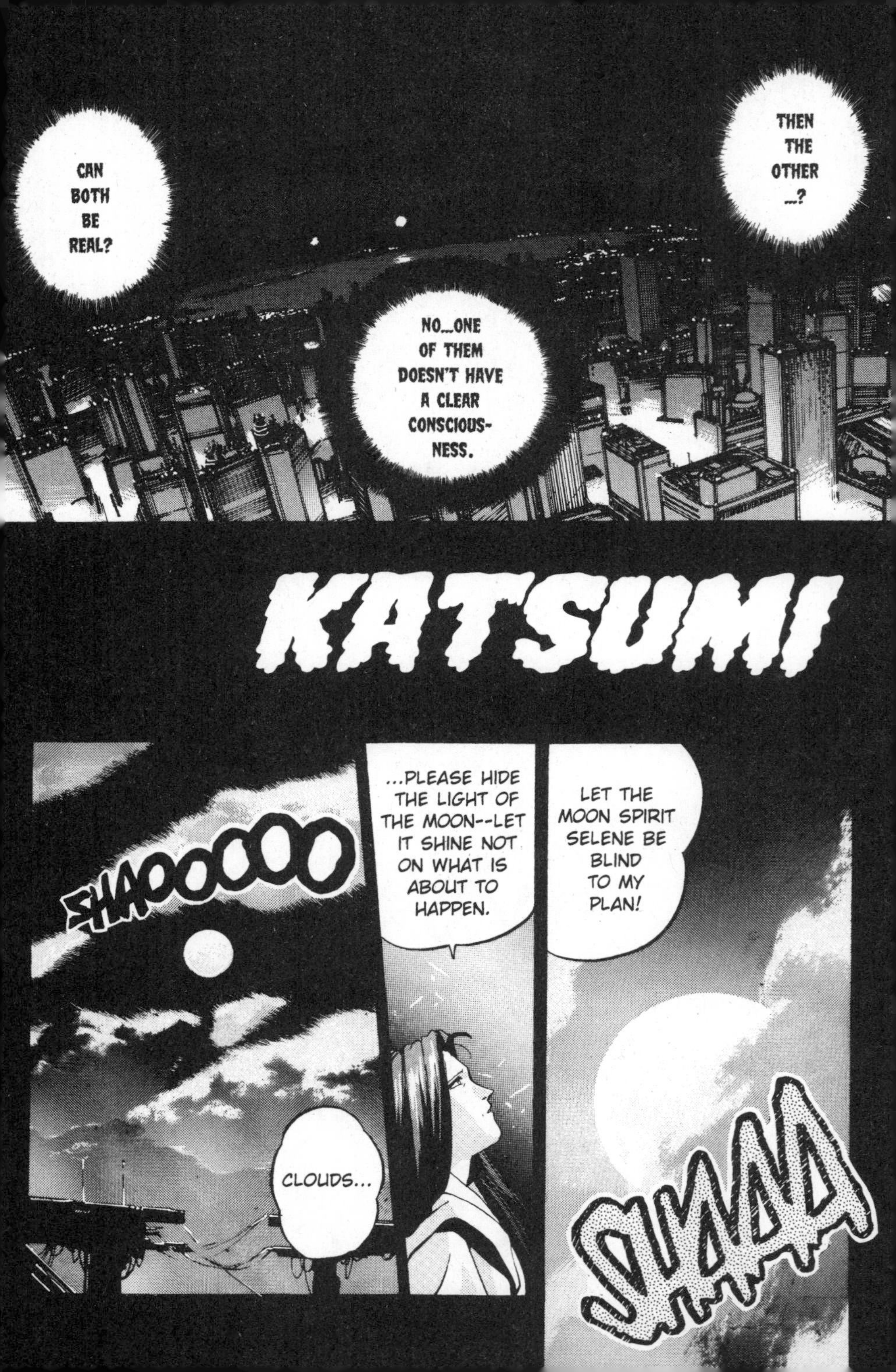
CAN BOTH BE REAL?
NO...ONE OF THEM DOESN'T HAVE A CLEAR CONSCIOUS-NESS.
THEN THE OTHER ...?
KATSUMI
SHAOOOOO
CLOUDS...
...PLEASE HIDE THE LIGHT OF THE MOON--LET IT SHINE NOT ON WHAT IS ABOUT TO HAPPEN.
LET THE MOON SPIRIT SELENE BE BLIND TO MY PLAN!
SHAAA

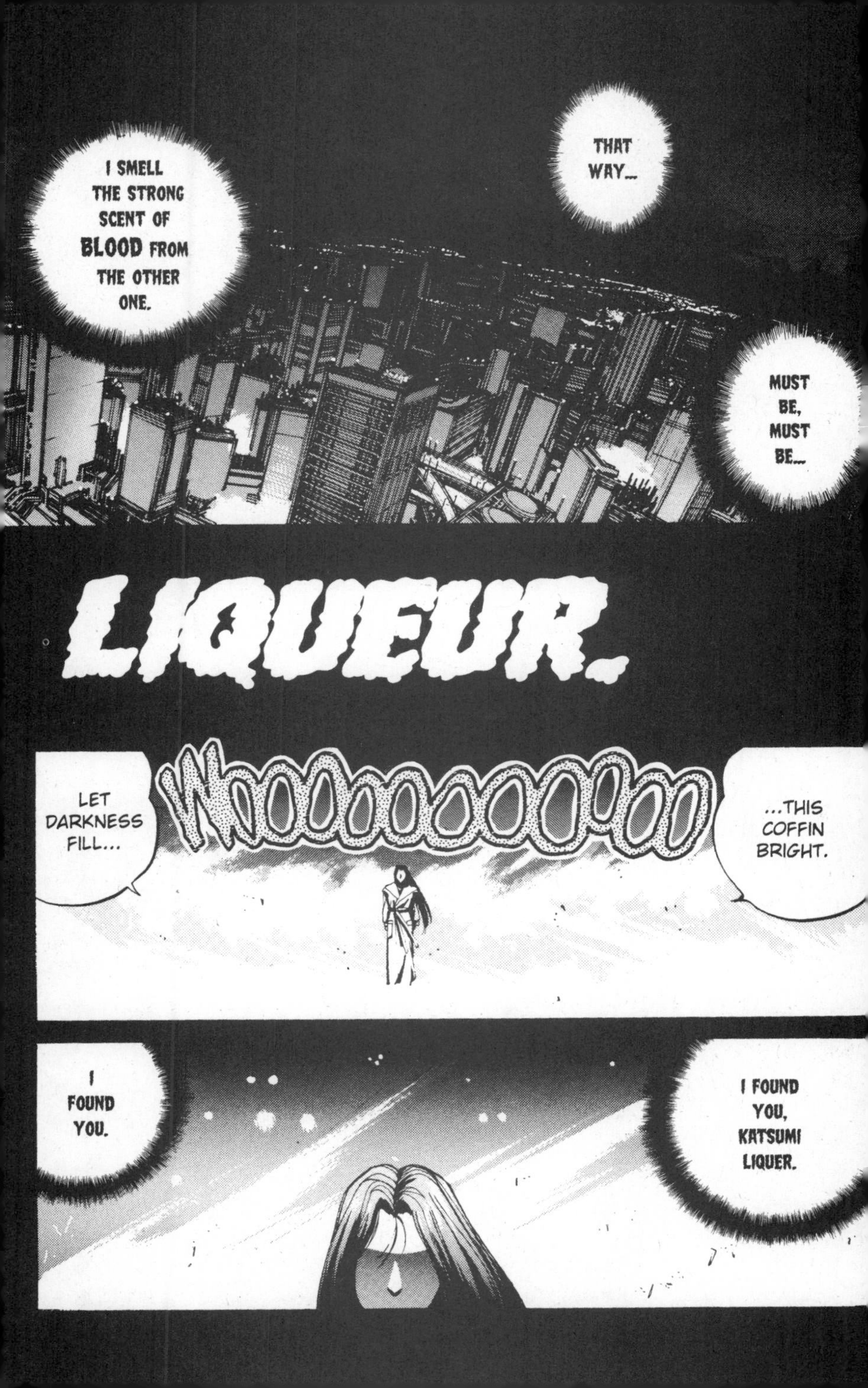
I SMELL THE STRONG SCENT OF BLOOD FROM THE OTHER ONE.
THAT WAY...
MUST BE, MUST BE...
LIQUEUR.
LET DARKNESS FILL...
WOOOOOOOOOOOOO
...THIS COFFIN BRIGHT.
I FOUND YOU.
I FOUND YOU, KATSUMI LIQUER.

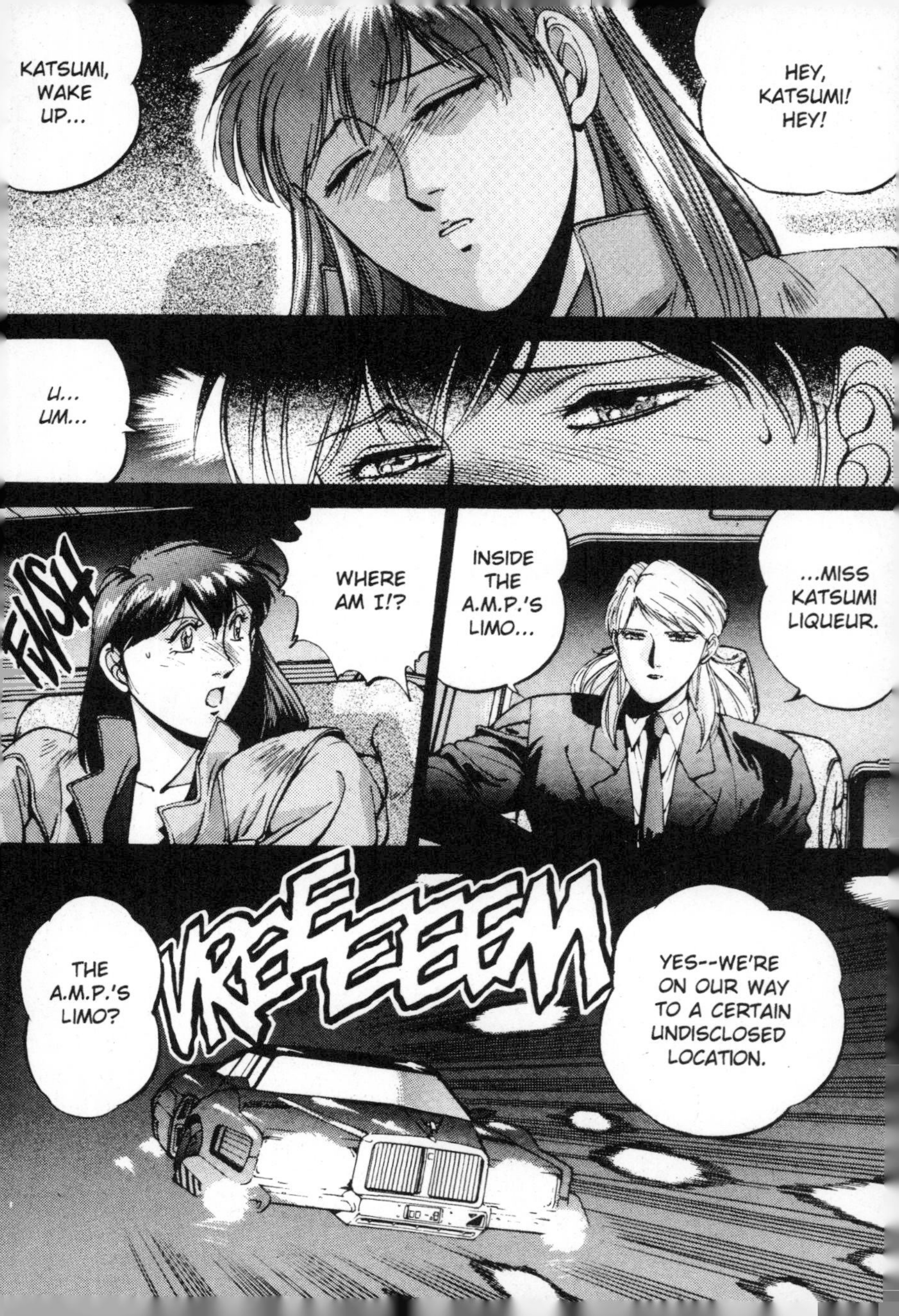
KATSUMI, WAKE UP...
HEY, KATSUMI! HEY!
U... UM...
FWSH
WHERE AM I!?
INSIDE THE A.M.P.'S LIMO...
...MISS KATSUMI LIQUEUR.
VREEEEEM
THE A.M.P.'S LIMO?
YES--WE'RE ON OUR WAY TO A CERTAIN UNDISCLOSED LOCATION.

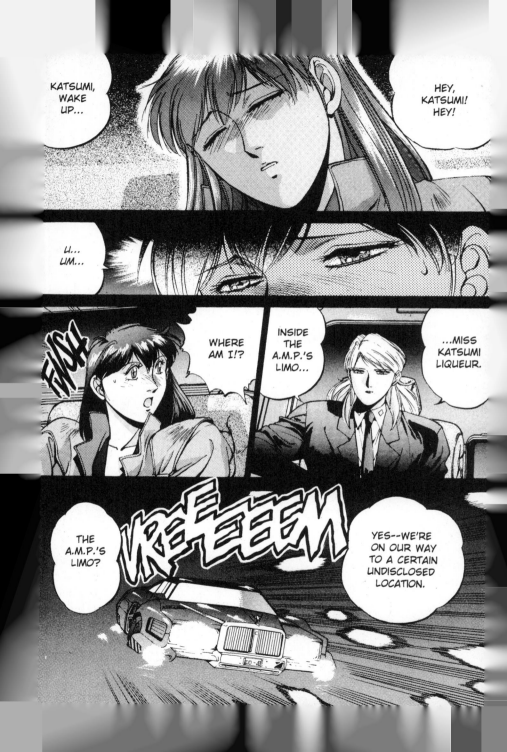

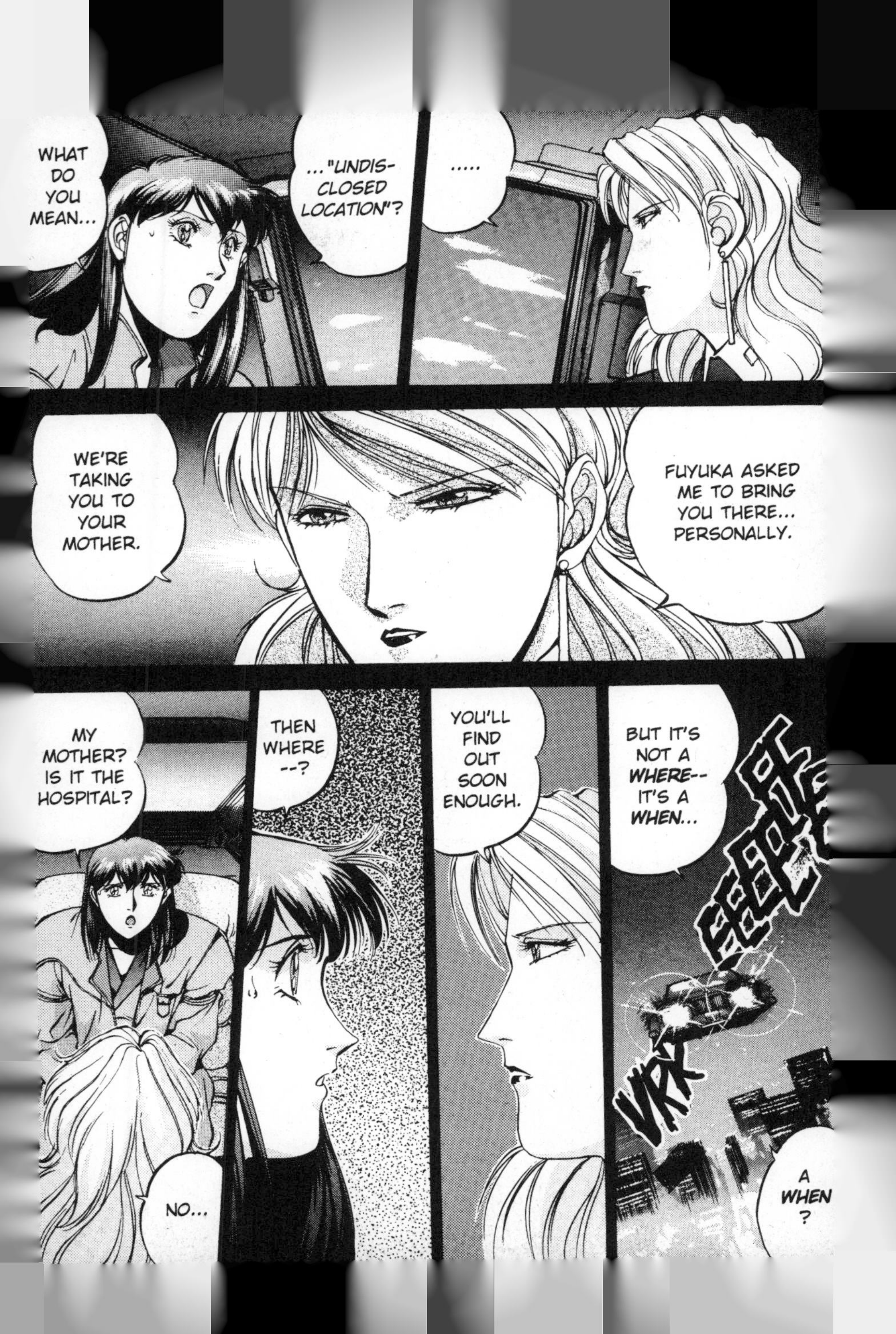
WHAT DO YOU MEAN...
..."UNDIS-CLOSED LOCATION"?
.....
WE'RE TAKING YOU TO YOUR MOTHER.
FUYUKA ASKED ME TO BRING YOU THERE... PERSONALLY.
MY MOTHER? IS IT THE HOSPITAL?
NO...
THEN WHERE --?
YOU'LL FIND OUT SOON ENOUGH.
BUT IT'S NOT A WHERE-- IT'S A WHEN...
EEEEEE
VRR
A WHEN?

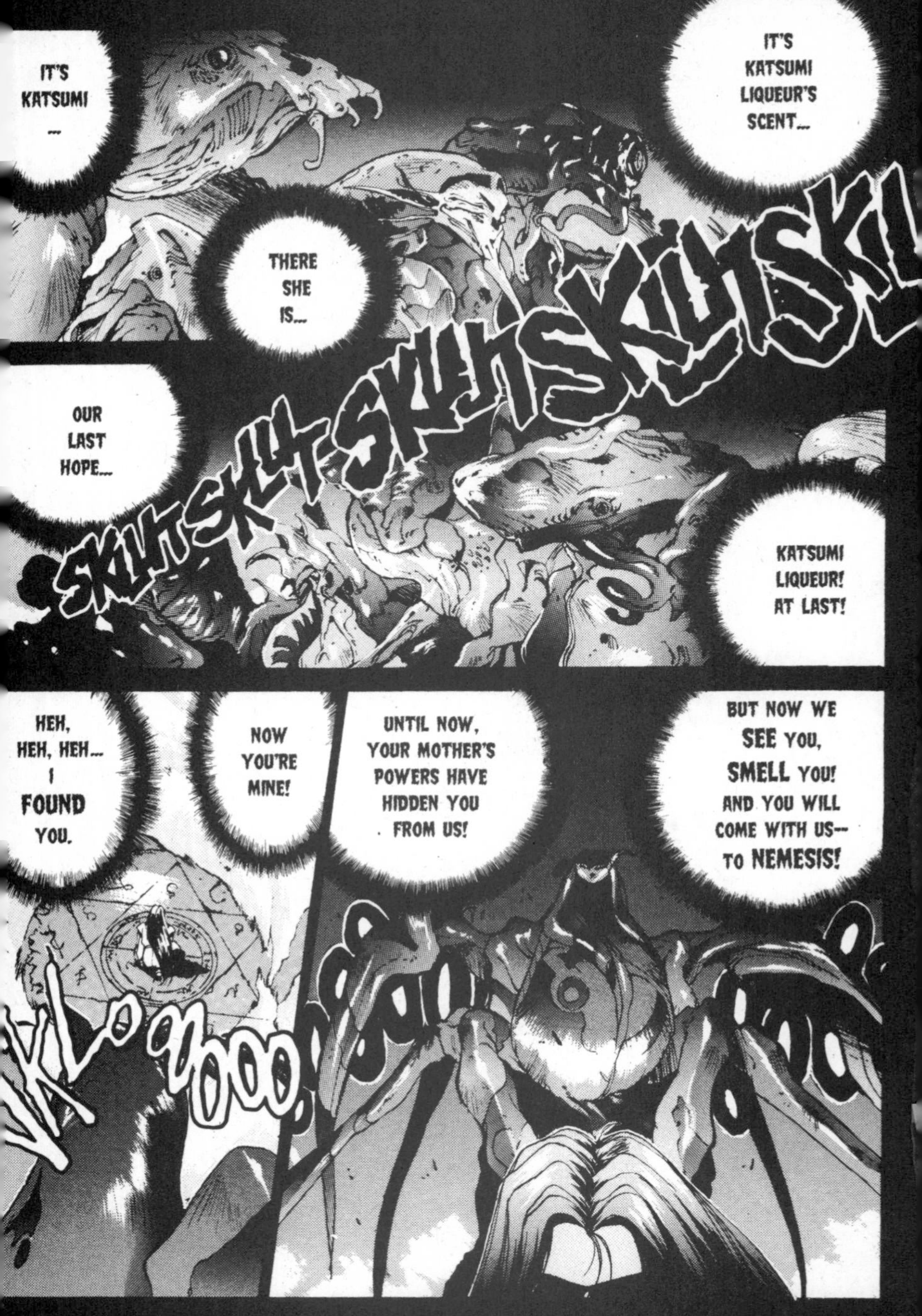
IT'S KATSUMI ...
THERE SHE IS...
IT'S KATSUMI LIQUEUR'S SCENT...
OUR LAST HOPE...
KATSUMI LIQUEUR! AT LAST!
HEH, HEH, HEH... I FOUND YOU.
NOW YOU'RE MINE!
UNTIL NOW, YOUR MOTHER'S POWERS HAVE HIDDEN YOU FROM US!
BUT NOW WE SEE YOU, SMELL YOU! AND YOU WILL COME WITH US-- TO NEMESIS!

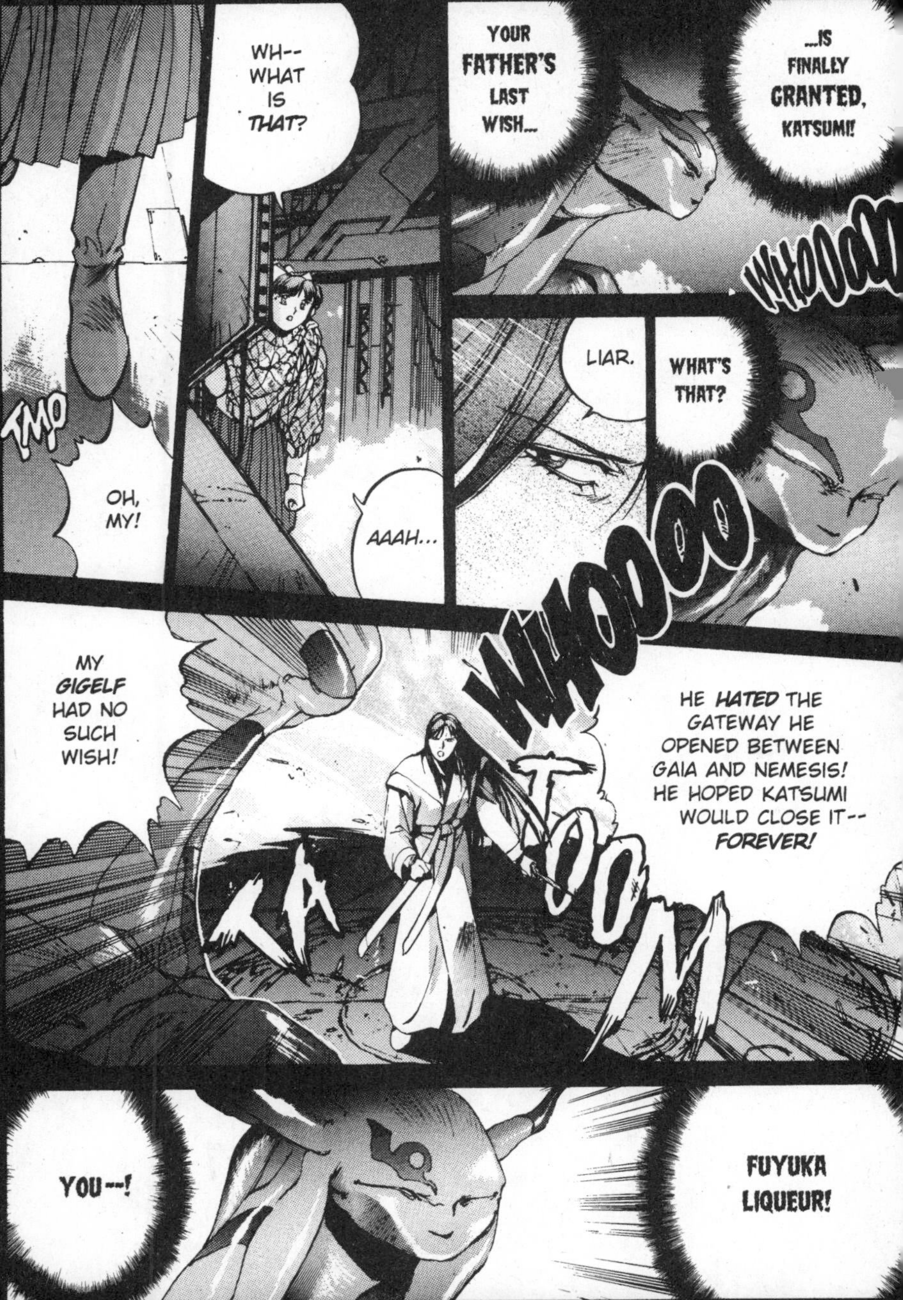
TMP
OH, MY!
WH-- WHAT IS THAT?
AAAH...
YOUR FATHER'S LAST WISH...
...IS FINALLY GRANTED, KATSUMI!
WHOOOO
LIAR.
WHAT'S THAT?
WHOOOO
MY GIGELF HAD NO SUCH WISH!
WHOOO
HE HATED THE GATEWAY HE OPENED BETWEEN GAIA AND NEMESIS! HE HOPED KATSUMI WOULD CLOSE IT-- FOREVER!
KA-TOOM
YOU--!
FUYUKA LIQUEUR!

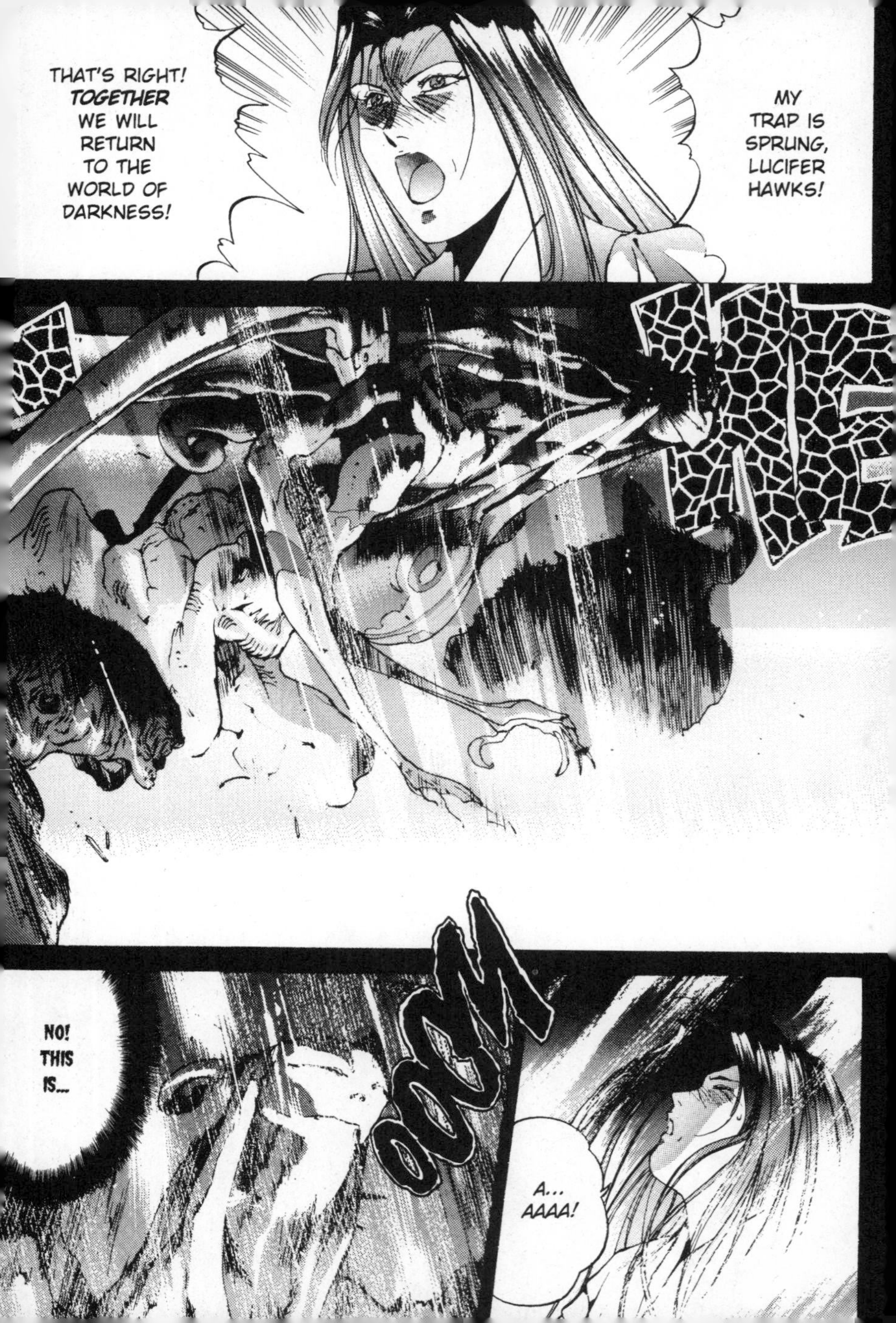
THAT'S RIGHT! TOGETHER WE WILL RETURN TO THE WORLD OF DARKNESS!
MY TRAP IS SPRUNG, LUCIFER HAWKS!
NO! THIS IS...
OOOM
A... AAAA!

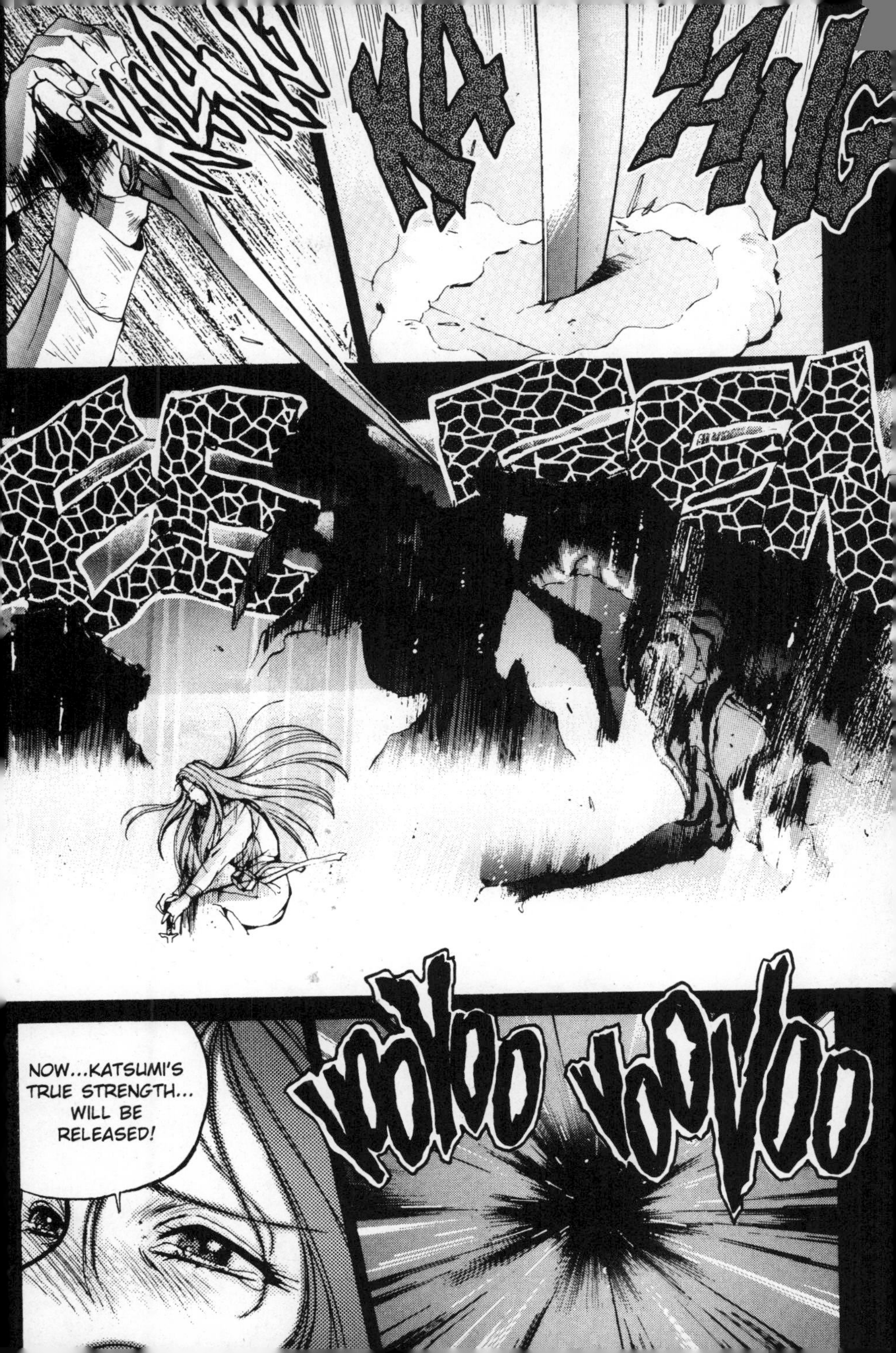
KA
ZANG
NOW...KATSUMI'S TRUE STRENGTH... WILL BE RELEASED!
VOOVOO VOOVOO

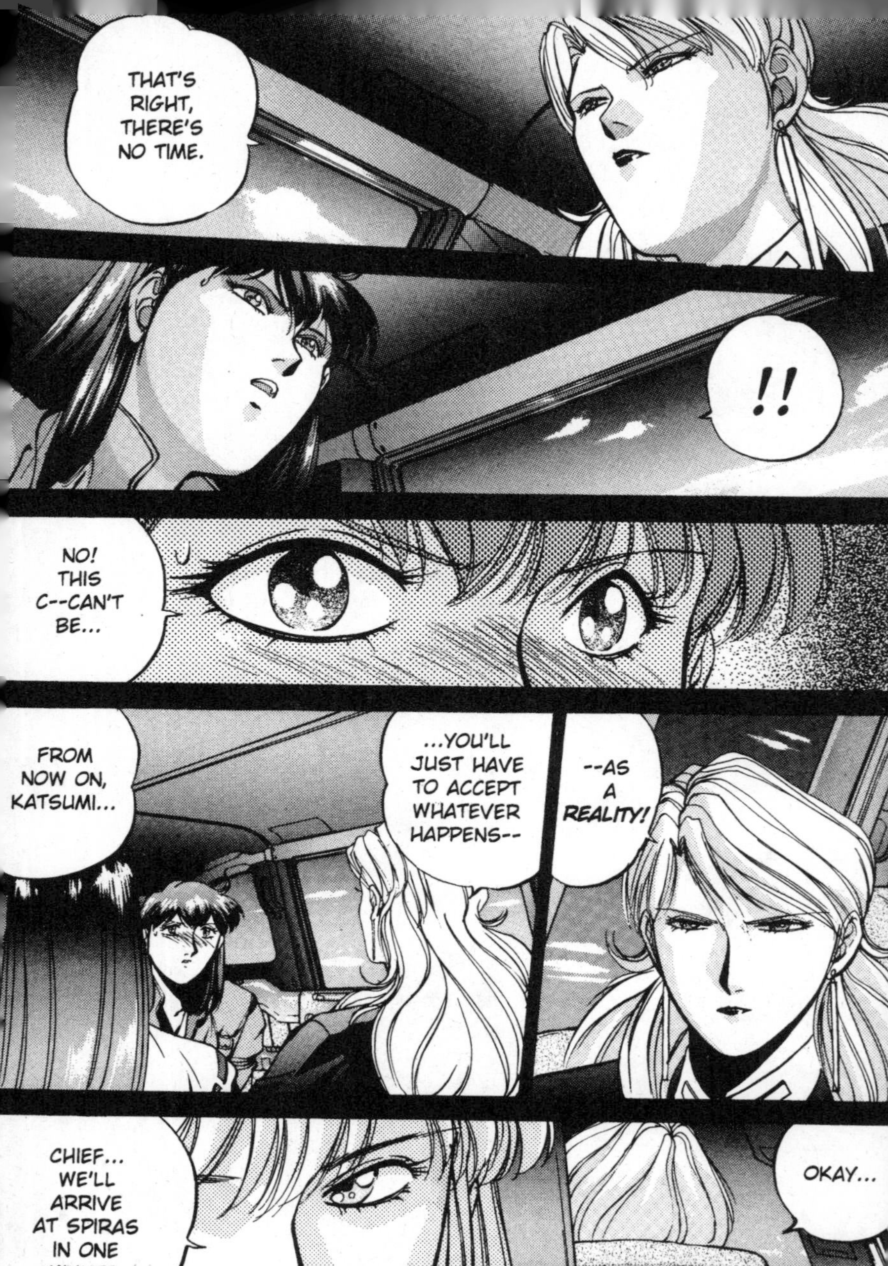
THAT'S RIGHT, THERE'S NO TIME.
!!
NO! THIS C--CAN'T BE...
FROM NOW ON, KATSUMI...
...YOU'LL JUST HAVE TO ACCEPT WHATEVER HAPPENS--
--AS A REALITY!
CHIEF... WE'LL ARRIVE AT SPIRAS IN ONE MINUTE.
OKAY...

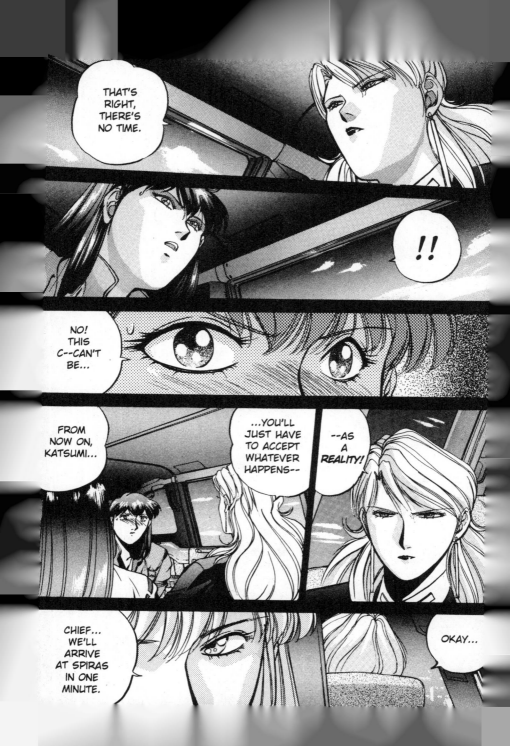

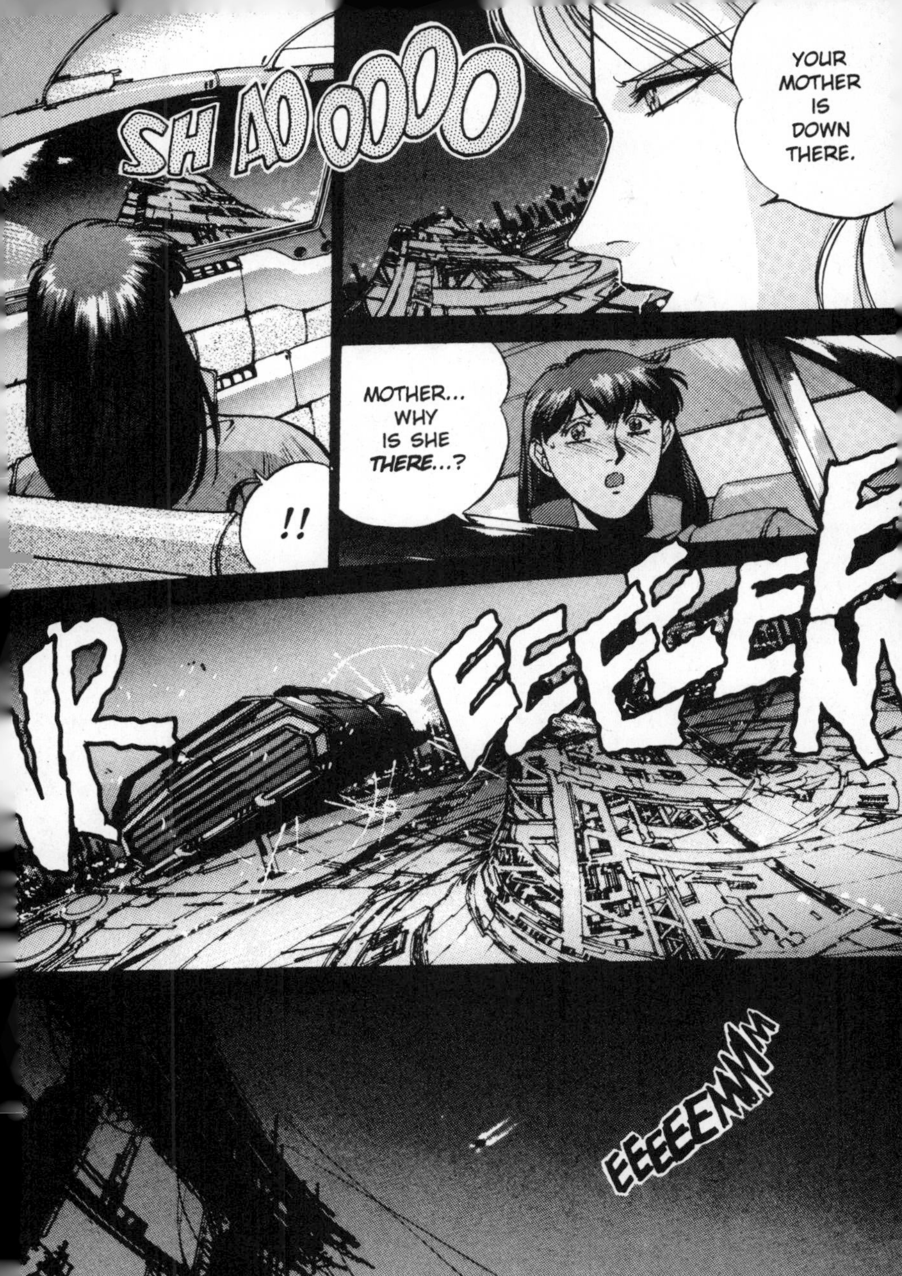
SH AO OOOO
!!
YOUR MOTHER IS DOWN THERE.
MOTHER... WHY IS SHE THERE...?
R EEEER
EEEEEMMM

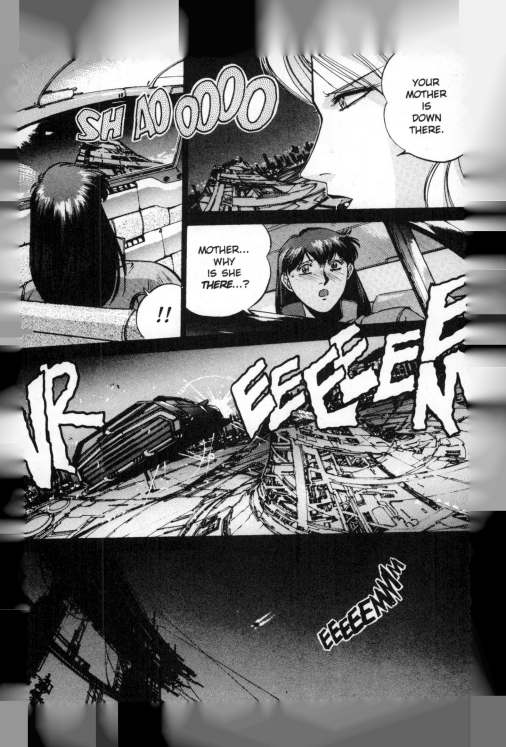

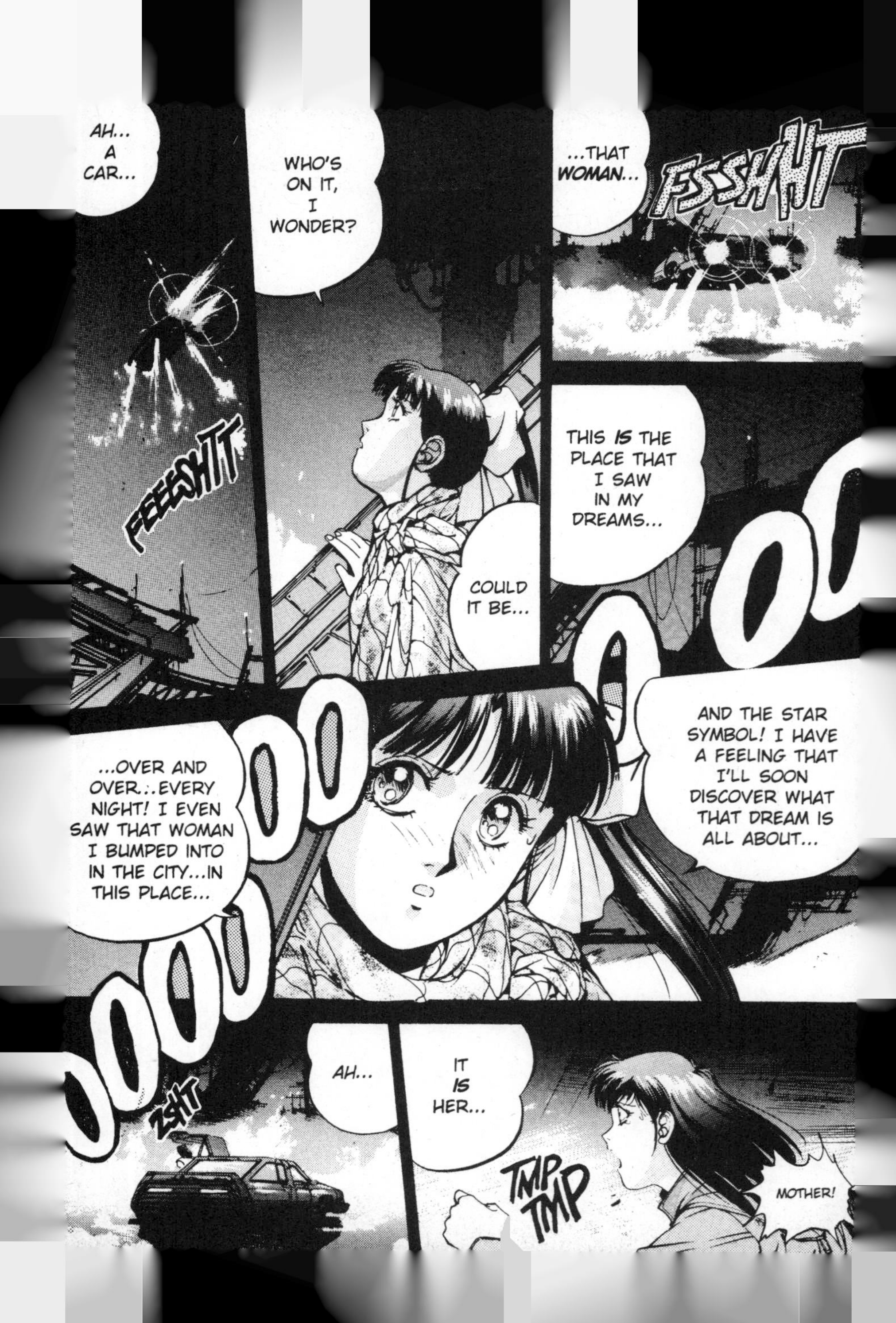
AH... A CAR...
FEEESHTT
WHO'S ON IT, I WONDER?
COULD IT BE...
...THAT WOMAN...
FSSSHHT
THIS IS THE PLACE THAT I SAW IN MY DREAMS...
...OVER AND OVER...EVERY NIGHT! I EVEN SAW THAT WOMAN I BUMPED INTO IN THE CITY...IN THIS PLACE...
AND THE STAR SYMBOL! I HAVE A FEELING THAT I'LL SOON DISCOVER WHAT THAT DREAM IS ALL ABOUT...
ZSHT
AH...
IT IS HER...
TMP TMP
MOTHER!

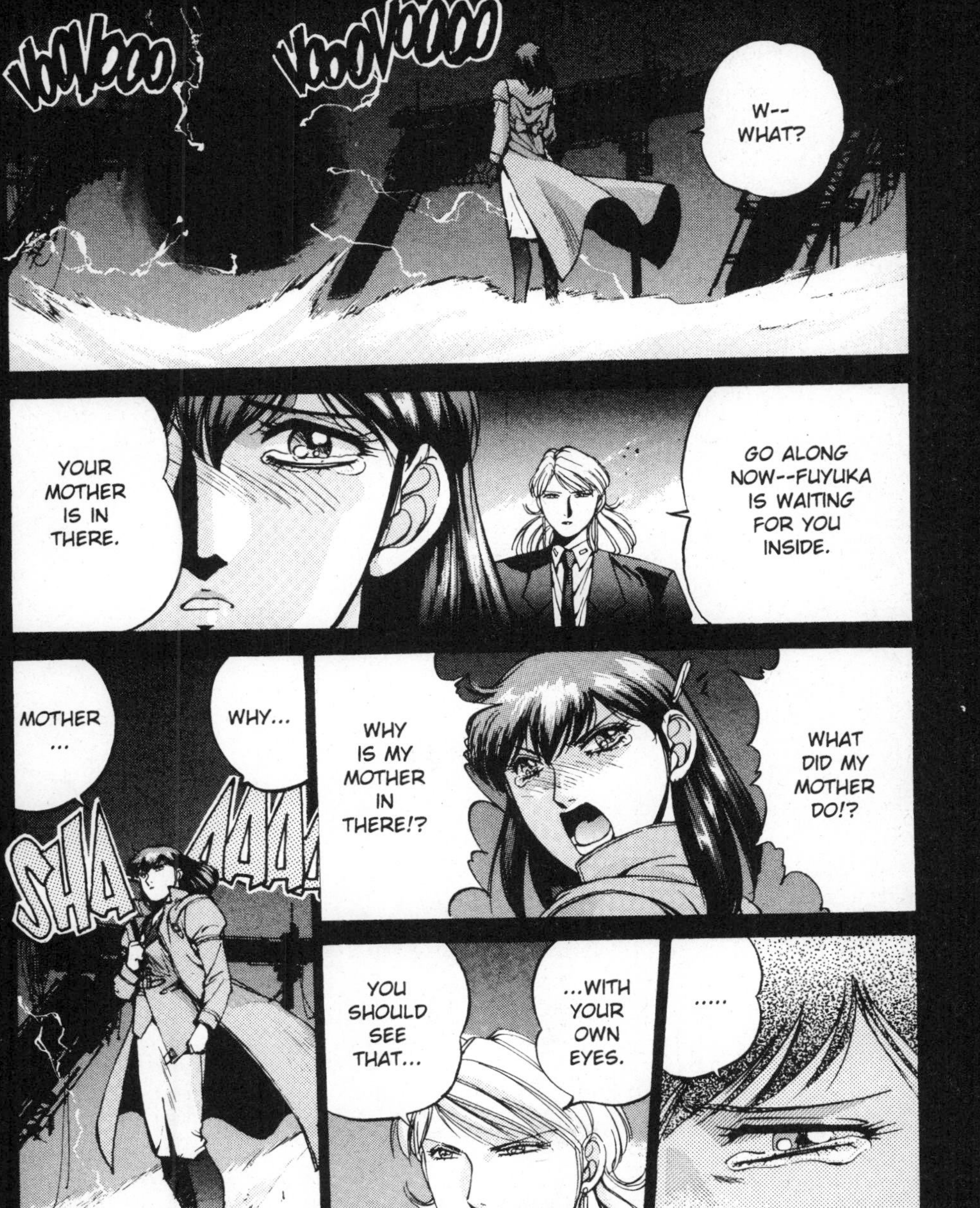
VOOVOOO
VOOOVOOOO
W-- WHAT?
YOUR MOTHER IS IN THERE.
GO ALONG NOW--FUYUKA IS WAITING FOR YOU INSIDE.
MOTHER ...
WHY...
SHAAAA
WHY IS MY MOTHER IN THERE!?
WHAT DID MY MOTHER DO!?
YOU SHOULD SEE THAT...
...WITH YOUR OWN EYES.
.....

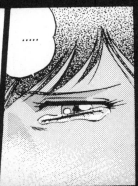

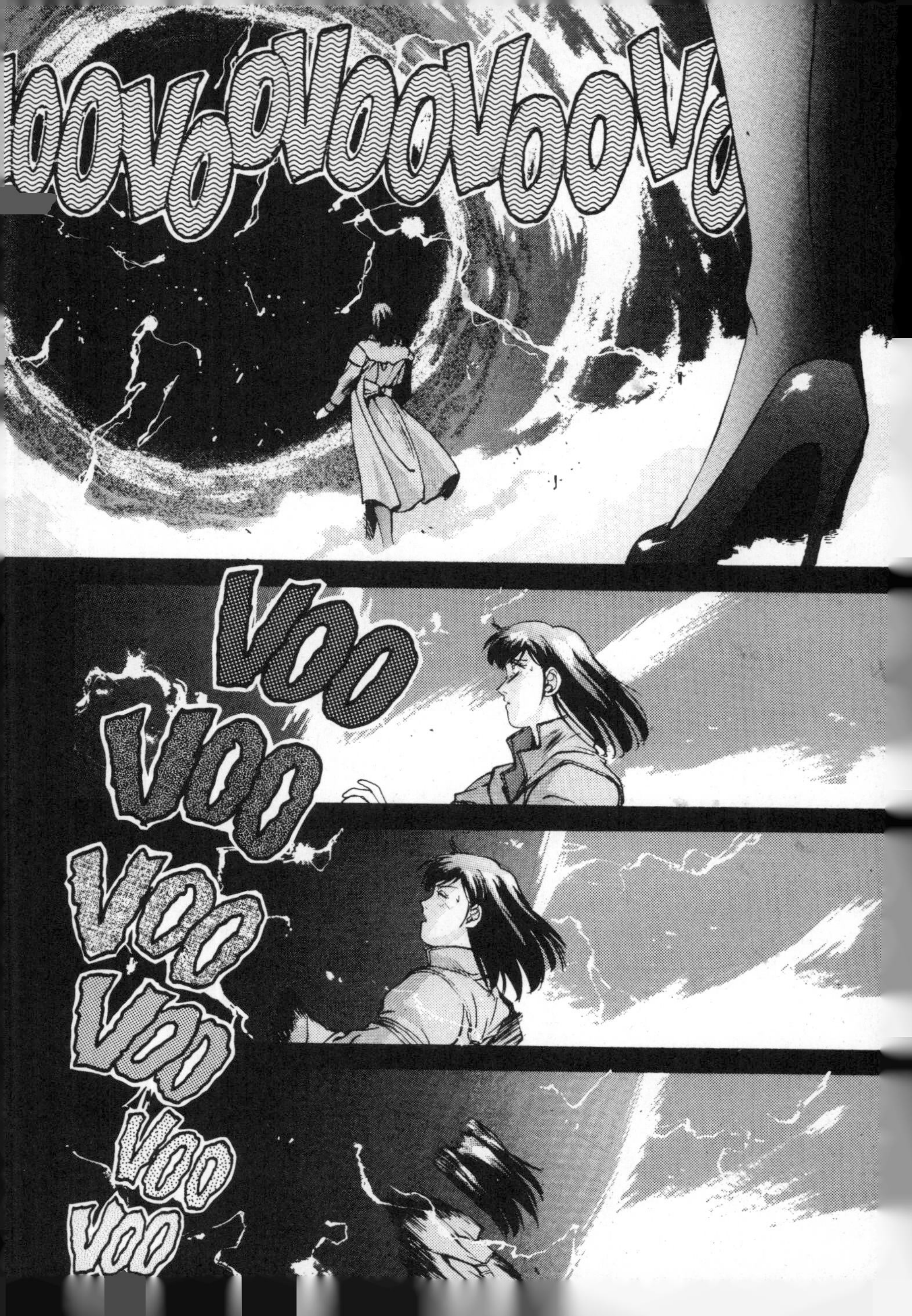
VOO
VOO
VOO
VOO
VOO
VOO

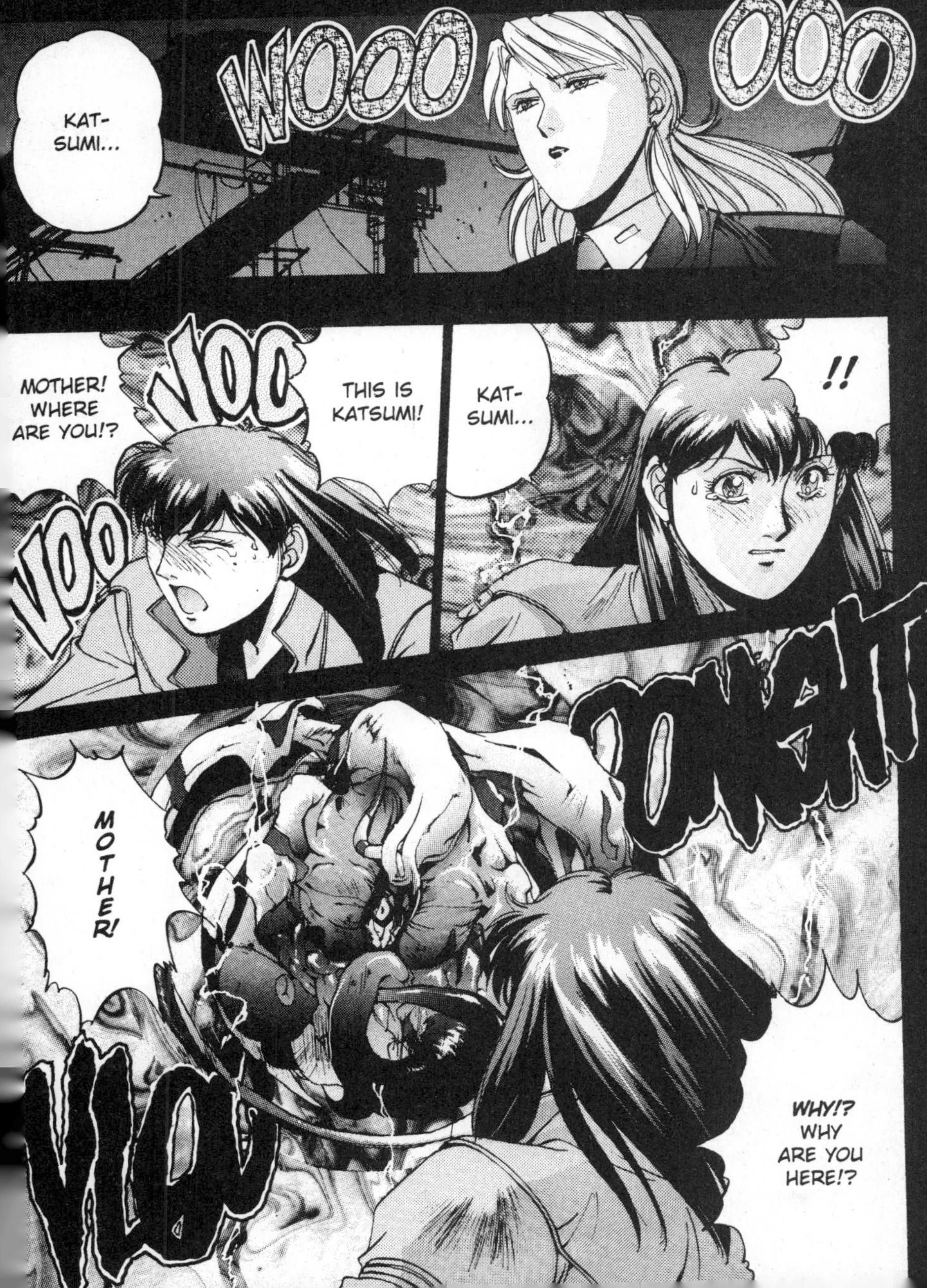
KAT-SUMI...
WOOO
OOO
MOTHER! WHERE ARE YOU!?
VOO
VOO
THIS IS KATSUMI!
KAT-SUMI...
!!
MOTHER!
WHY!? WHY ARE YOU HERE!?

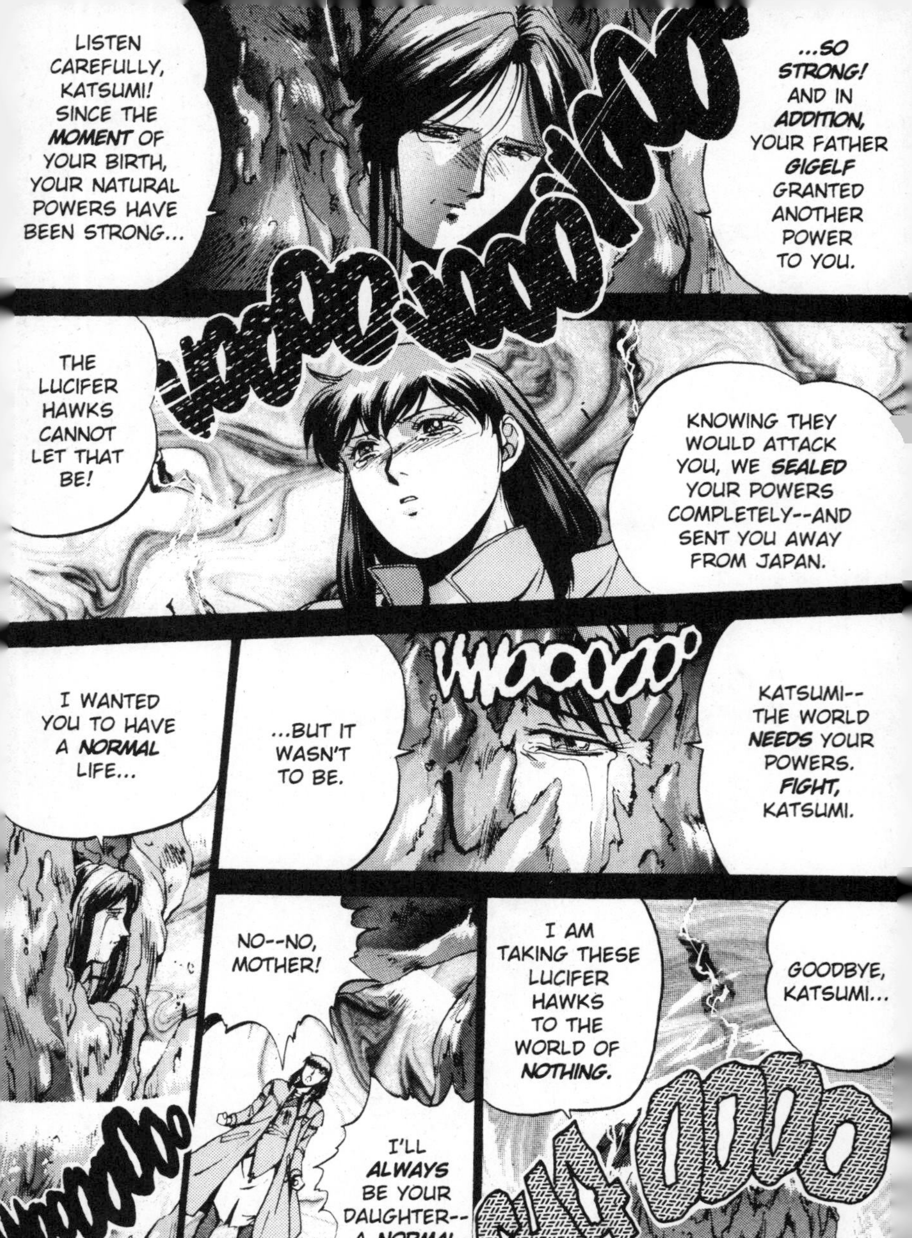
LISTEN CAREFULLY, KATSUMI! SINCE THE MOMENT OF YOUR BIRTH, YOUR NATURAL POWERS HAVE BEEN STRONG...
...SO STRONG! AND IN ADDITION, YOUR FATHER GIGELF GRANTED ANOTHER POWER TO YOU.
THE LUCIFER HAWKS CANNOT LET THAT BE!
KNOWING THEY WOULD ATTACK YOU, WE SEALED YOUR POWERS COMPLETELY--AND SENT YOU AWAY FROM JAPAN.
I WANTED YOU TO HAVE A NORMAL LIFE...
...BUT IT WASN'T TO BE.
KATSUMI-- THE WORLD NEEDS YOUR POWERS. FIGHT, KATSUMI.
NO--NO, MOTHER!
I'LL ALWAYS BE YOUR DAUGHTER-- A NORMAL GIRL!
I AM TAKING THESE LUCIFER HAWKS TO THE WORLD OF NOTHING.
GOODBYE, KATSUMI...

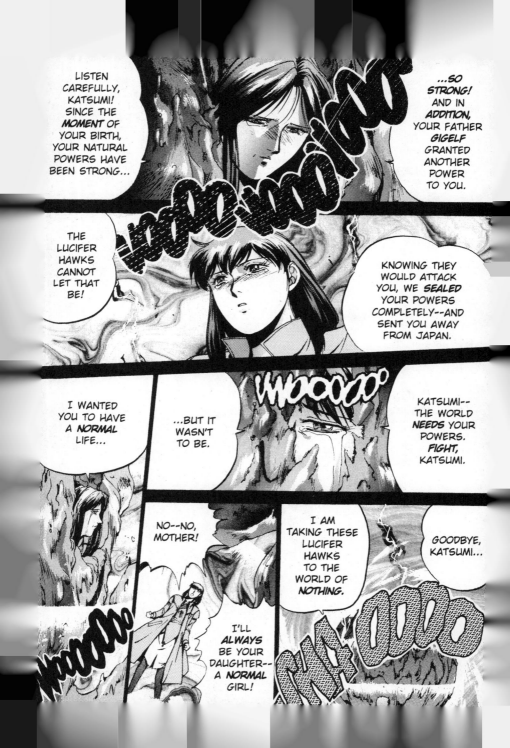

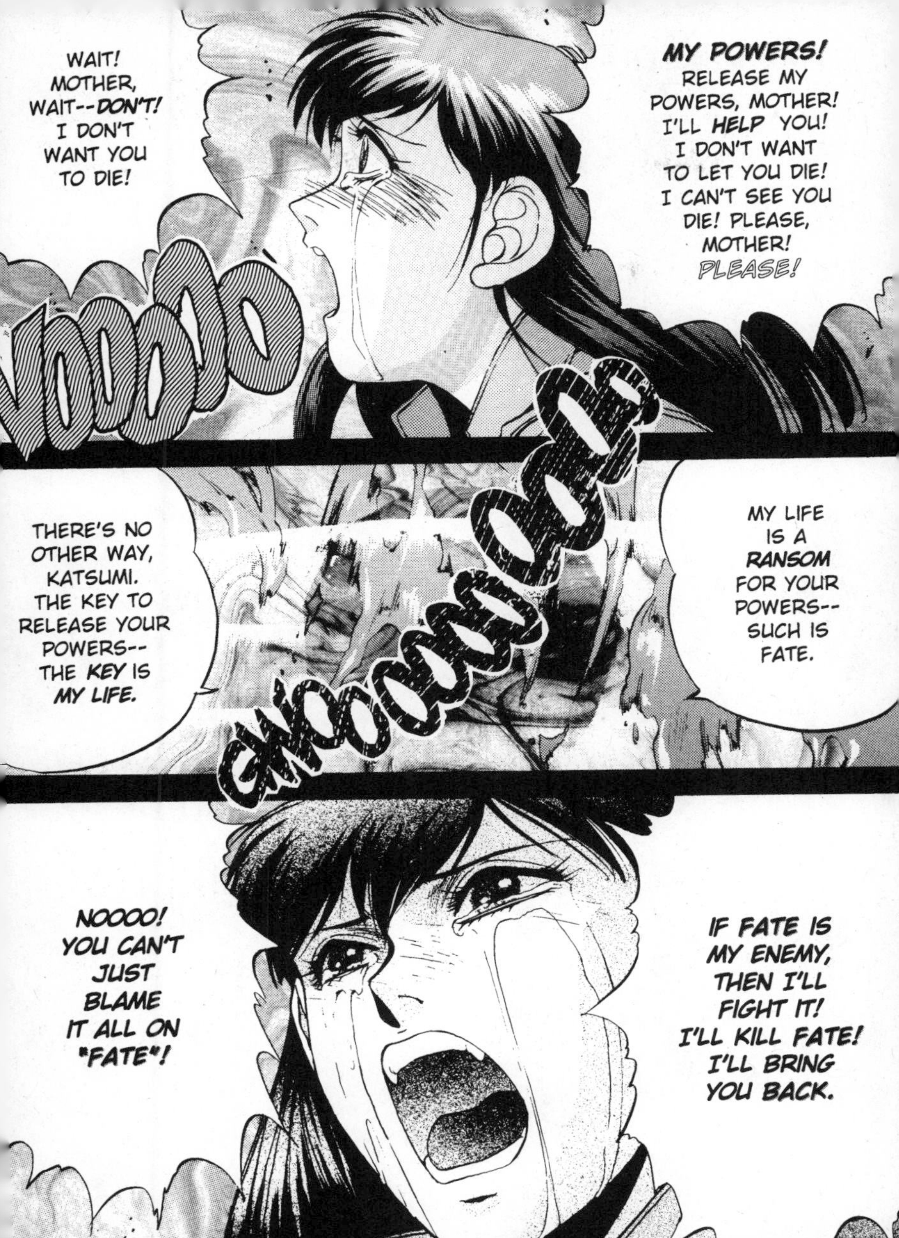
WAIT! MOTHER, WAIT--DON'T! I DON'T WANT YOU TO DIE!
MY POWERS! RELEASE MY POWERS, MOTHER! I'LL HELP YOU! I DON'T WANT TO LET YOU DIE! I CAN'T SEE YOU DIE! PLEASE, MOTHER! PLEASE!
VOOOOO
THERE'S NO OTHER WAY, KATSUMI. THE KEY TO RELEASE YOUR POWERS-- THE KEY IS MY LIFE.
MY LIFE IS A RANSOM FOR YOUR POWERS-- SUCH IS FATE.
NOOOO! YOU CAN'T JUST BLAME IT ALL ON "FATE"!
IF FATE IS MY ENEMY, THEN I'LL FIGHT IT! I'LL KILL FATE! I'LL BRING YOU BACK.

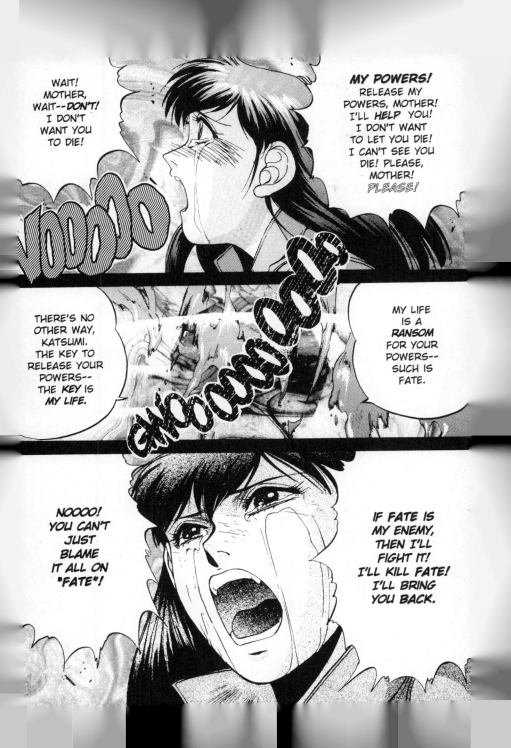

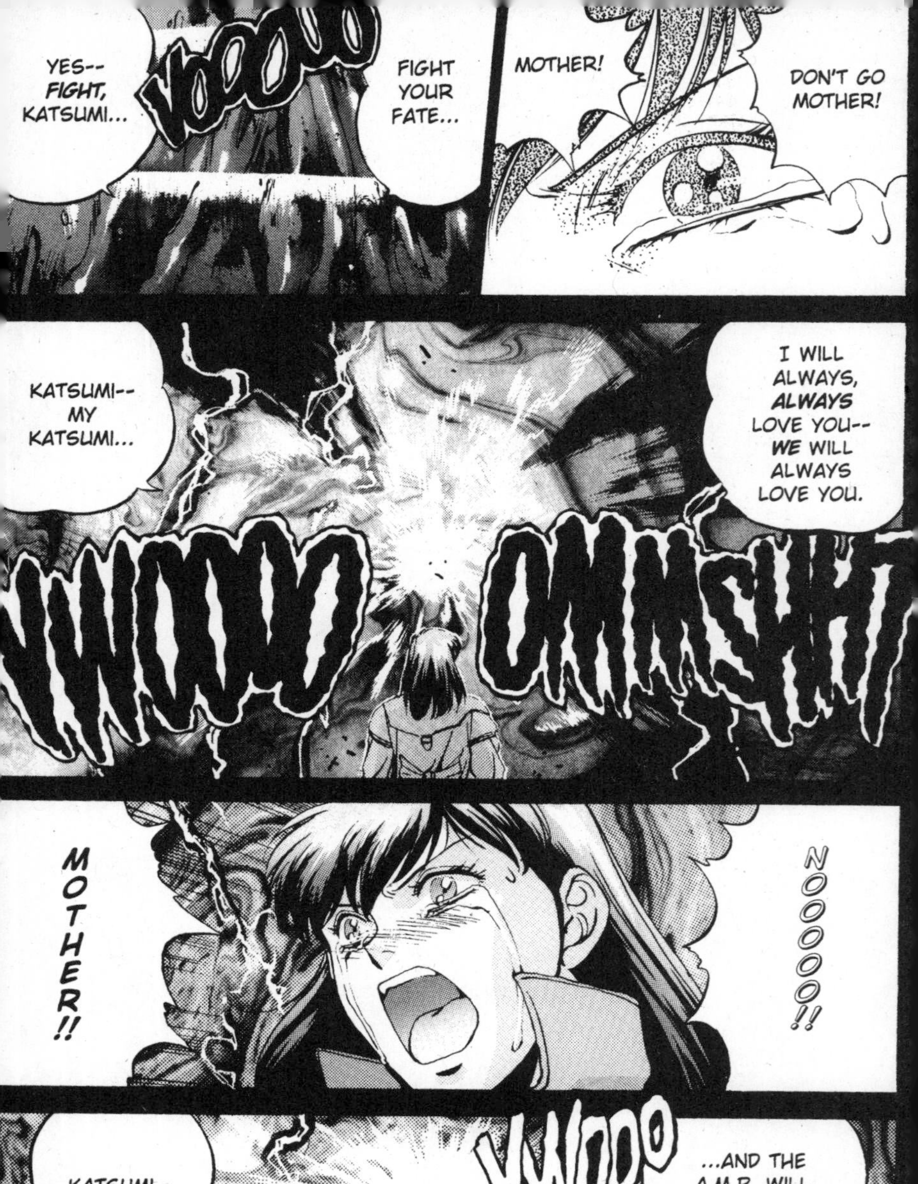
YES-- *FIGHT,* KATSUMI...
FIGHT YOUR FATE...
MOTHER!
DON'T GO MOTHER!
KATSUMI-- MY KATSUMI...
I WILL ALWAYS, **ALWAYS** LOVE YOU-- **WE** WILL ALWAYS LOVE YOU.
MOTHER!!
NOOOOOO!!
KATSUMI-- CHIEF RALLY...
VWOOO
...AND THE A.M.P. WILL TAKE CARE OF YOU... GOODBYE...

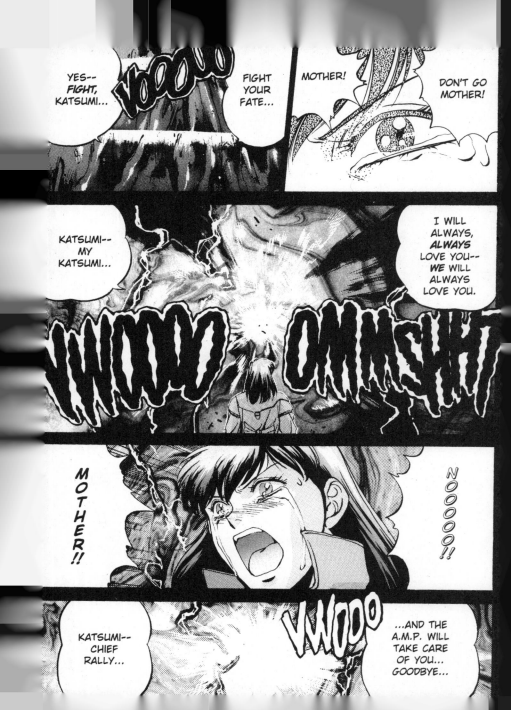

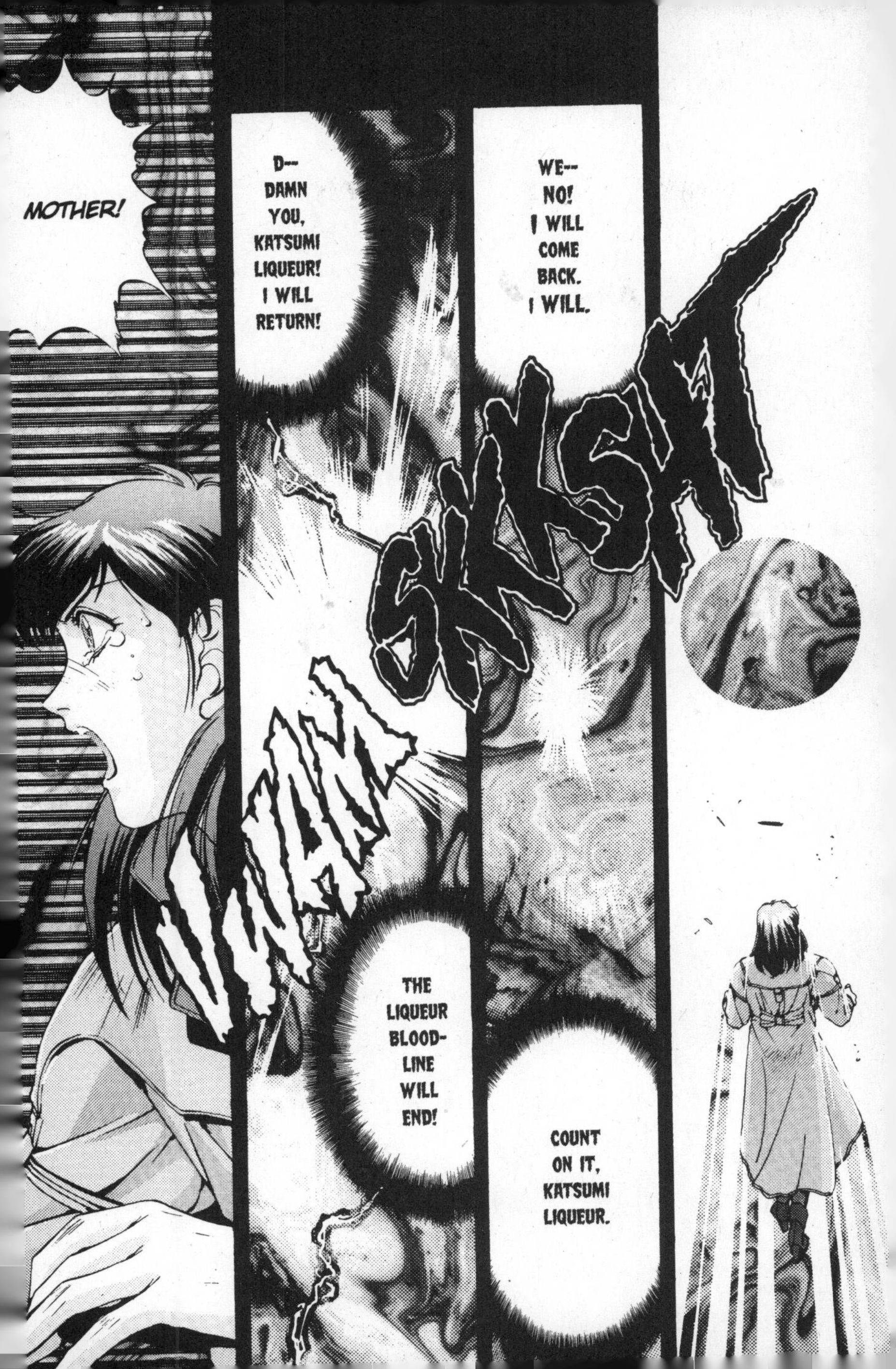
MOTHER!
D-- DAMN YOU, KATSUMI LIQUEUR! I WILL RETURN!
THE LIQUEUR BLOOD-LINE WILL END!
WE-- NO! I WILL COME BACK. I WILL.
SKKSHT
COUNT ON IT, KATSUMI LIQUEUR.

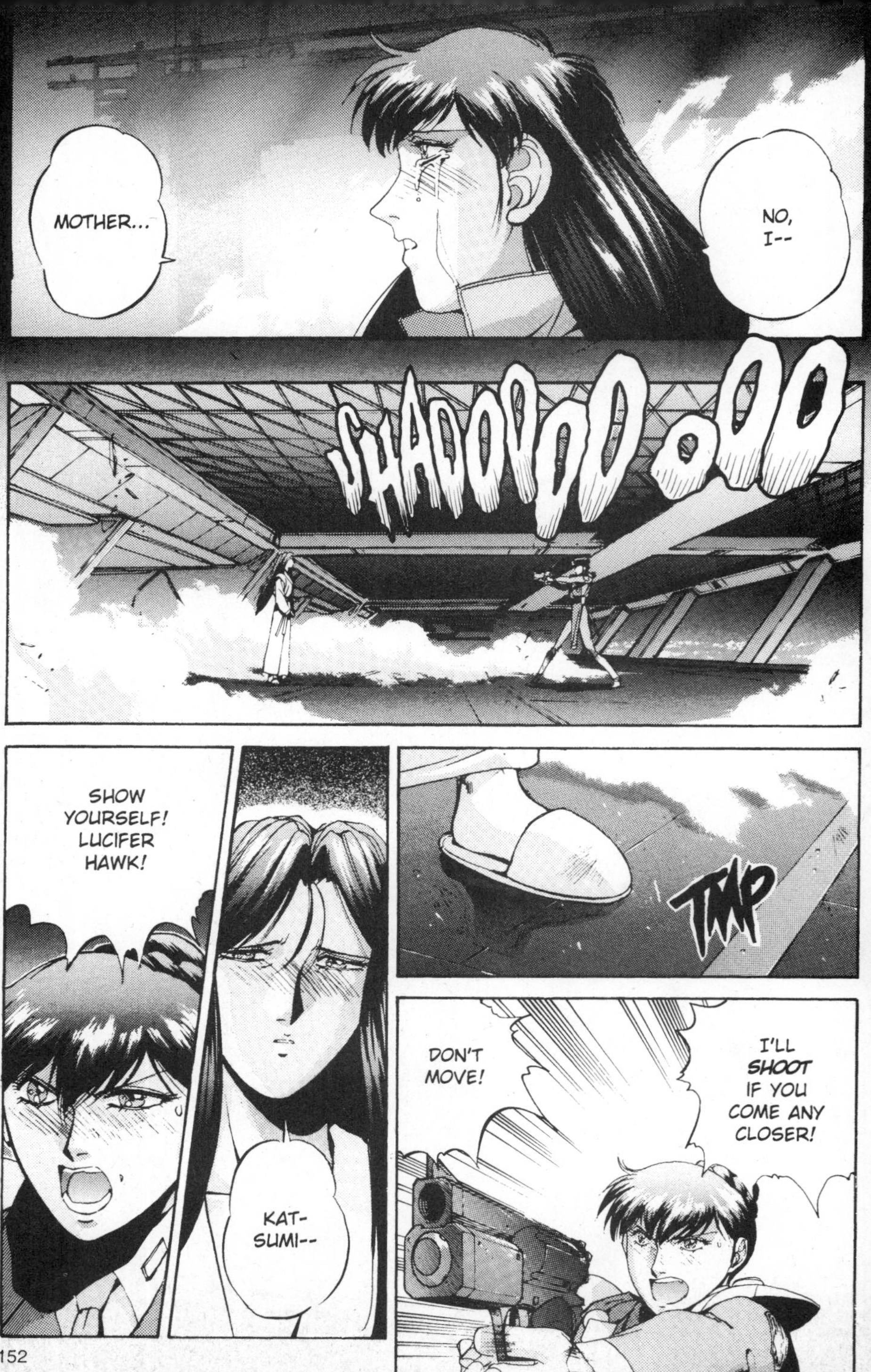
MOTHER...
NO, I--
SHADOOOOO OOO
SHOW YOURSELF! LUCIFER HAWK!
KAT-SUMI--
TAP
DON'T MOVE!
I'LL SHOOT IF YOU COME ANY CLOSER!

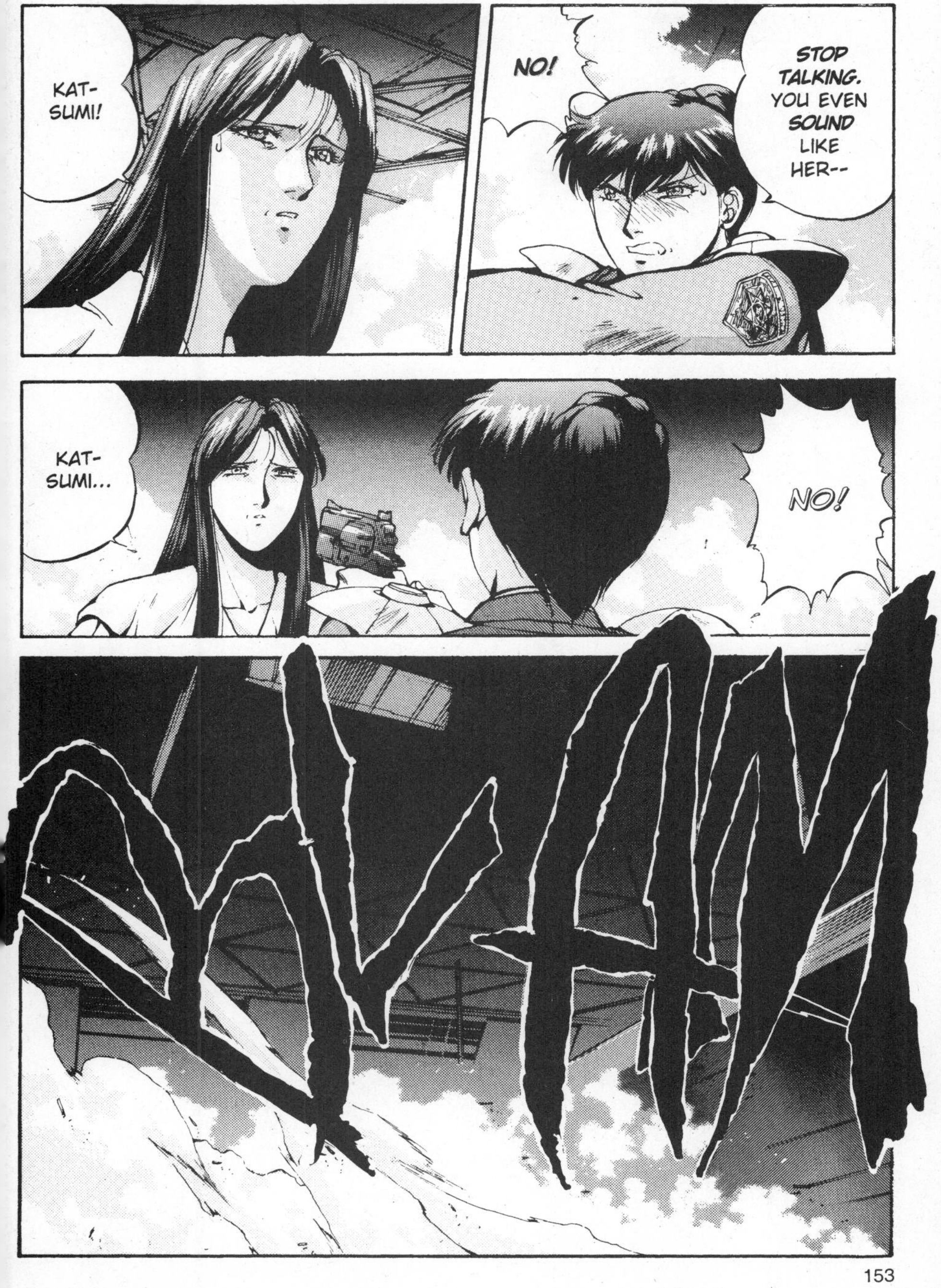
KAT-SUMI!
NO!
STOP TALKING. YOU EVEN SOUND LIKE HER--
KAT-SUMI...
NO!

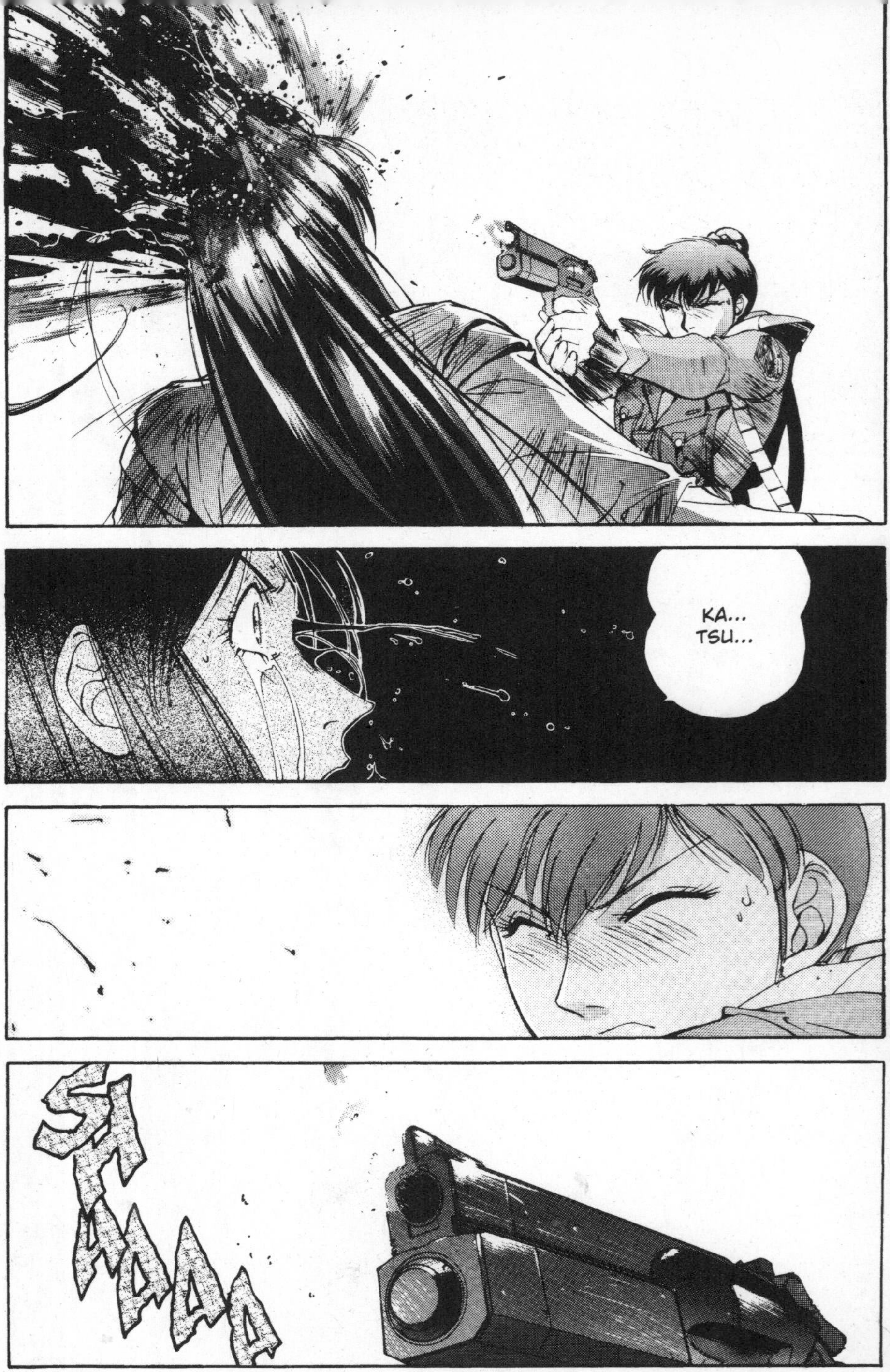
KA...
TSU...
SHAAAA

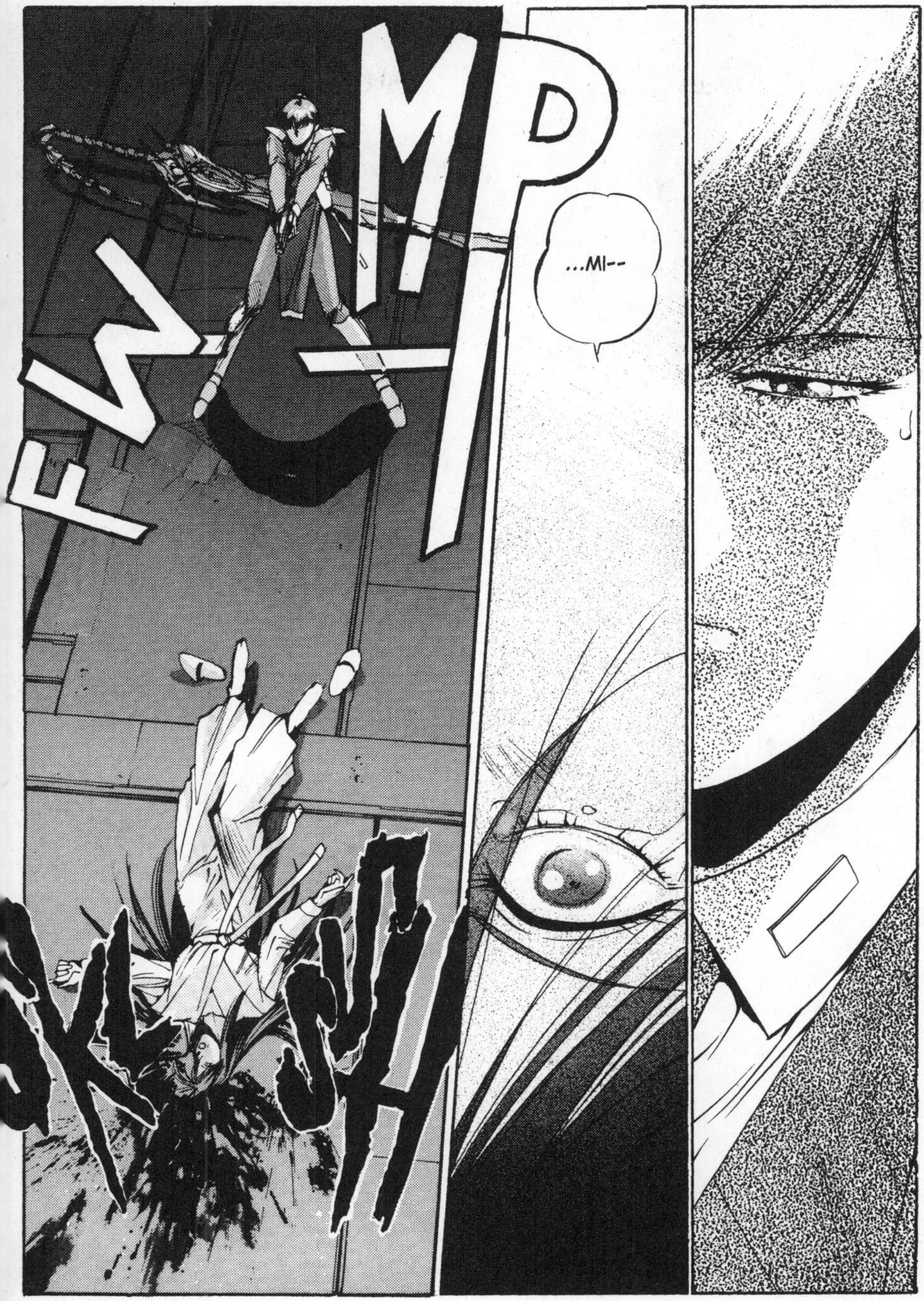
FWUMP
...MI--
SKLUCH

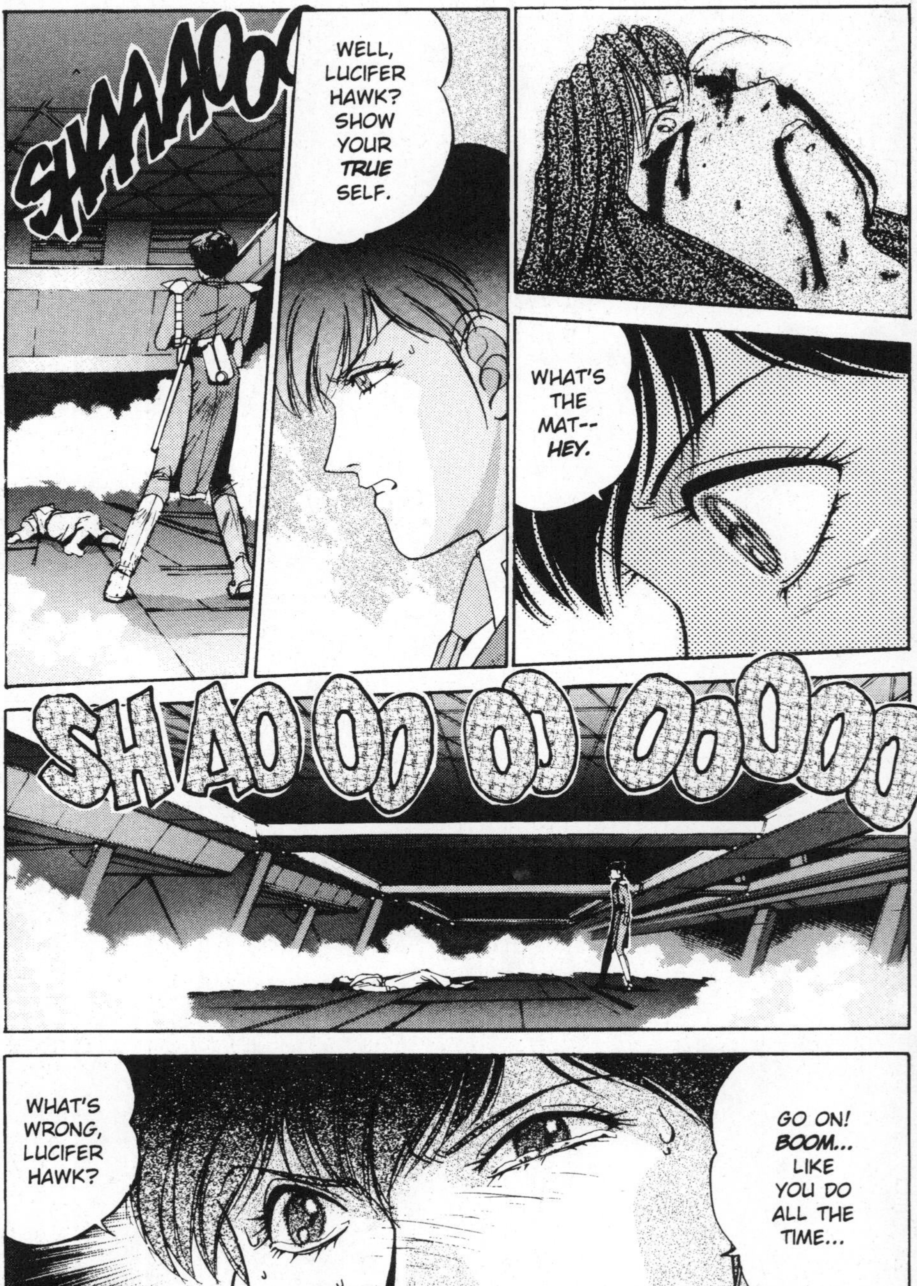
SHAAAOOO
WELL, LUCIFER HAWK? SHOW YOUR TRUE SELF.
WHAT'S THE MAT-- HEY.
SHAOOOOOOOOOOO
WHAT'S WRONG, LUCIFER HAWK?
GO ON! BOOM... LIKE YOU DO ALL THE TIME...

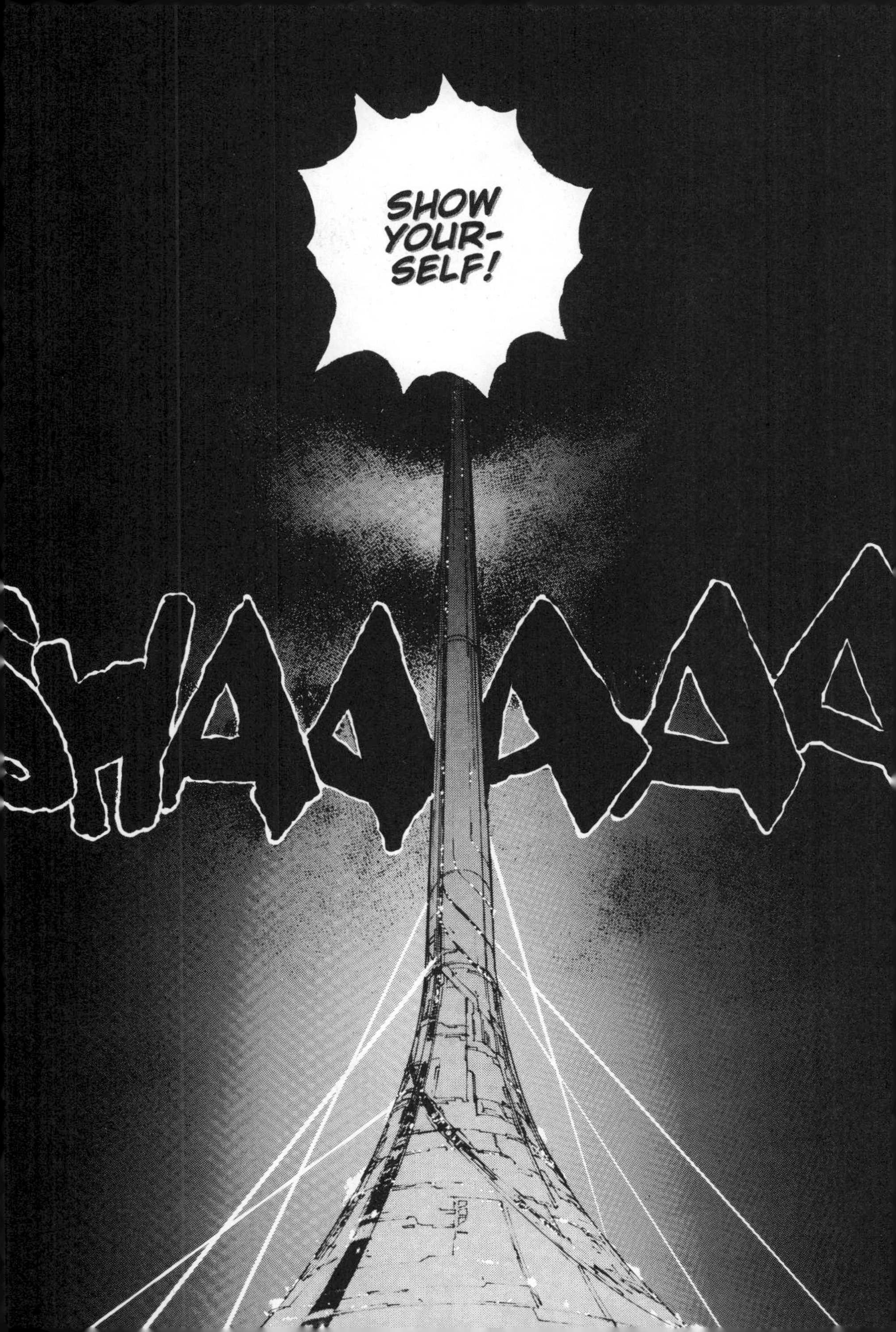
SHOW YOUR-SELF!
SHAAAAA

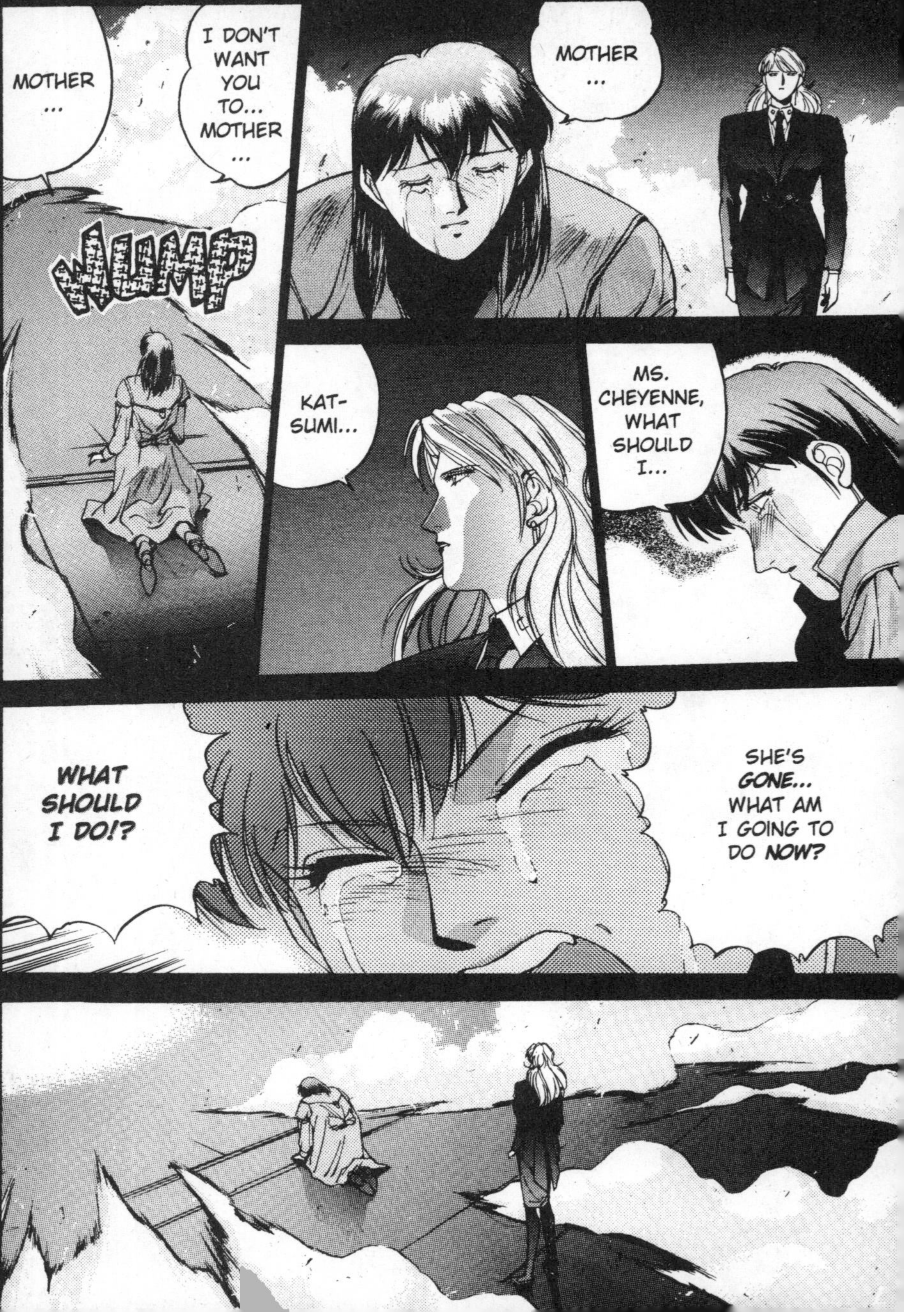
MOTHER ...
I DON'T WANT YOU TO... MOTHER ...
WUMP
MOTHER ...
KAT-SUMI...
MS. CHEYENNE, WHAT SHOULD I...
WHAT SHOULD I DO!?
SHE'S GONE... WHAT AM I GOING TO DO NOW?

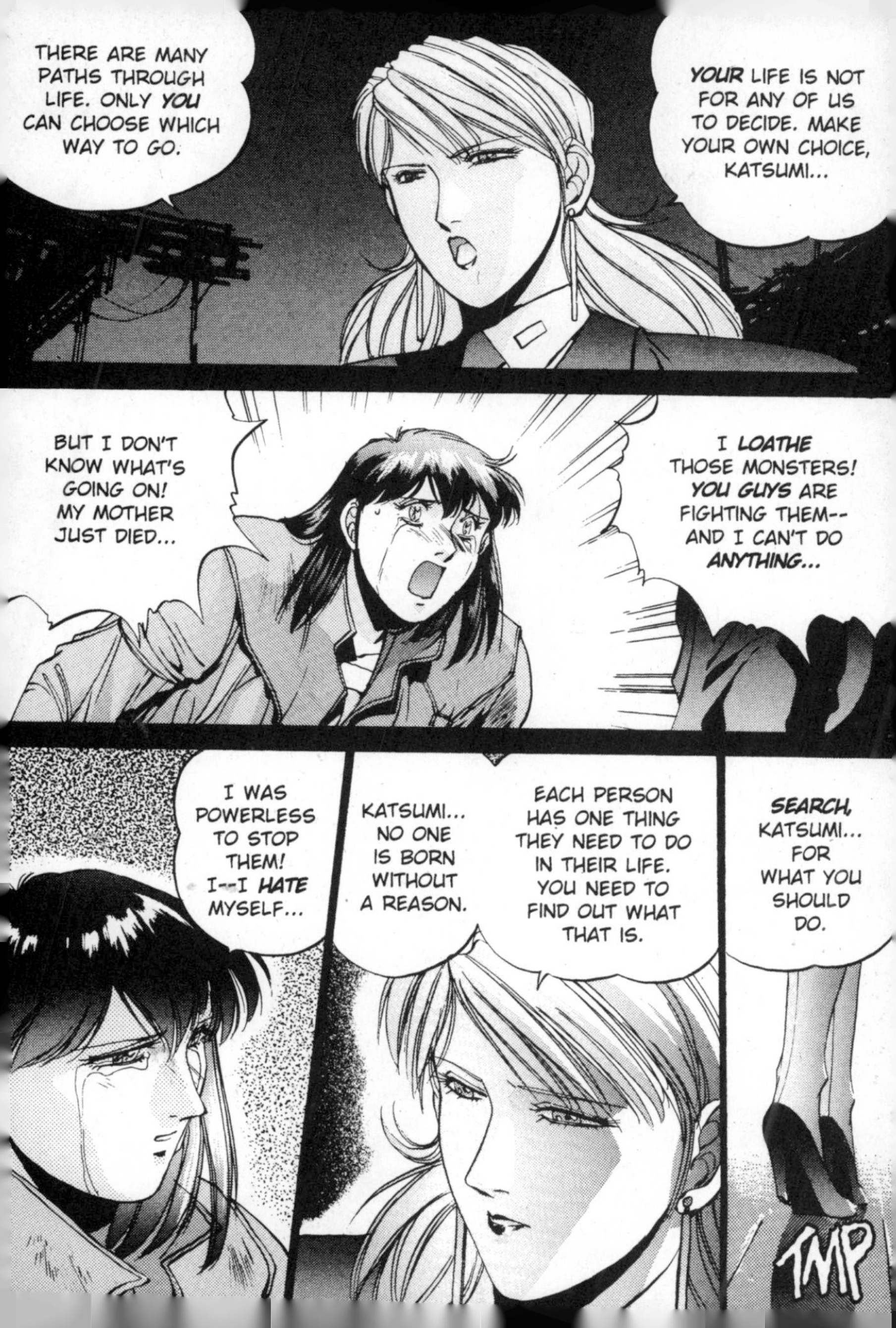
THERE ARE MANY PATHS THROUGH LIFE. ONLY YOU CAN CHOOSE WHICH WAY TO GO.
YOUR LIFE IS NOT FOR ANY OF US TO DECIDE. MAKE YOUR OWN CHOICE, KATSUMI...
BUT I DON'T KNOW WHAT'S GOING ON! MY MOTHER JUST DIED...
I LOATHE THOSE MONSTERS! YOU GUYS ARE FIGHTING THEM-- AND I CAN'T DO ANYTHING...
I WAS POWERLESS TO STOP THEM! I--I HATE MYSELF...
KATSUMI... NO ONE IS BORN WITHOUT A REASON.
EACH PERSON HAS ONE THING THEY NEED TO DO IN THEIR LIFE. YOU NEED TO FIND OUT WHAT THAT IS.
SEARCH, KATSUMI... FOR WHAT YOU SHOULD DO.
TMP

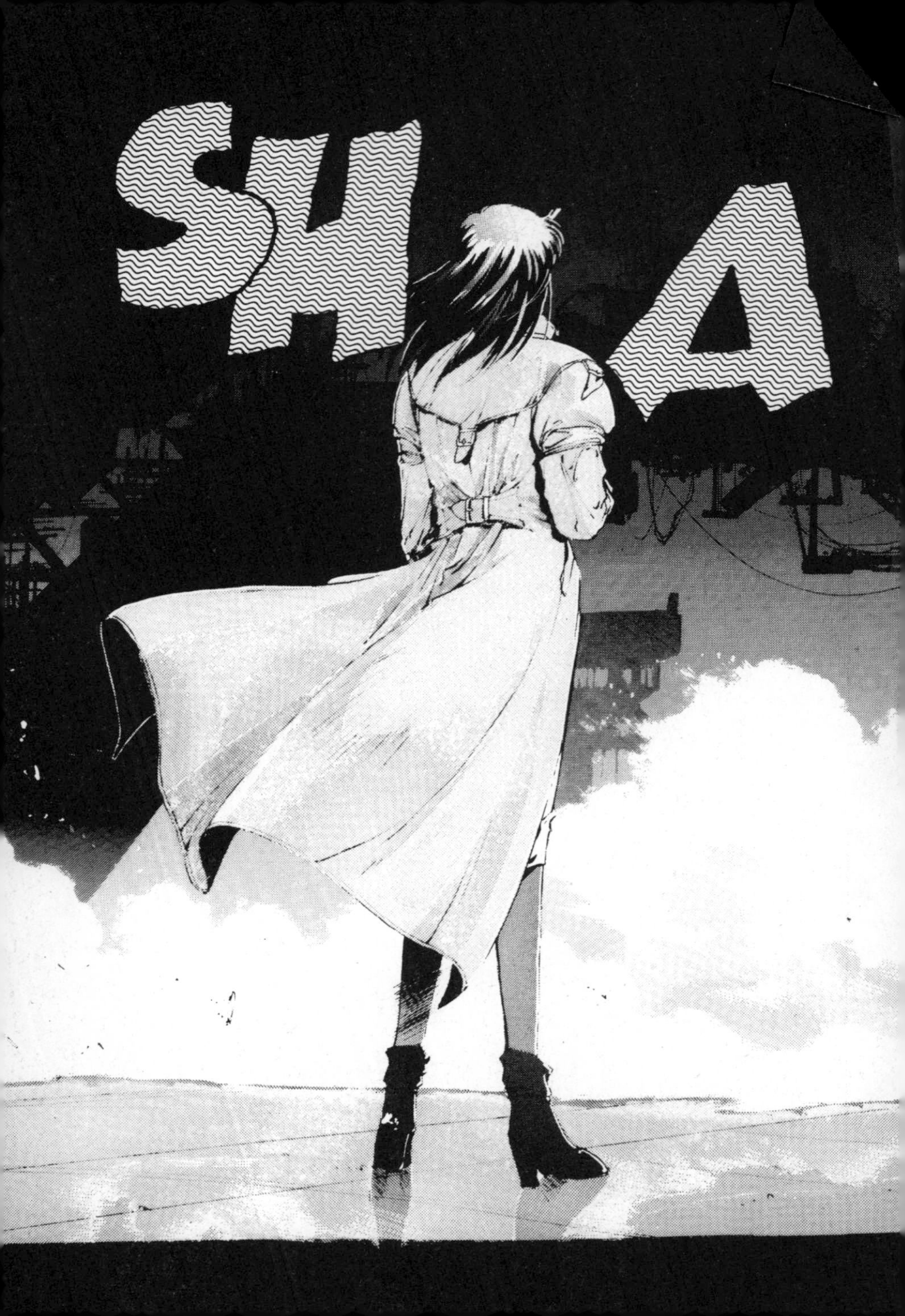
SH A

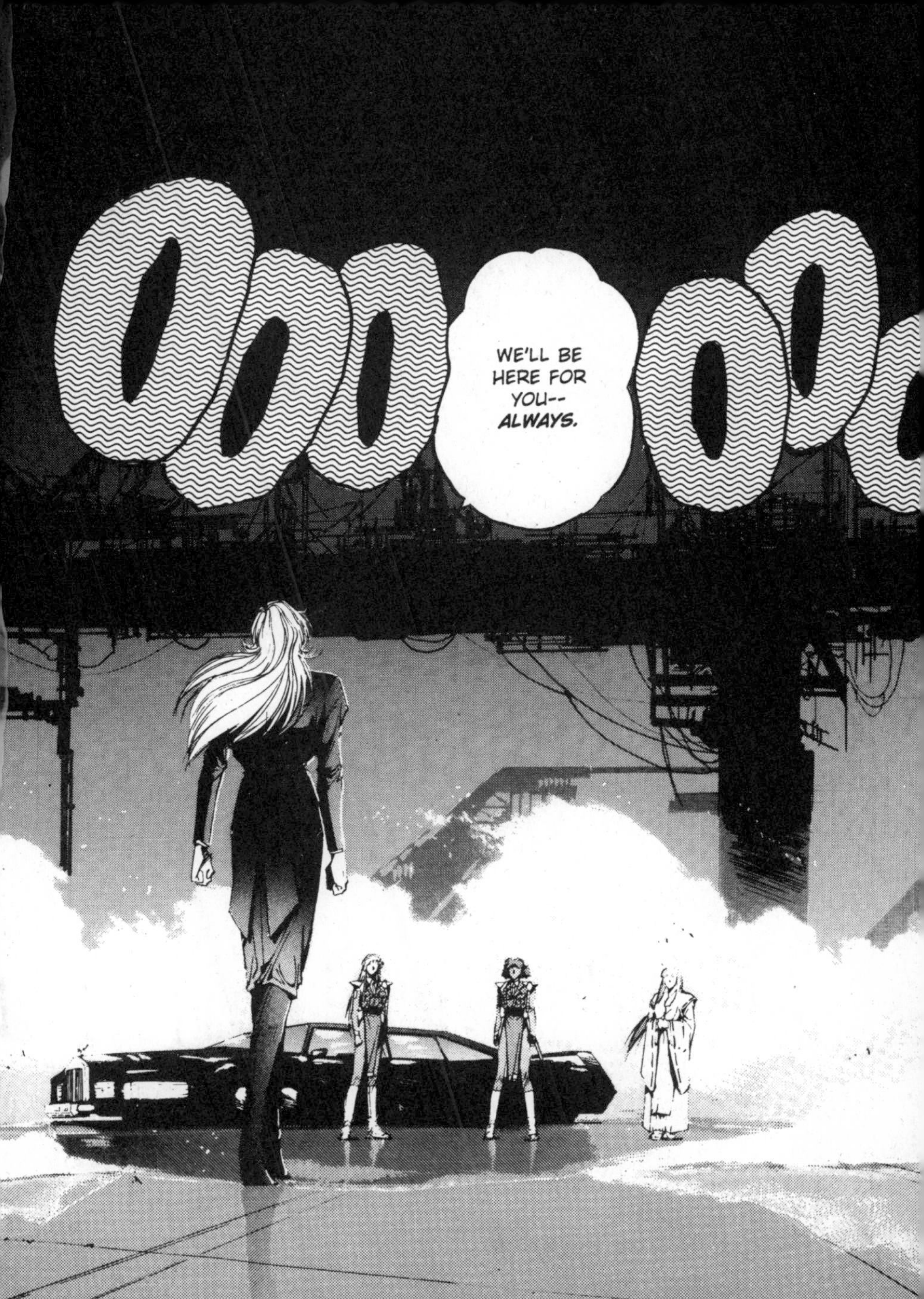
WE'LL BE HERE FOR YOU-- ALWAYS.

IT...
IT CAN'T
BE...
MOTHER...

I...KILLED...
MY REAL...
MOTHER.

UNGH
...

*tch tch
tch tch*

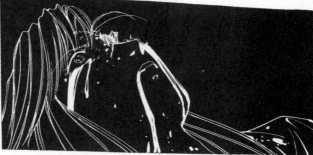

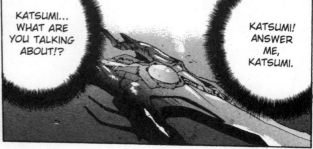

KATSUMI...
WHAT ARE
YOU TALKING
ABOUT!?

KATSUMI!
ANSWER
ME,
KATSUMI.

162

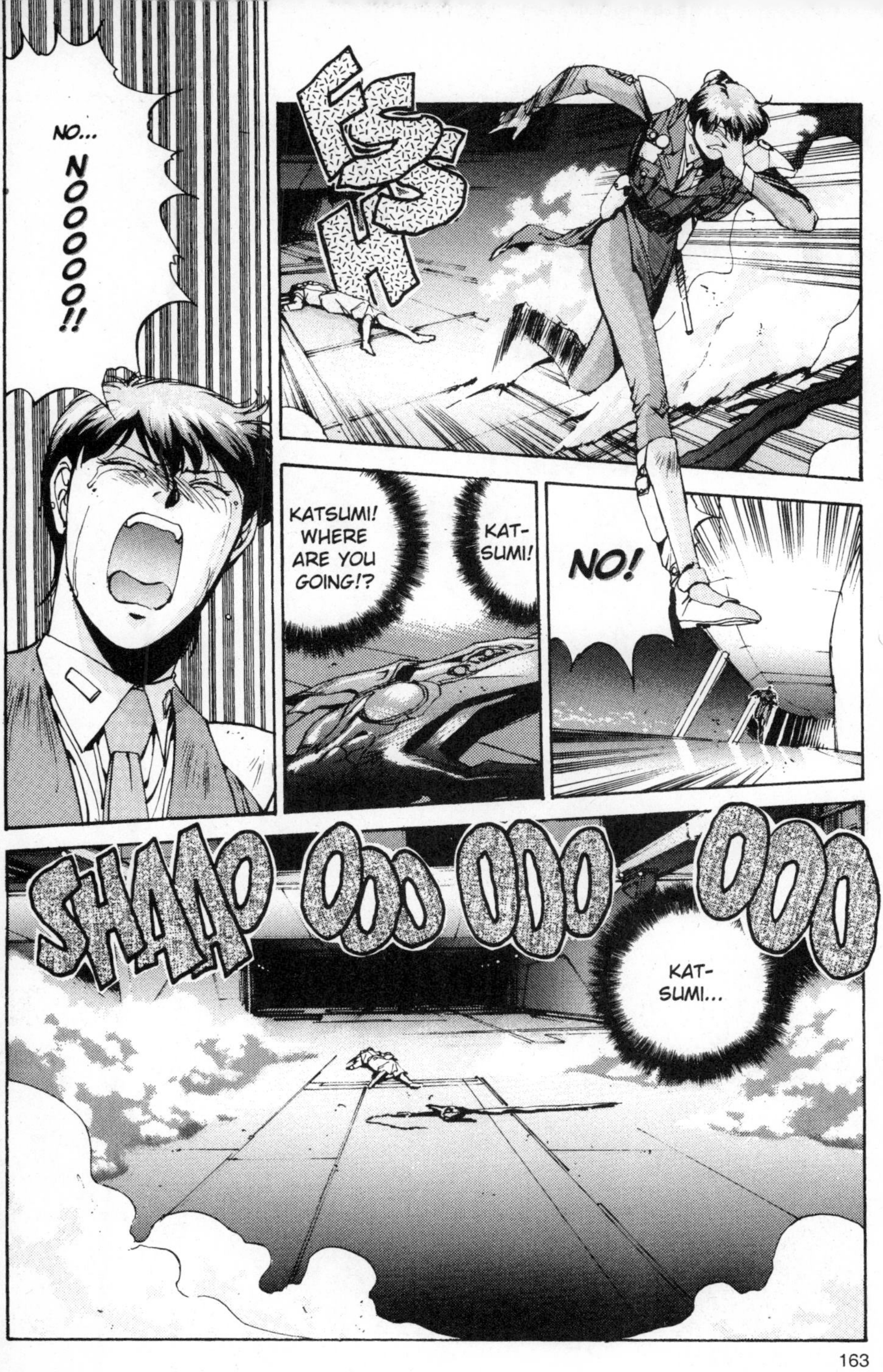
NO...
NOOOOOOO!!
FSSH
KATSUMI! WHERE ARE YOU GOING!?
KAT-SUMI!
NO!
SHAAO OOO OOO OOO
KAT-SUMI...

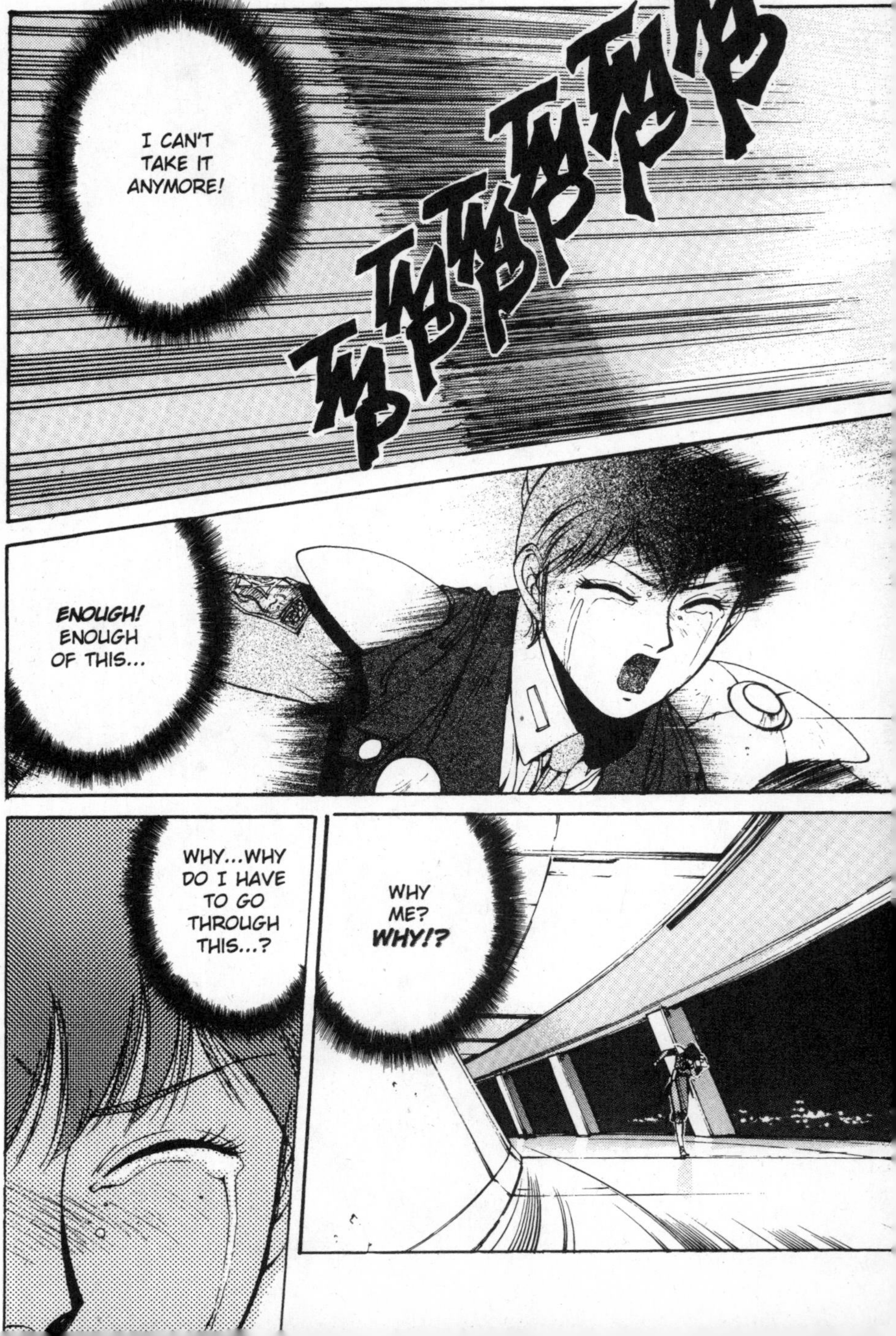
I CAN'T TAKE IT ANYMORE!
ENOUGH! ENOUGH OF THIS...
WHY...WHY DO I HAVE TO GO THROUGH THIS...?
WHY ME? **WHY!?**

I HATE IT!

LUCIFER HAWKS, A.M.P., THIS WRETCHED WORLD!

IF THIS IS MY *FATE*-- I WANT *OUT!* *OUT!*

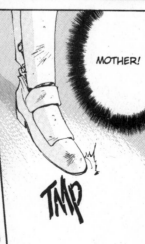

MOTHER!

TMP

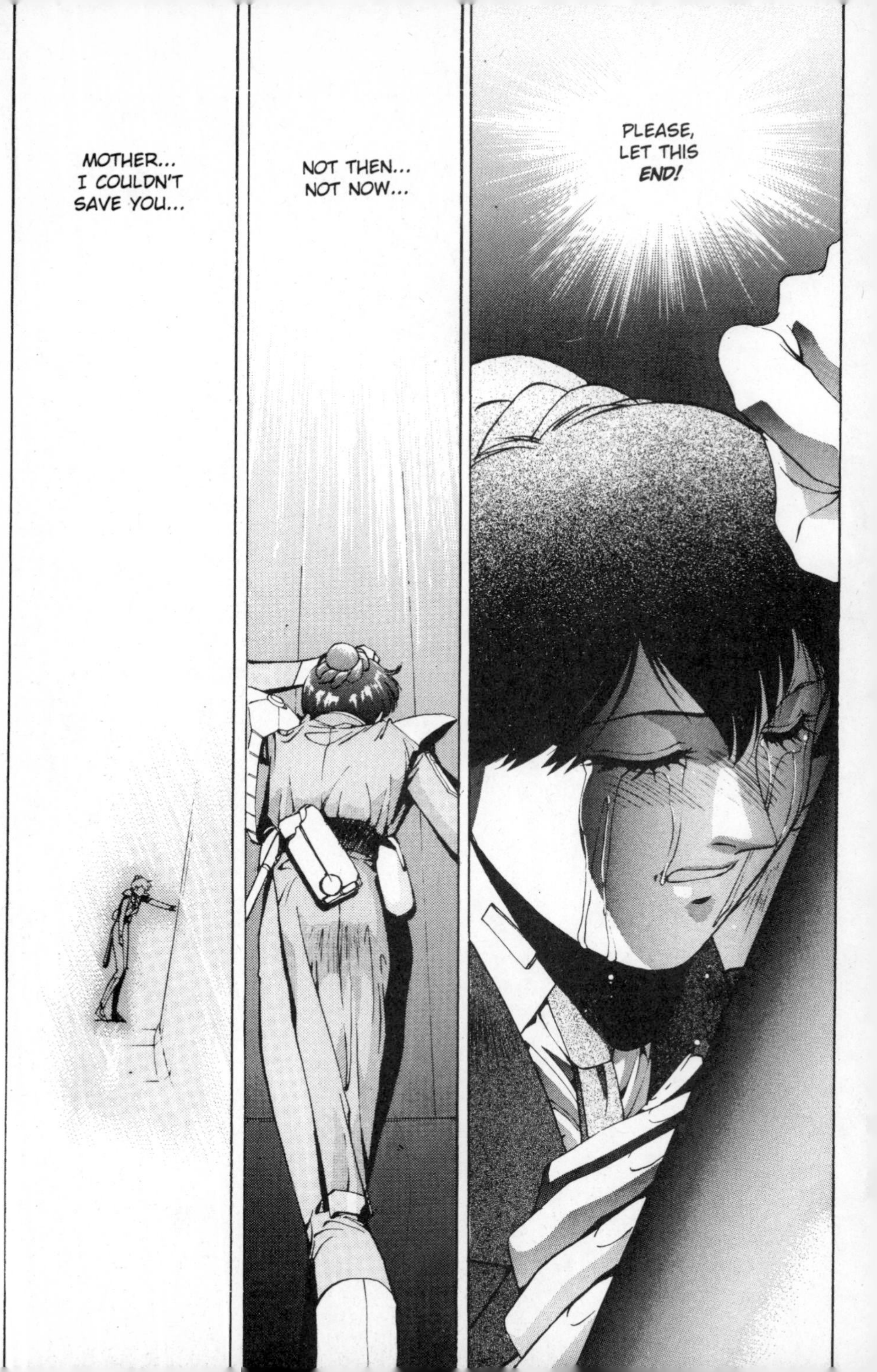
MOTHER... I COULDN'T SAVE YOU...
NOT THEN... NOT NOW...
PLEASE, LET THIS *END!*

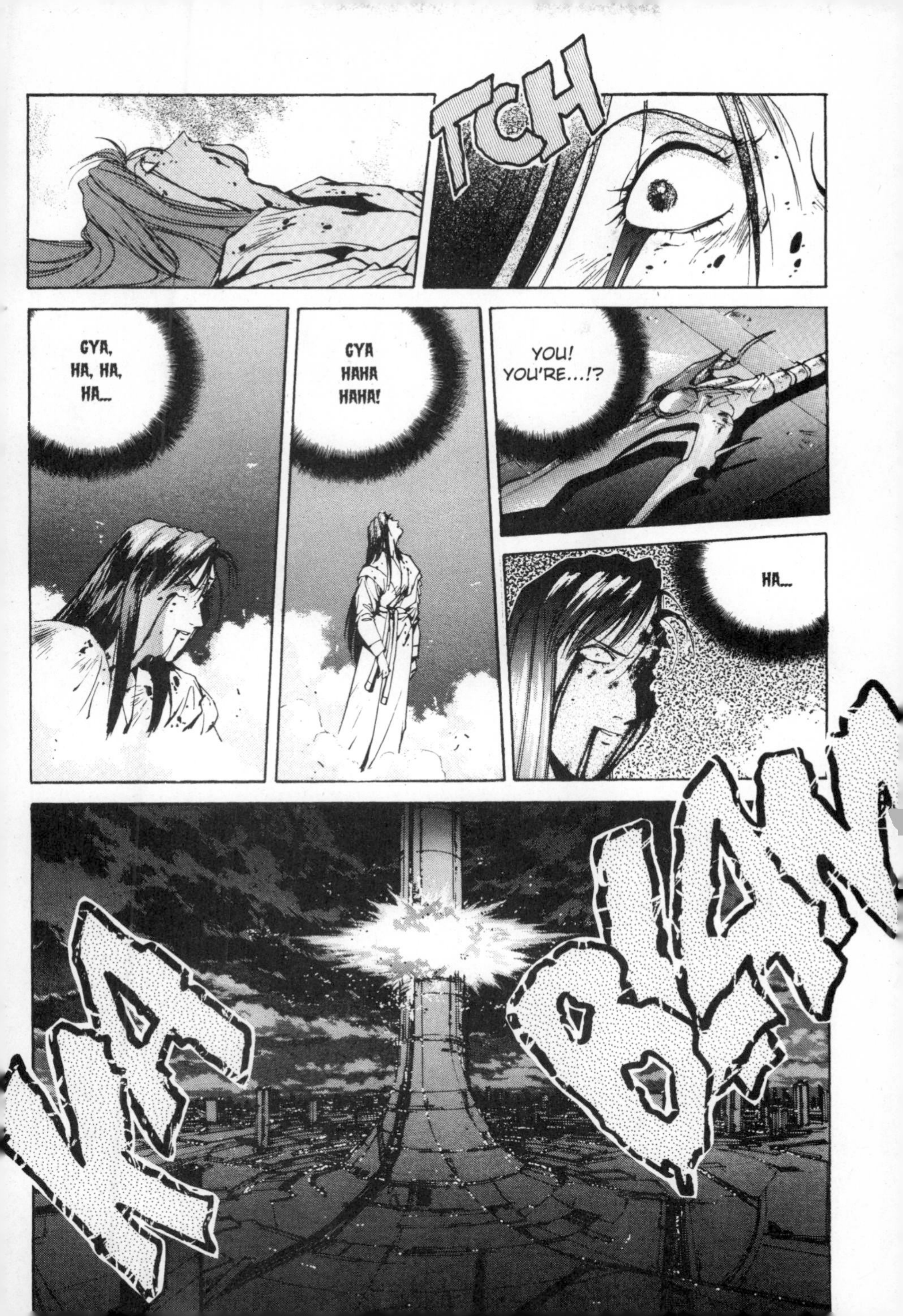
TCH
GYA, HA, HA, HA...
GYA HAHA HAHA!
YOU! YOU'RE...!?
HA...
KA-BAM

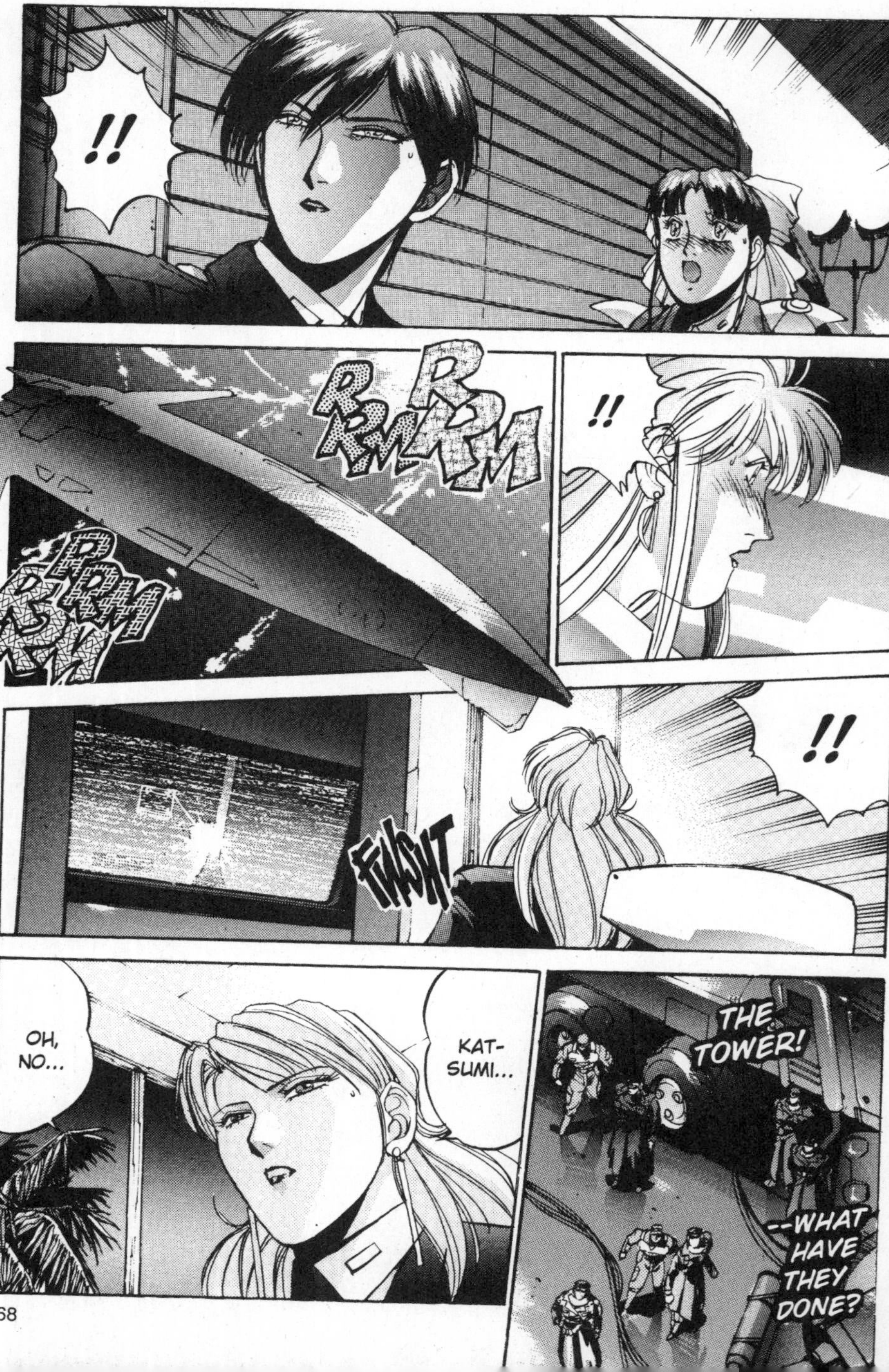
!!
!!
!!
FWSHT
THE TOWER!
--WHAT HAVE THEY DONE?
KAT-SUMI...
OH, NO...

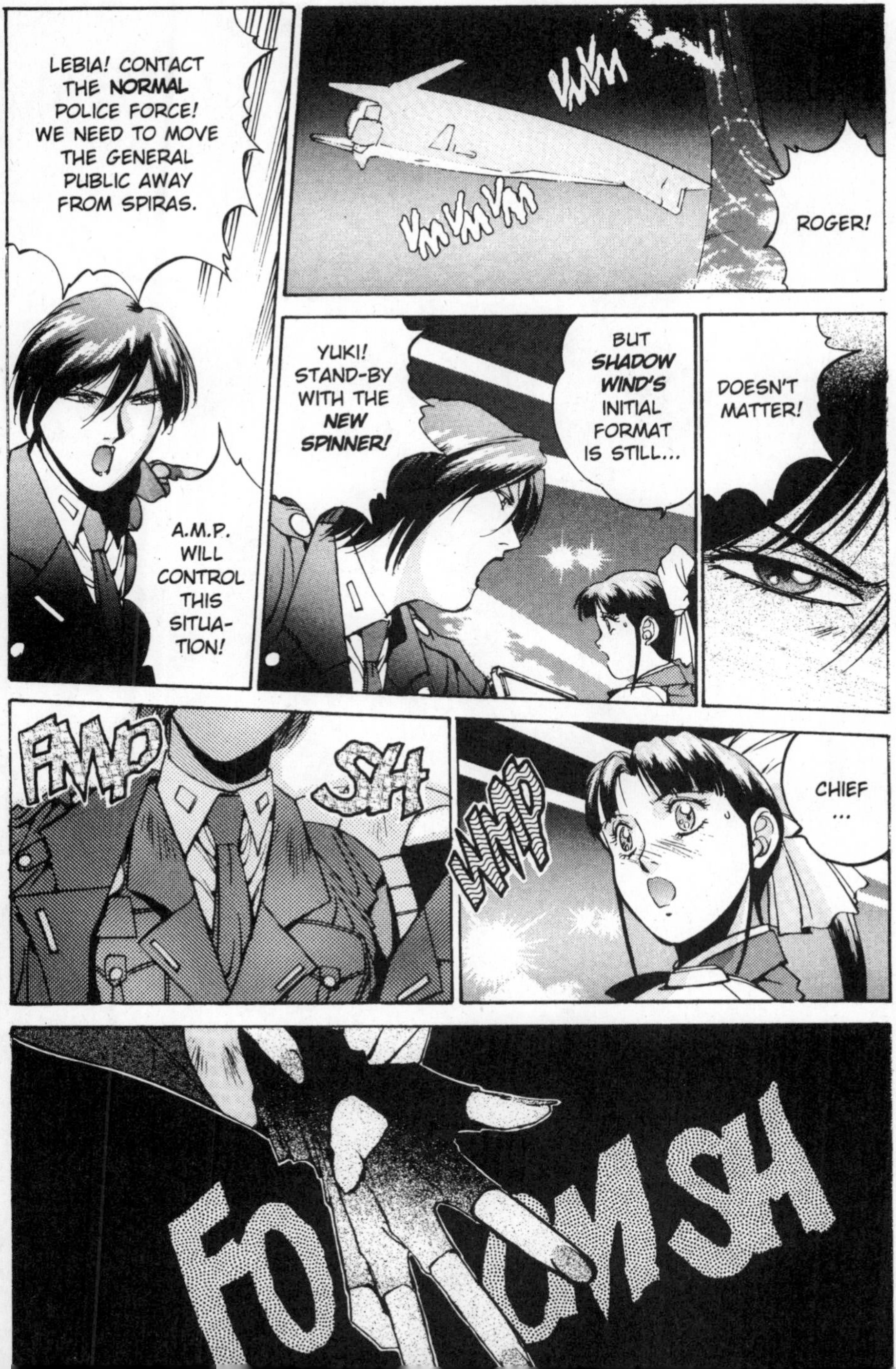
LEBIA! CONTACT THE **NORMAL** POLICE FORCE! WE NEED TO MOVE THE GENERAL PUBLIC AWAY FROM SPIRAS.
A.M.P. WILL CONTROL THIS SITUA-TION!
VMVM
VMVMVM
ROGER!
YUKI! STAND-BY WITH THE ***NEW SPINNER!***
BUT ***SHADOW WIND'S*** INITIAL FORMAT IS STILL...
DOESN'T MATTER!
FWIP
SH
WHIP
CHIEF ...
FOOMSH

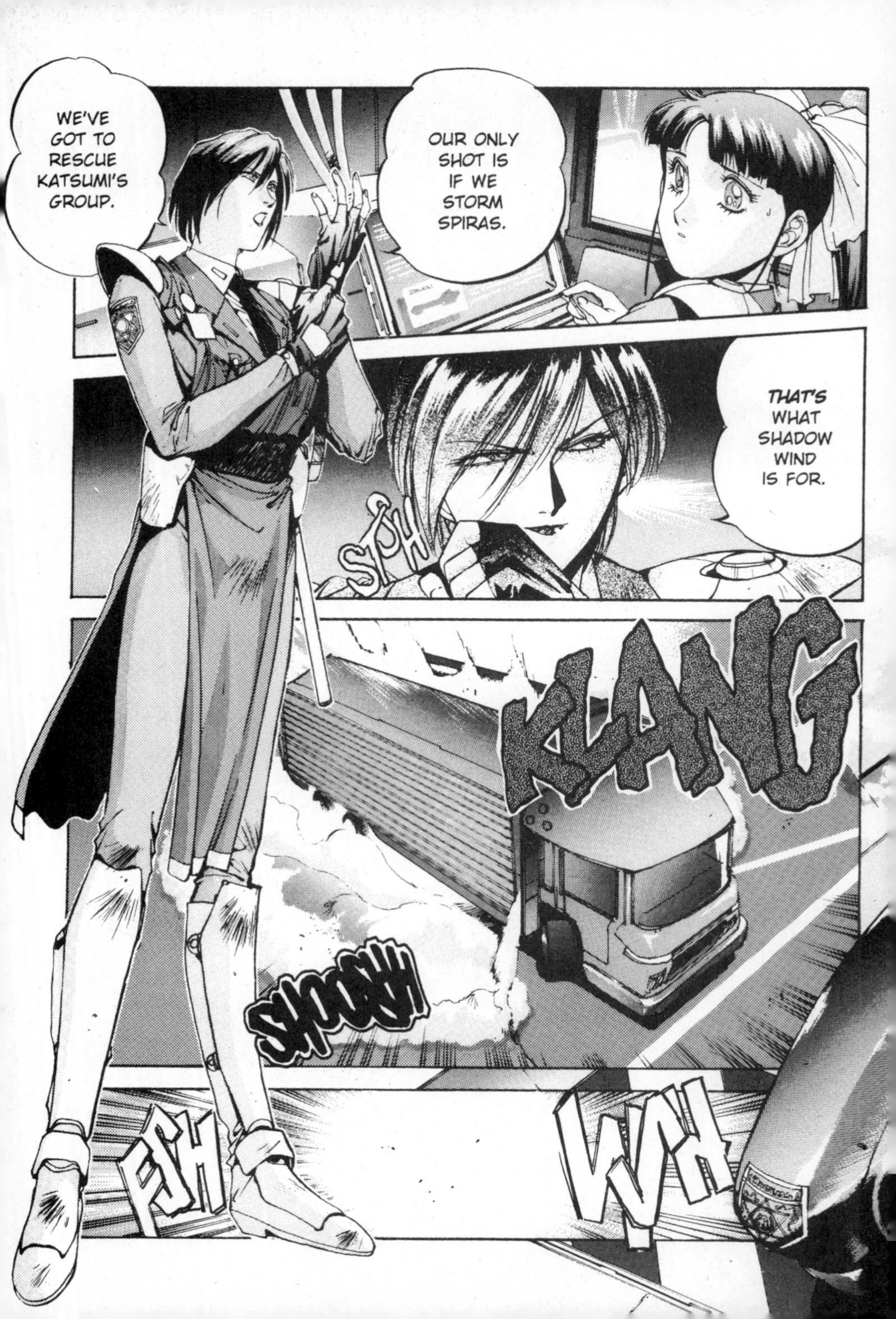
WE'VE GOT TO RESCUE KATSUMI'S GROUP.
OUR ONLY SHOT IS IF WE STORM SPIRAS.
SPH
THAT'S WHAT SHADOW WIND IS FOR.
KLANG
SHOOSH
FSH
WA

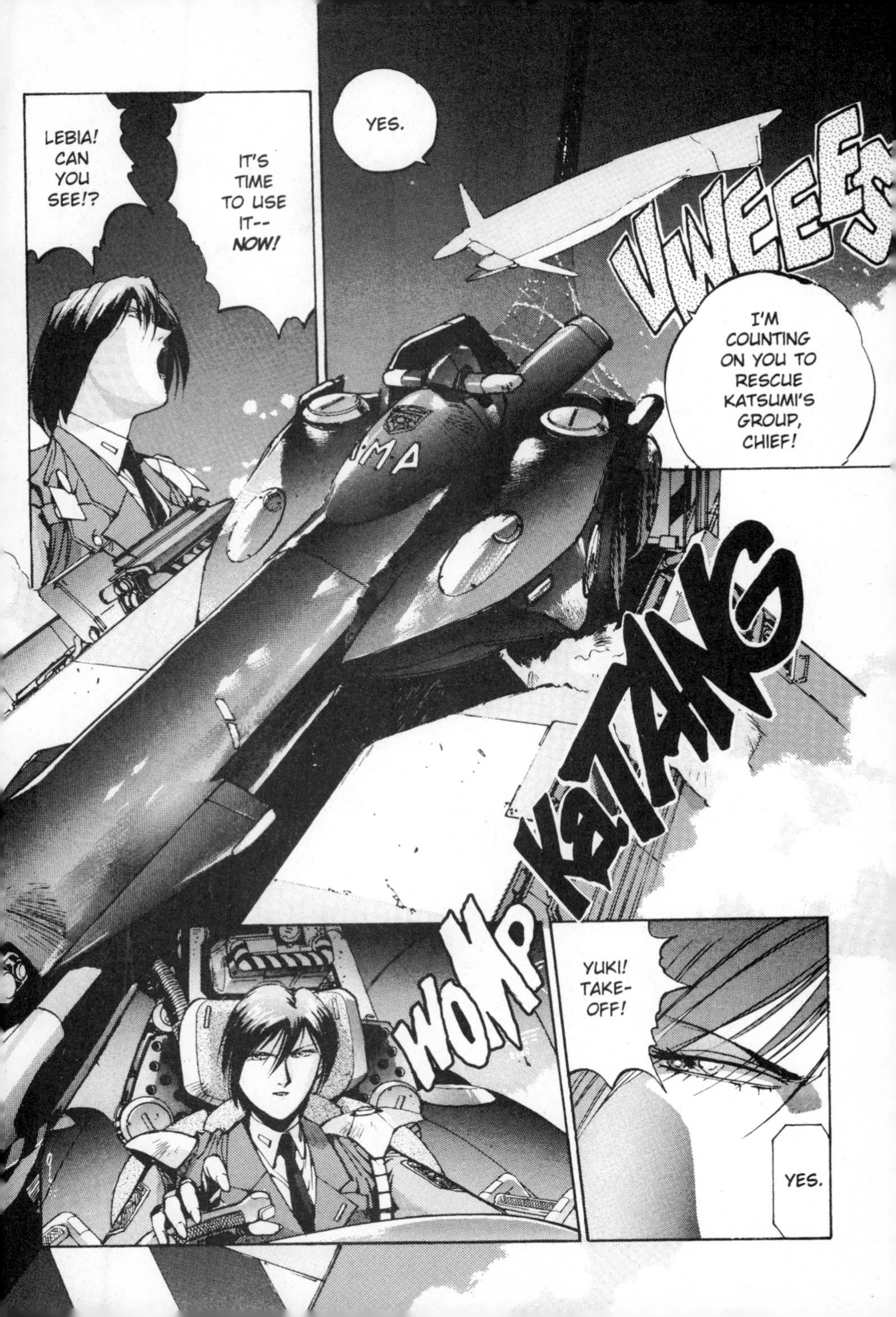
LEBIA! CAN YOU SEE!?
IT'S TIME TO USE IT-- NOW!
YES.
VWEEE
I'M COUNTING ON YOU TO RESCUE KATSUMI'S GROUP, CHIEF!
KATANG
WOMP
YUKI! TAKE-OFF!
YES.

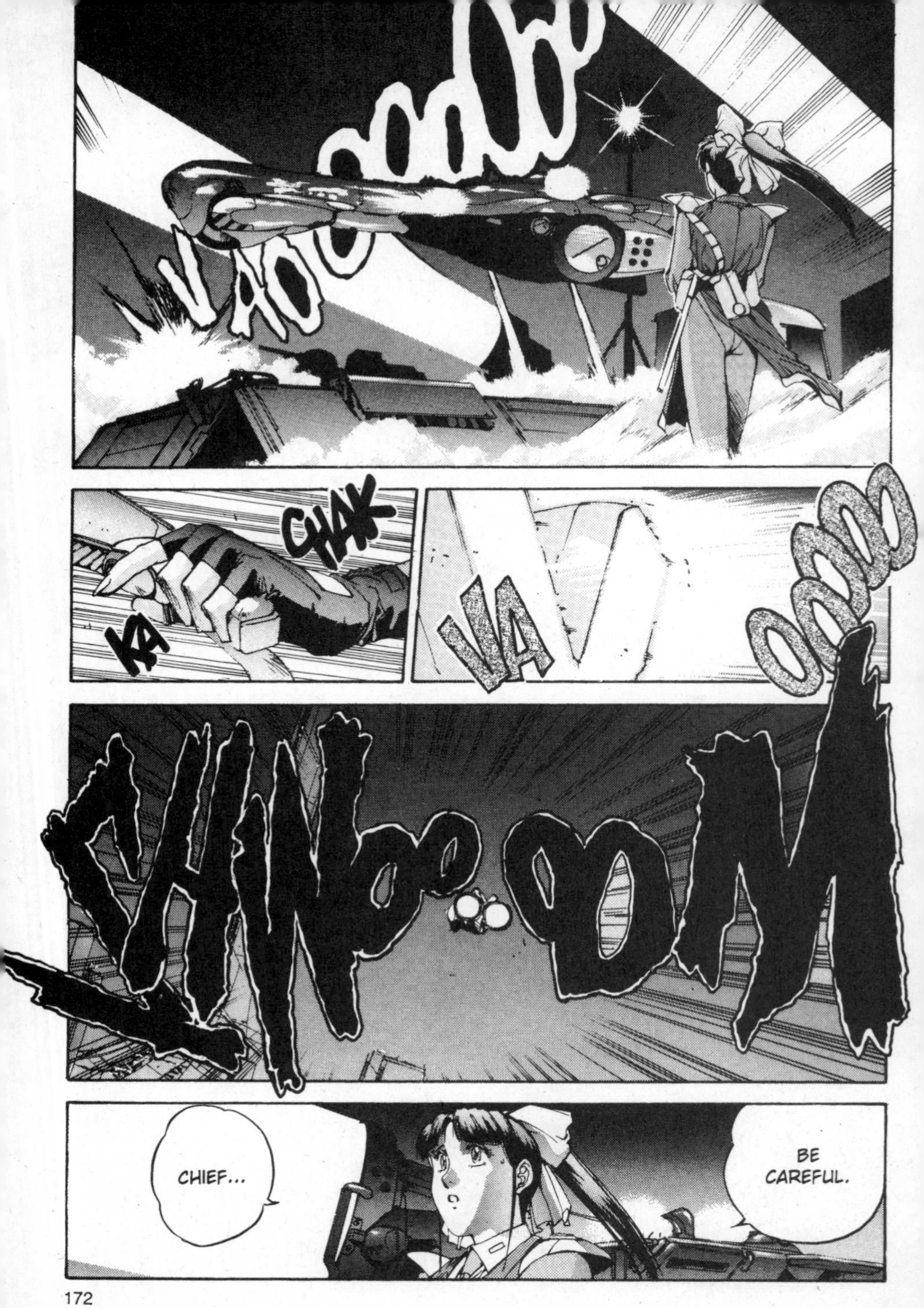
VAOOOOO
KA
CHAK
VA
OOOOO
CHNOOOOM
CHIEF...
BE CAREFUL.

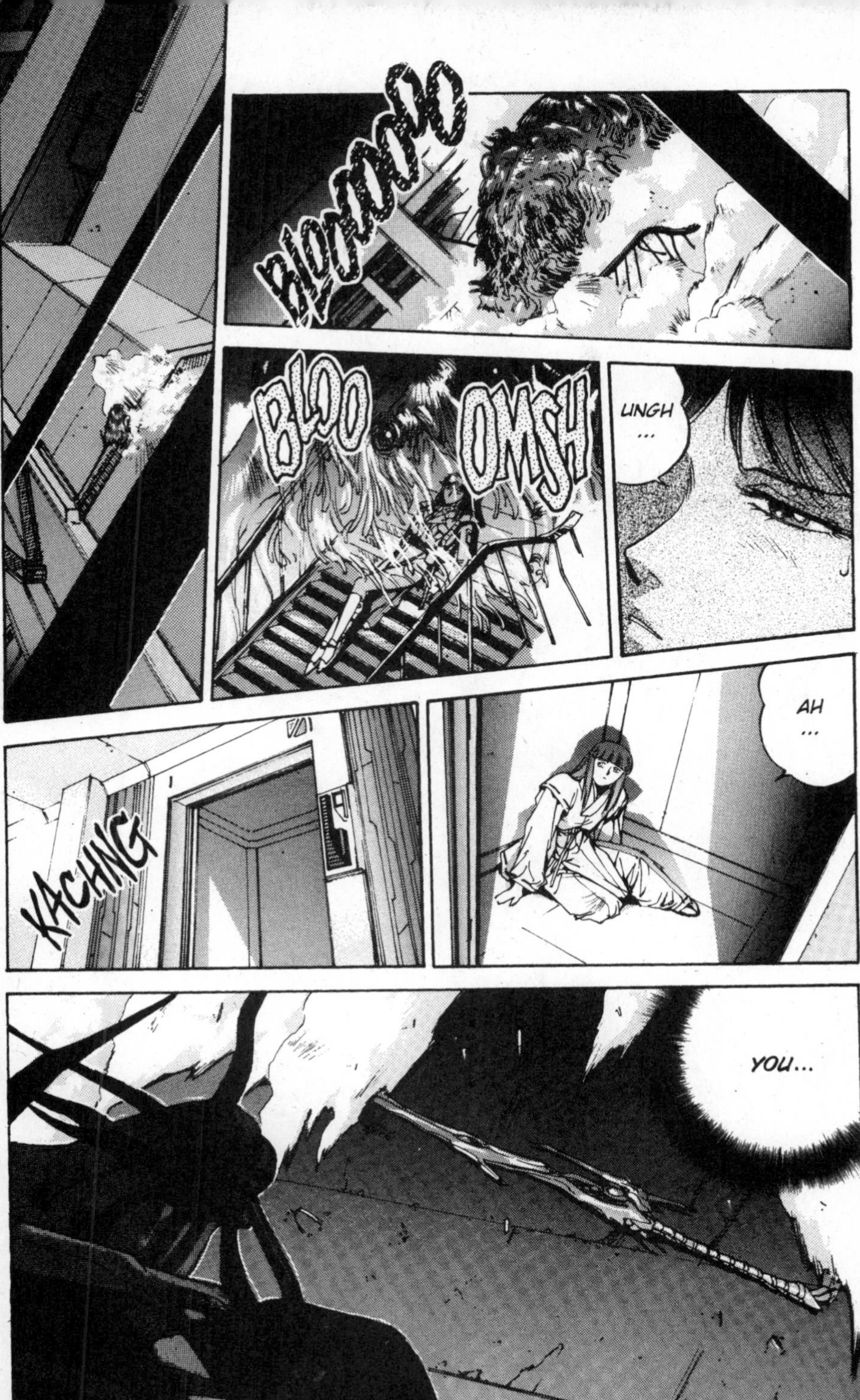
BLOOOOOO
BLOO OMSH
UNGH ...
KACHNG
AH ...
YOU...

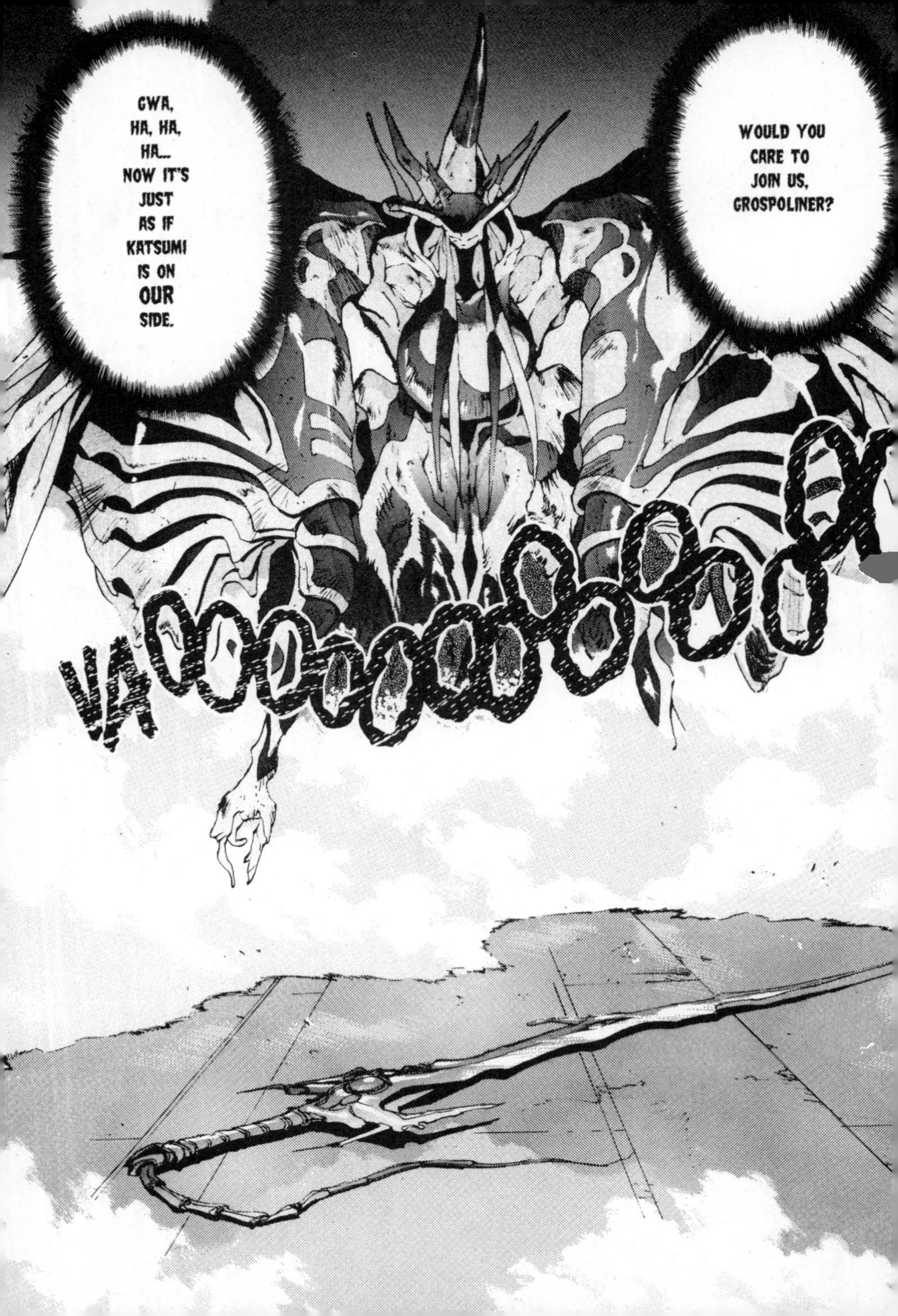
GWA, HA, HA, HA... NOW IT'S JUST AS IF KATSUMI IS ON OUR SIDE.
WOULD YOU CARE TO JOIN US, GROSPOLINER?
VAOOOOOOOOOOOOX

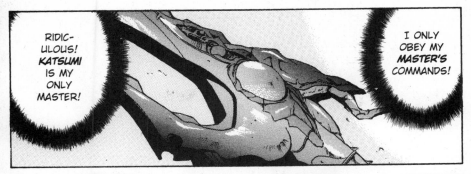

RIDIC-ULOUS! **KATSUMI** IS MY ONLY MASTER!

I ONLY OBEY MY **MASTER'S** COMMANDS!

QUITE REASONABLE. BUT--

--SPIRAS HAS BECOME PART OF MY BODY. SOON I SHALL SWALLOW YOU AS WELL.

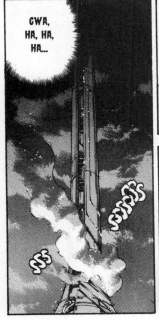

GWA, HA, HA, HA...

AH... WHAT A NICE VIEW!

THE CITY'S LIGHTS ALL TWINKLING ...

I'D BETTER GO HOME NOW-- BEFORE I GET SCOLDED.

UM, YEAH... HAVE TO GO **HOME** NOW.

175

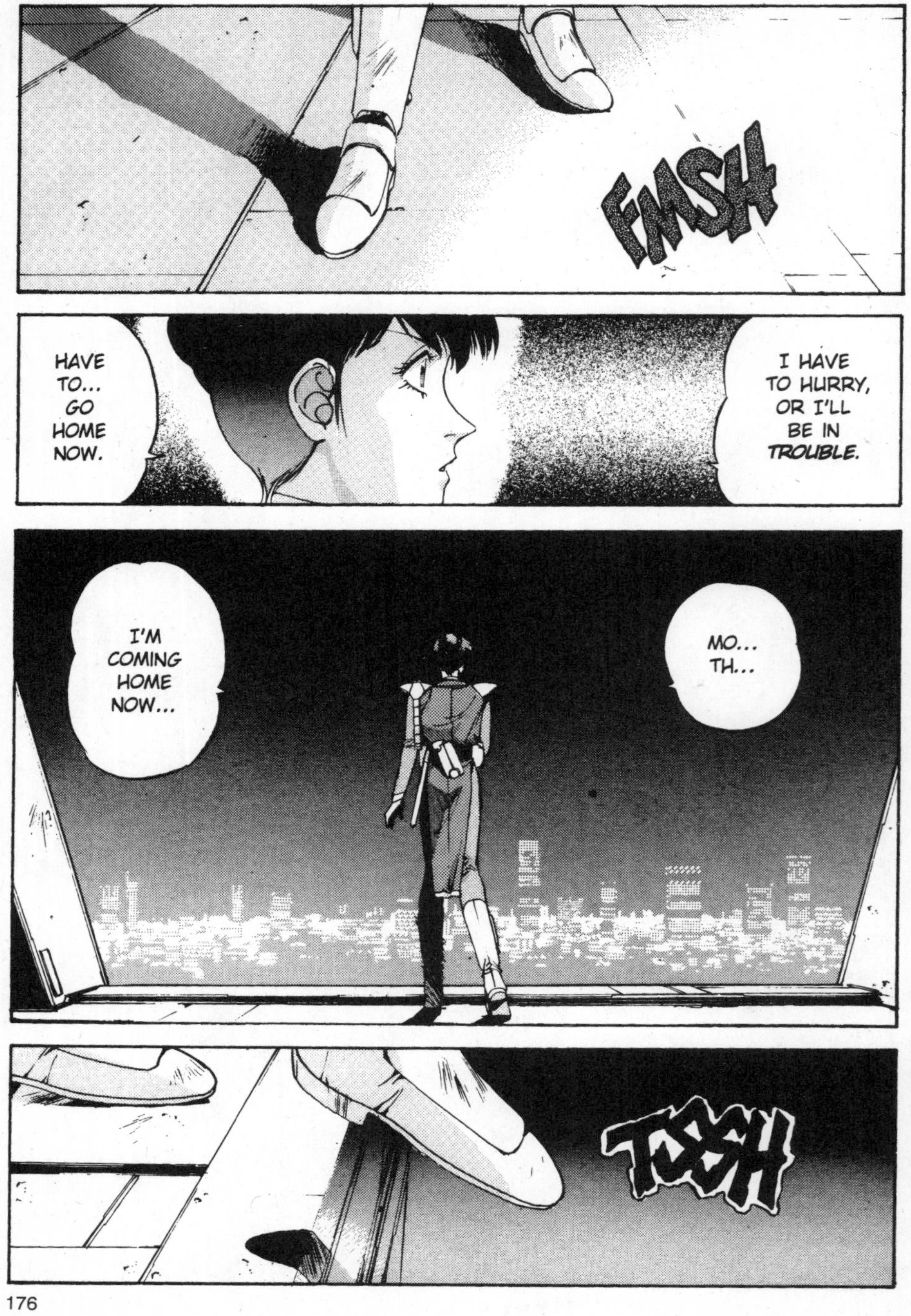
FMSH
HAVE TO... GO HOME NOW.
I HAVE TO HURRY, OR I'LL BE IN *TROUBLE.*
I'M COMING HOME NOW...
MO... TH...
TOSH

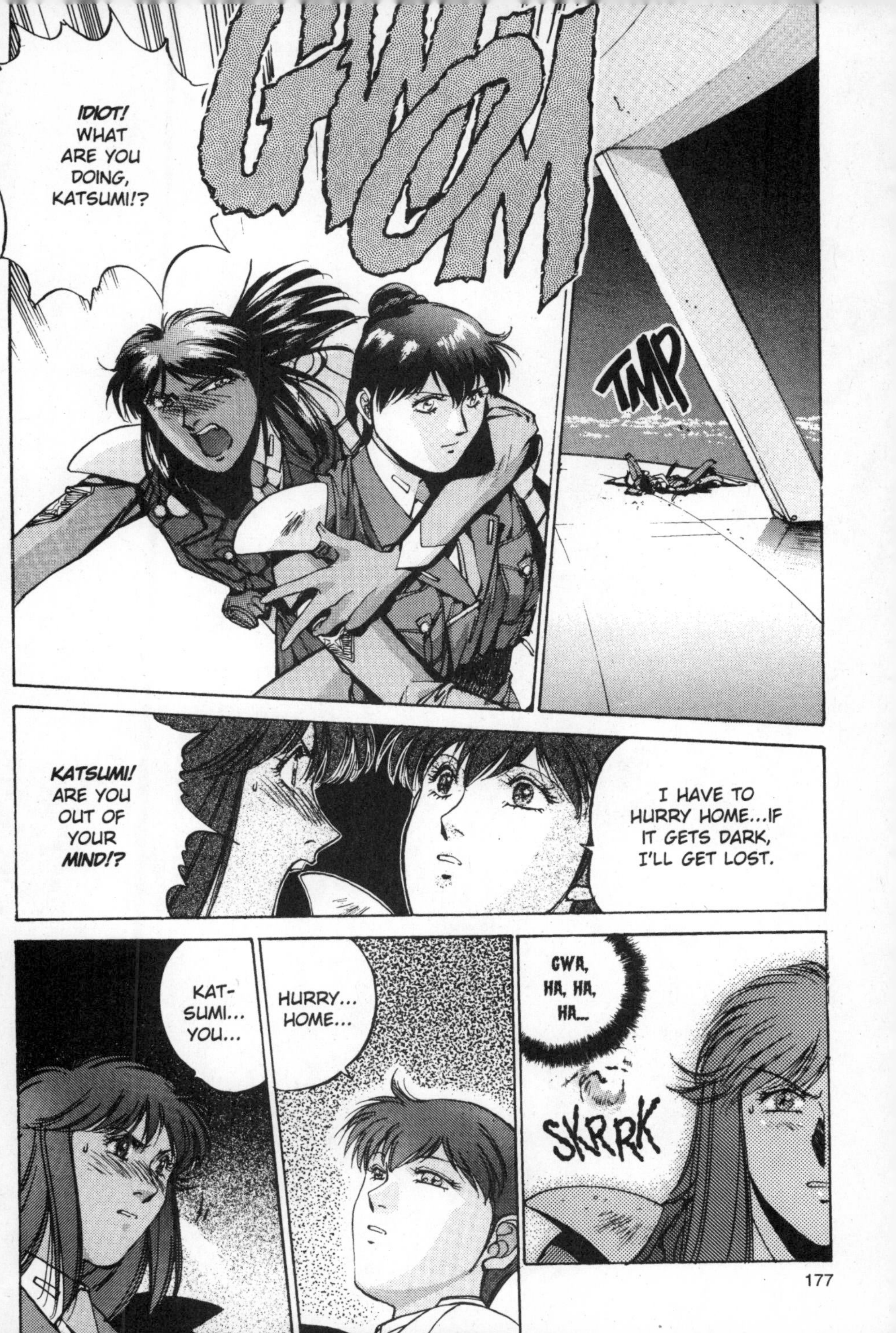
IDIOT! WHAT ARE YOU DOING, KATSUMI!?
GHOOM
TMP
KATSUMI! ARE YOU OUT OF YOUR MIND!?
I HAVE TO HURRY HOME...IF IT GETS DARK, I'LL GET LOST.
KAT-SUMI... YOU...
HURRY... HOME...
GWA, HA, HA, HA...
SKRRK

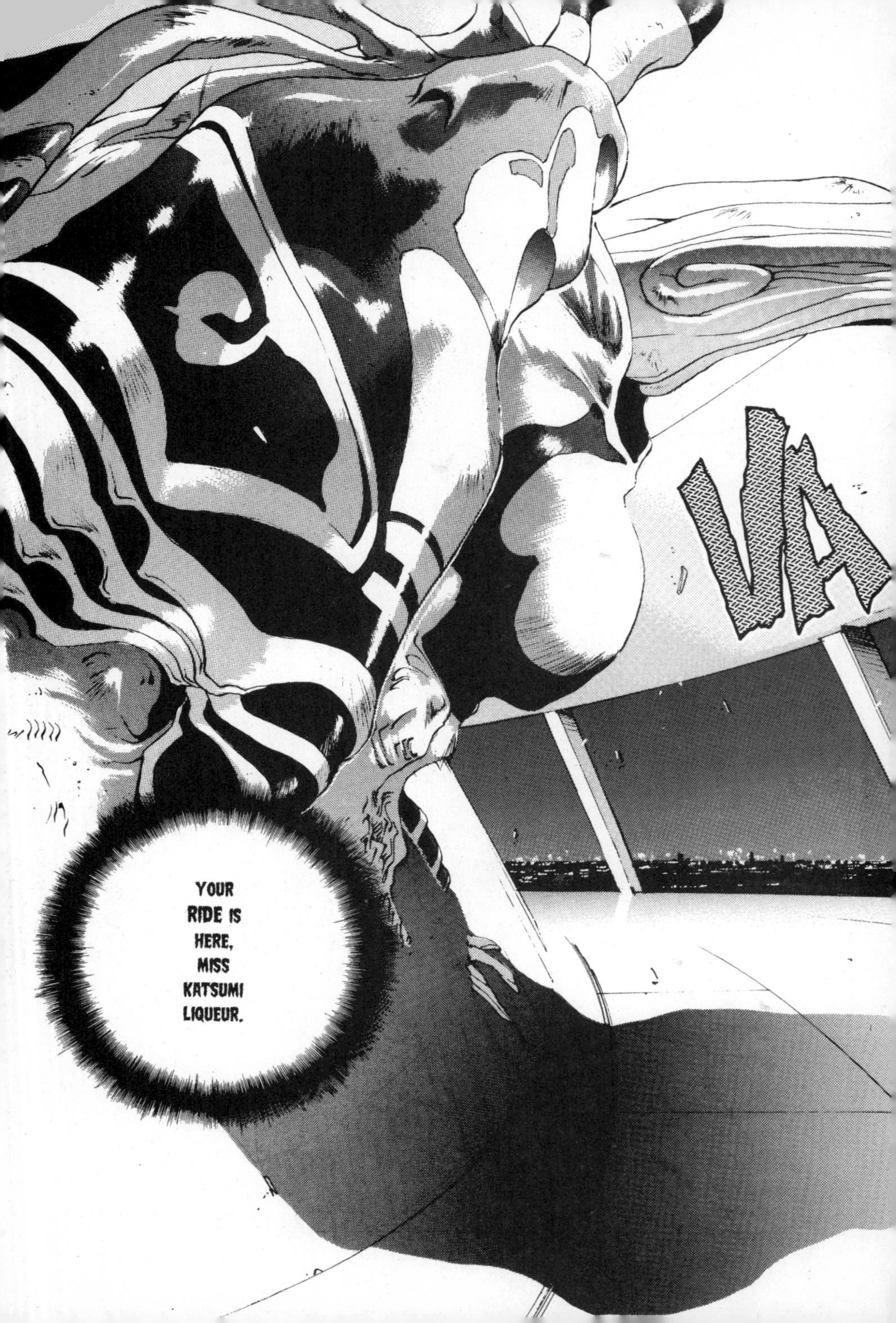
VA
YOUR RIDE IS HERE, MISS KATSUMI LIQUEUR.

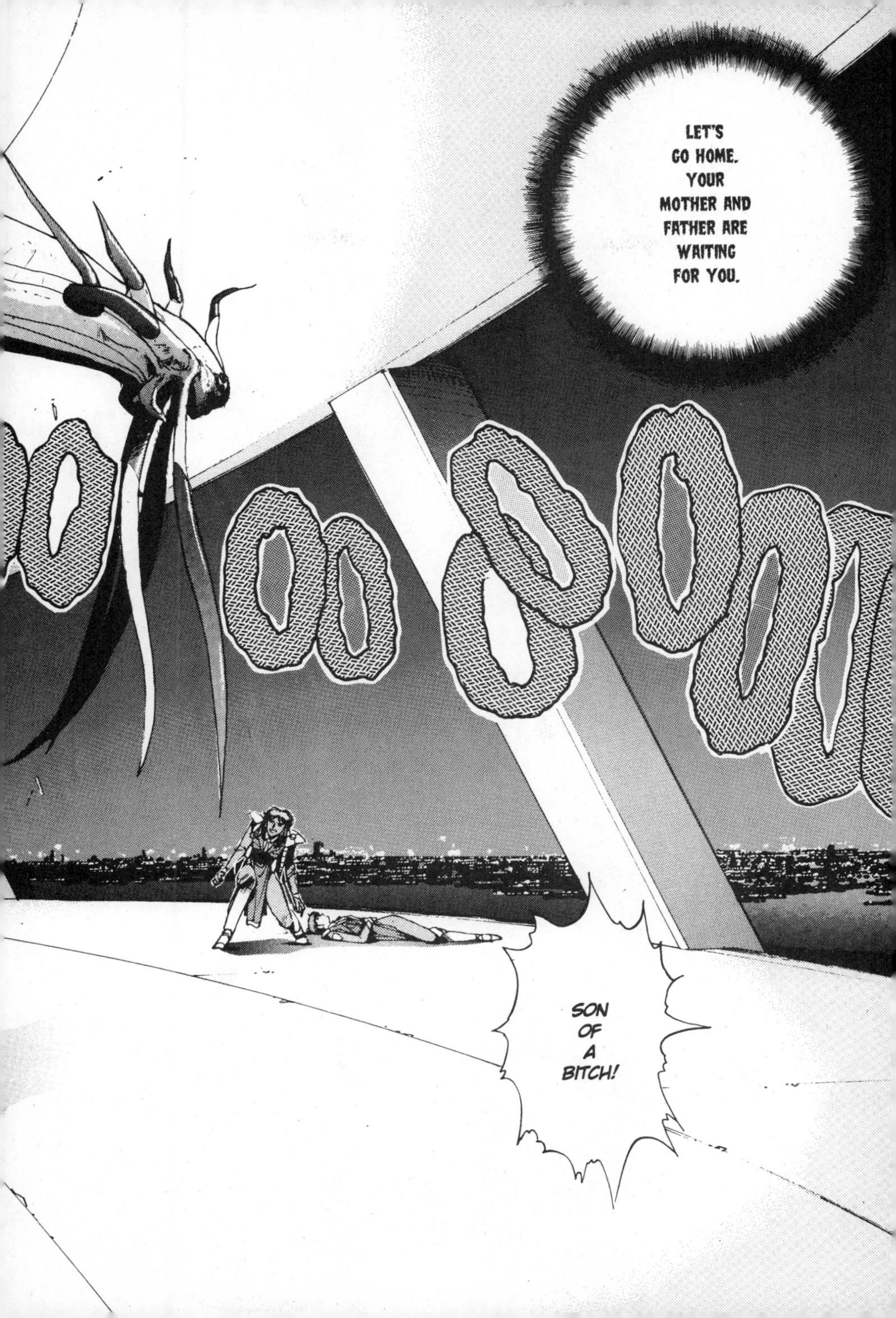
LET'S GO HOME. YOUR MOTHER AND FATHER ARE WAITING FOR YOU.
SON OF A BITCH!

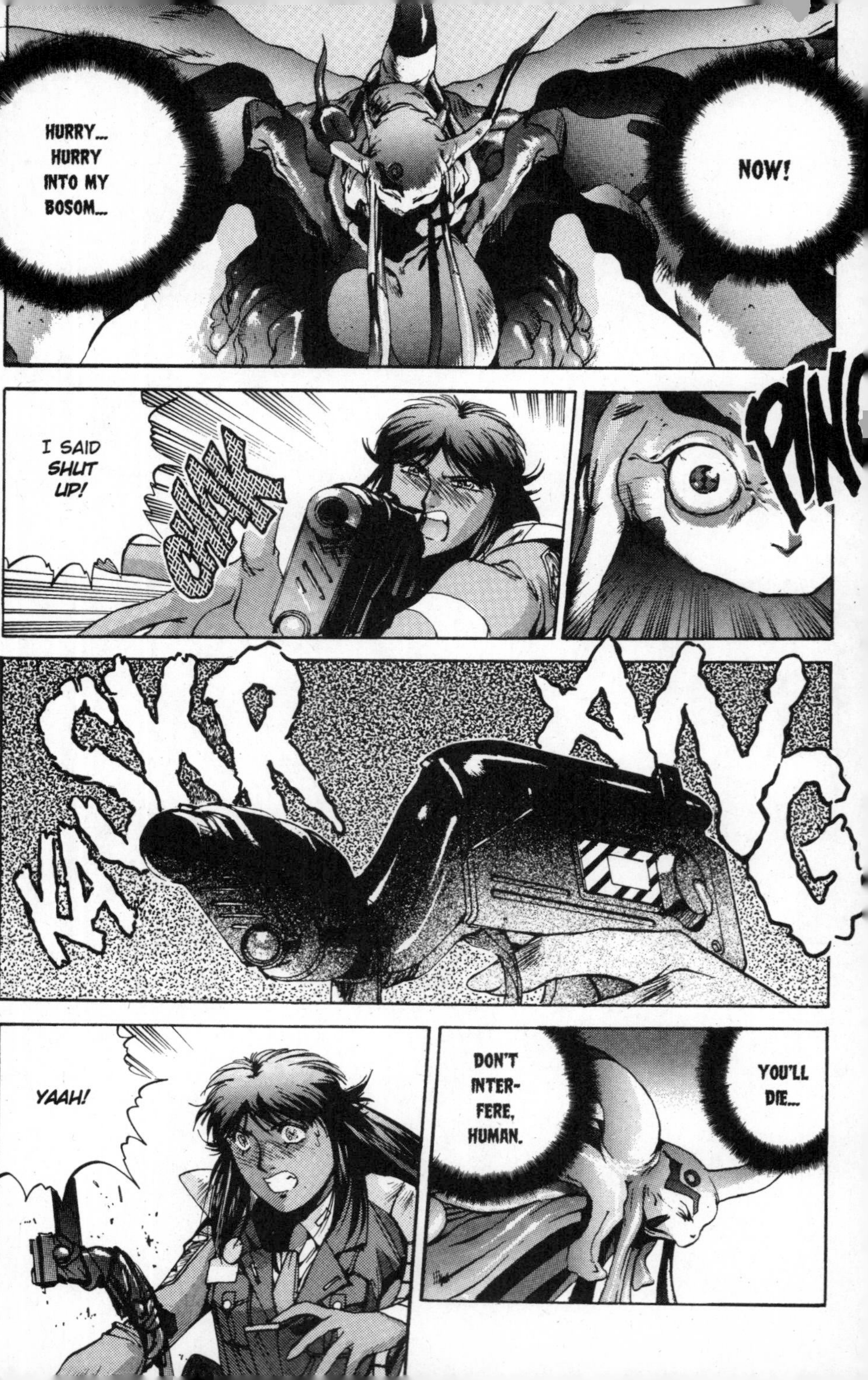
HURRY... HURRY INTO MY BOSOM...
NOW!
I SAID SHUT UP!
CHAK
PING
KASKRANG
YAAH!
DON'T INTER-FERE, HUMAN.
YOU'LL DIE...

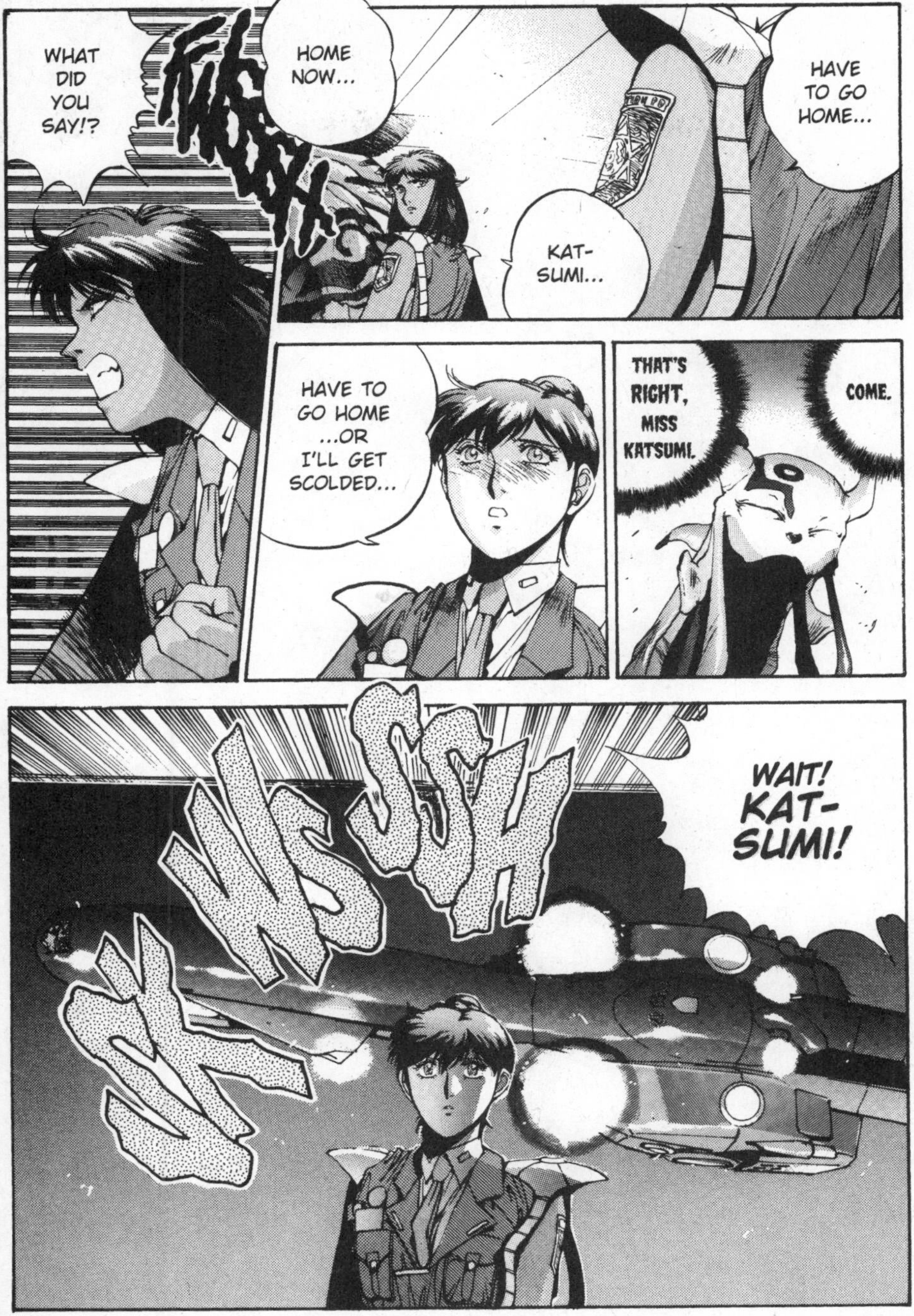
WHAT DID YOU SAY!?
HOME NOW...
HAVE TO GO HOME...
KAT-SUMI...
HAVE TO GO HOME ...OR I'LL GET SCOLDED...
THAT'S RIGHT, MISS KATSUMI.
COME.
WAIT! KAT-SUMI!

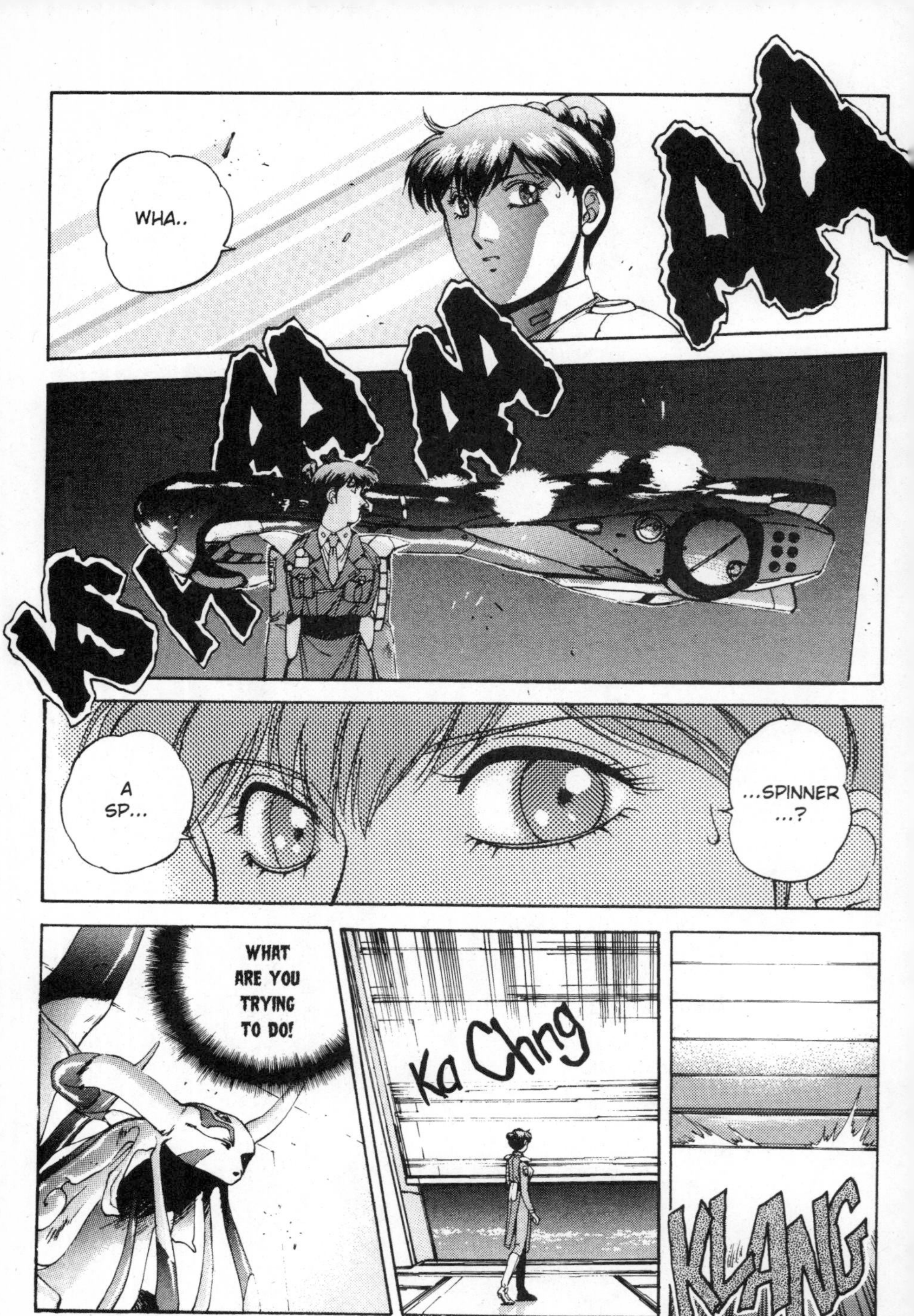
WHA..
A SP...
...SPINNER ...?
WHAT ARE YOU TRYING TO DO!
Ka Chng
KLANG

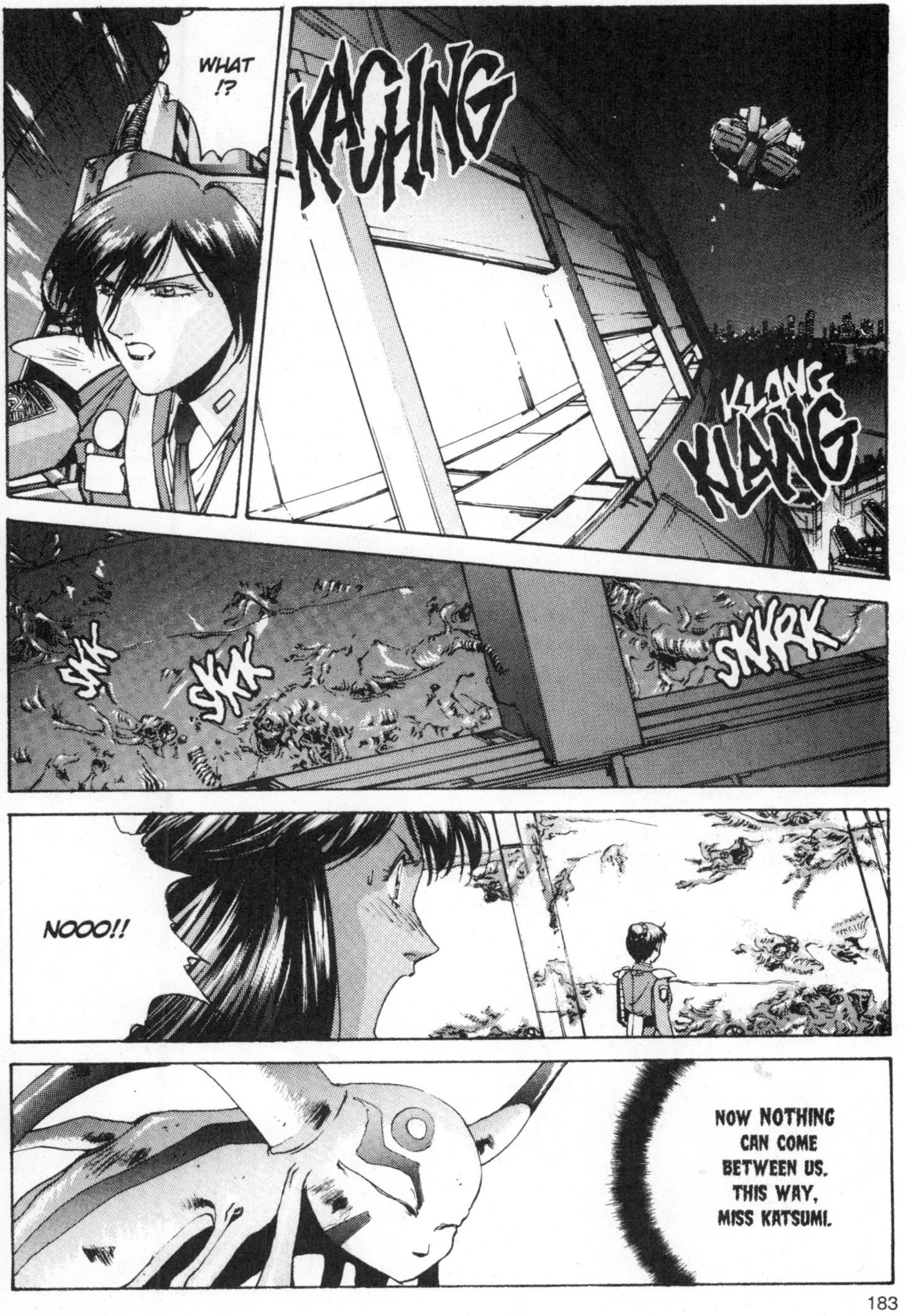
WHAT !?
KACHING
KLONG
KLANG
SKK
SKK
SKKRK
NOOO!!
NOW NOTHING CAN COME BETWEEN US. THIS WAY, MISS KATSUMI.

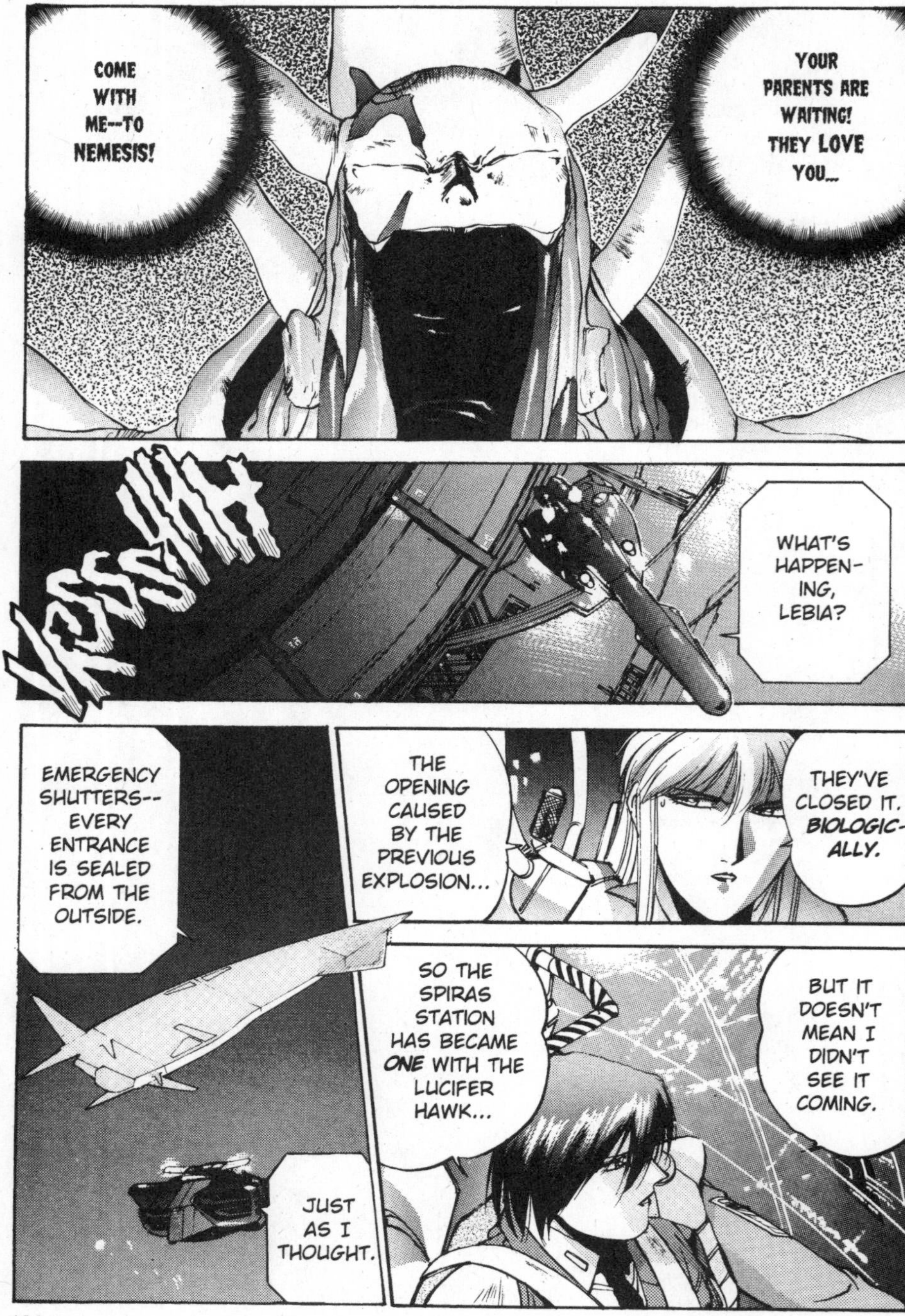
COME WITH ME--TO NEMESIS!
YOUR PARENTS ARE WAITING! THEY LOVE YOU...
WHAT'S HAPPEN-ING, LEBIA?
EMERGENCY SHUTTERS--EVERY ENTRANCE IS SEALED FROM THE OUTSIDE.
JUST AS I THOUGHT.
THE OPENING CAUSED BY THE PREVIOUS EXPLOSION...
THEY'VE CLOSED IT. *BIOLOGIC-ALLY.*
SO THE SPIRAS STATION HAS BECAME *ONE* WITH THE LUCIFER HAWK...
BUT IT DOESN'T MEAN I DIDN'T SEE IT COMING.

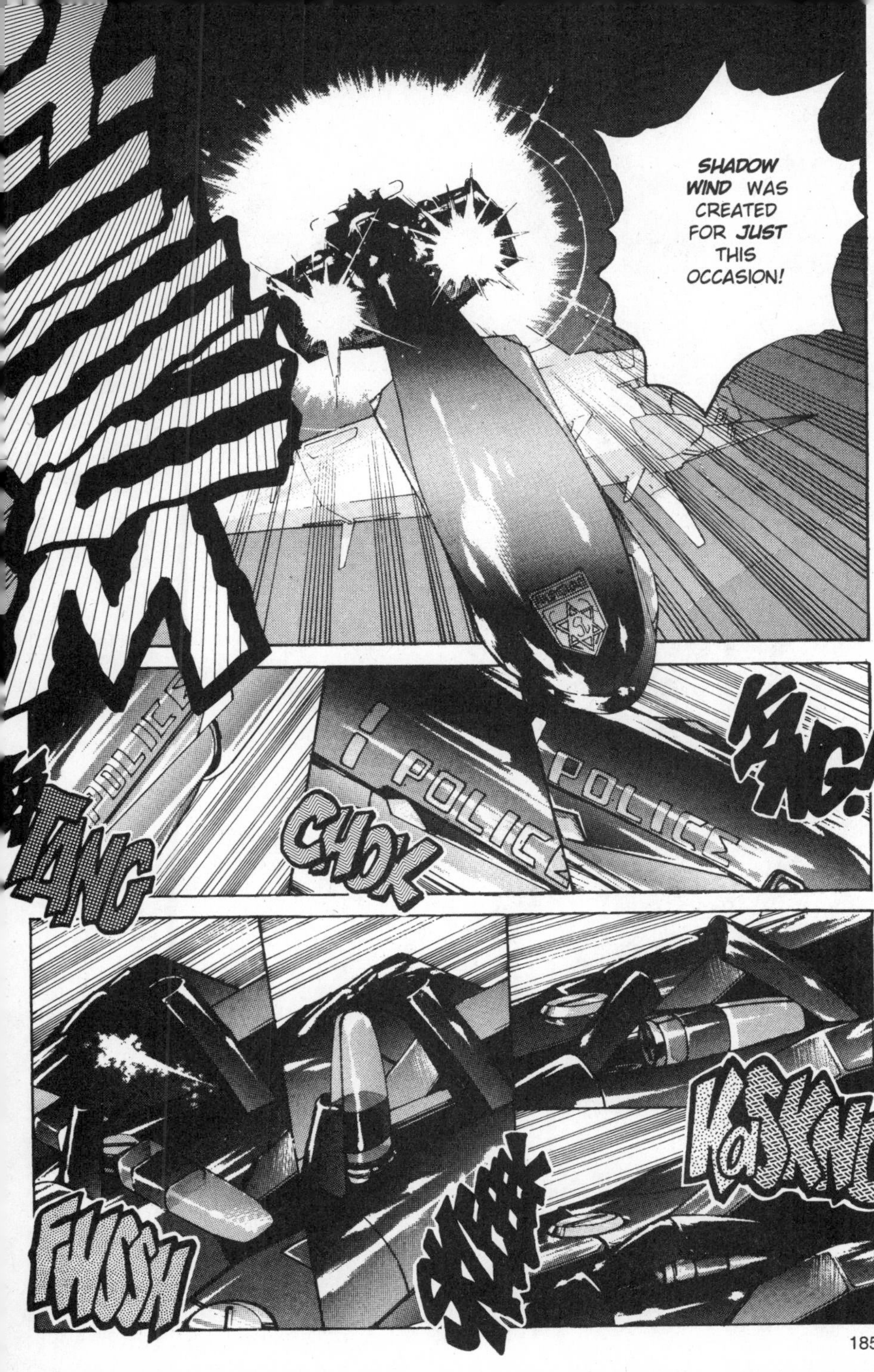
SHADOW WIND WAS CREATED FOR JUST THIS OCCASION!
POLICE
CHOK
POLICE
KANG!

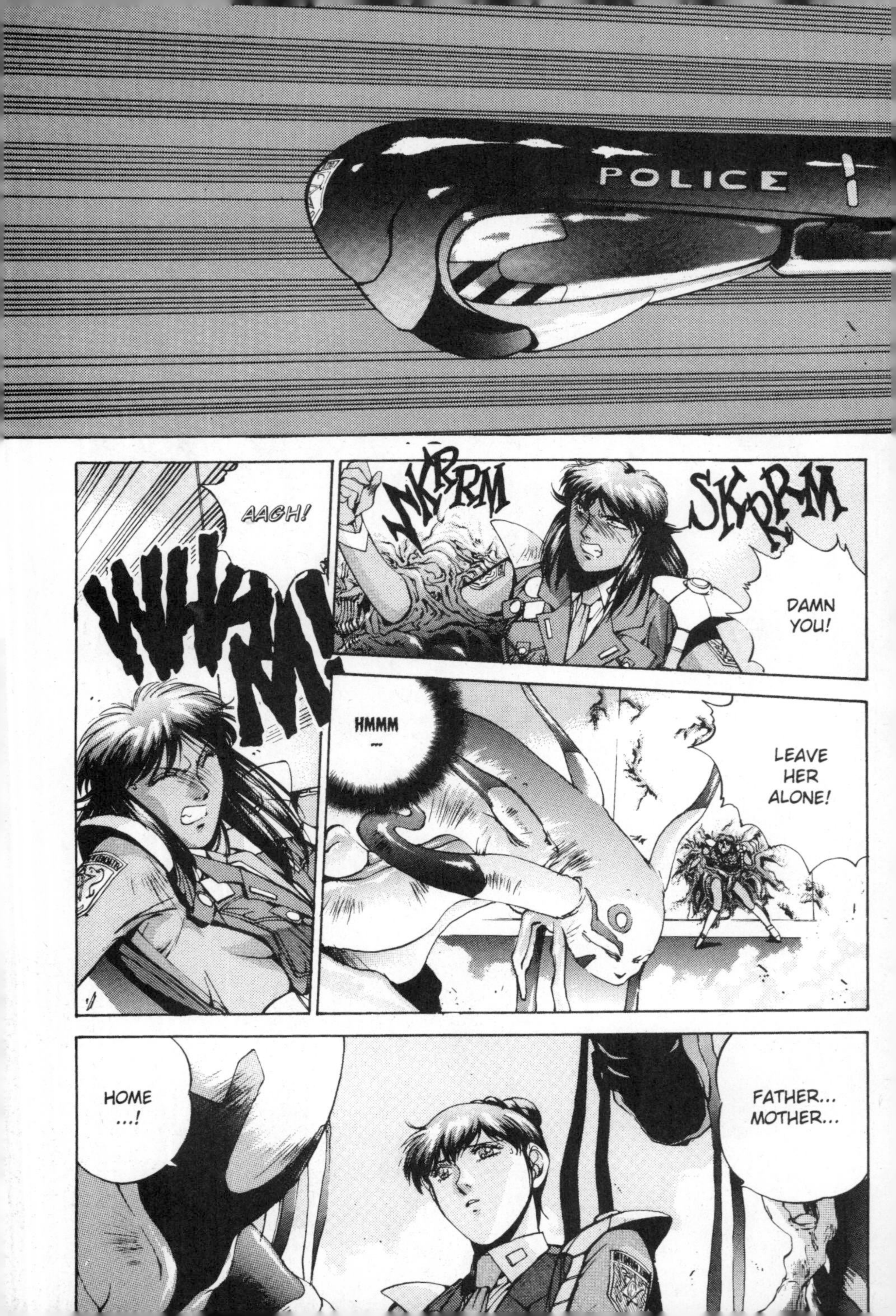
POLICE
AAGH!
WHAM!
SKRRM
SKRRM
DAMN YOU!
HMMM ...
LEAVE HER ALONE!
HOME ...!
FATHER... MOTHER...

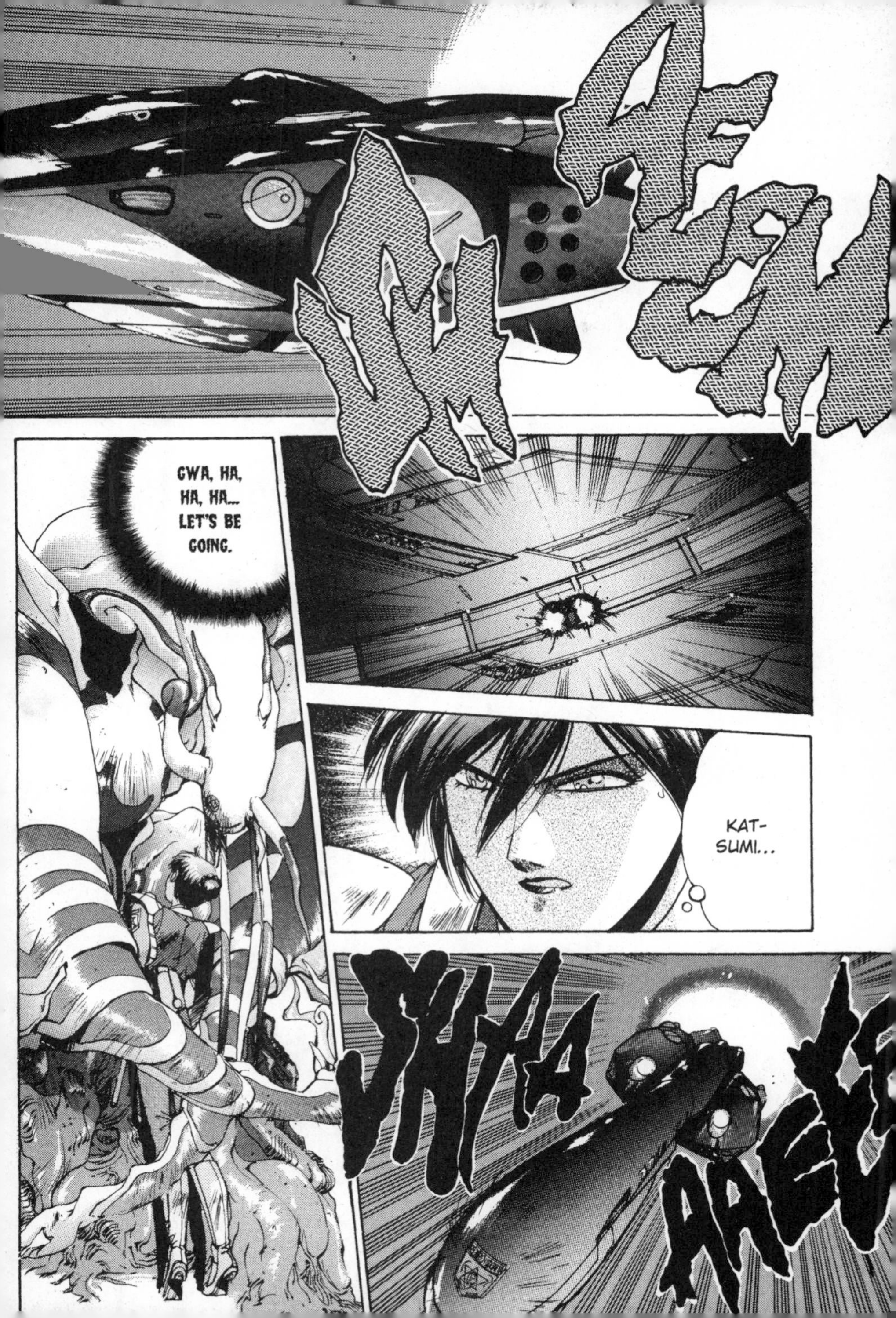
GWA, HA, HA, HA... LET'S BE GOING.
KAT-SUMI...

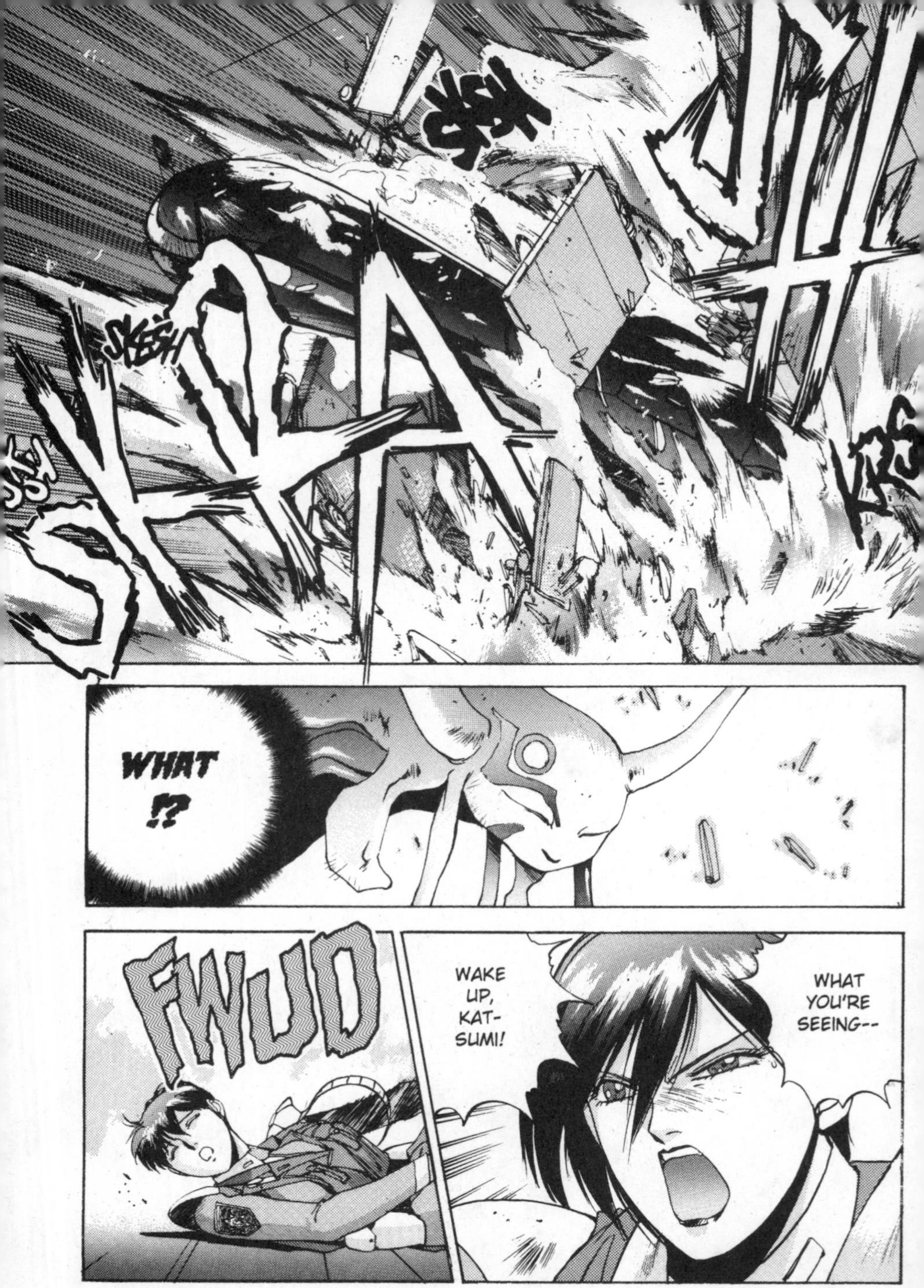
SKSH
SKESH
KRS
WHAT !?
FWUD
WAKE UP, KAT-SUMI!
WHAT YOU'RE SEEING--

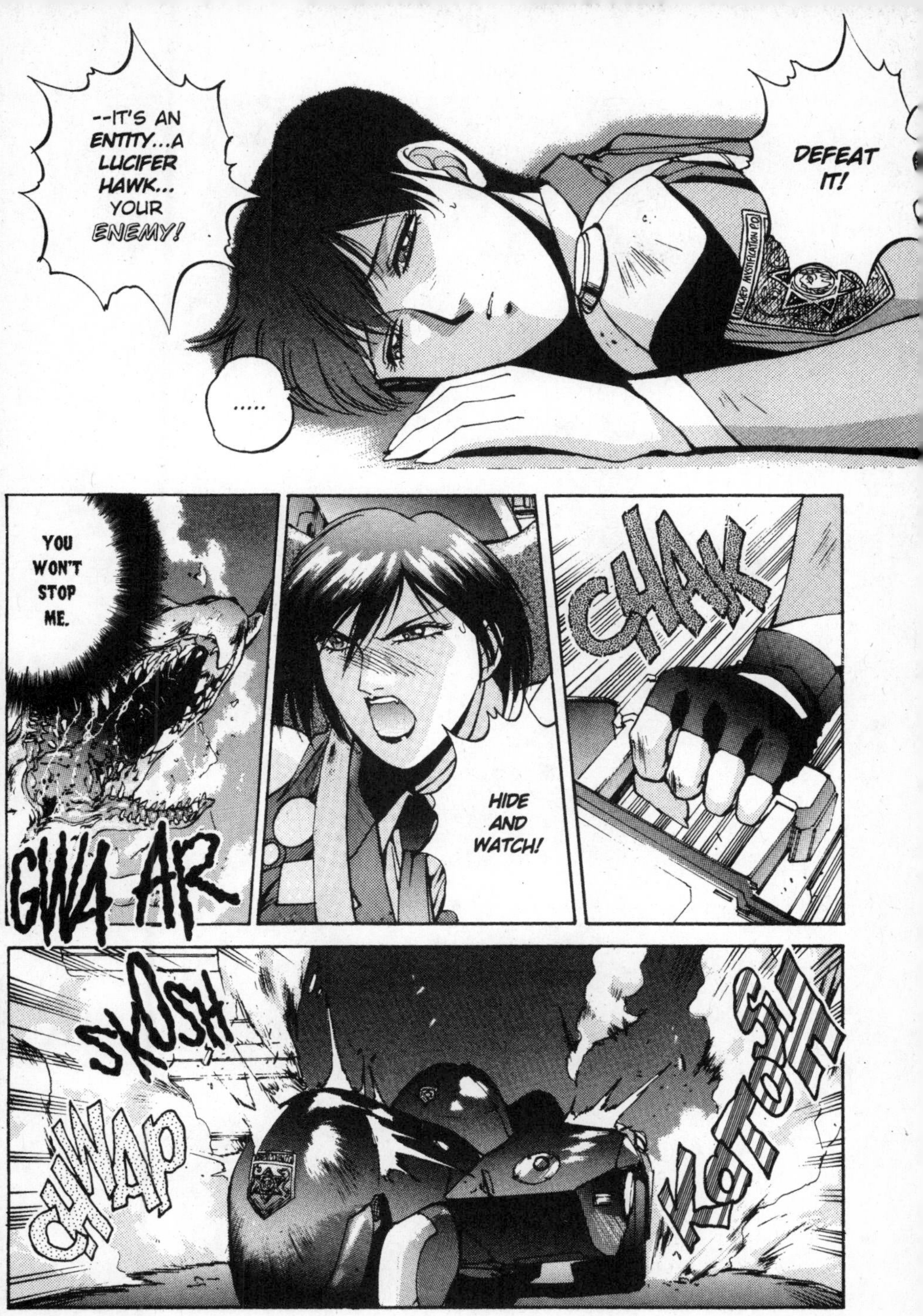
--IT'S AN ENTITY...A LUCIFER HAWK... YOUR ENEMY!
DEFEAT IT!
.....
YOU WON'T STOP ME.
GWA AR
HIDE AND WATCH!
CHAK
SKOSH
CHWAP

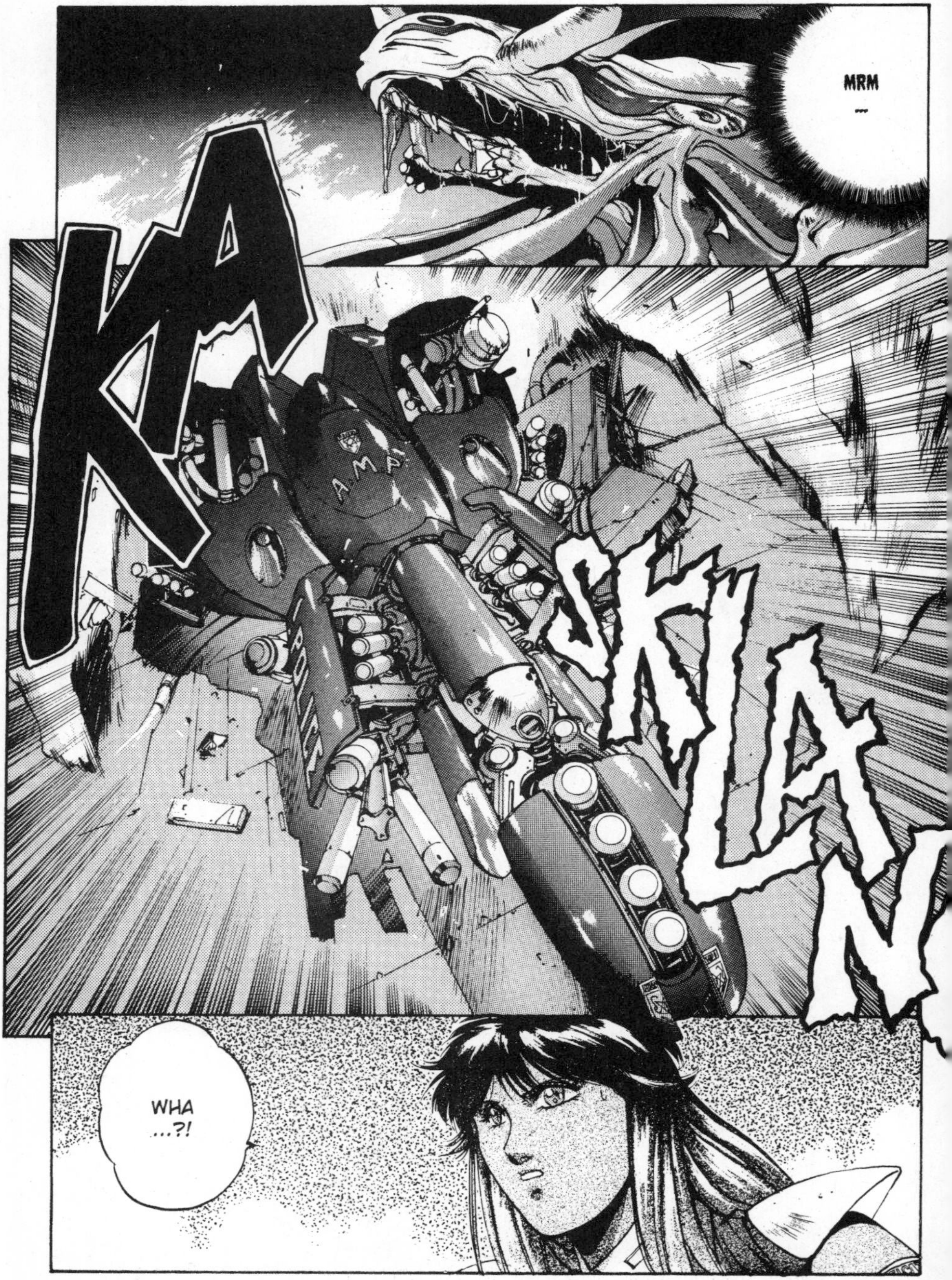

MRM
...
KA
SKLAN
WHA
...?!

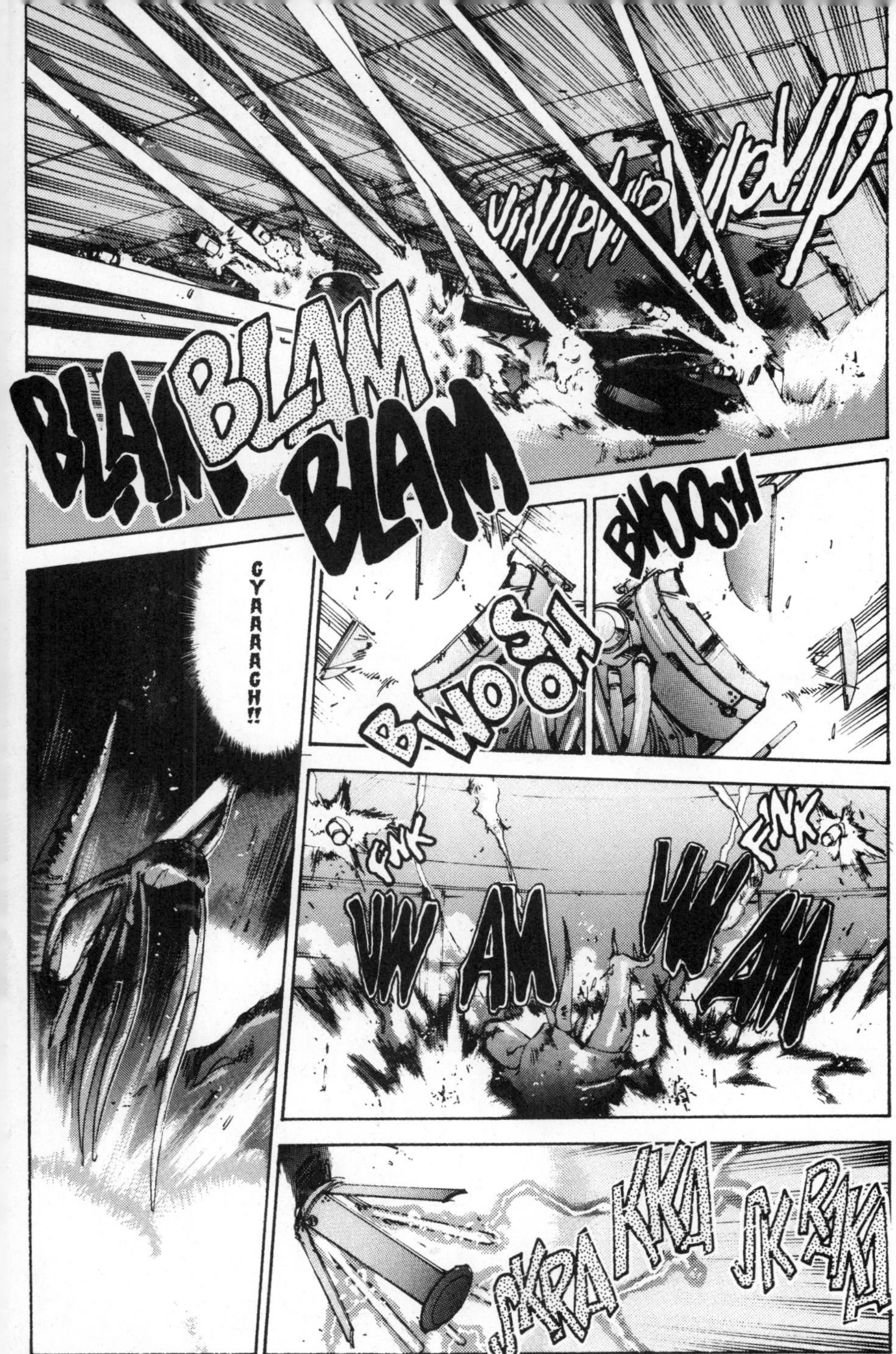
BLAM
BLAM
BLAM
GYAAAAGH!!
BWOOSH
BWOOOSH
FINK
WWAM
FINK
WWAM
SKRAKKA
SKRAKKA

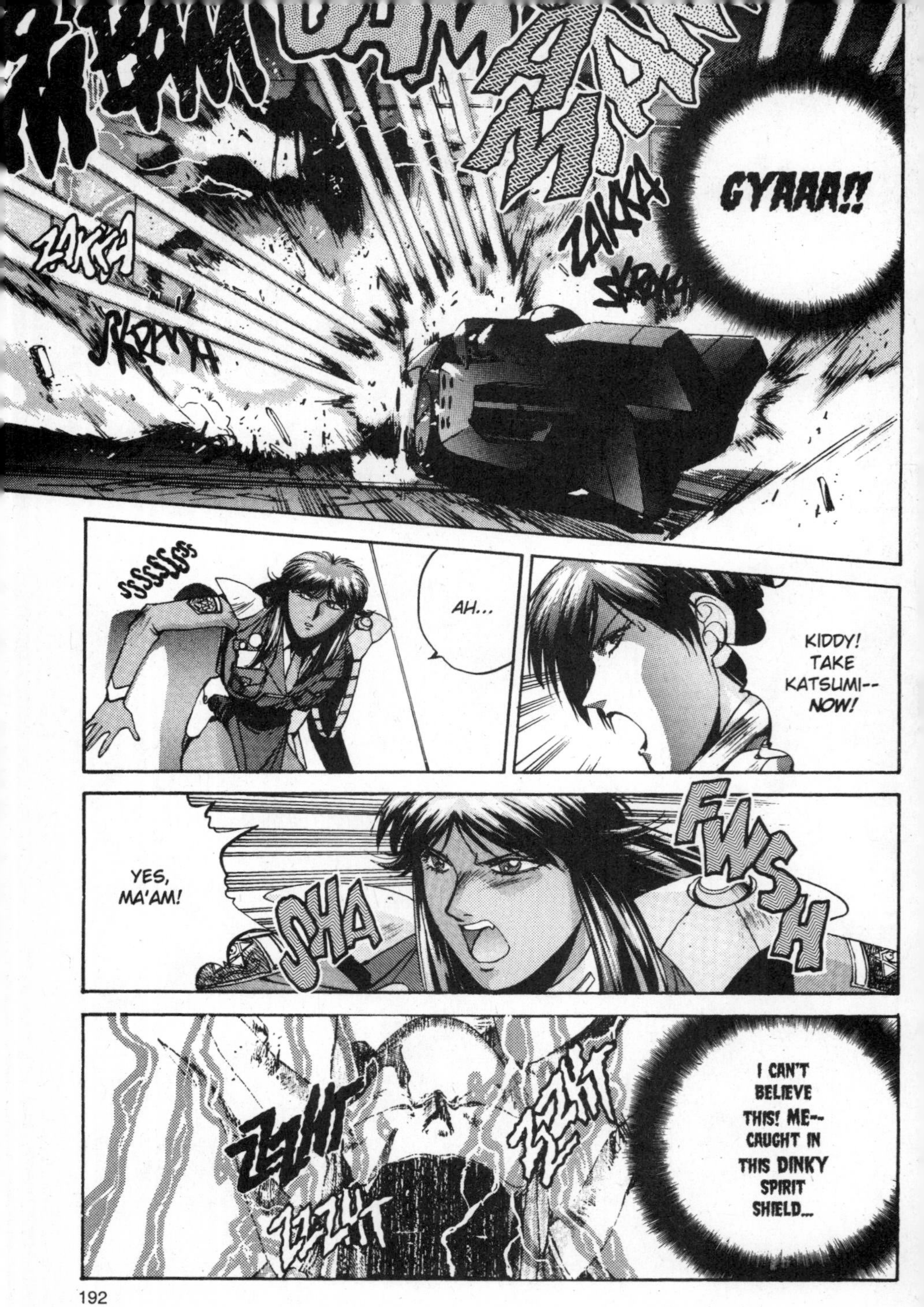
ZAKKA
ZAKKA
GYAAA!!
AH...
KIDDY! TAKE KATSUMI-- NOW!
YES, MA'AM!
SHA
FWSH
I CAN'T BELIEVE THIS! ME-- CAUGHT IN THIS DINKY SPIRIT SHIELD...

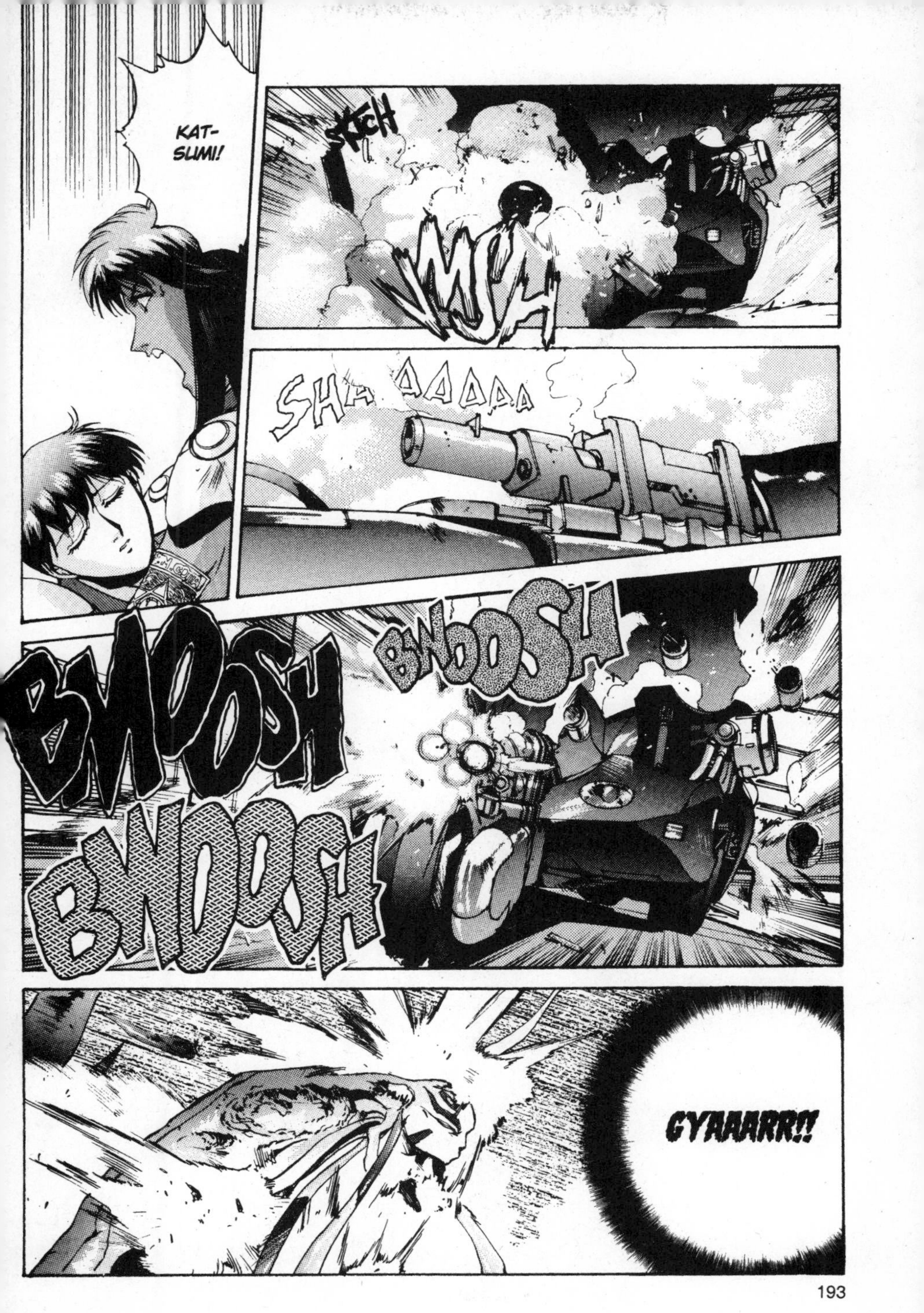
KAT-
SUMI!
SKTCH
WMSH
SHAAAAA
BWOOSH
BWOOSH
BWOOSH
GYAAARR!!

CHAK

.....

VEEEEEM

SHAAAAAAAAAA

A.M.P.

CHIEF! KATSUMI'S SAFE!

VWEE

OOSH

BLAM

SKRAKA

GYAAAAOOO!!

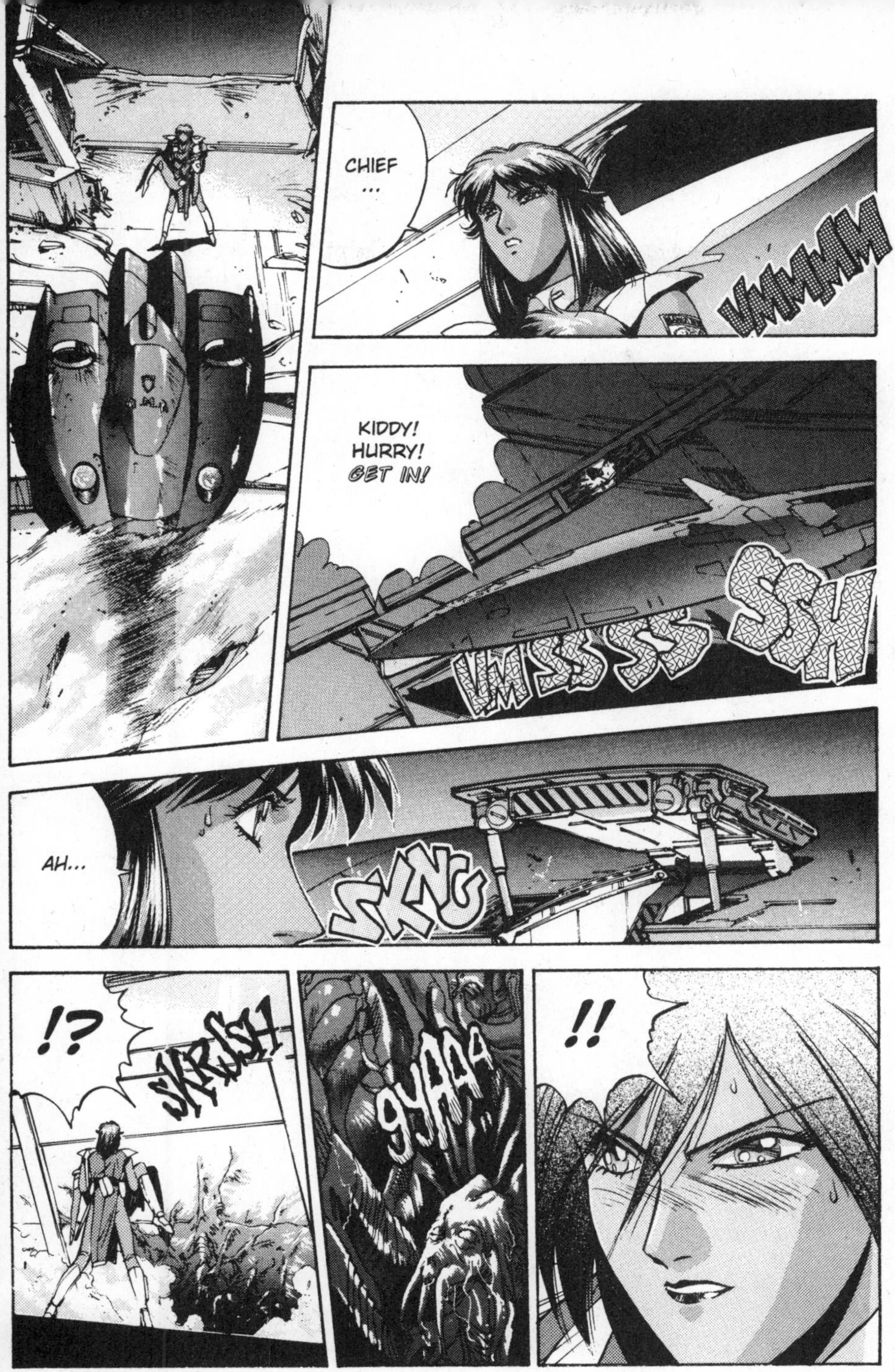
CHIEF ...
VMMMM
KIDDY! HURRY! GET IN!
VMSSSSSSH
AH...
SKNG
!?
SKRSH
GYAAA
!!

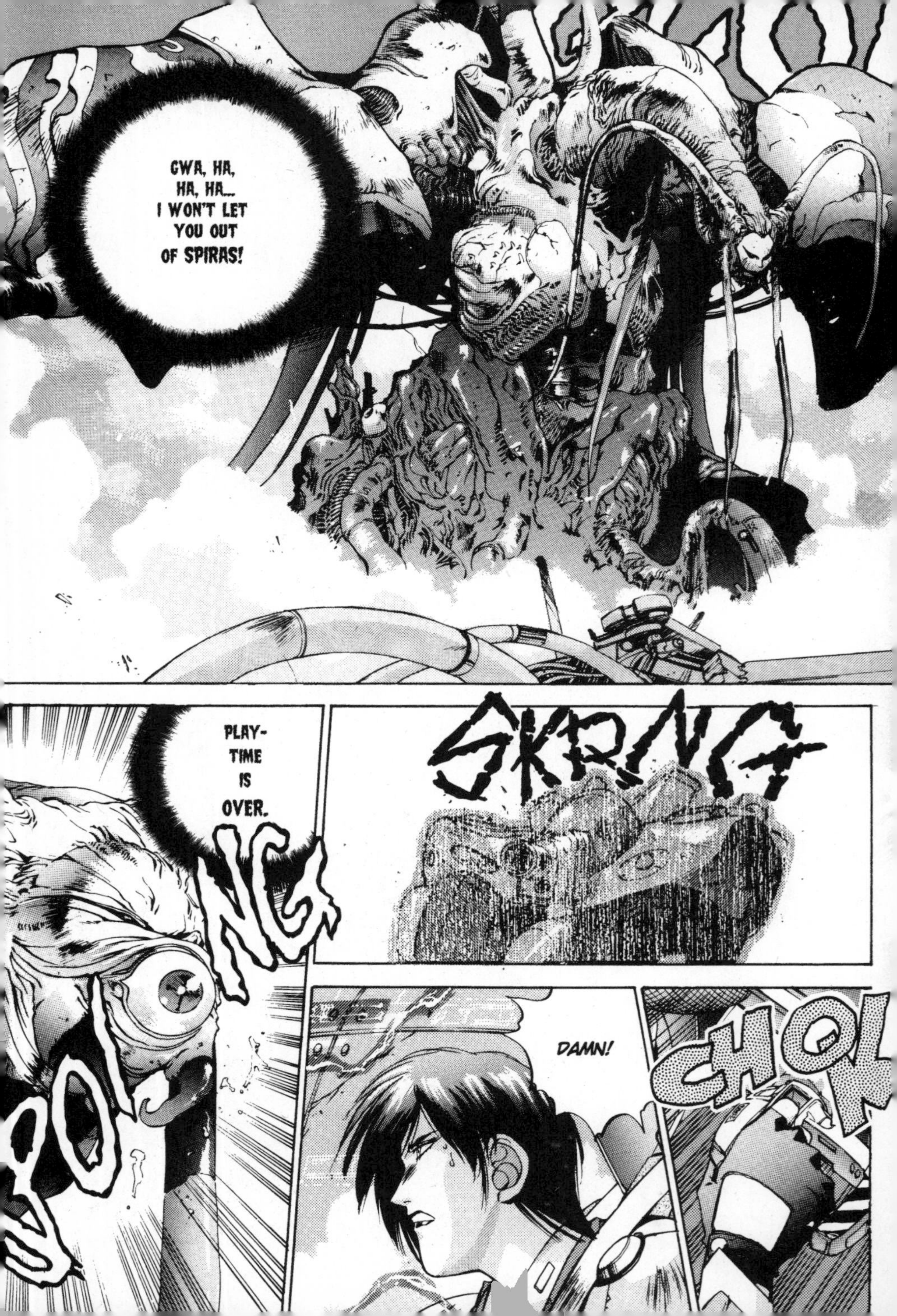
GWA, HA, HA, HA... I WON'T LET YOU OUT OF SPIRAS!
PLAY-TIME IS OVER.
SKRNG
DAMN!

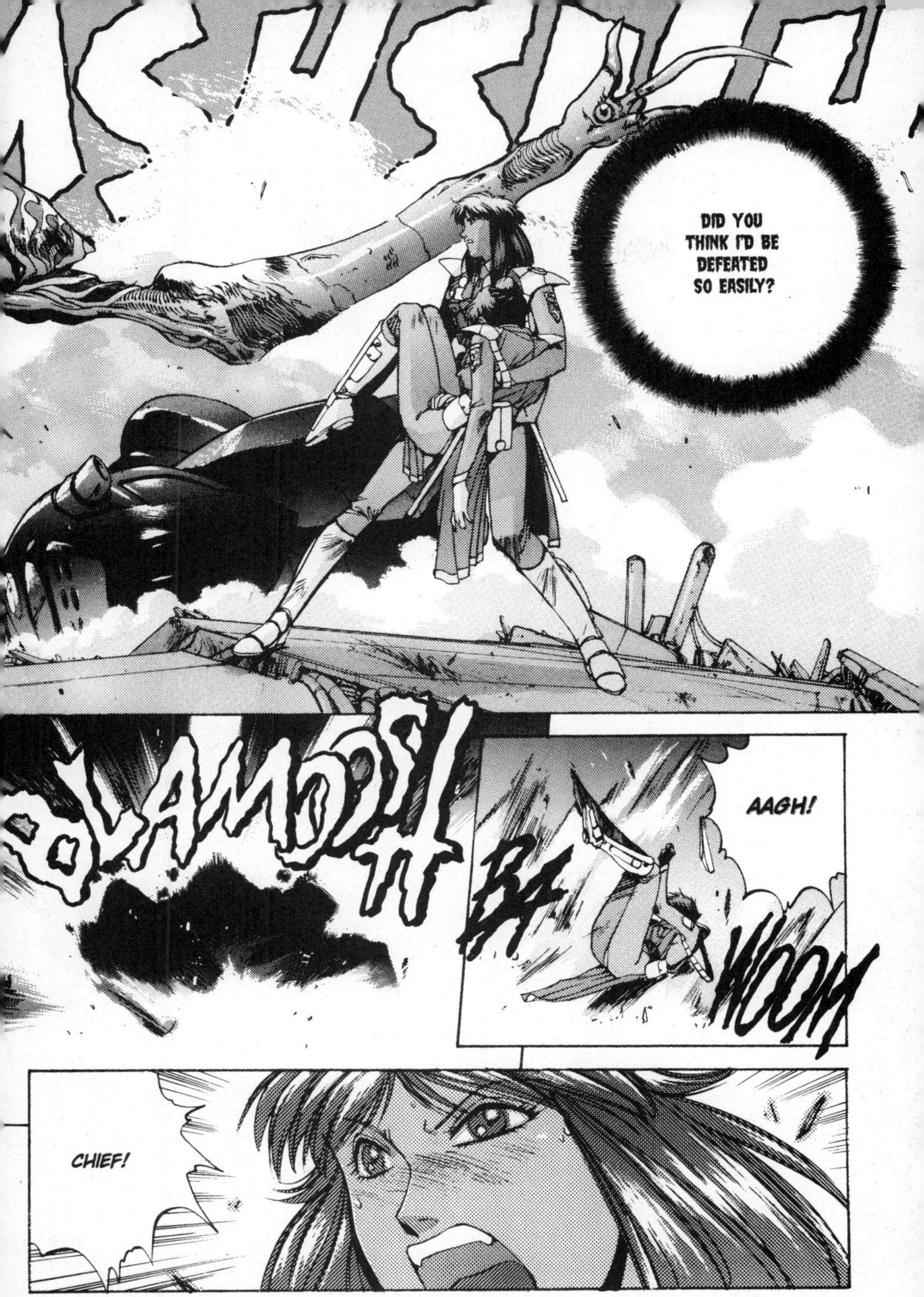
DID YOU THINK I'D BE DEFEATED SO EASILY?
AAGH!
BA
WOOM
CHIEF!

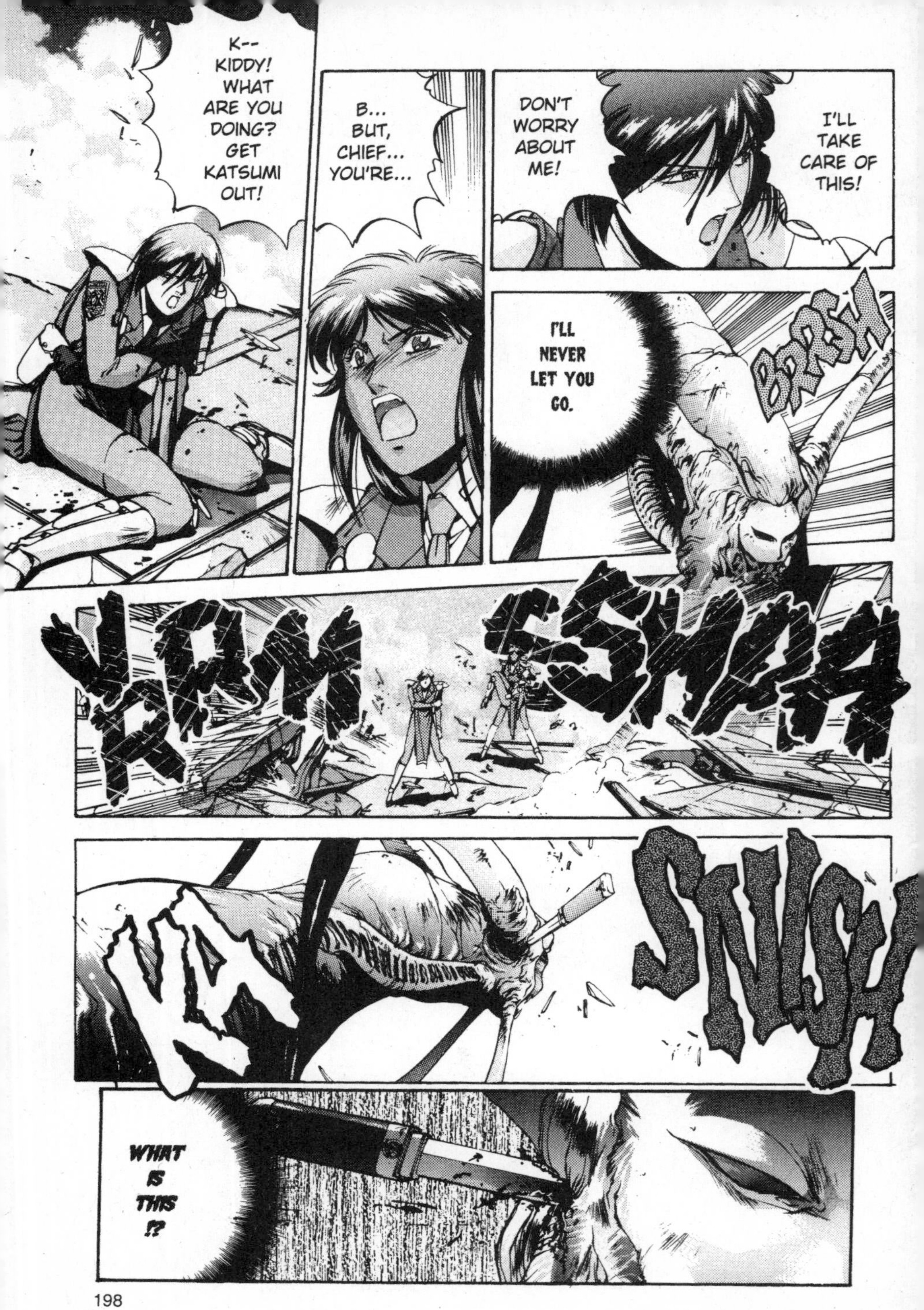
K-- KIDDY! WHAT ARE YOU DOING? GET KATSUMI OUT!
B... BUT, CHIEF... YOU'RE...
DON'T WORRY ABOUT ME!
I'LL TAKE CARE OF THIS!
I'LL NEVER LET YOU GO.
WHAT IS THIS !?

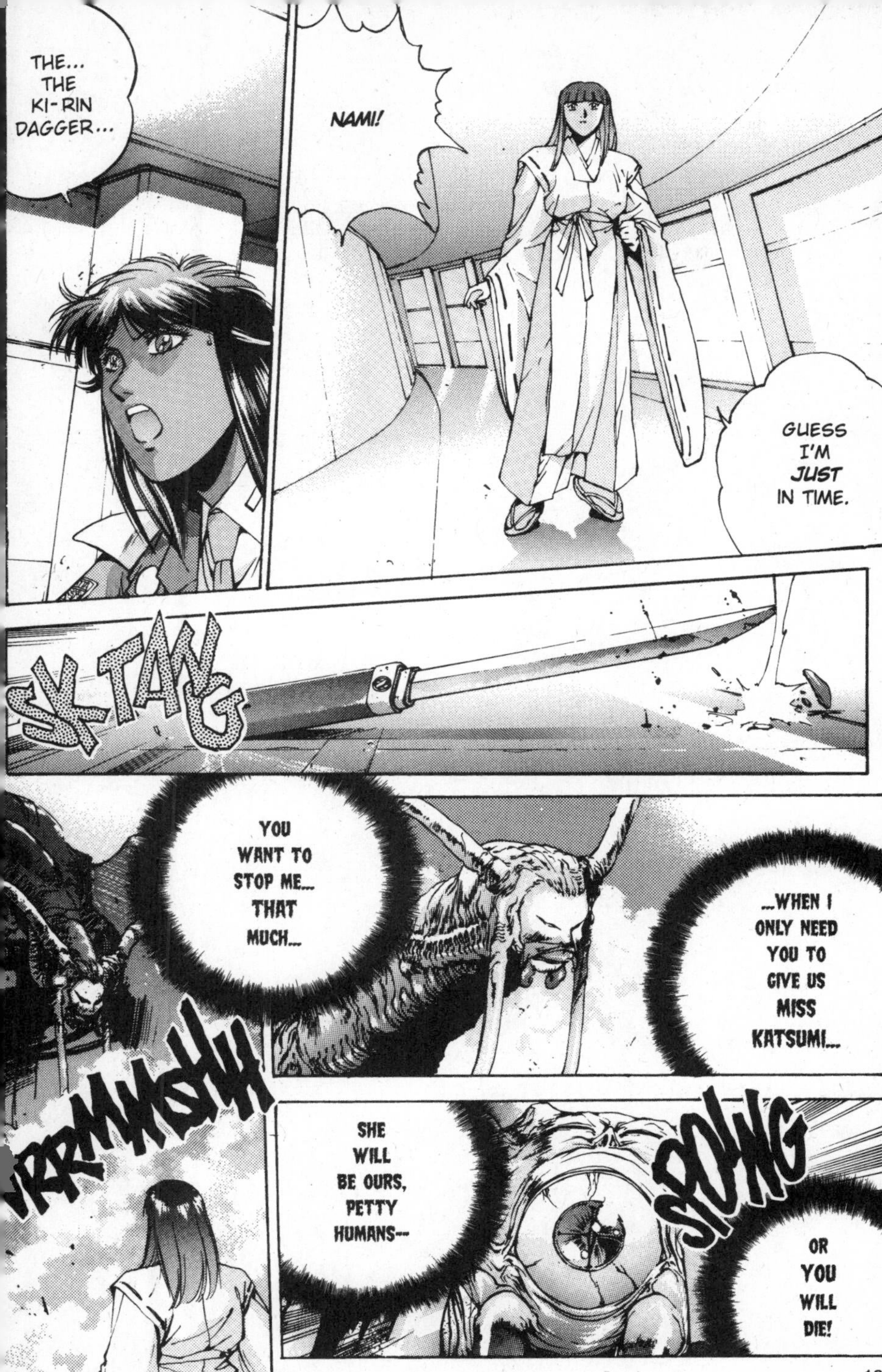
THE... THE KI-RIN DAGGER...
NAMI!
GUESS I'M *JUST* IN TIME.
SK-TANG
YOU WANT TO STOP ME... THAT MUCH...
...WHEN I ONLY NEED YOU TO GIVE US MISS KATSUMI...
RRMMSHH
SHE WILL BE OURS, PETTY HUMANS--
SPONG
OR YOU WILL DIE!

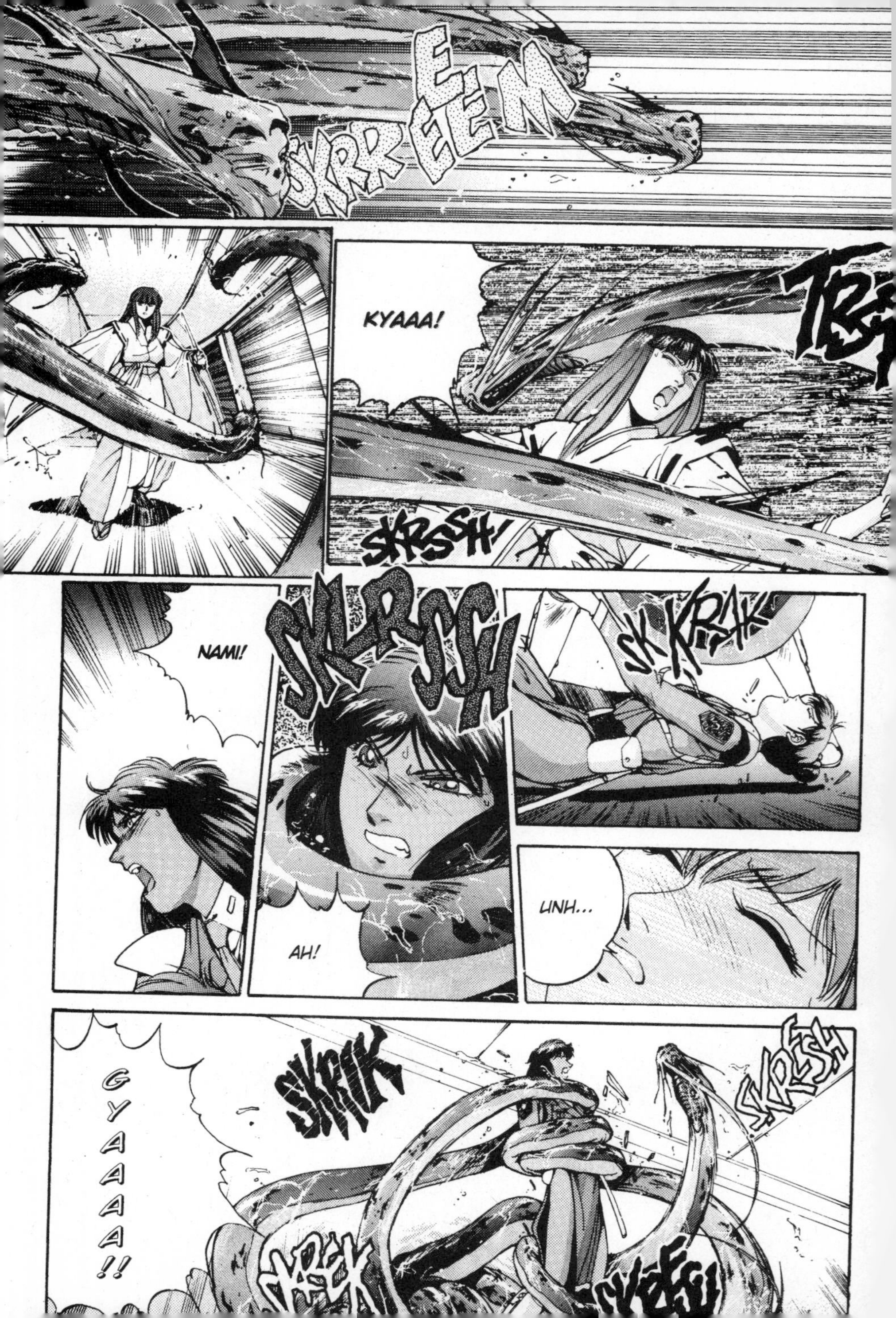
SKRREEEEM
KYAAA!
SKRSSH!
NAMI!
SKLRSCH
AH!
SK KRAK
UNH...
GYAAAAAA!!
SKRIIK
SKRESH

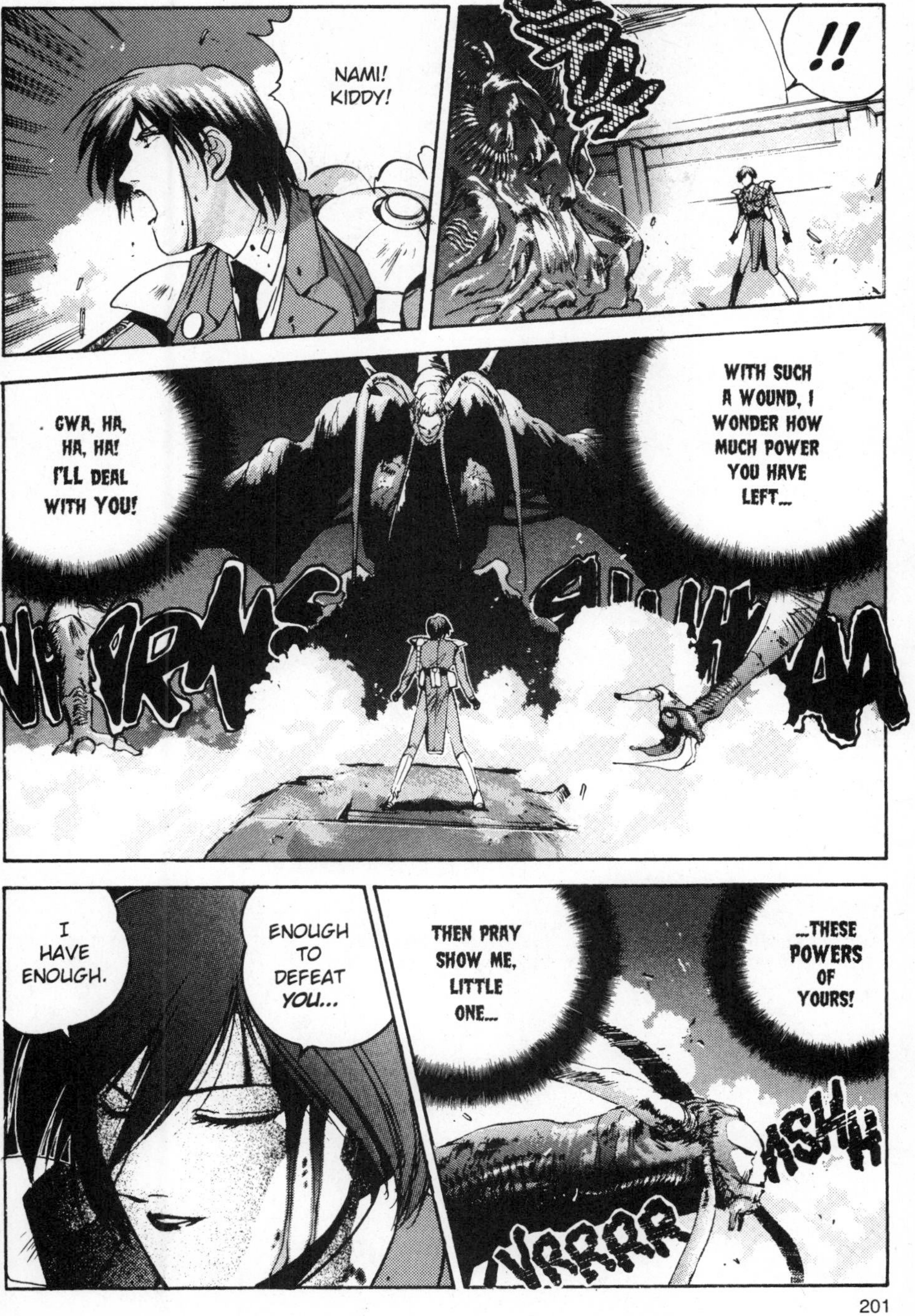
NAMI! KIDDY!
!!
. GWA, HA, HA, HA! I'LL DEAL WITH YOU!
WITH SUCH A WOUND, I WONDER HOW MUCH POWER YOU HAVE LEFT...
I HAVE ENOUGH.
ENOUGH TO DEFEAT YOU...
THEN PRAY SHOW ME, LITTLE ONE...
...THESE POWERS OF YOURS!
VRRRR

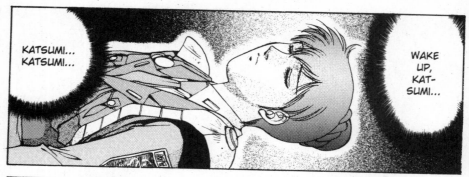

KATSUMI... KATSUMI...
WAKE UP, KATSUMI...
IT'S TIME TO STOP BEING A CHILD, KATSUMI...
AH...
OPEN YOUR EYES! PULL YOURSELF TOGETHER!
YOU'VE BEEN GONE FROM US TOO LONG.
WHO IS IT...?
THE PAST IS PAST, ISN'T IT?
NOW IS ALL THAT COUNTS, KATSUMI! EVERY DEMON THAT CAN BE CONQUERED IS IN THE NOW!
WHAT... WHAT CAN I...
WHAT CAN I DO?!
OPEN YOUR EYES TO THE PRESENT!
ONLY THEN WILL YOU KNOW WHAT TO DO!

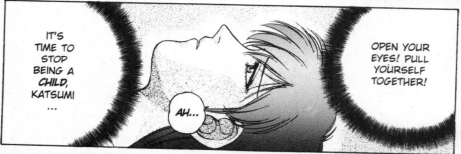

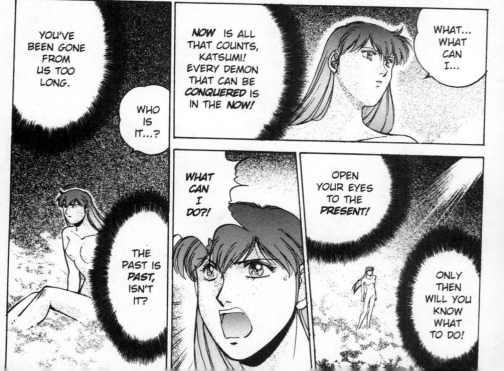

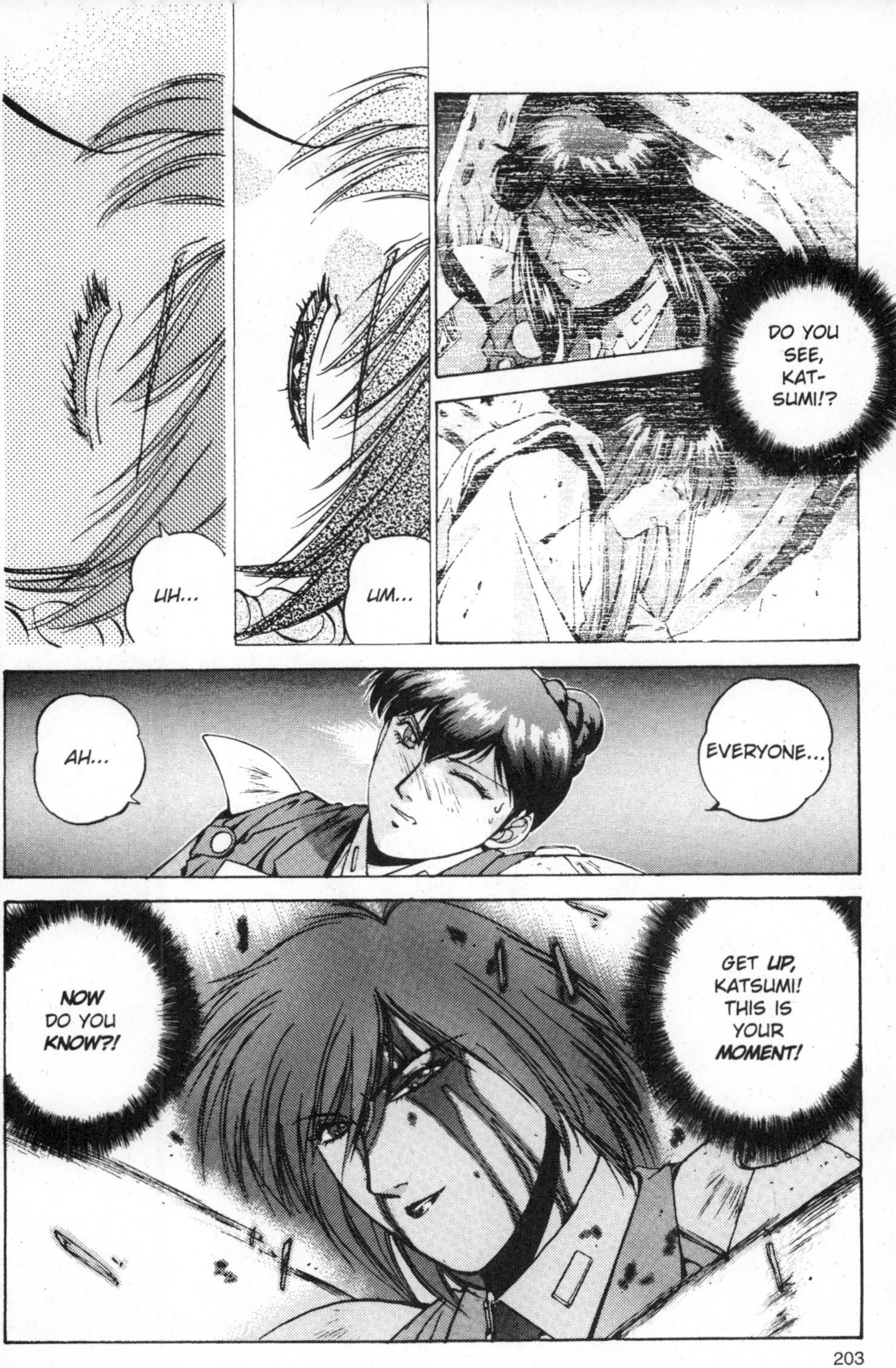
UH...
UM...
DO YOU SEE, KAT-SUMI!?
AH...
EVERYONE...
NOW DO YOU KNOW?!
GET UP, KATSUMI! THIS IS YOUR MOMENT!

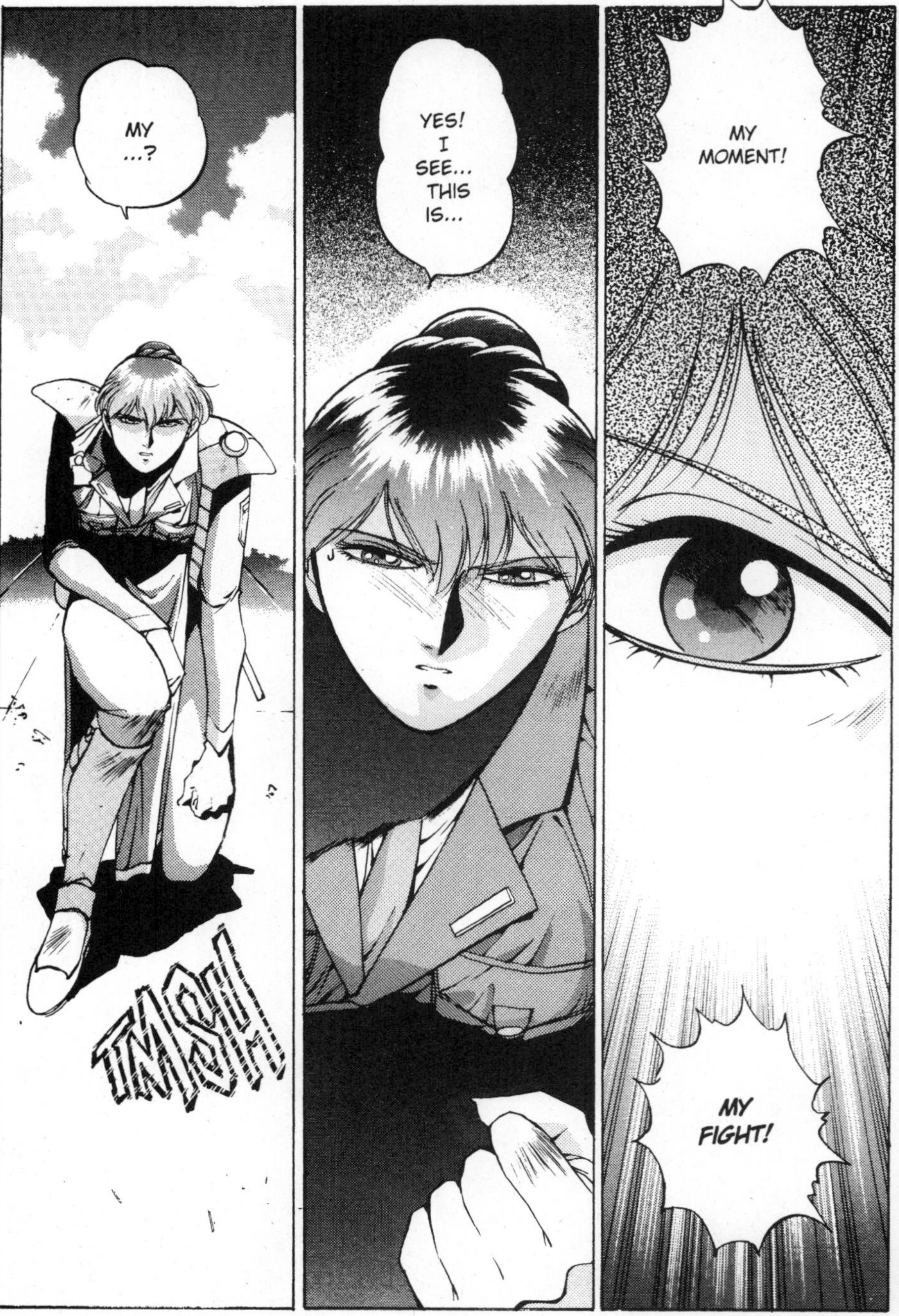
MY ...?
TMSH!
YES! I SEE... THIS IS...
MY MOMENT!
MY FIGHT!

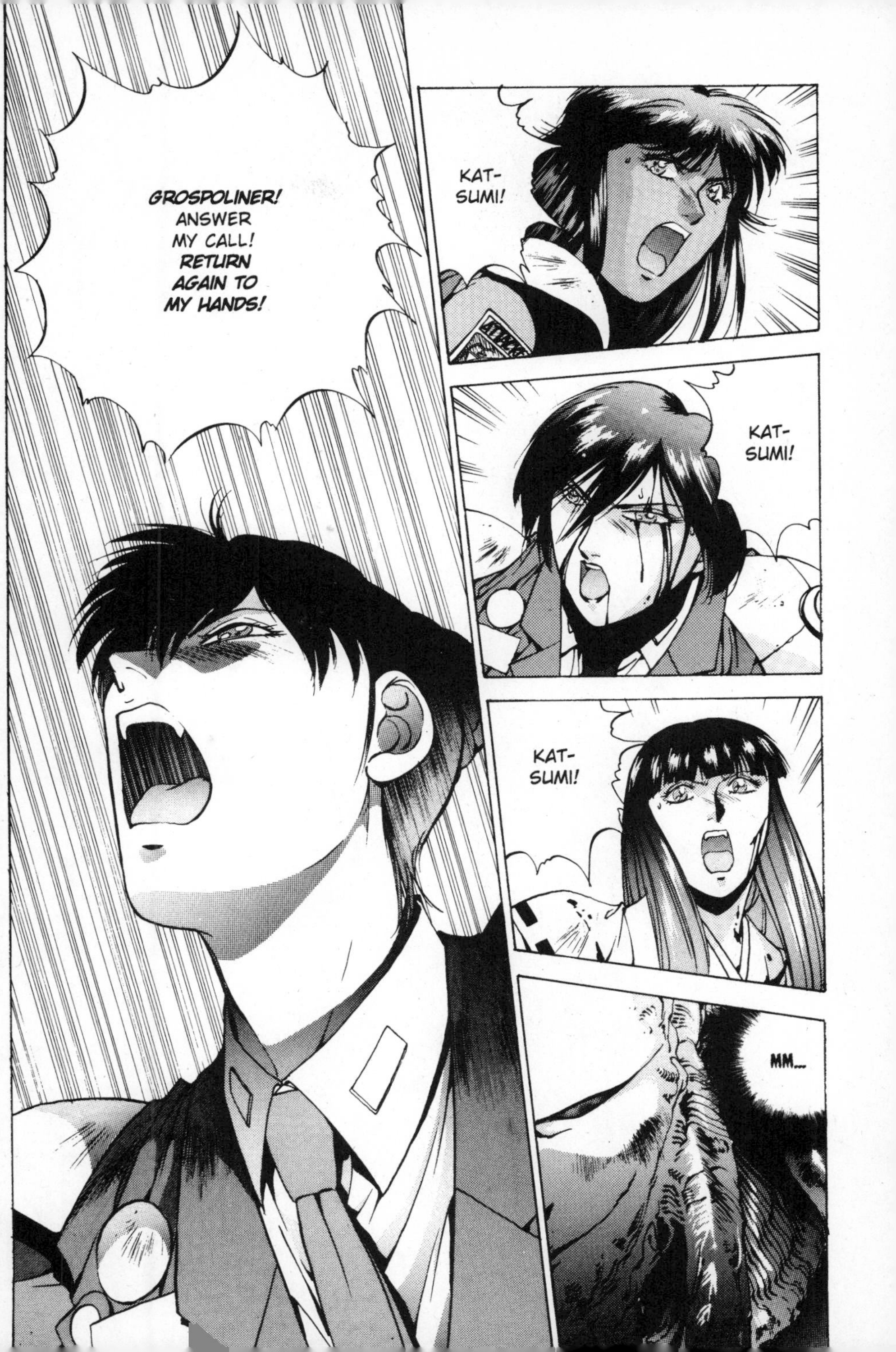
GROSPOLINER! ANSWER MY CALL! RETURN AGAIN TO MY HANDS!
KAT-SUMI!
KAT-SUMI!
KAT-SUMI!
MM...

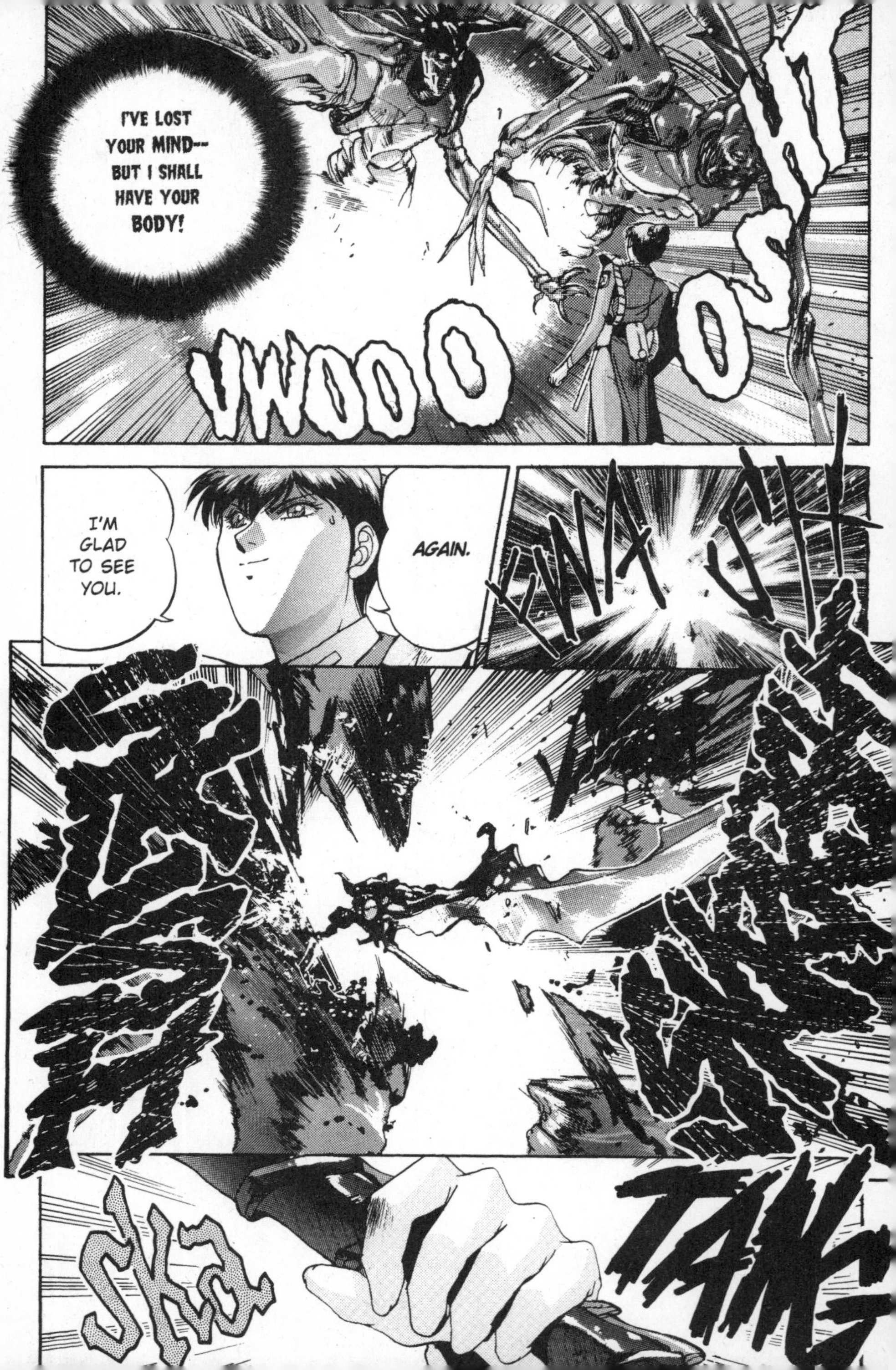
I'VE LOST YOUR MIND-- BUT I SHALL HAVE YOUR BODY!
VWOOOOSH!!
I'M GLAD TO SEE YOU.
AGAIN.
SKA
TANG

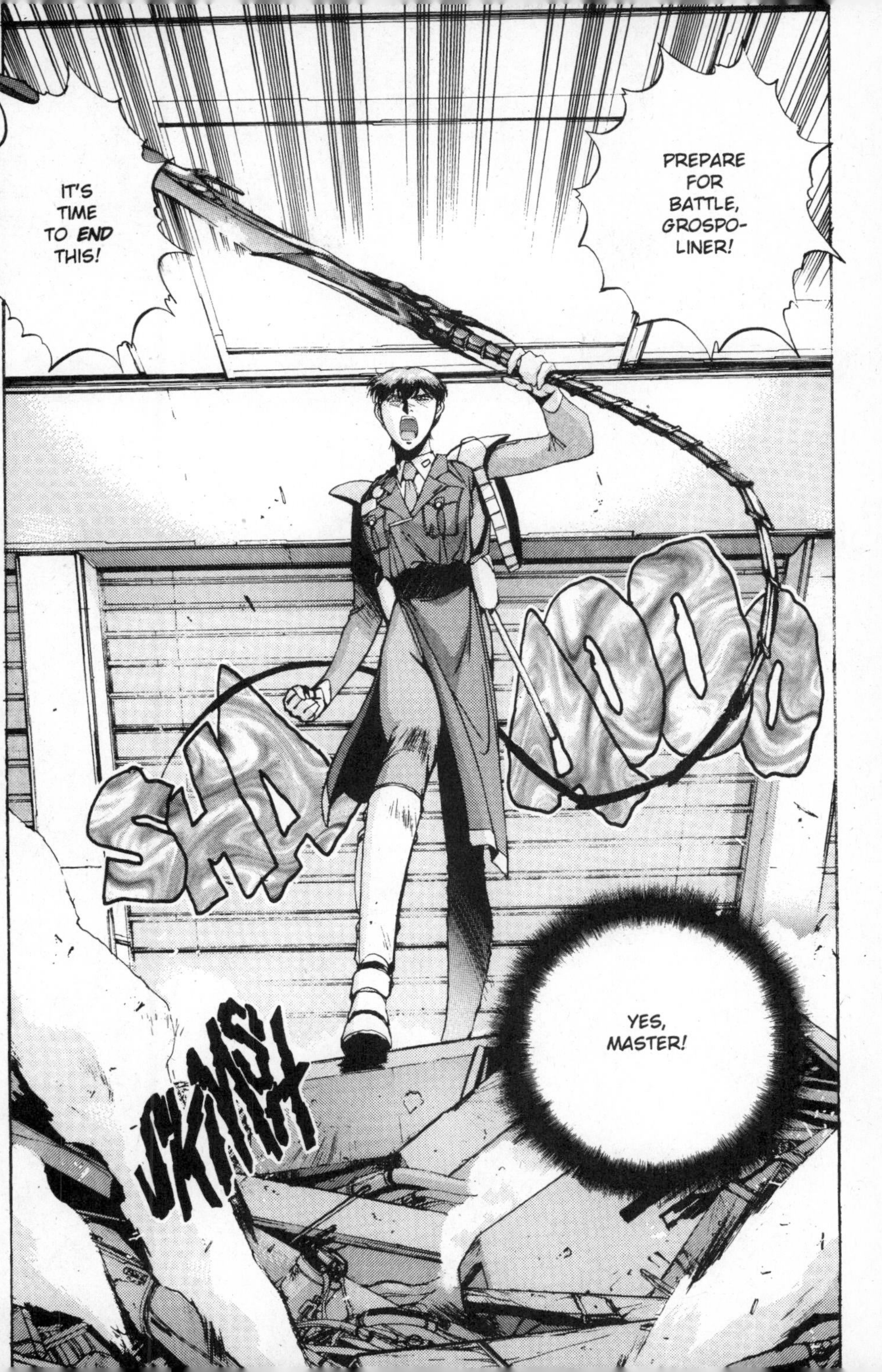

IT'S TIME TO END THIS!
PREPARE FOR BATTLE, GROSPO-LINER!
SHA-WOOO
SKASH!
YES, MASTER!

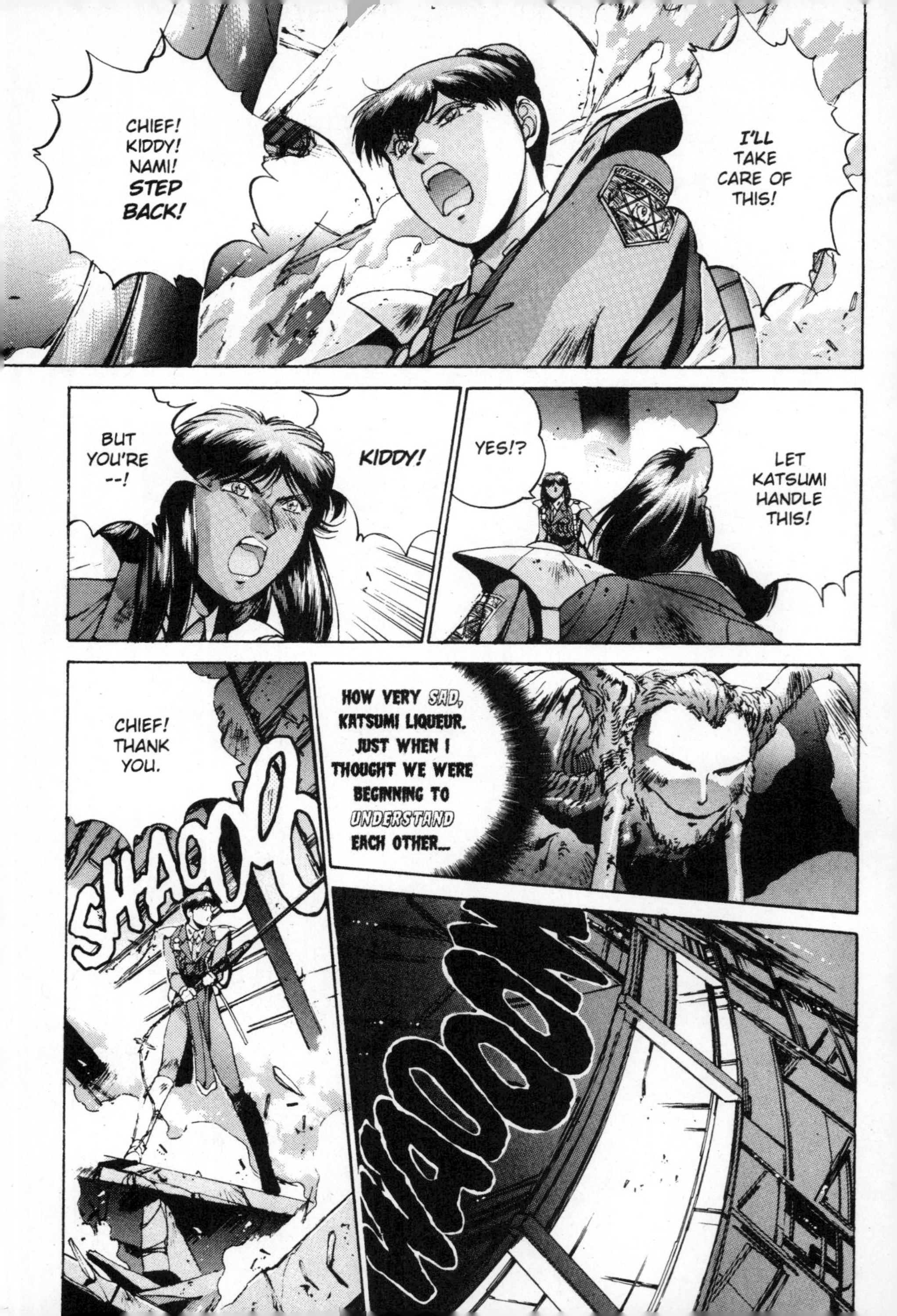
CHIEF! KIDDY! NAMI! STEP BACK!
I'LL TAKE CARE OF THIS!
BUT YOU'RE --!
KIDDY!
YES!?
LET KATSUMI HANDLE THIS!
CHIEF! THANK YOU.
HOW VERY SAD, KATSUMI LIQUEUR. JUST WHEN I THOUGHT WE WERE BEGINNING TO UNDERSTAND EACH OTHER...
SHAOOM
WHOOOM

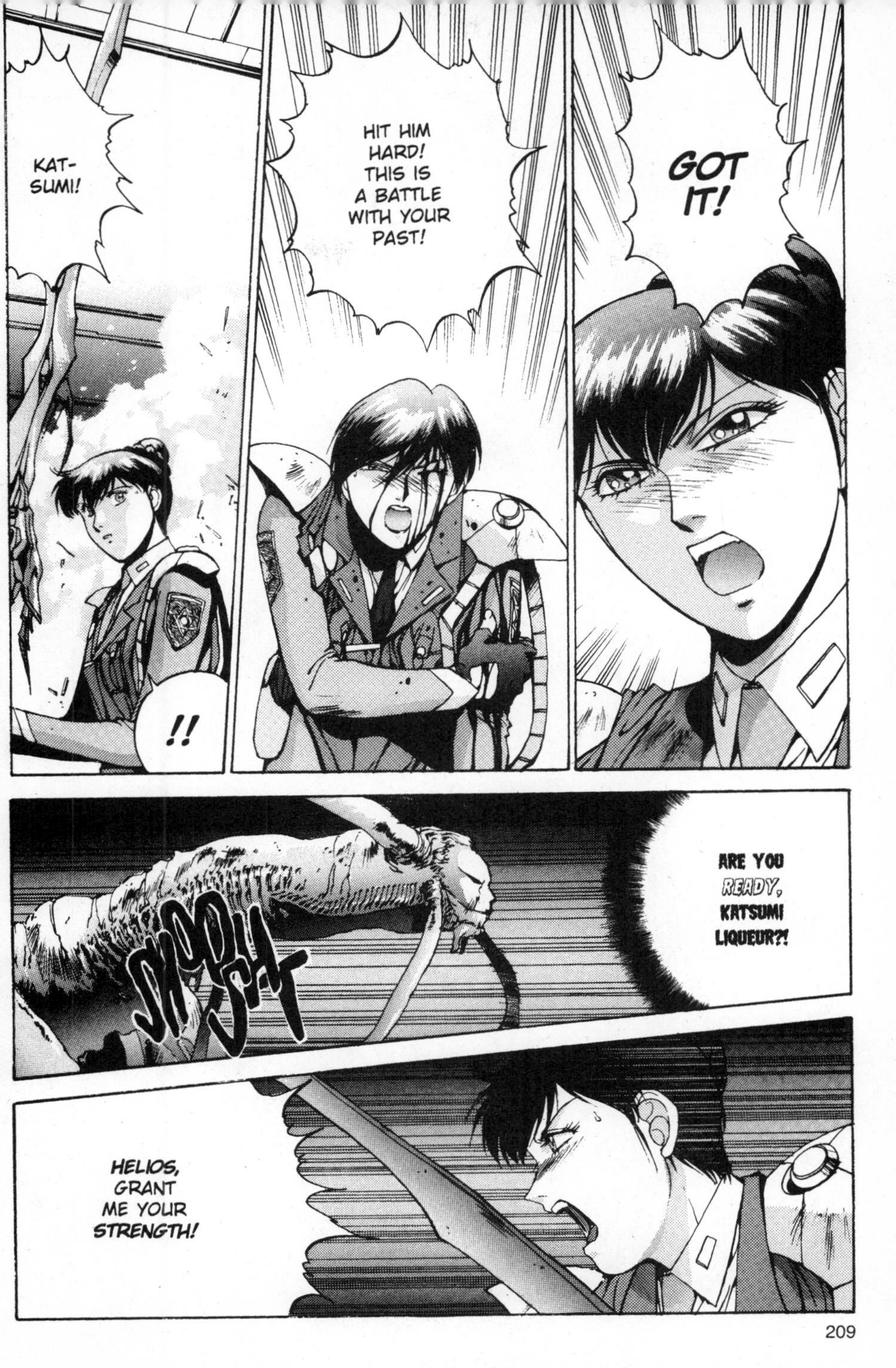
KAT-SUMI!
!!
HIT HIM HARD! THIS IS A BATTLE WITH YOUR PAST!
GOT IT!
SHOOSH
ARE YOU READY, KATSUMI LIQUEUR?!
HELIOS, GRANT ME YOUR STRENGTH!

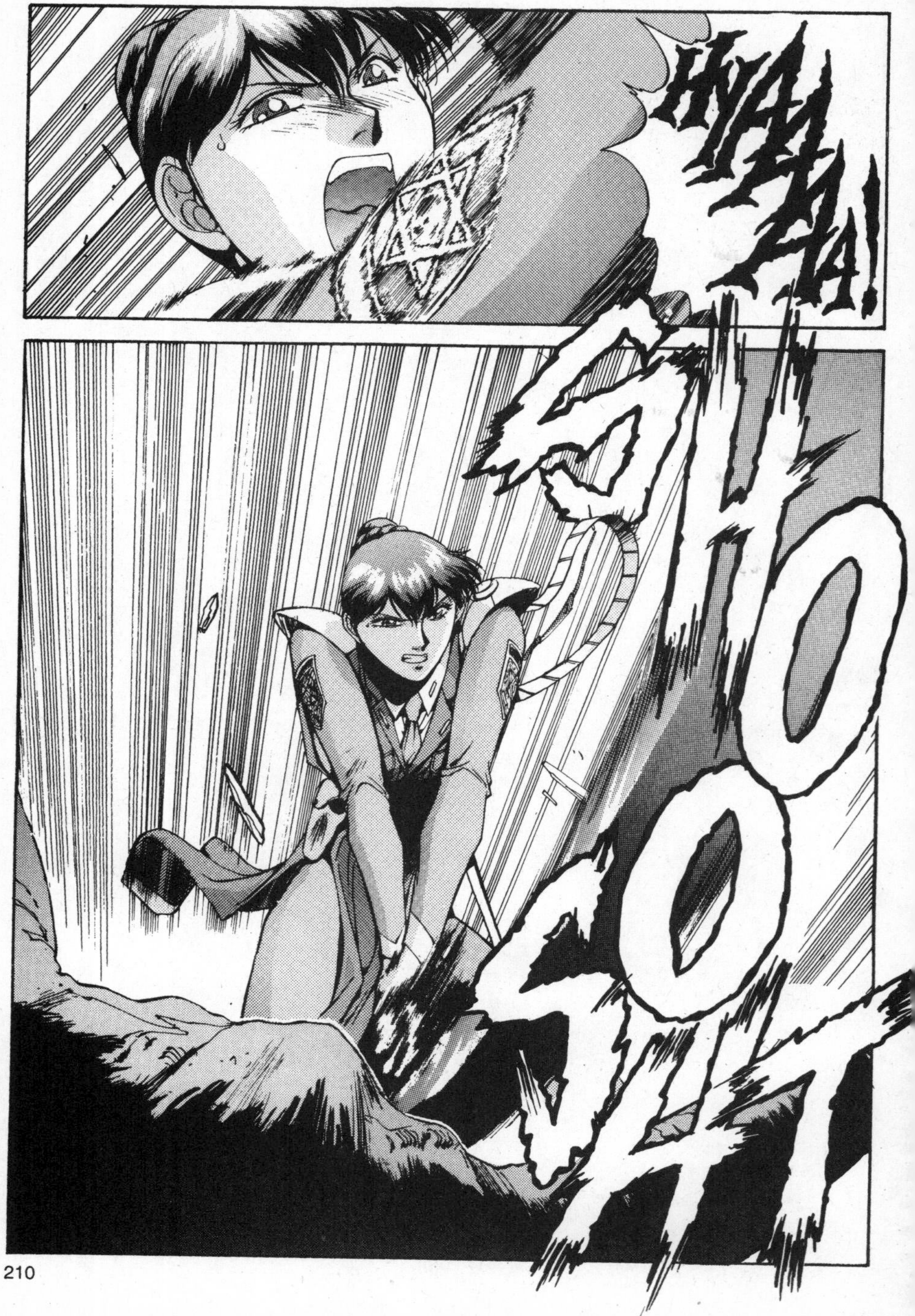
HYAAAA!

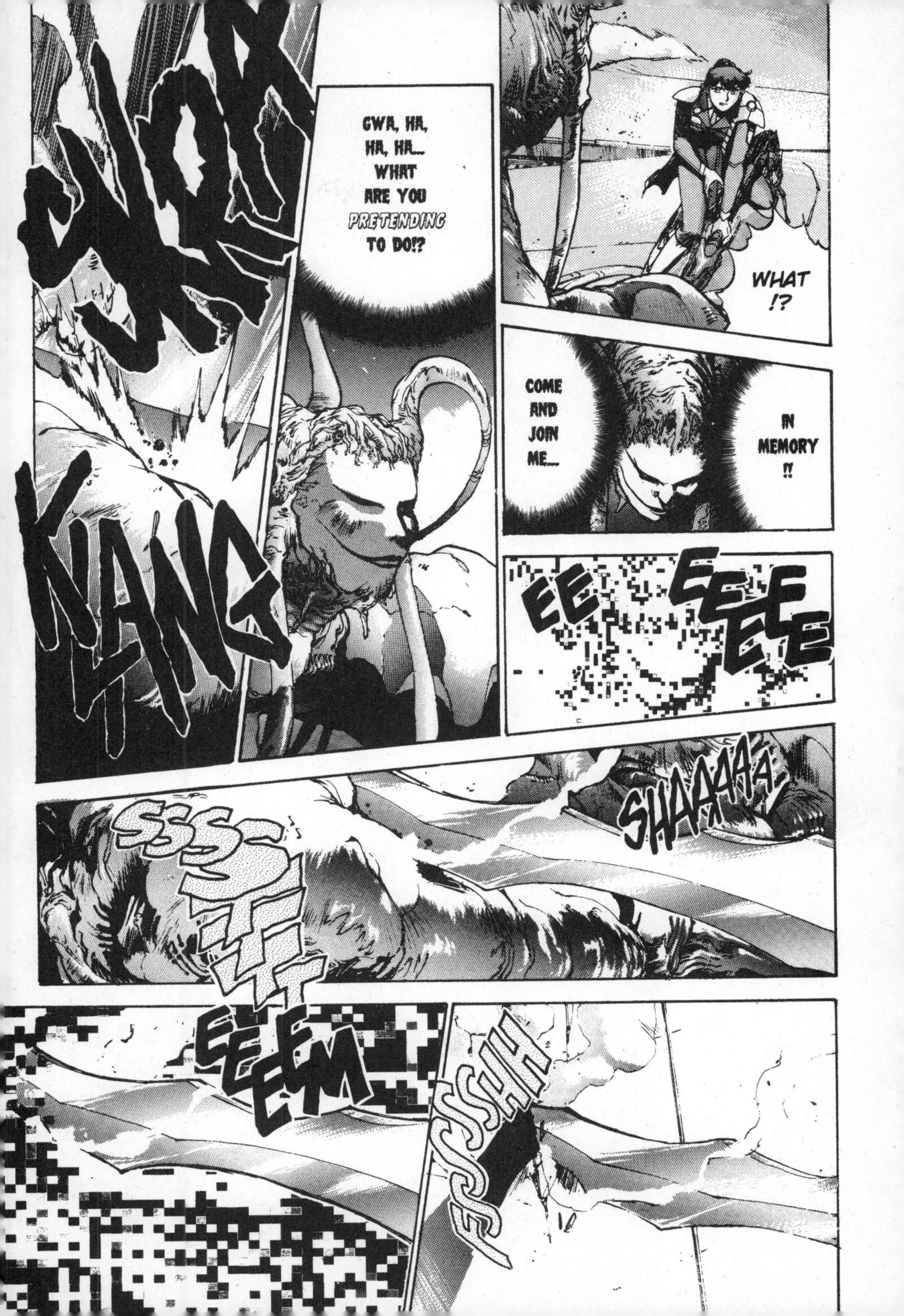
KLANG
GWA, HA, HA, HA... WHAT ARE YOU *PRETENDING* TO DO!?
WHAT !?
COME AND JOIN ME...
IN MEMORY !!

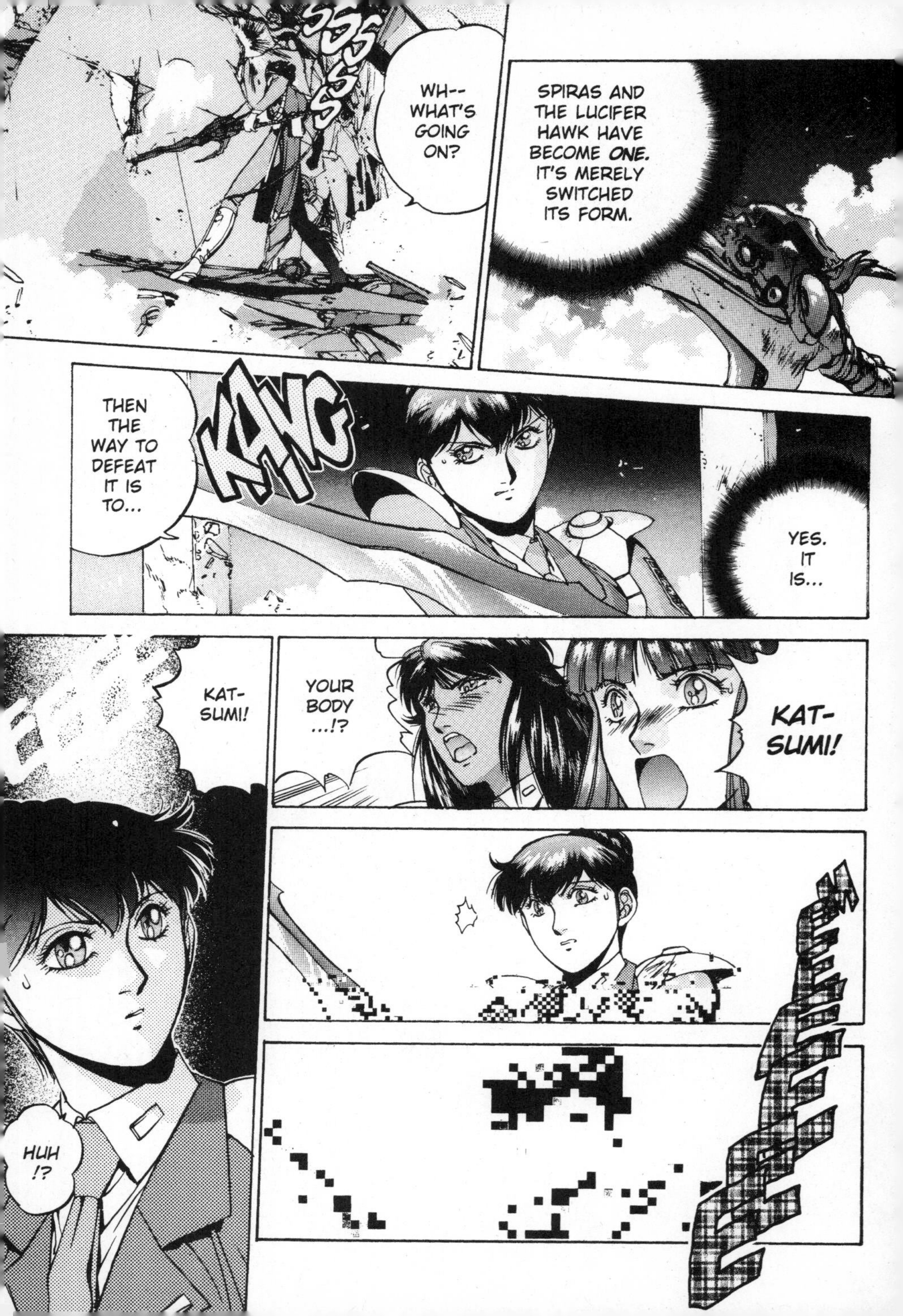

SSSSSSS
WH-- WHAT'S GOING ON?
SPIRAS AND THE LUCIFER HAWK HAVE BECOME *ONE.* IT'S MERELY SWITCHED ITS FORM.
THEN THE WAY TO DEFEAT IT IS TO...
KANG
YES. IT IS...
KAT-SUMI!
HUH !?
YOUR BODY ...!?
KAT-SUMI!

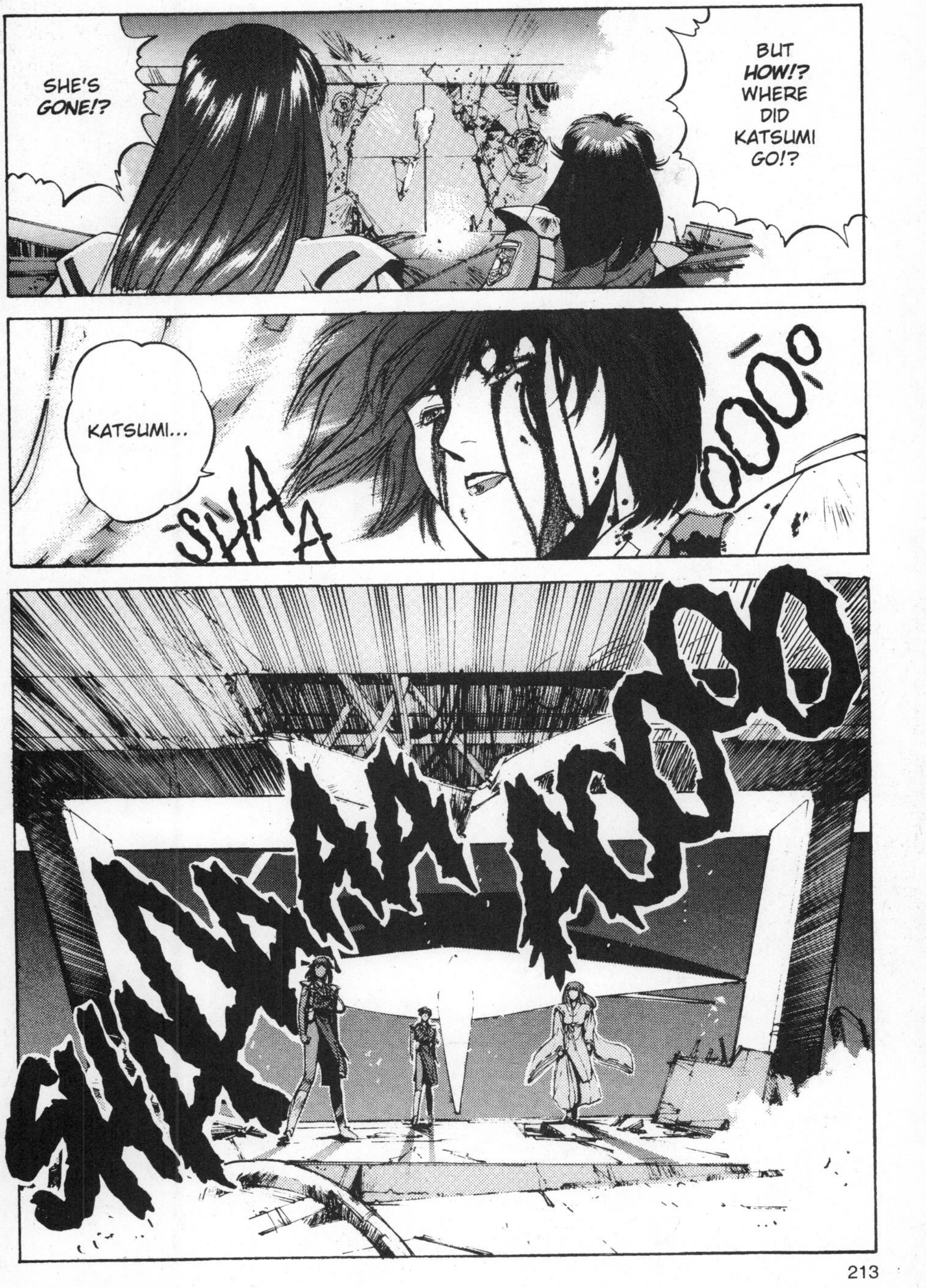
SHE'S GONE!?
BUT HOW!? WHERE DID KATSUMI GO!?
KATSUMI...

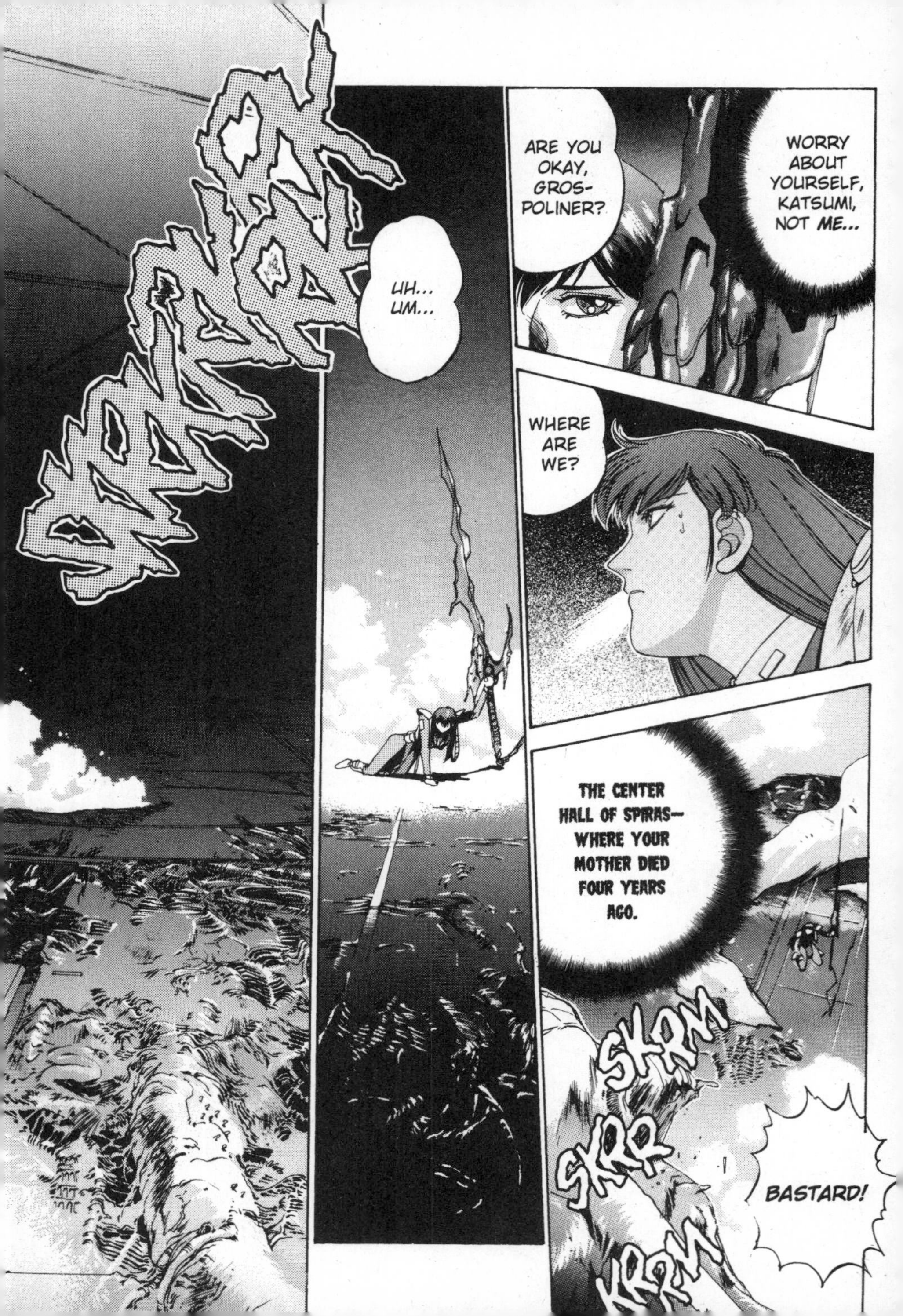
UH... UM...
ARE YOU OKAY, GROS-POLINER?
WORRY ABOUT YOURSELF, KATSUMI, NOT ME...
WHERE ARE WE?
THE CENTER HALL OF SPIRAS-- WHERE YOUR MOTHER DIED FOUR YEARS AGO.
SKRM
SKRR
BASTARD!

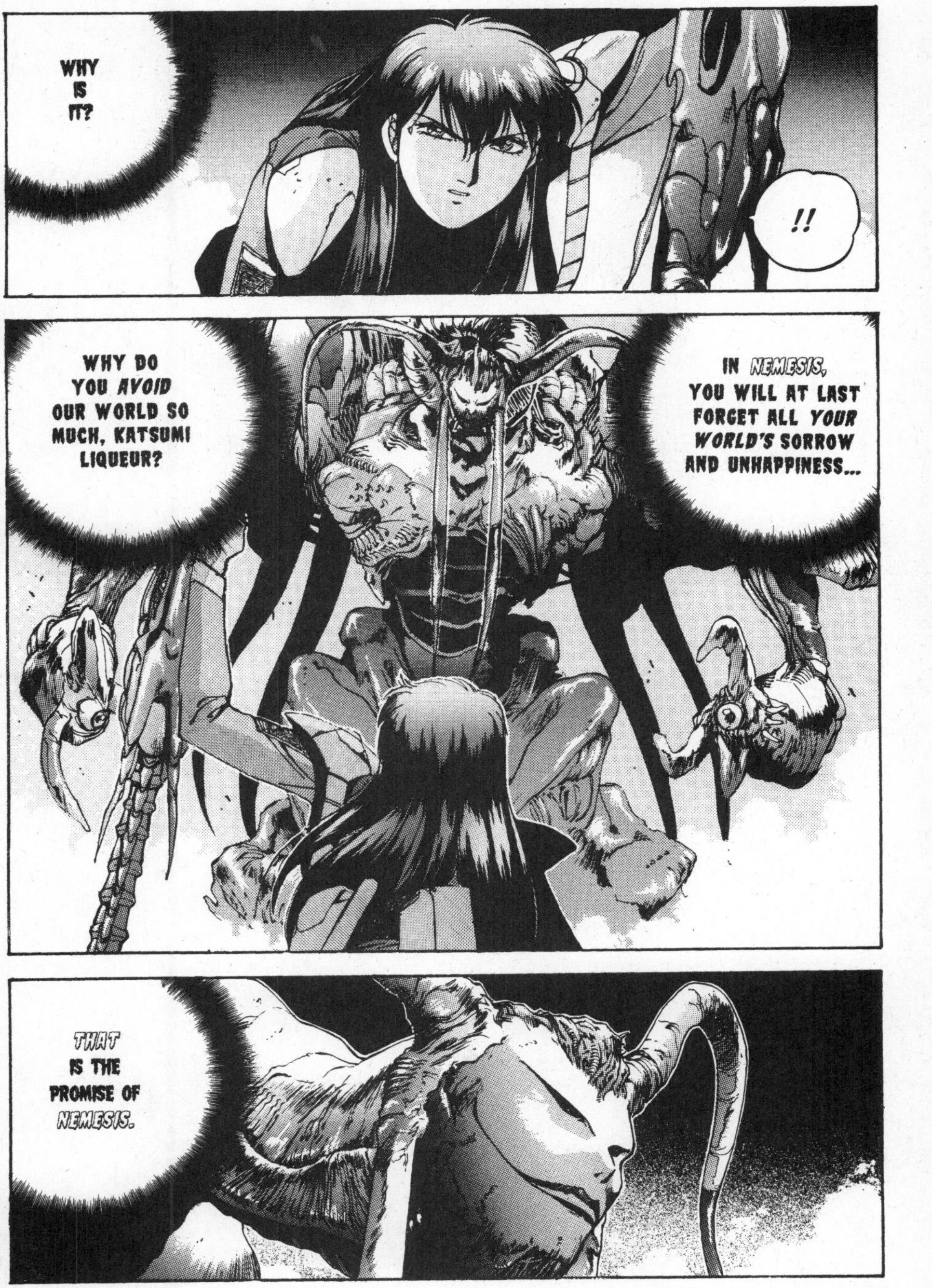
WHY IS IT?
!!
WHY DO YOU *AVOID* OUR WORLD SO MUCH, KATSUMI LIQUEUR?
IN *NEMESIS*, YOU WILL AT LAST FORGET ALL *YOUR WORLD'S* SORROW AND UNHAPPINESS...
THAT IS THE PROMISE OF *NEMESIS*.

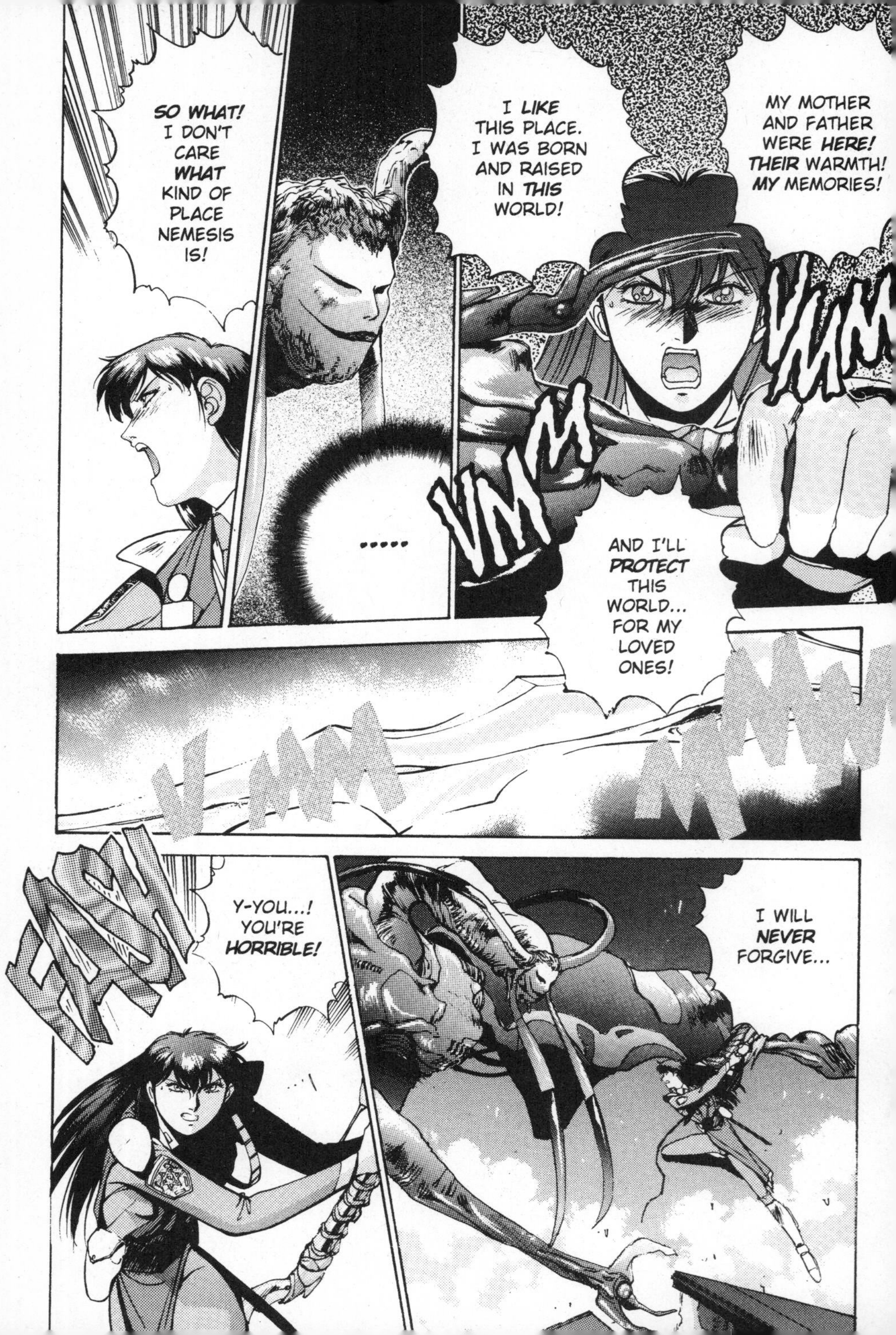
SO WHAT! I DON'T CARE WHAT KIND OF PLACE NEMESIS IS!
......
I LIKE THIS PLACE. I WAS BORN AND RAISED IN THIS WORLD!
MY MOTHER AND FATHER WERE HERE! THEIR WARMTH! MY MEMORIES!
VMM
VMM
AND I'LL PROTECT THIS WORLD... FOR MY LOVED ONES!
Y-YOU...! YOU'RE HORRIBLE!
...!
I WILL NEVER FORGIVE...

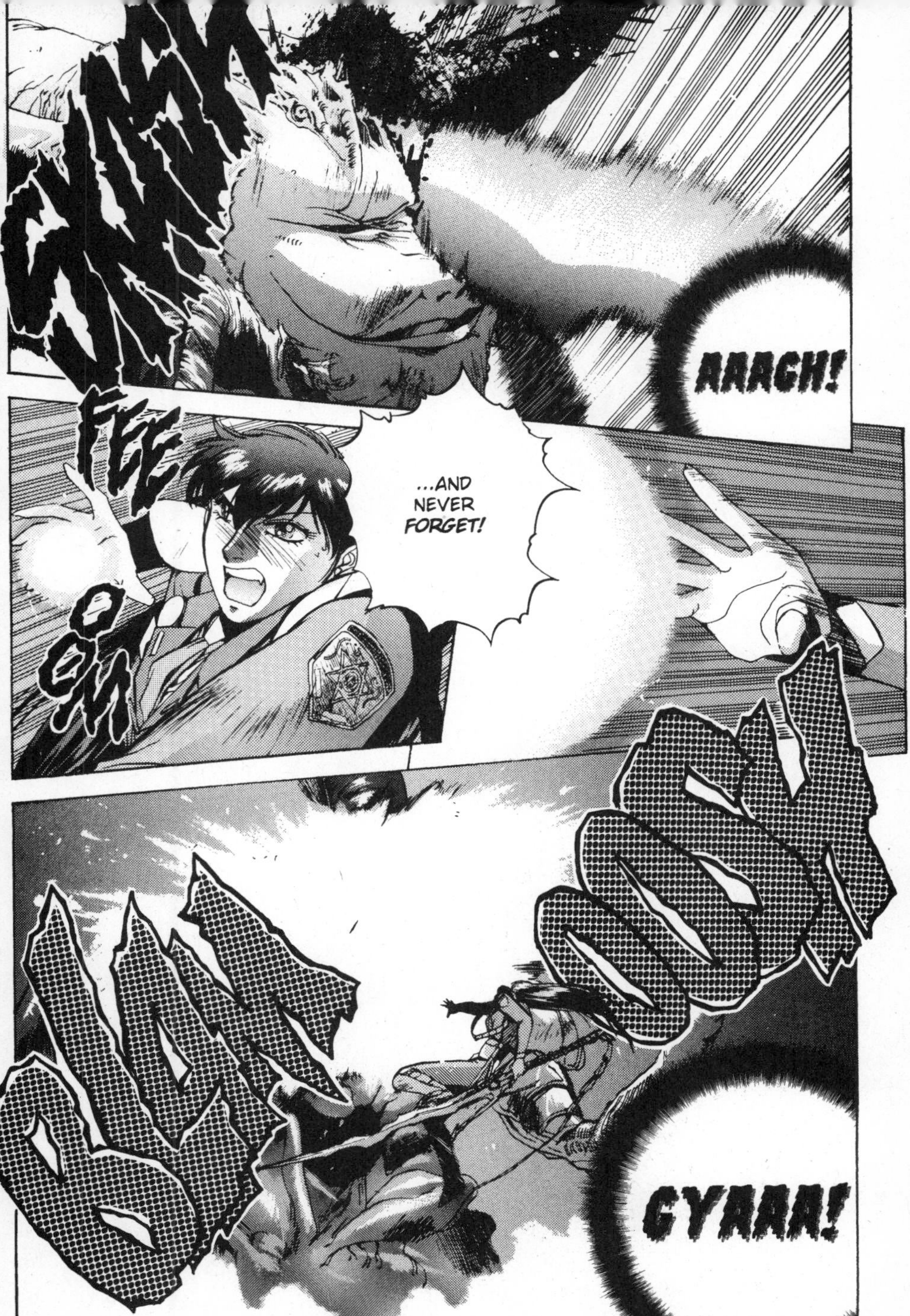
AAACH!
FEE
...AND NEVER FORGET!
GYAAA!

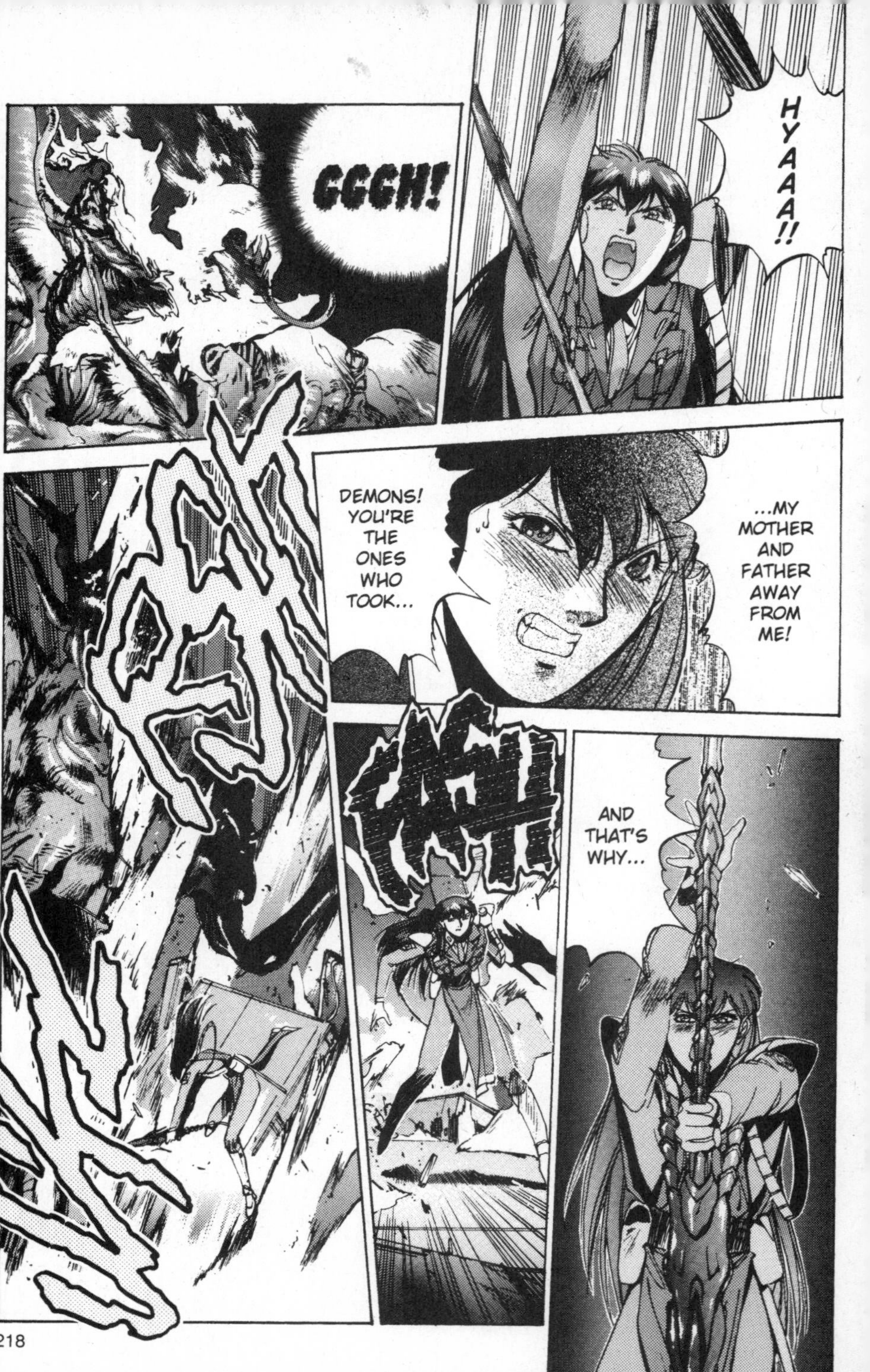
GGGH!
HYAAAA!!
DEMONS! YOU'RE THE ONES WHO TOOK...
...MY MOTHER AND FATHER AWAY FROM ME!
AND THAT'S WHY...

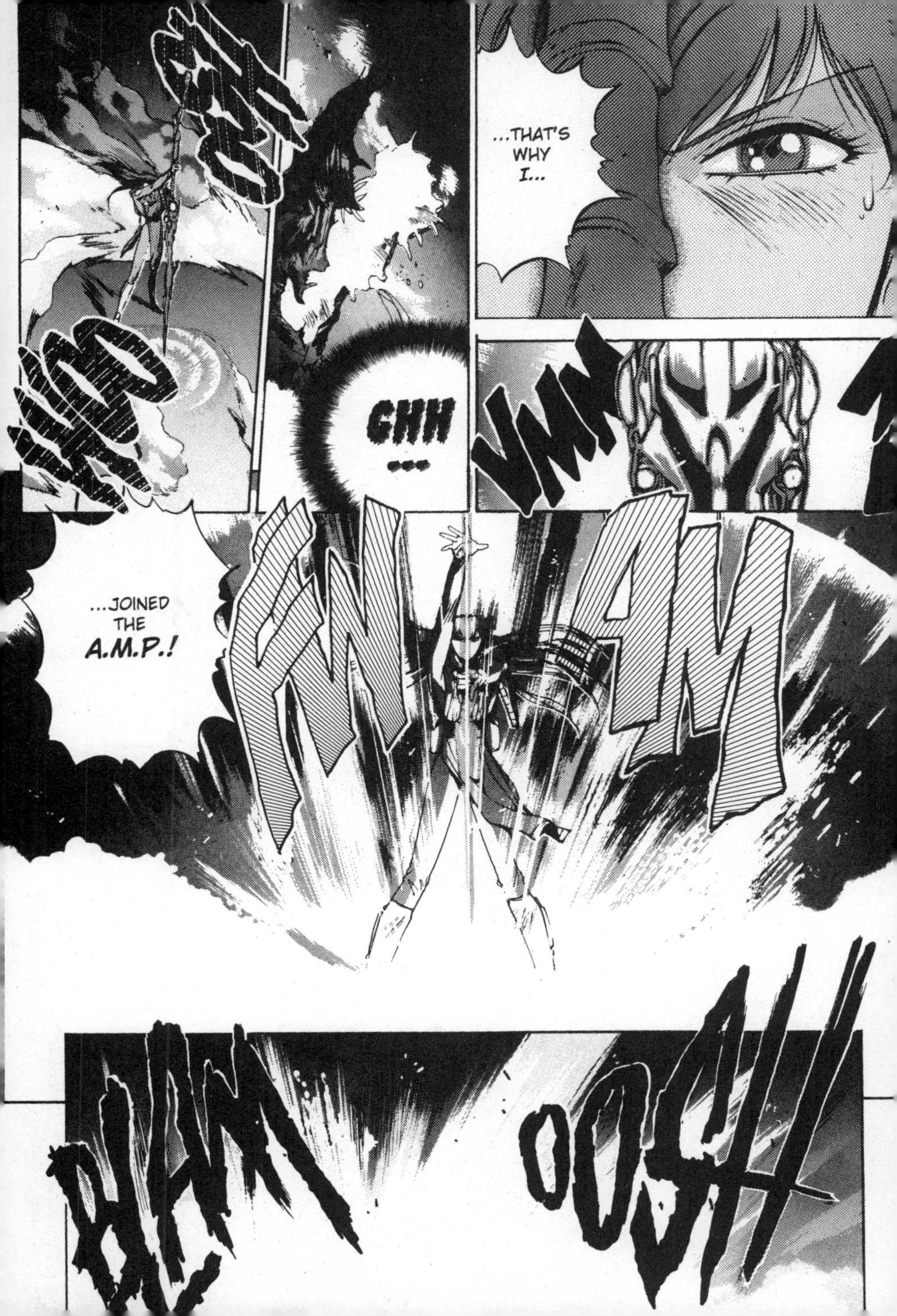
GHH
...THAT'S WHY I...
...JOINED THE A.M.P.!
WHAM

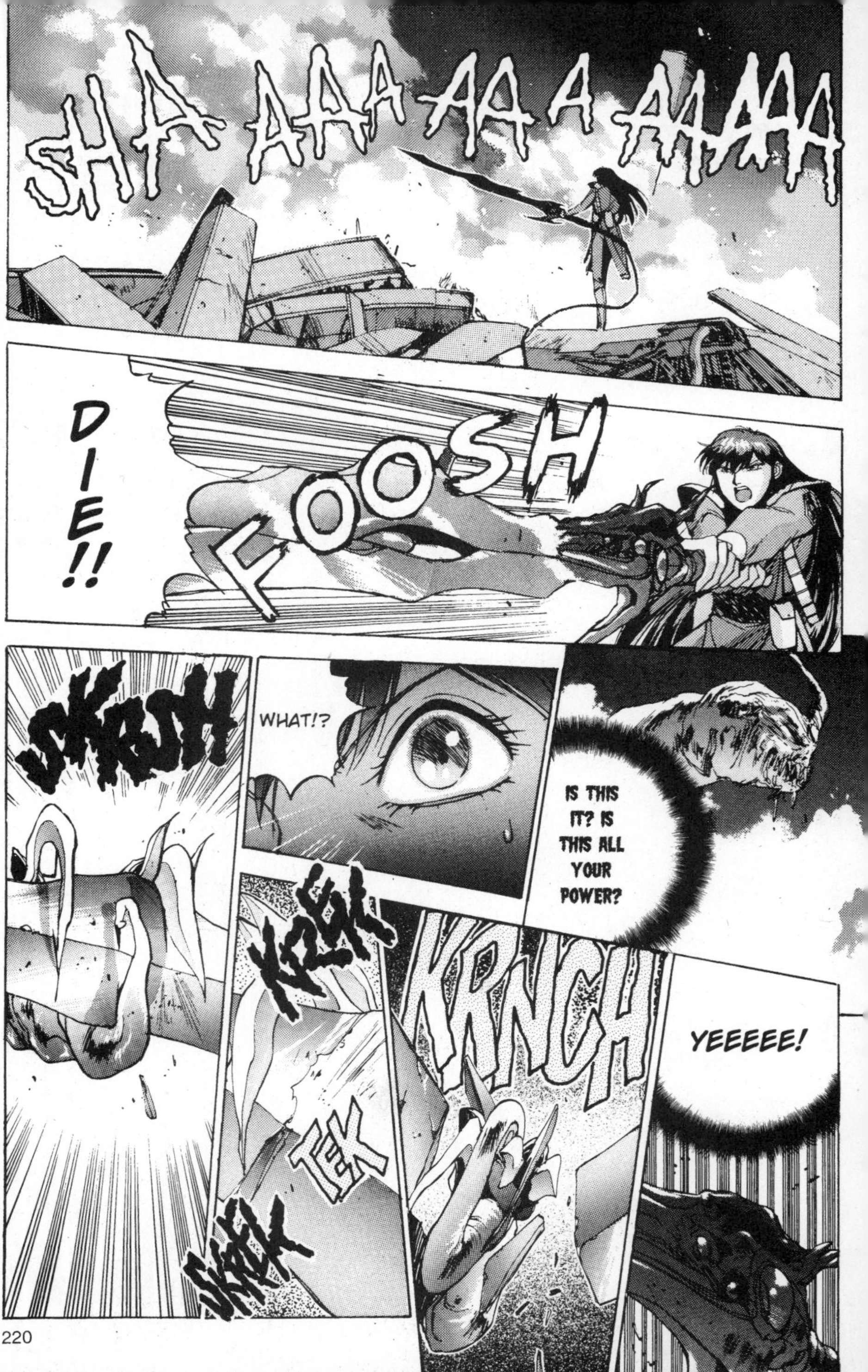
SHA AAA AA A AAAA
DIE!!
FOOSH
WHAT!?
IS THIS IT? IS THIS ALL YOUR POWER?
TECK
KRNCH
YEEEEE!

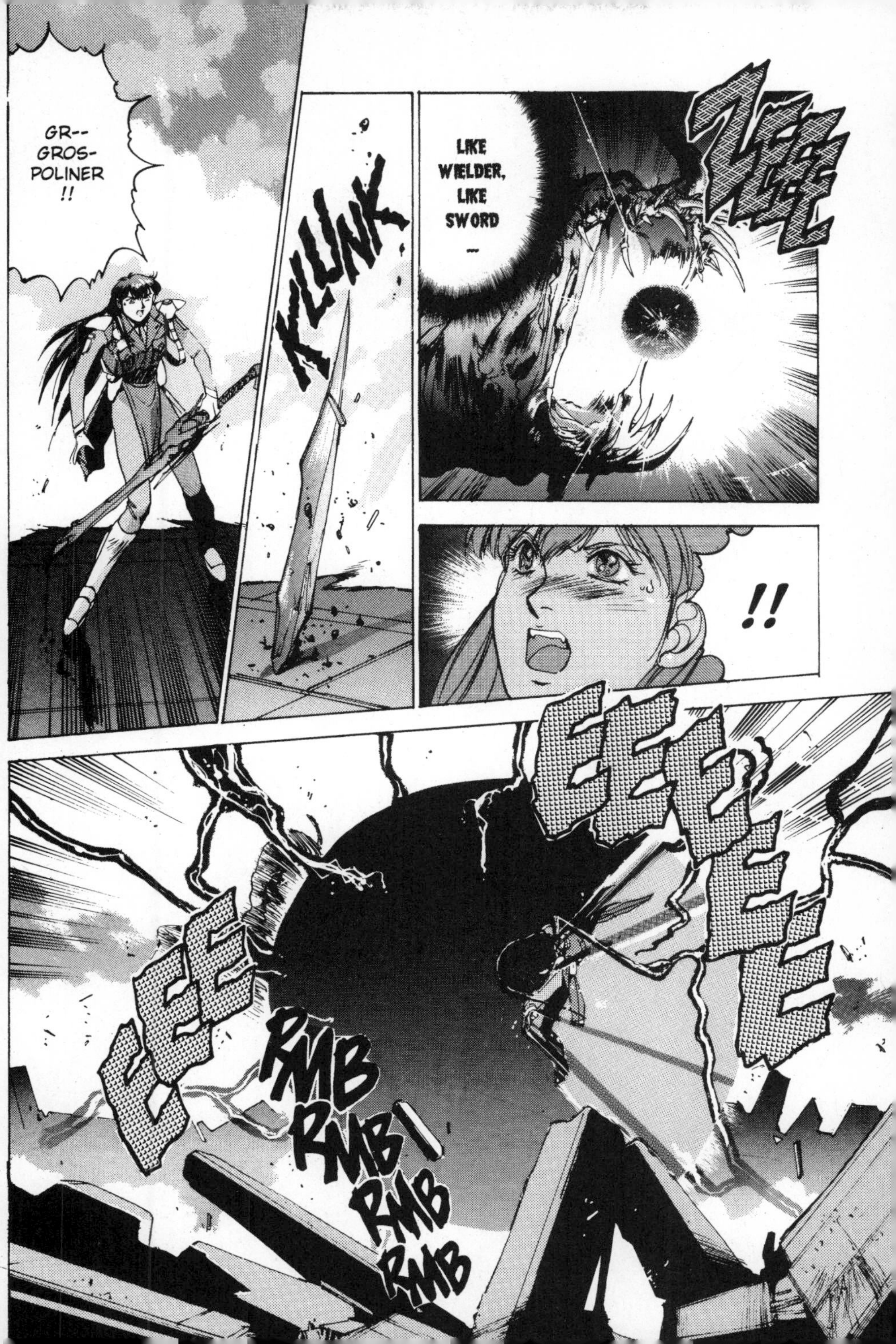
GR--
GROS-
POLINER
!!
KLUNK
LIKE
WIELDER,
LIKE
SWORD
...
!!
RMB
RMB
RMB
RMB

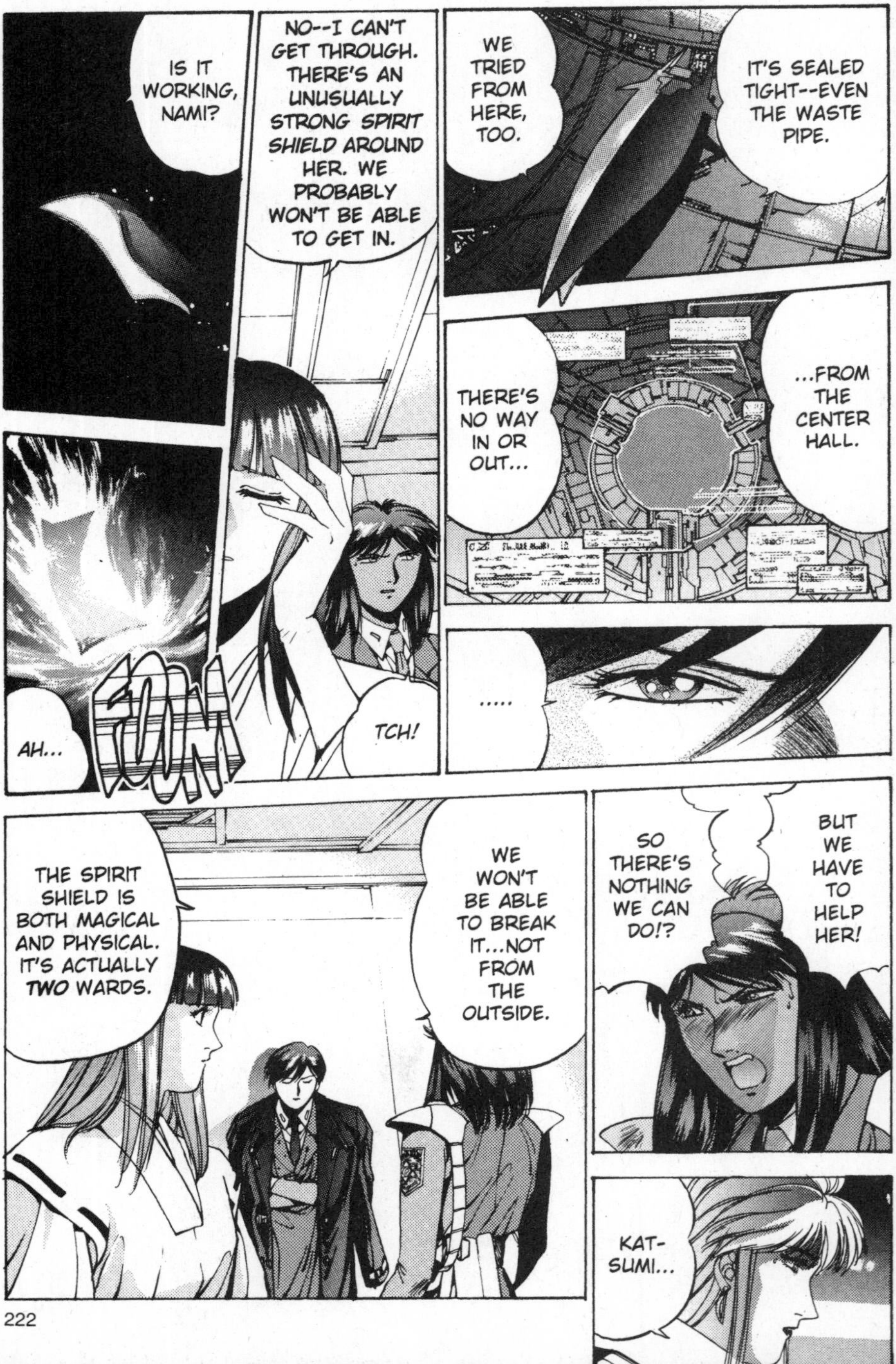
IS IT WORKING, NAMI?
NO--I CAN'T GET THROUGH. THERE'S AN UNUSUALLY STRONG SPIRIT SHIELD AROUND HER. WE PROBABLY WON'T BE ABLE TO GET IN.
WE TRIED FROM HERE, TOO.
IT'S SEALED TIGHT--EVEN THE WASTE PIPE.
THERE'S NO WAY IN OR OUT...
...FROM THE CENTER HALL.
AH...
FOOM
TCH!
.....
THE SPIRIT SHIELD IS BOTH MAGICAL AND PHYSICAL. IT'S ACTUALLY TWO WARDS.
WE WON'T BE ABLE TO BREAK IT...NOT FROM THE OUTSIDE.
SO THERE'S NOTHING WE CAN DO!?
BUT WE HAVE TO HELP HER!
KAT-SUMI...

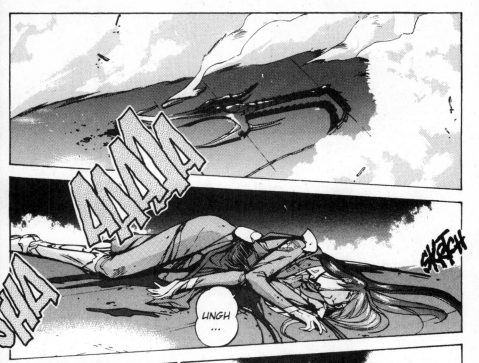

UNGH
...

YOU DIS-
APPOINT ME,
KATSUMI
LIQUEUR.

I THOUGHT YOU'D
HAVE GREATER
POWERS—BUT
YOU'VE ONLY *HALF*
YOUR PARENTS'
MIGHT.

NO!
SHE
STAYS
HERE!

STILL,
NEMESIS
NEEDS
YOU.

UH...

COME,
I'LL
SHOW
YOU...

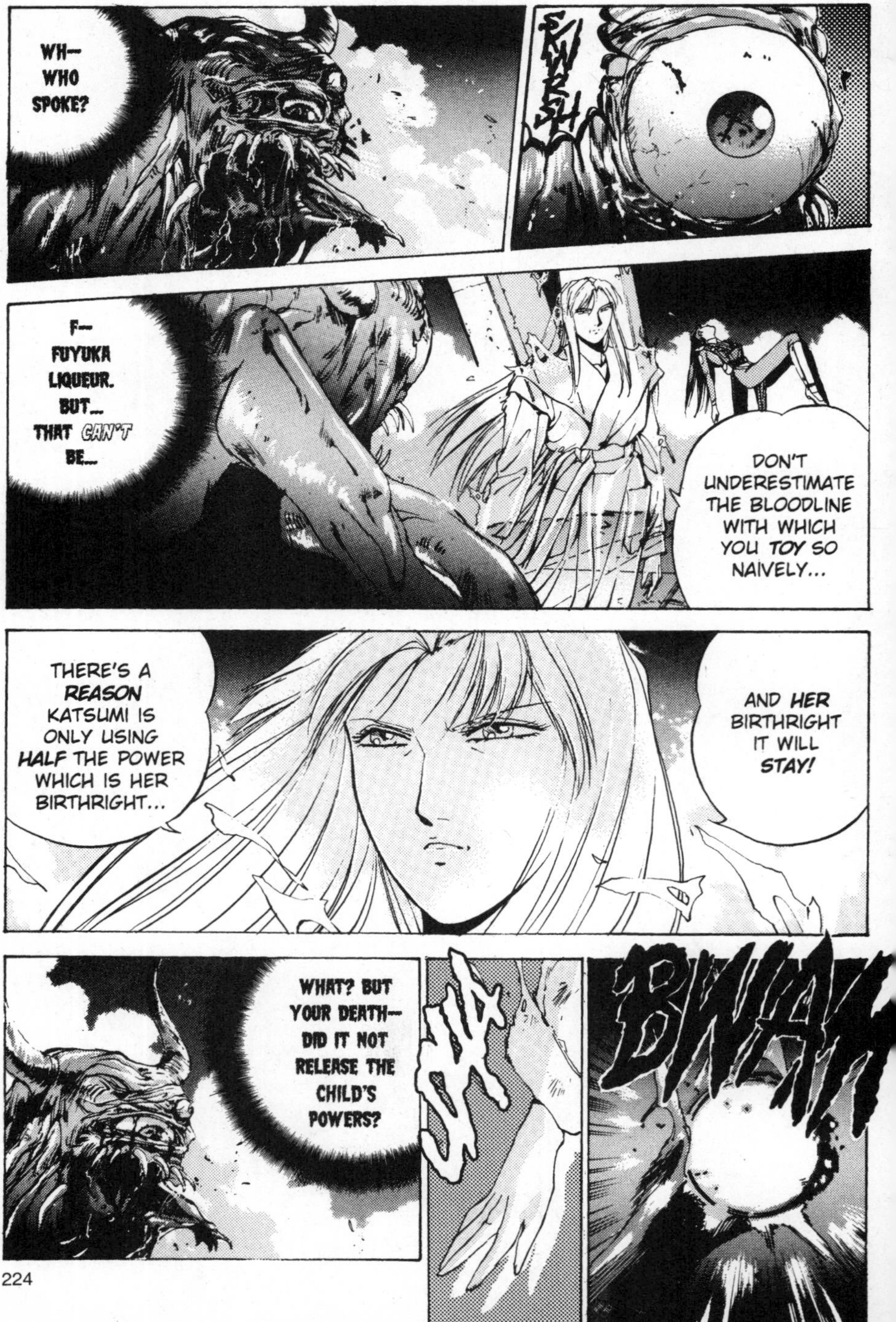
WH— WHO SPOKE?
SKWRSH
F— FUYUKA LIQUEUR. BUT... THAT CAN'T BE...
DON'T UNDERESTIMATE THE BLOODLINE WITH WHICH YOU TOY SO NAIVELY...
THERE'S A REASON KATSUMI IS ONLY USING HALF THE POWER WHICH IS HER BIRTHRIGHT...
AND HER BIRTHRIGHT IT WILL STAY!
WHAT? BUT YOUR DEATH— DID IT NOT RELEASE THE CHILD'S POWERS?
BWAK

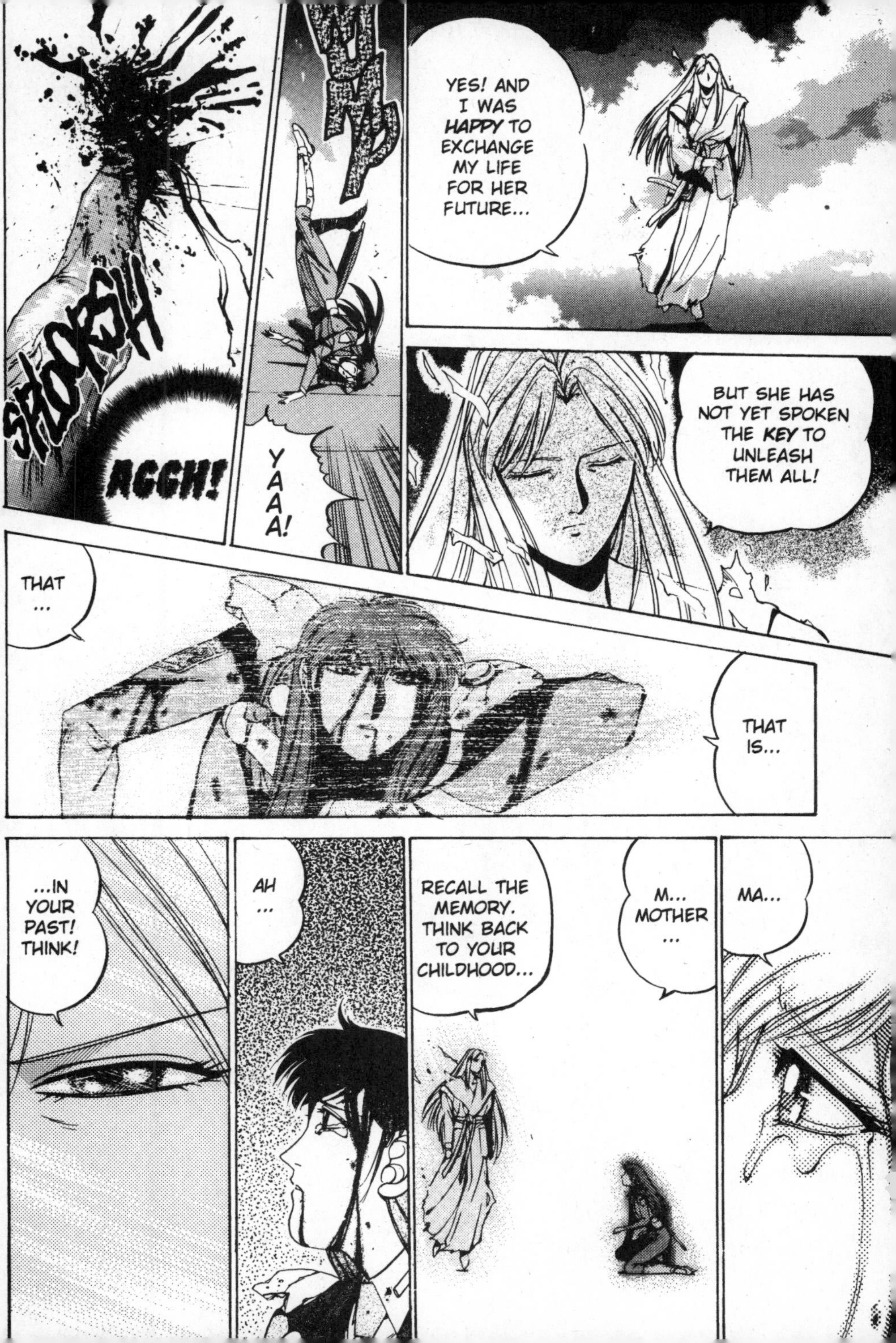

SHOOSH
AGGH!
YAAAA!
YES! AND I WAS HAPPY TO EXCHANGE MY LIFE FOR HER FUTURE...
BUT SHE HAS NOT YET SPOKEN THE KEY TO UNLEASH THEM ALL!
THAT ...
THAT IS...
...IN YOUR PAST! THINK!
AH ...
RECALL THE MEMORY. THINK BACK TO YOUR CHILDHOOD...
M... MOTHER ...
MA...

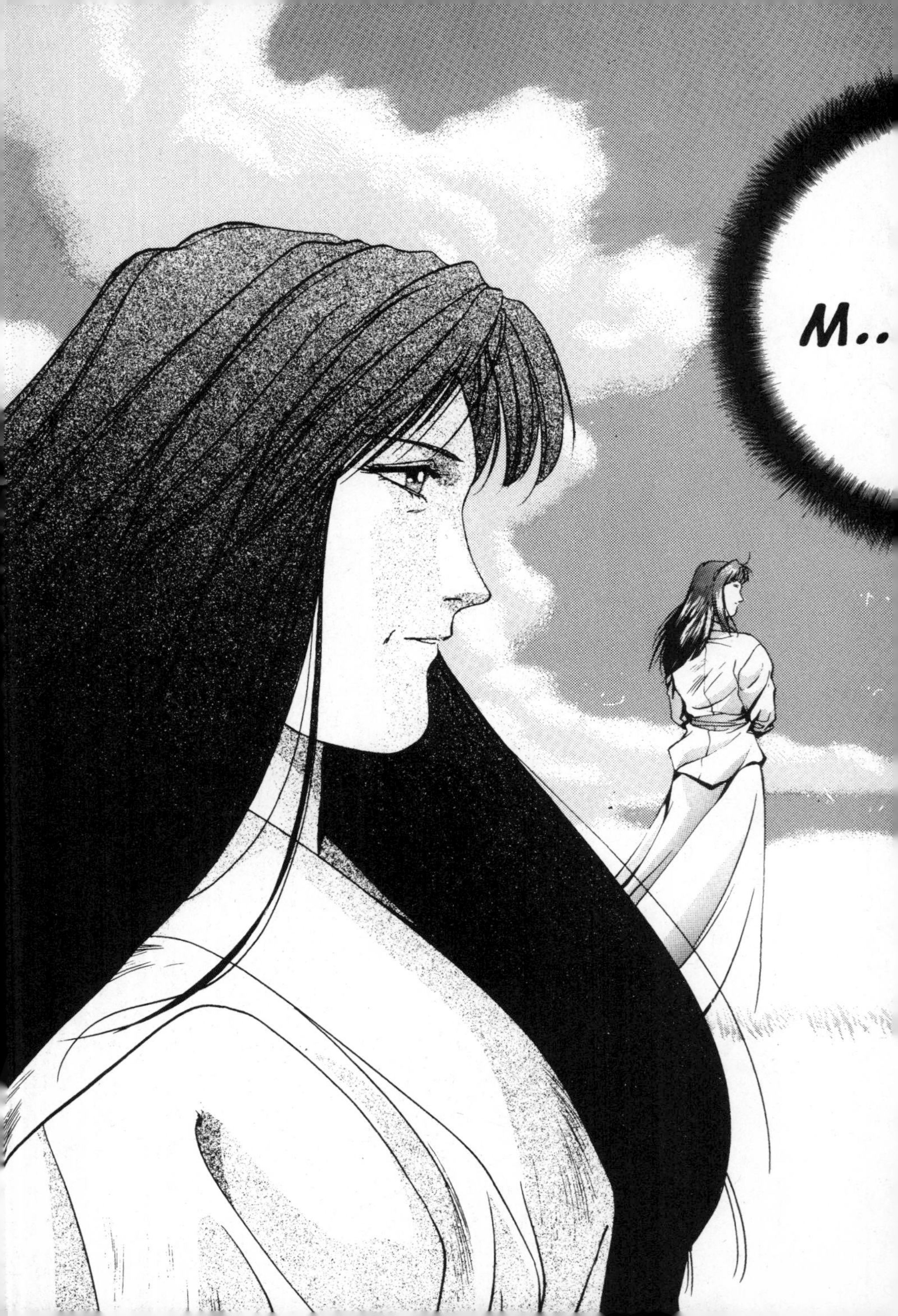
M..

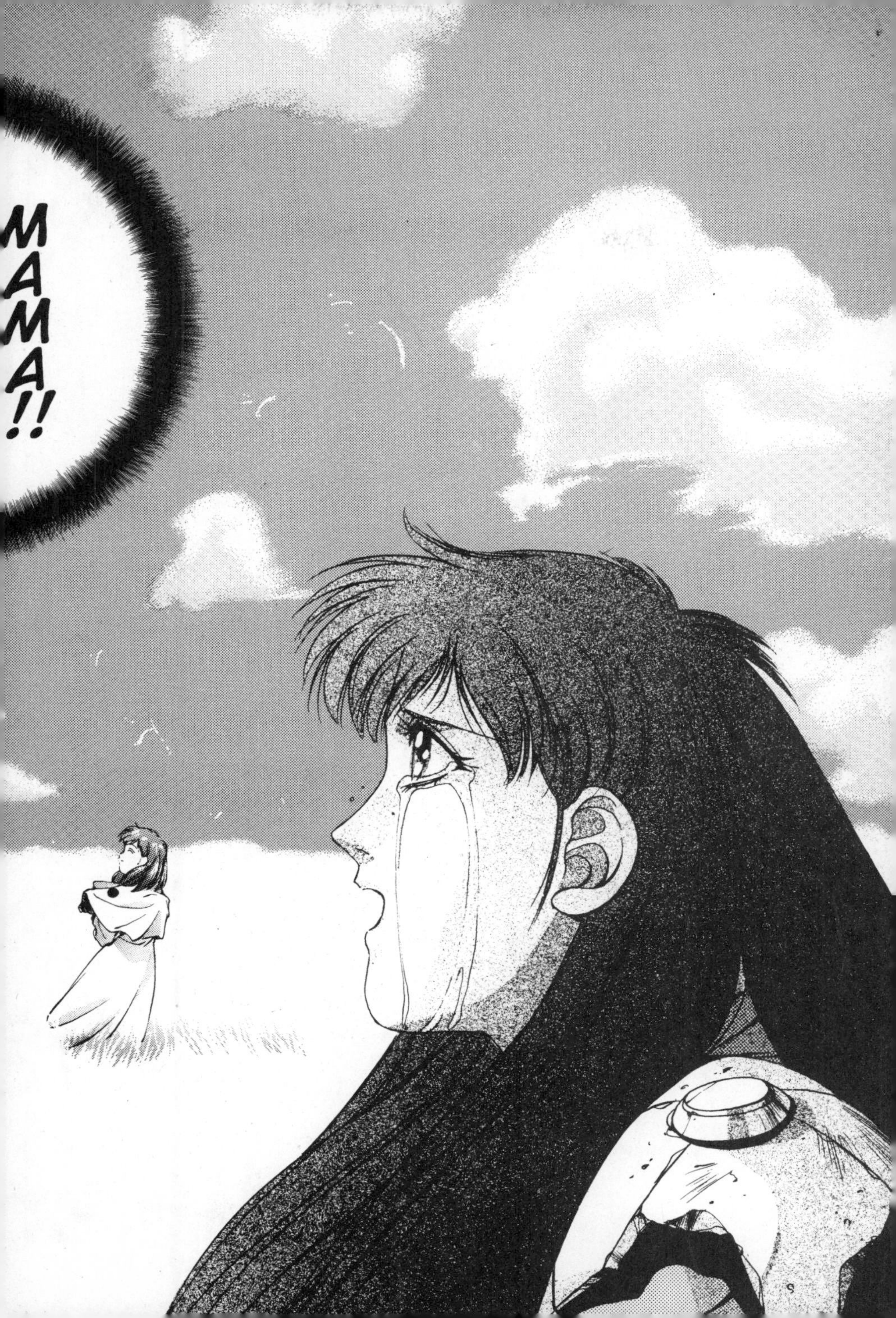
MAMA!!

GYEEE!

SKLAMM

FMM FMM FMM FMM

CENTER HALL'S SPIRIT SHIELD HAS BROKEN!

KAT-SUMI!

KAT-SUMI!

GYAAGH!!

FWOOOOOSS

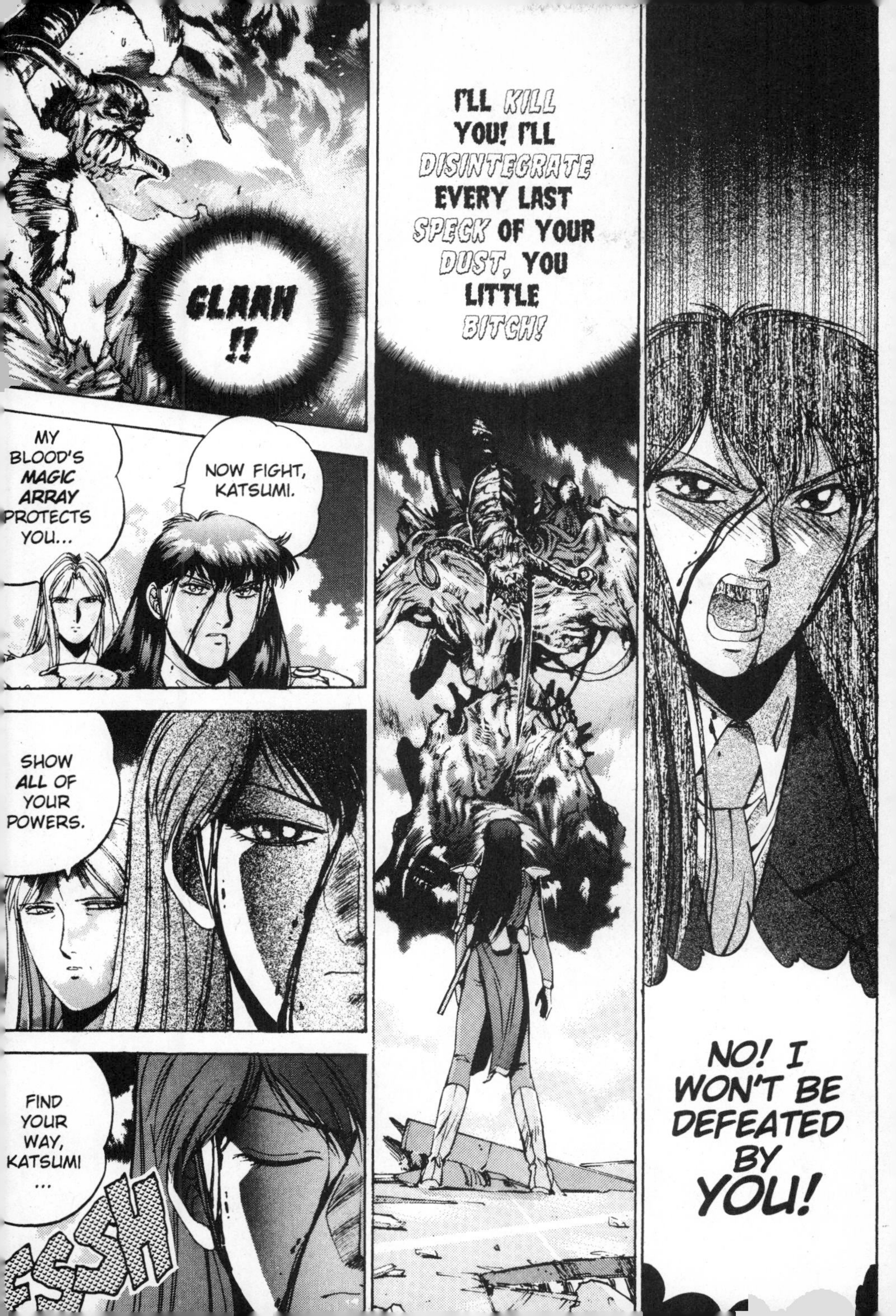
GLAAH !!
MY BLOOD'S MAGIC ARRAY PROTECTS YOU...
NOW FIGHT, KATSUMI.
SHOW ALL OF YOUR POWERS.
FIND YOUR WAY, KATSUMI ...
I'LL KILL YOU! I'LL DISINTEGRATE EVERY LAST SPECK OF YOUR DUST, YOU LITTLE BITCH!
NO! I WON'T BE DEFEATED BY YOU!

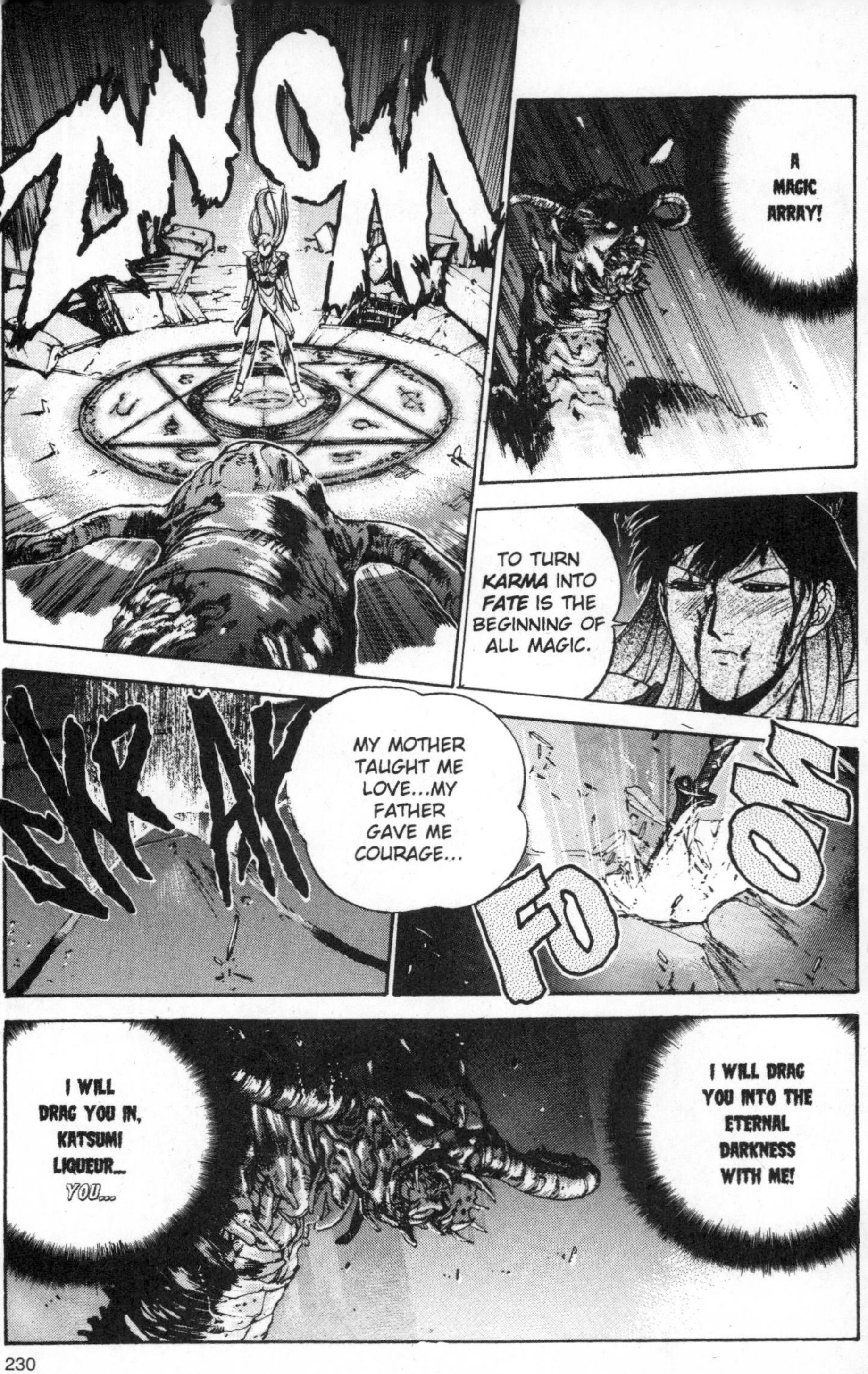
A MAGIC ARRAY!
TO TURN KARMA INTO FATE IS THE BEGINNING OF ALL MAGIC.
CRAK
MY MOTHER TAUGHT ME LOVE...MY FATHER GAVE ME COURAGE...
FOOM
I WILL DRAG YOU IN, KATSUMI LIQUEUR... YOU...
I WILL DRAG YOU INTO THE ETERNAL DARKNESS WITH ME!

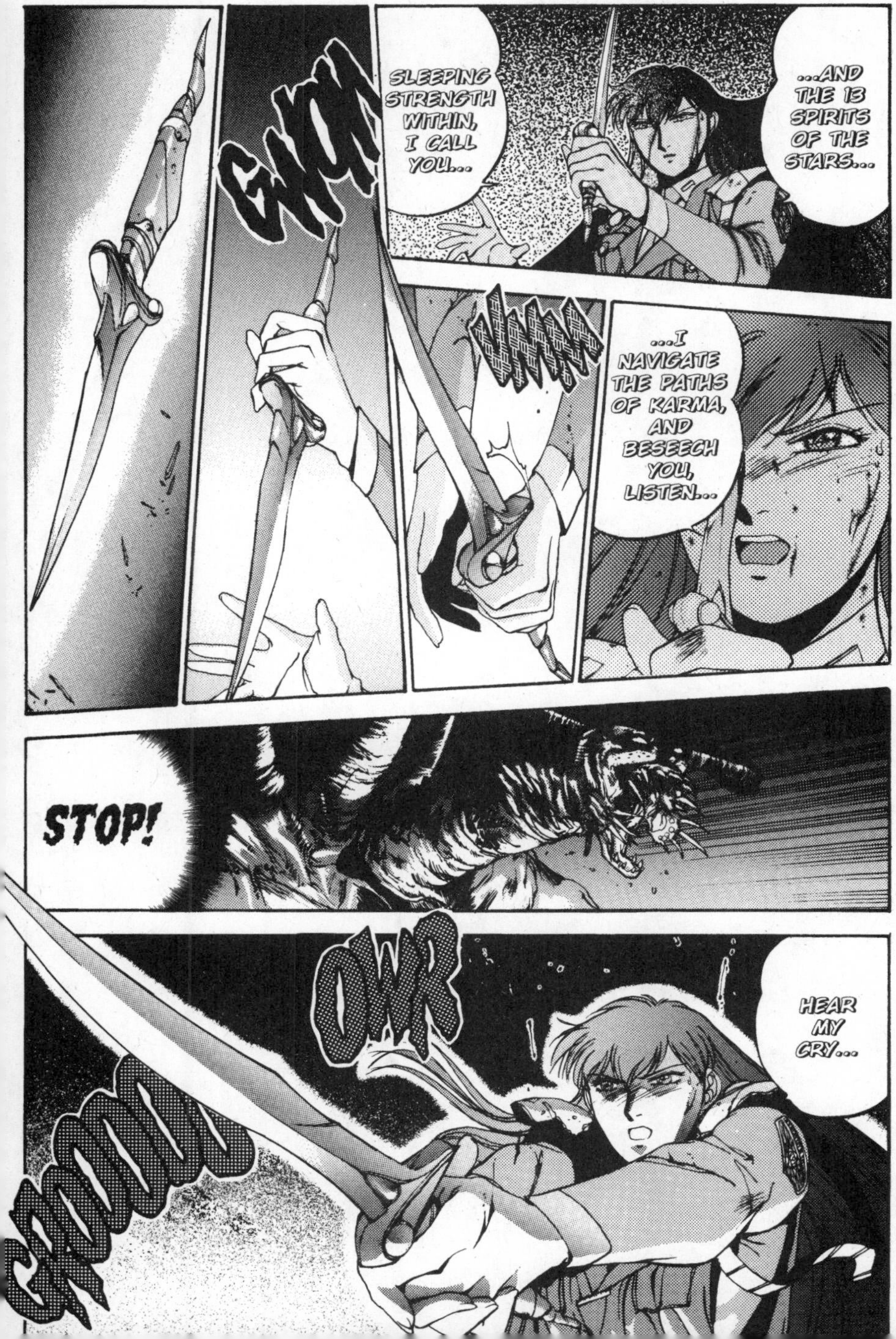
SLEEPING STRENGTH WITHIN, I CALL YOU...
...AND THE 13 SPIRITS OF THE STARS...
...I NAVIGATE THE PATHS OF KARMA, AND BESEECH YOU, LISTEN...
STOP!
HEAR MY CRY...

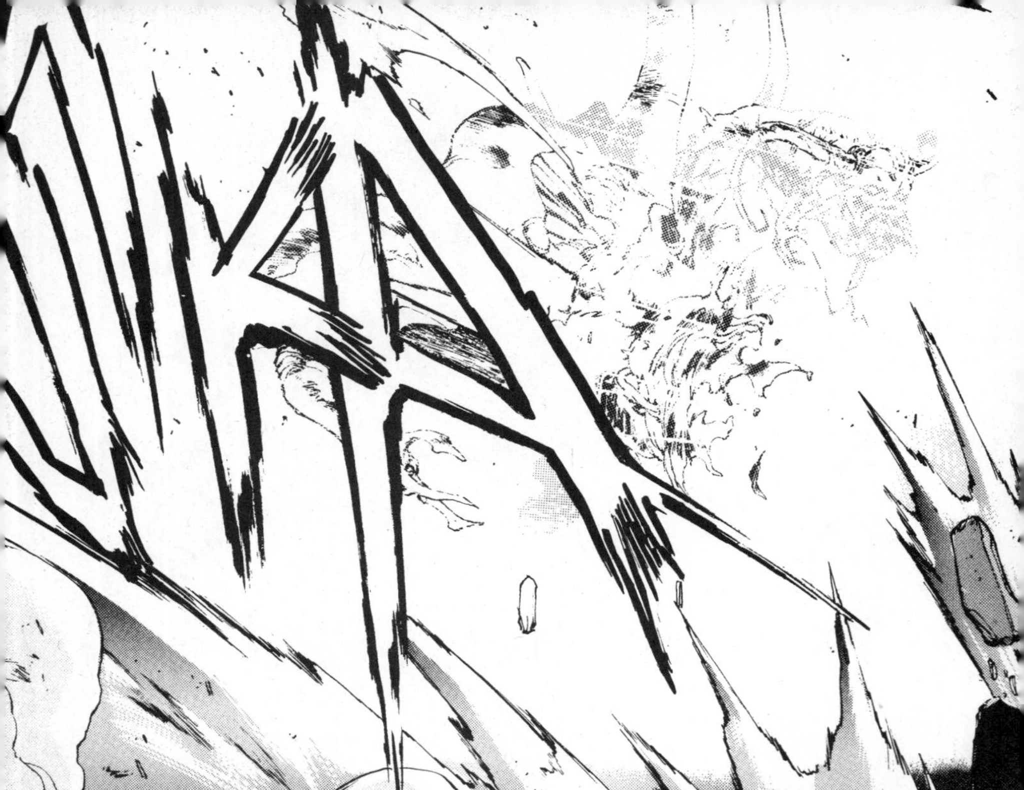
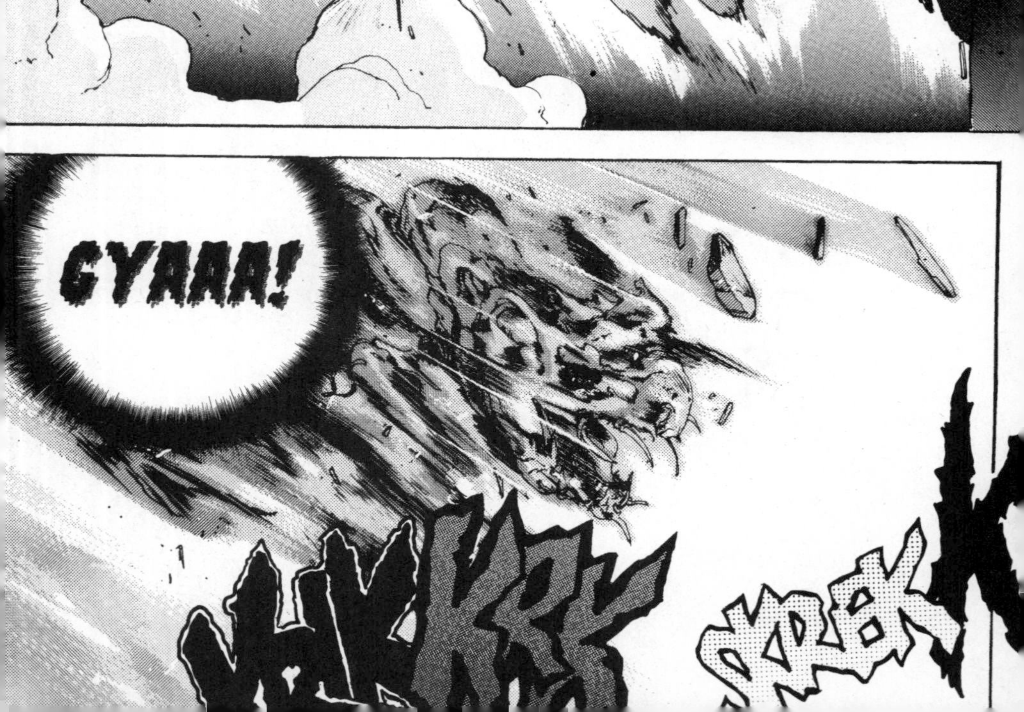
GYAAA!

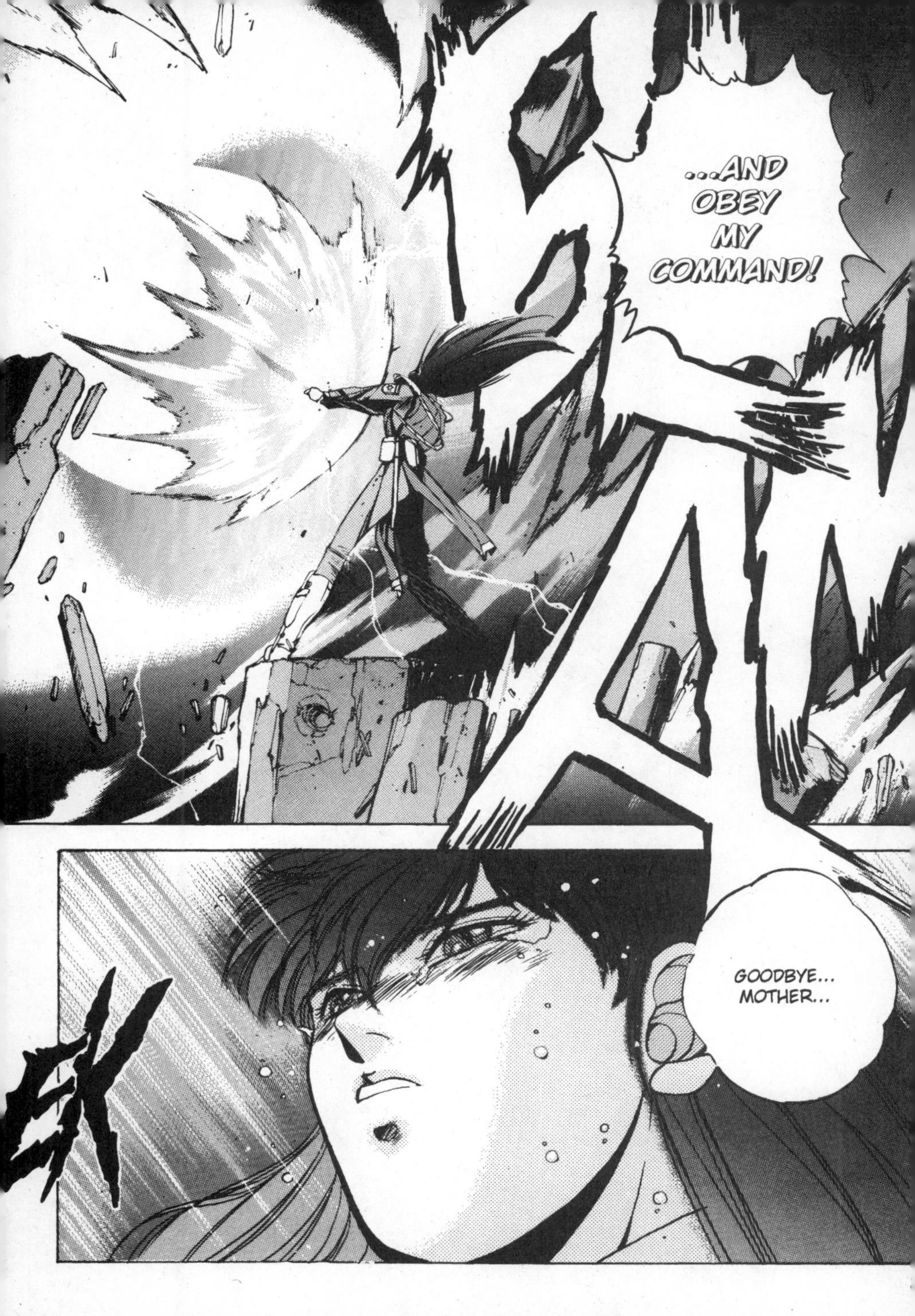
...AND OBEY MY COMMAND!
GOODBYE... MOTHER...

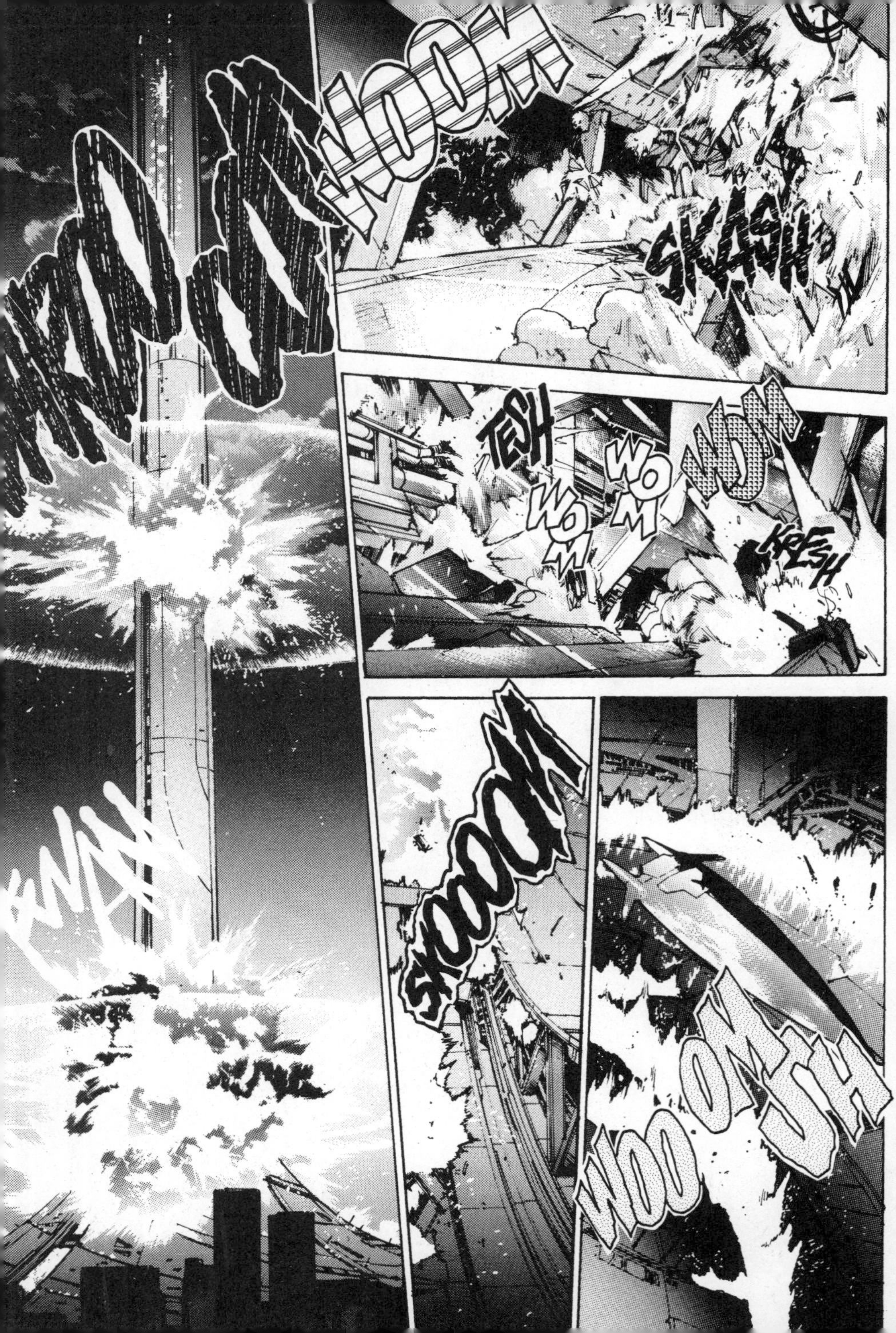
WOOOM
SKASH
TESH
WOM
WOM
WOM
KRESH
SKOOOOM
WOOOMSH

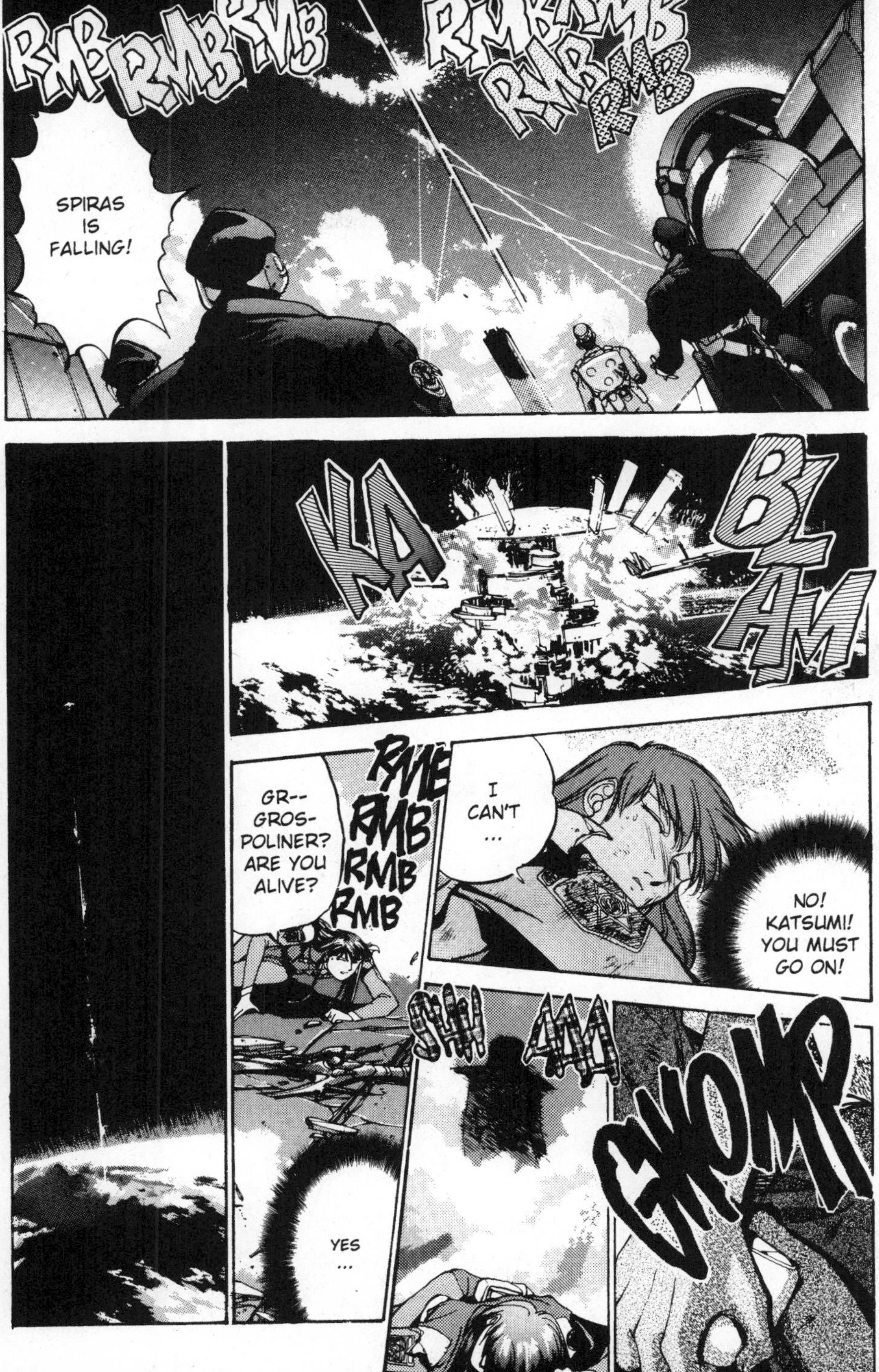

RMB RMB RMB
RMB RMB RMB RMB RMB
SPIRAS IS FALLING!
KA BLAM
GR-- GROS-POLINER? ARE YOU ALIVE?
RMB RMB RMB RMB
I CAN'T ...
NO! KATSUMI! YOU MUST GO ON!
SHHAAA
YES ...
CHOMP

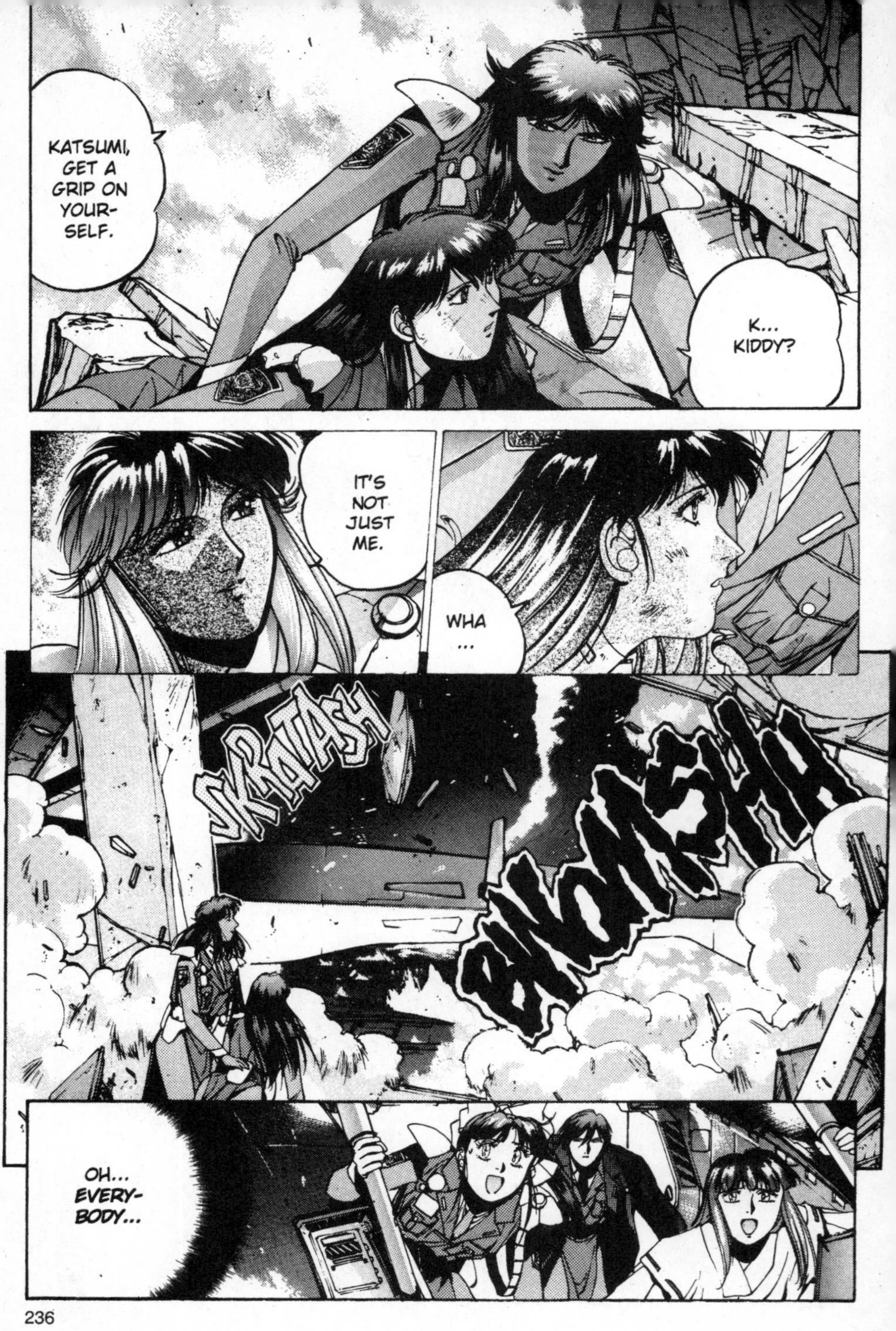
KATSUMI, GET A GRIP ON YOUR-SELF.
K... KIDDY?
IT'S NOT JUST ME.
WHA ...
SKRATASH
OH... EVERY-BODY...

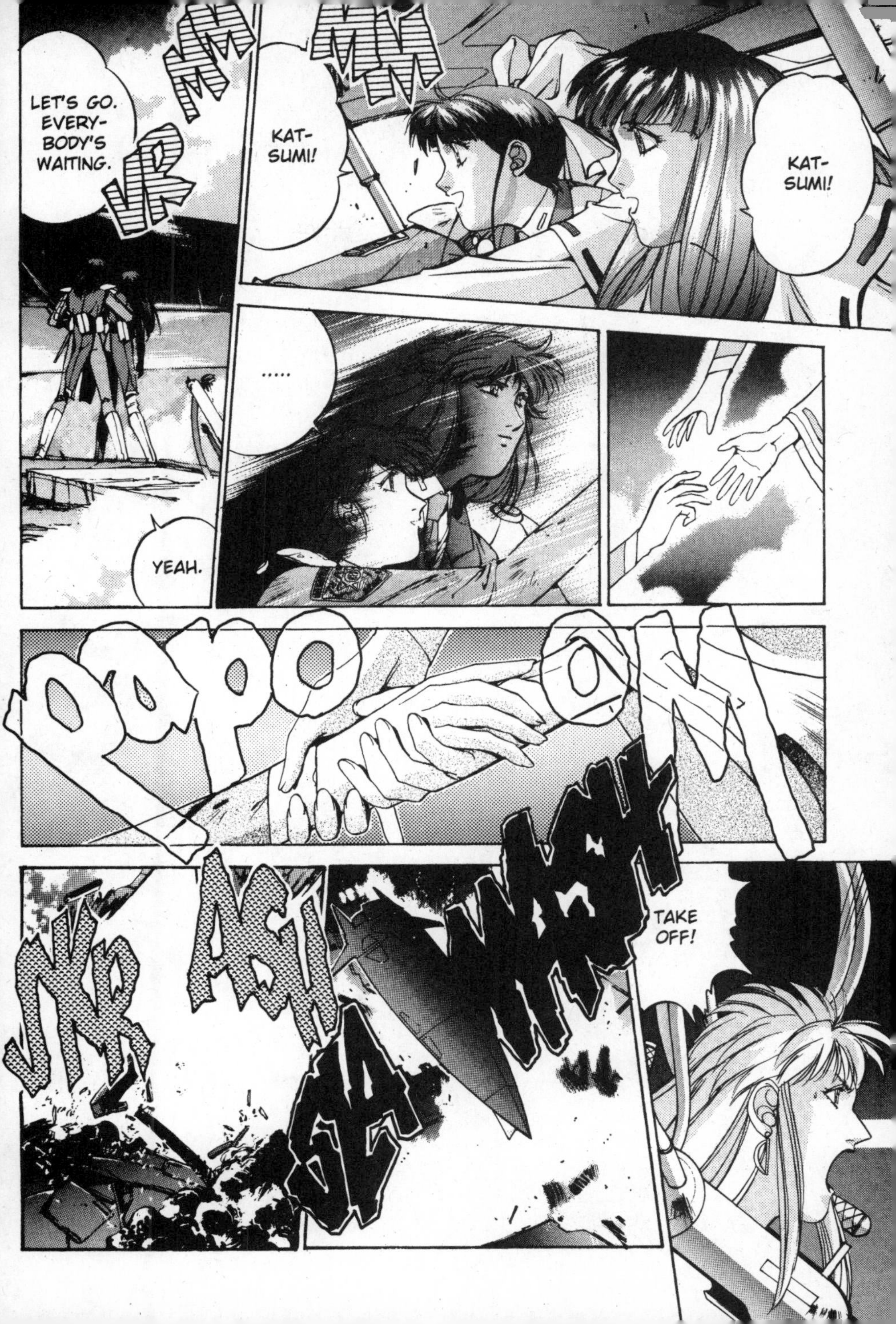

LET'S GO. EVERY-BODY'S WAITING.
YEAH.
KAT-SUMI!
KAT-SUMI!
.....
TAKE OFF!

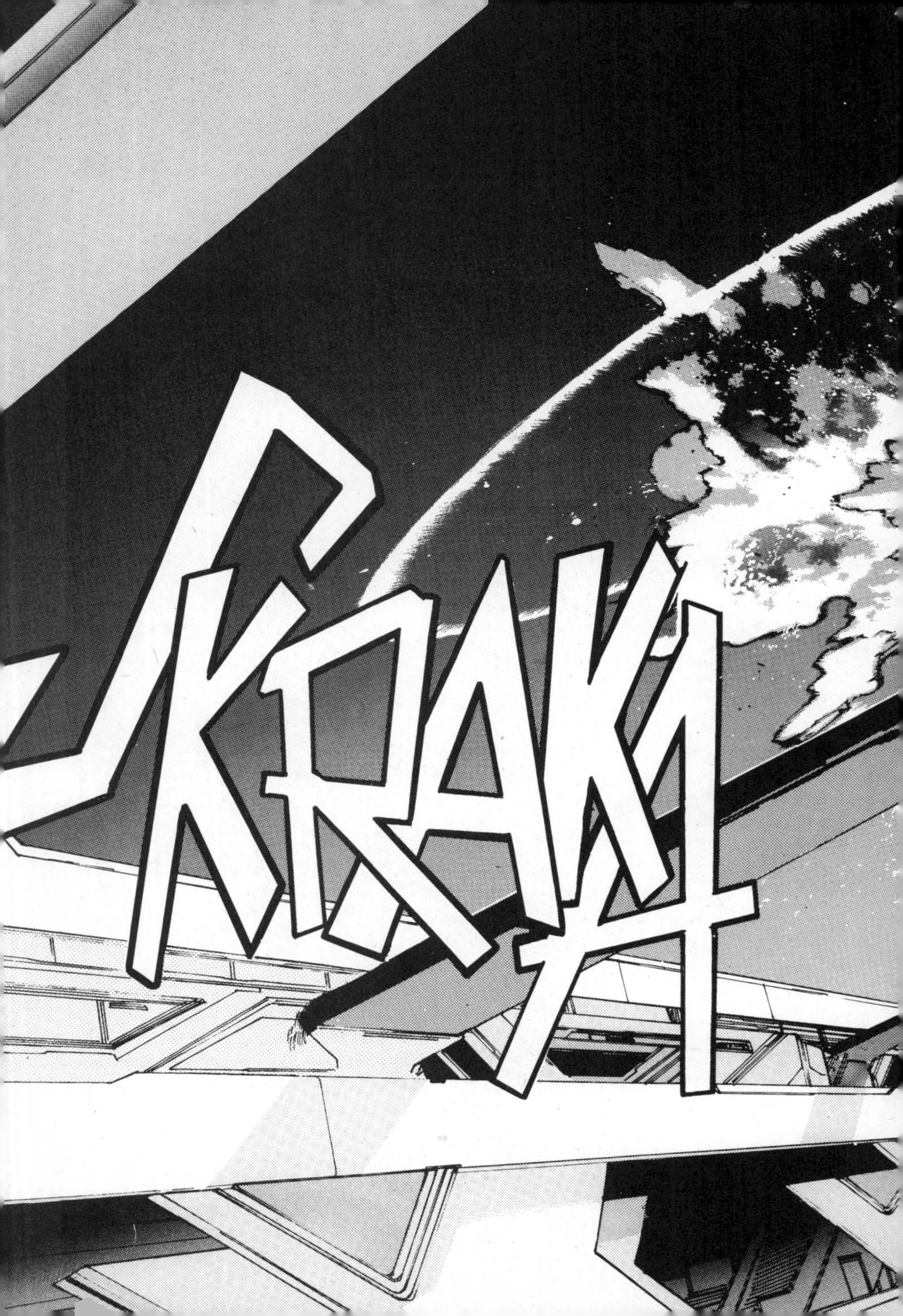
KRAKA

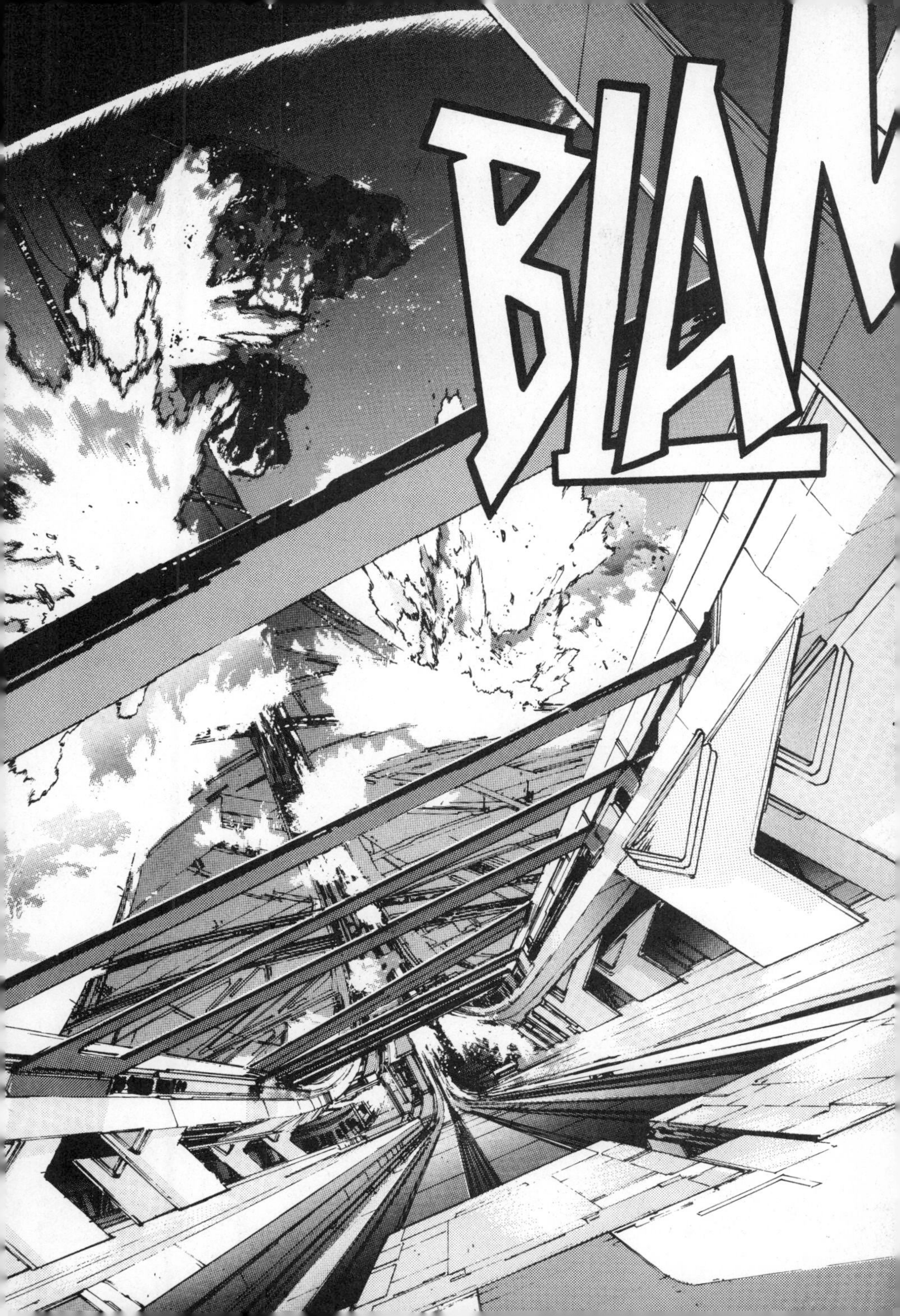
BLA

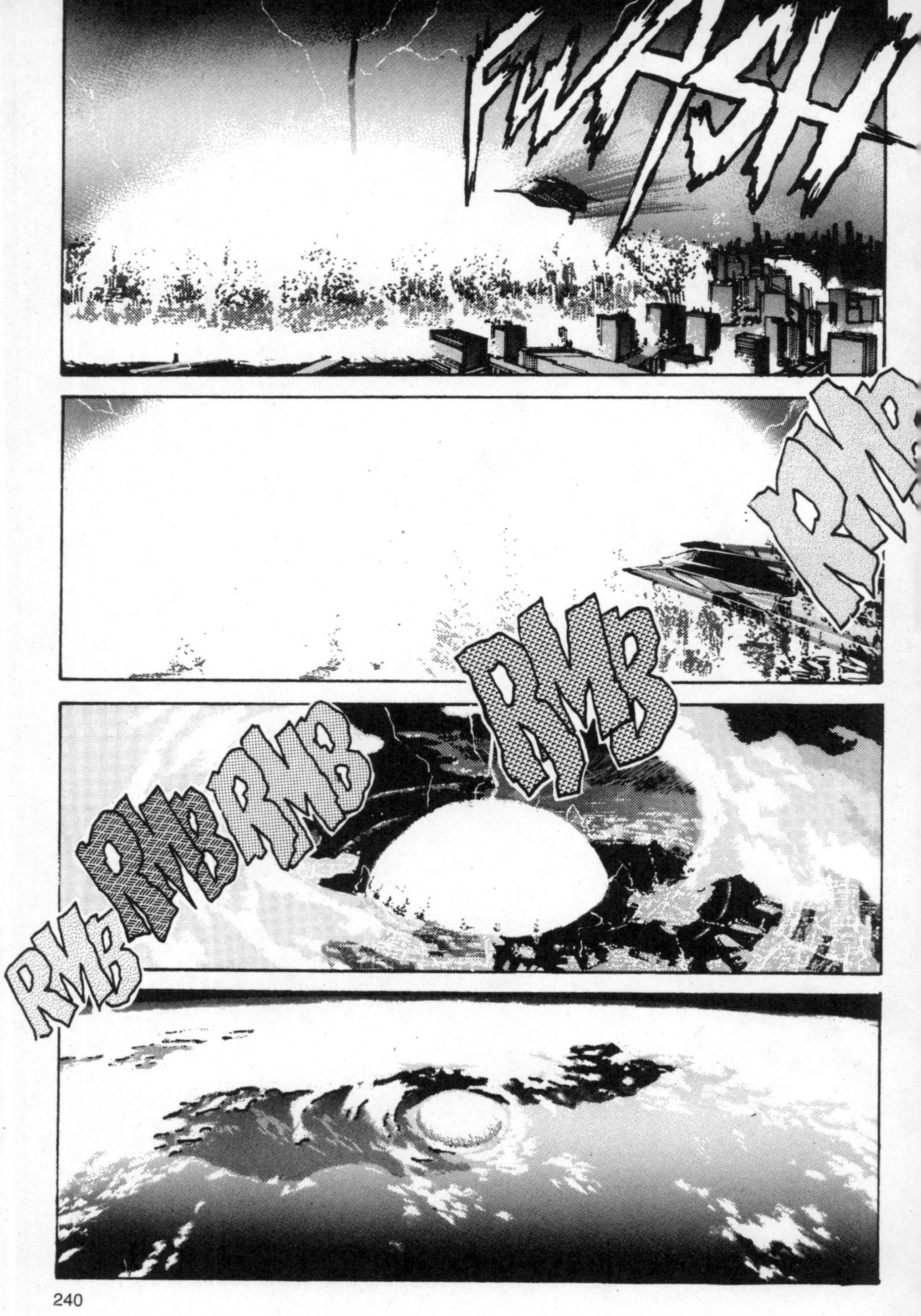
FLASH
RMB
RMB
RMB RMB RMB RMB

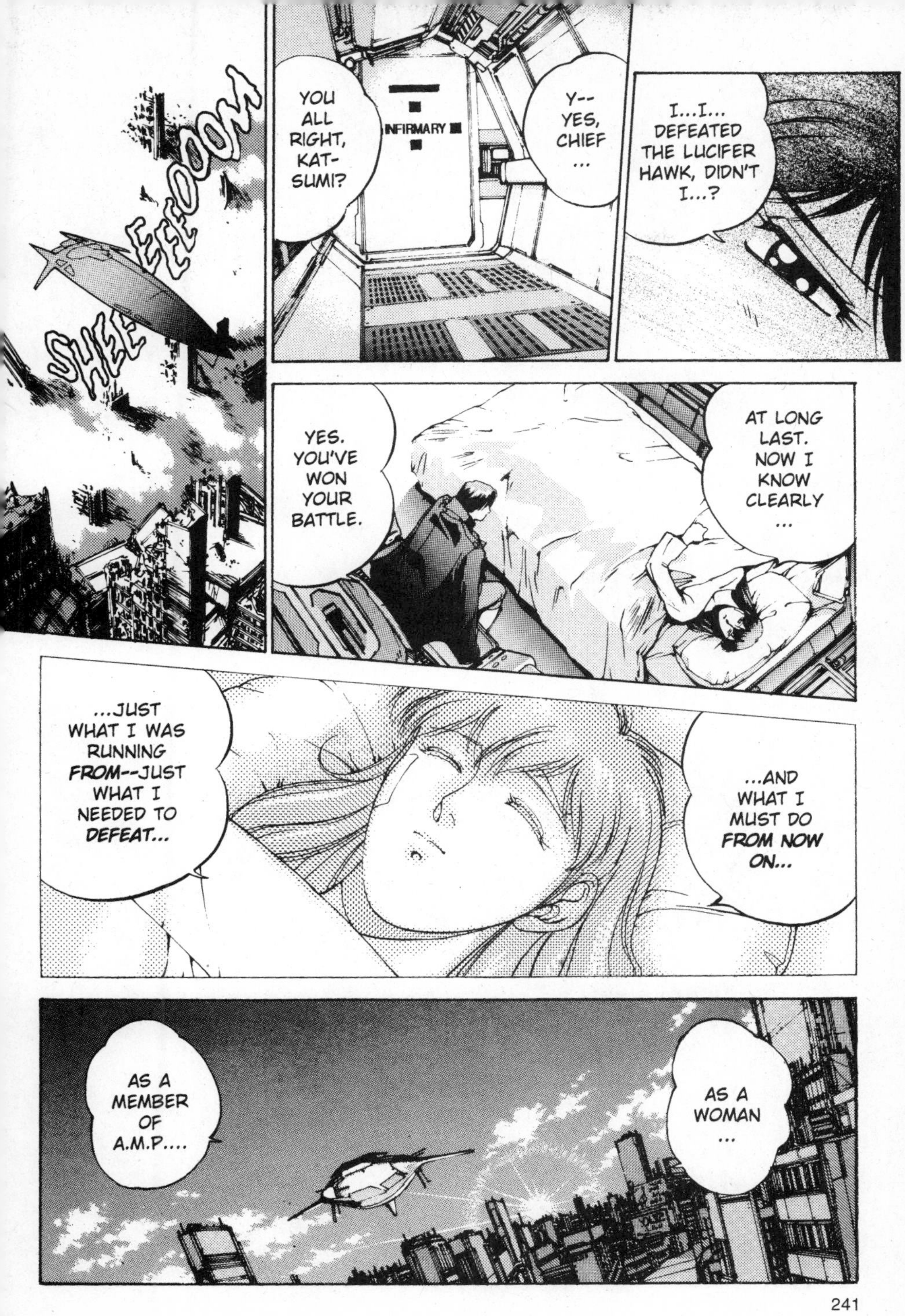
SHEEEEOOOM
YOU ALL RIGHT, KATSUMI?
INFIRMARY
Y-- YES, CHIEF ...
I...I... DEFEATED THE LUCIFER HAWK, DIDN'T I...?
YES. YOU'VE WON YOUR BATTLE.
AT LONG LAST. NOW I KNOW CLEARLY ...
...JUST WHAT I WAS RUNNING FROM--JUST WHAT I NEEDED TO DEFEAT...
...AND WHAT I MUST DO FROM NOW ON...
AS A MEMBER OF A.M.P....
AS A WOMAN ...

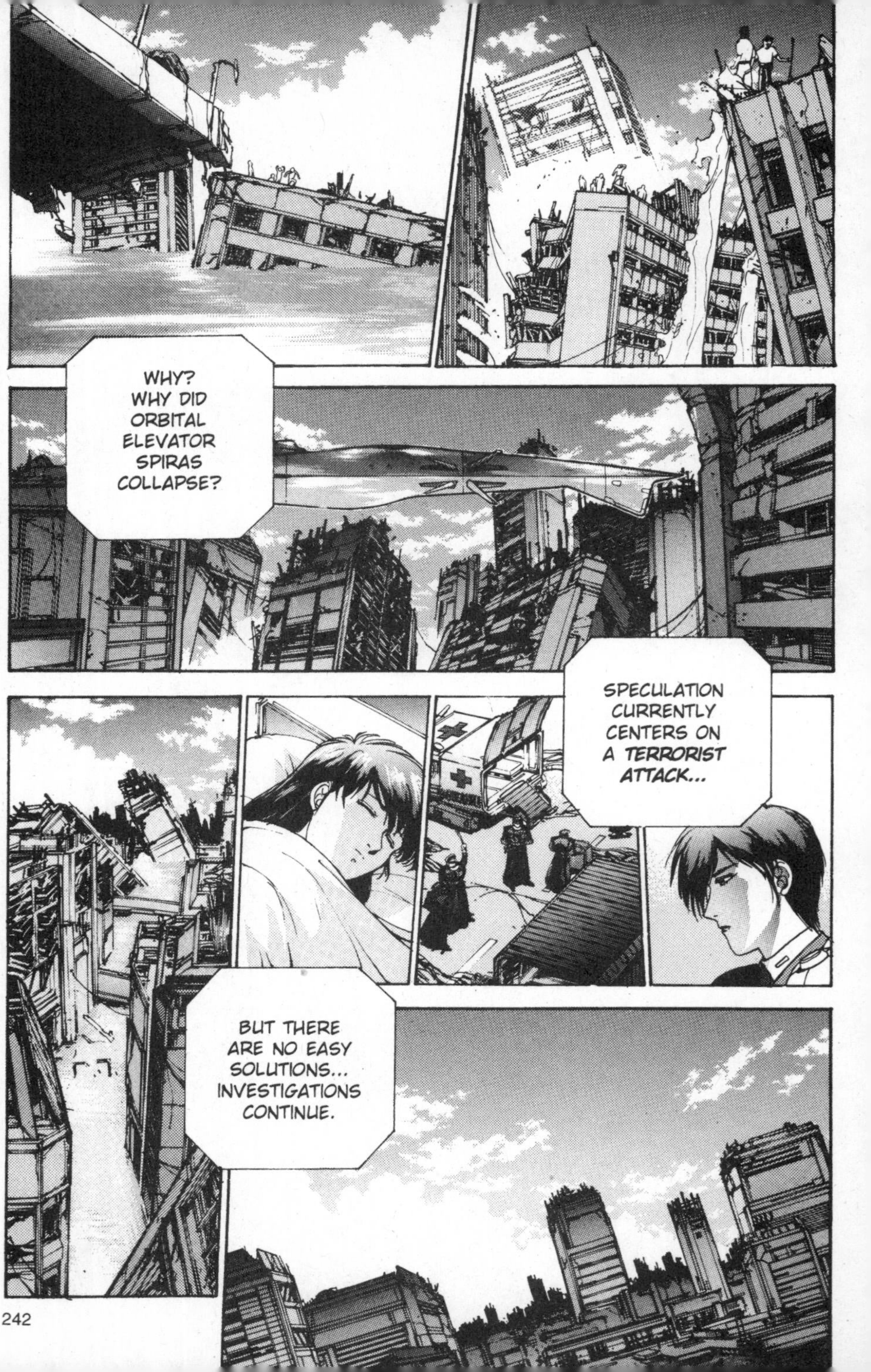
WHY? WHY DID ORBITAL ELEVATOR SPIRAS COLLAPSE?
SPECULATION CURRENTLY CENTERS ON A *TERRORIST* ATTACK...
BUT THERE ARE NO EASY SOLUTIONS... INVESTIGATIONS CONTINUE.

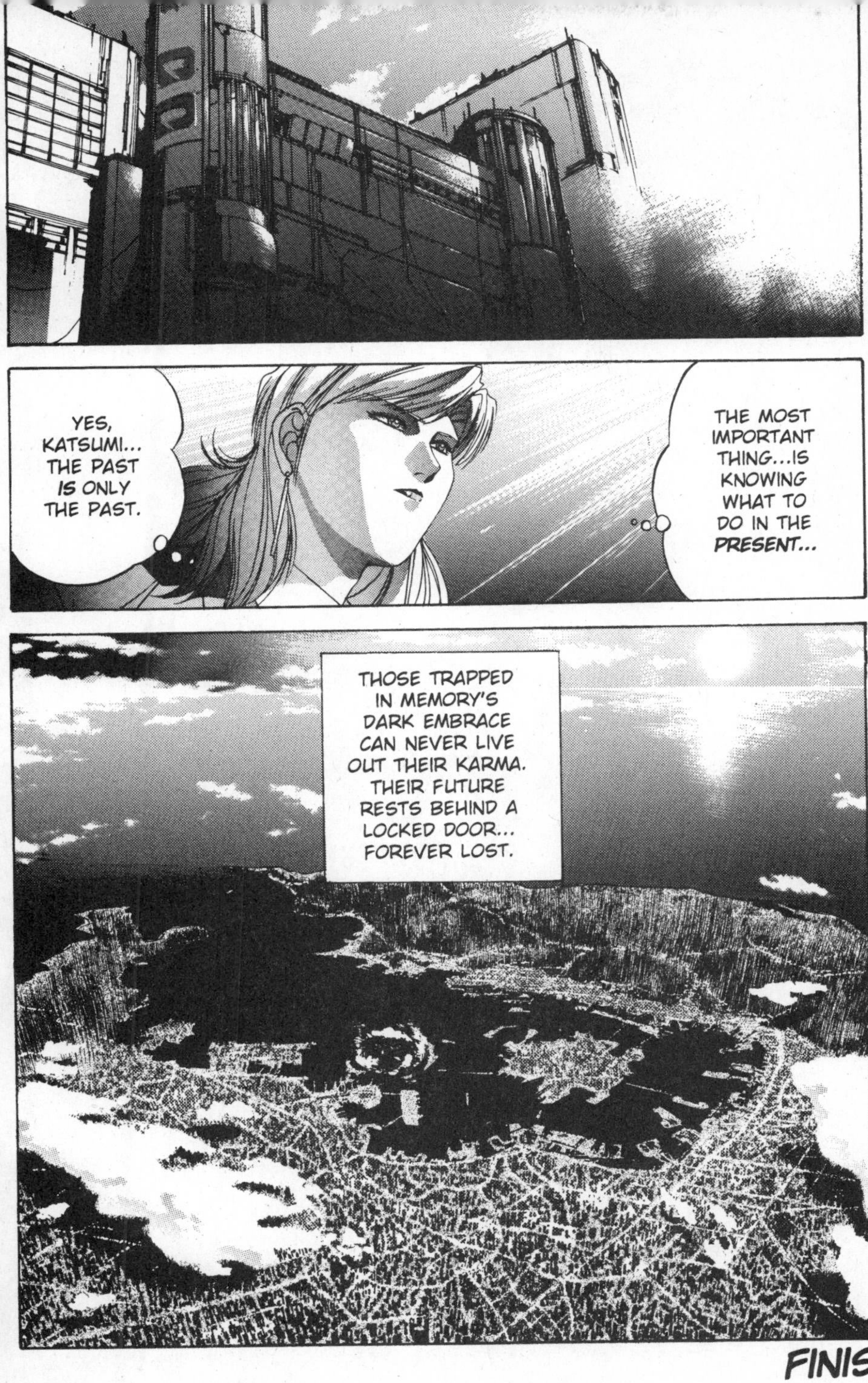
YES, KATSUMI... THE PAST IS ONLY THE PAST.
THE MOST IMPORTANT THING...IS KNOWING WHAT TO DO IN THE PRESENT...
THOSE TRAPPED IN MEMORY'S DARK EMBRACE CAN NEVER LIVE OUT THEIR KARMA. THEIR FUTURE RESTS BEHIND A LOCKED DOOR... FOREVER LOST.

FINIS

KIA ASAMIYA GALLERY

These illustrations were originally printed on the inside of the dust-jackets of the Japanese **Silent Möbius** graphic novels (Vols. 2-5).

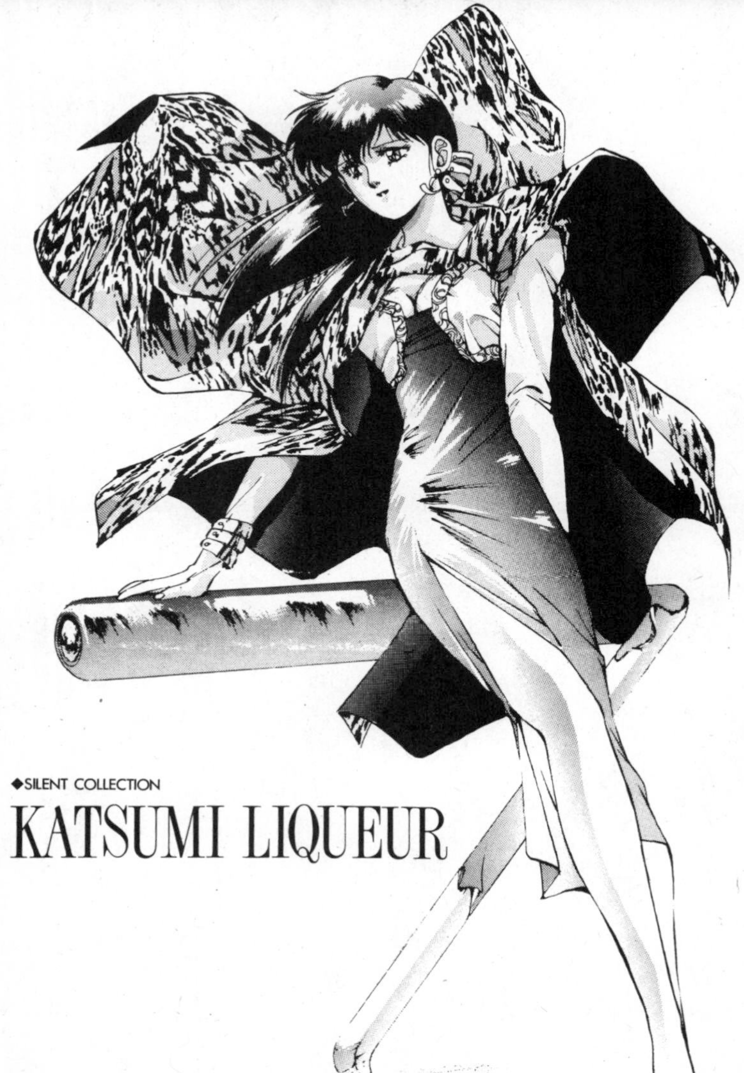
◆SILENT COLLECTION
KATSUMI LIQUEUR

◆SILENT COLLECTION

YUKI SAIKO

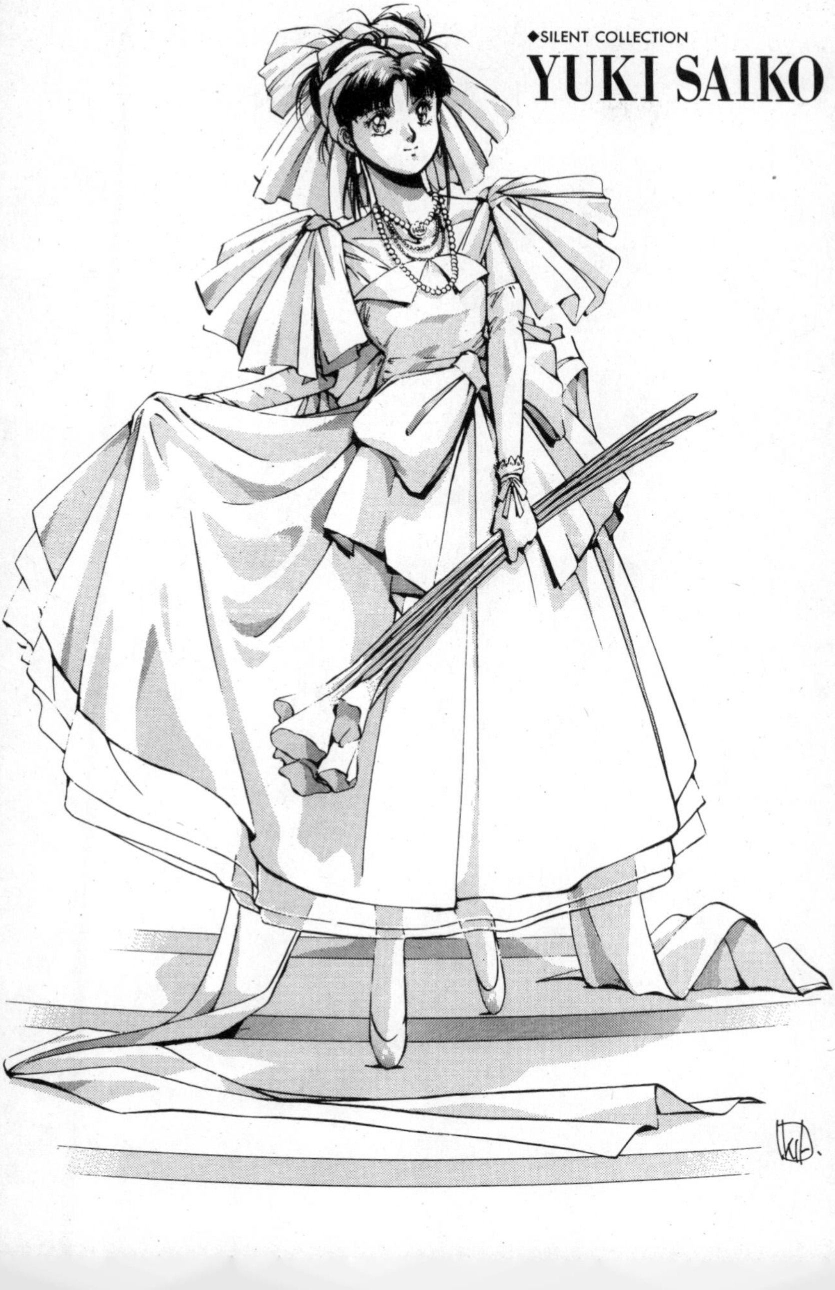

◆SILENT COLLECTION

LEBIA MAVERICK

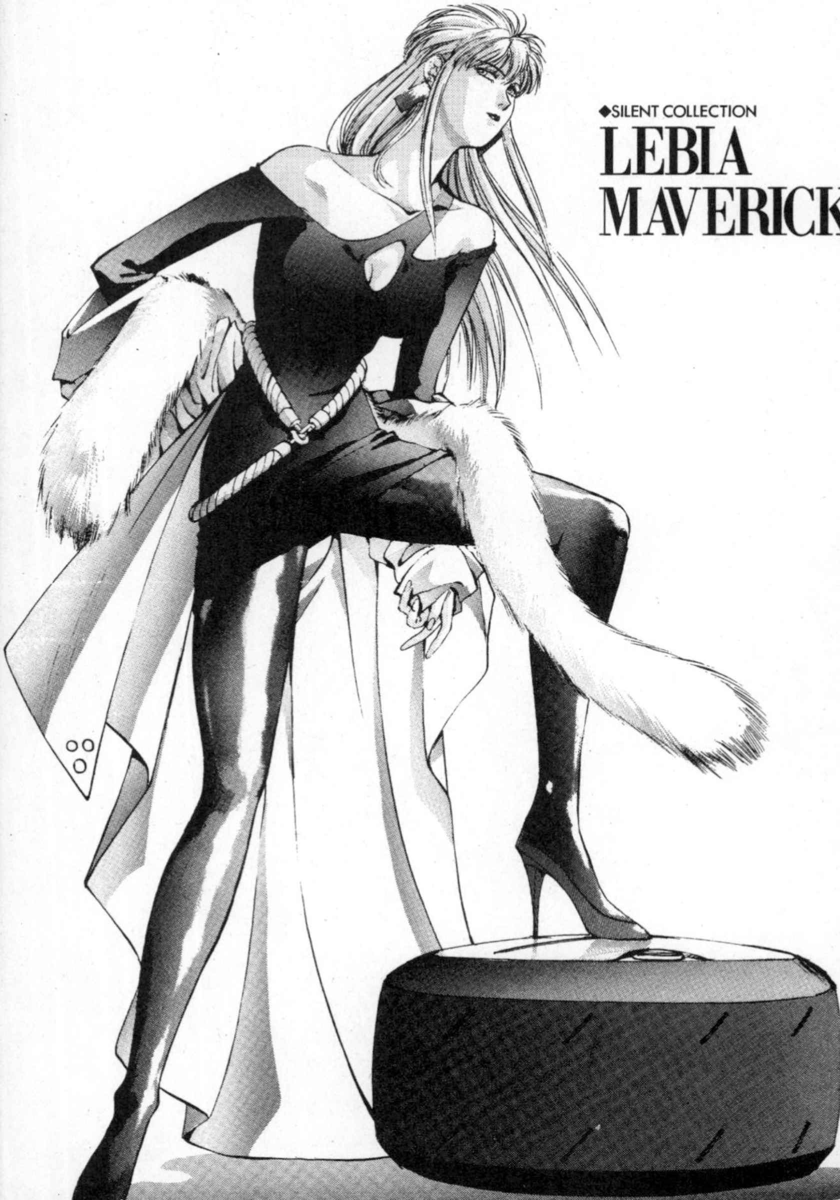

◆SILENT COLLECTION

NAMI
YAMIGUMO